LEAVING THE TWENTIETH CENTURY

SITUATIONIST REVOLUTIONS

McKENZIE WARK

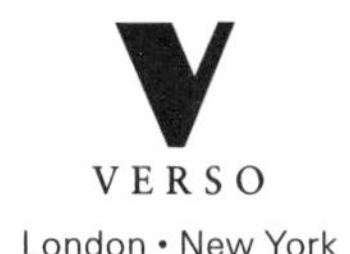

London • New York

This one-volume edition first published by Verso 2024
The Beach Beneath the Street first published by Verso 2011
The Spectacle of Disintegration first published by Verso 2013

1 3 5 7 9 10 8 6 4 2

Verso
UK: 6 Meard Street, London W1F 0EG
US: 388 Atlantic Avenue, Brooklyn, NY 11217
versobooks.com

Verso is the imprint of New Left Books

ISBN-13: 978-1-80429-486-4
ISBN-13: 978-1-80429-488-8 (US EBK)
ISBN-13: 978-1-80429-487-1 (UK EBK)

British Library Cataloguing in Publication Data
A catalogue record for this book is available from the British Library

Library of Congress Cataloging-in-Publication Data
A catalog record for this book is available from the Library of Congress

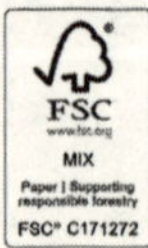

Typeset in Cochin by MJ & N Gavan, Truro, Cornwall
Printed and bound by CPI Group (UK) Ltd, Croydon CR0 4YY

Contents

Leaving the Twentieth Century: Situationist Revolutions

Sous les pavés, la plage! Beneath the paving stones, the beach! Or to keep the alliteration: below the bricks, the beach! A friend who engaged in the Paris street struggles of May 1968 once explained to me that the cobblestones nest in a bed of sand. Ambivalent things once you dug them up, constructive and destructive, for building barricades or chucking at cops.

There are enough books about May '68 to build many barricades. This is not one of them. That now-mythic event forms the (almost) absent center of this book. *Leaving the Twentieth Century* was originally two books: *The Beach Beneath the Street,* which extracted concepts and practices from Situationists and friends up until 1968, and *The Spectacle of Disintegration,* which did the same for the period after 1968, the time of defeat.[1]

Leaving the twentieth century is what did not happen. Sure, the calendar ticked over, but the various revolutions against the society of the spectacle did not succeed in overthrowing it in its totality. It mutated into something worse, worldwide. The Paris of May '68 was a mere part of a global revolutionary project, and the Situationists a mere part of those Paris events. A fragment of a fragment, a trace of an ambition for the world, dashed against the rocks of its inertia.

Why revisit the Situationists? They were a particularly inventive lot, tossing out not so much ideas as practices. They were as free as was possible at the time from the constraints of the party, the academy, the media and the art world, the four institutions that at various times have recuperated the radical impulse. And here I know of what I speak given that my own work has felt the snares of all four.

The literature on the Situationists now fills a long wall of shelves. My objective was not just to contribute another brick. Nor did I have any interest in the petty world of the "Debord boys," who appear to have learned nothing from the veneration of Guy Debord, their Situationist saint, other than the schoolyard art of the insult. My interest was, and remains, to write for those who would rather be making revolution, but who in the absence of revolutionary conditions make practices within everyday life that generate situations and concepts that might point toward another city for another life.

Nor did I want to pick sides in the various feuds and splits among the Situationists. They were the sum of their differences. There were many who had something to contribute. I wanted to put the women back into the story, as they are too often left out. I wanted to decenter it away from Paris, as that city had already lost its place as the fantasy capital of revolution. I present the Situationists as a medley of stories, a conceptual novel, with occasional flashbacks and leaps into present time.

What is now the first part of this book is the "before" story, full of piss and vinegar. It starts not with the theory and practice of the labor movement but the theory and practice of delinquent layabouts, some of whom then joined forces with revolutionary artists, to collectively produce the possibility of living otherwise.[2] Questions come up along the way. Can one love without making the beloved one's property? What is the relation of creative work to labor? What form would a city take that responded to our needs and wants? These were some of the questions at stake in the revolution that was to be.

The second part follows our characters and their concepts through the years of learning to live with, and from, defeat. There is deeper work on the long history of the society of the spectacle, and on the surprisingly practical remedies offered in utopian thought. There are tactics of discretion learned from those whose whole lives are under surveillance. There's formal, aesthetic questions about what kinds of work might not so much enlighten as enliven us as to how to act tactically.

In the second part, I also advance my own modest contribution to this conceptual story: the *spectacle of disintegration*. The society of the spectacle is one in which the commodity form doubles itself in the form of an image, the spectacle, which in turn becomes the means of self-knowledge, and self-delusion, of commodity production itself. It forms a totality that absorbs, into its double form of thing and image, the whole planet. Its dynamism reproduces sameness on an ever-expanding scale. The revolution in and against it tried, and failed, to interrupt its temporality with a dash of historical time.

The time of the spectacle is uniform and empty, absorbing the historical time of difference by turning even revolt into an image. Revolution becomes one of its sidelines. In the absence of historical struggle, the spectacle drifts and degrades, feeding on itself, fragmenting, eroding its own conditions of ongoingness. It may require different tactics to engage with it in its declining years. The post-Situationist characters and concepts, whose stories unfold across the second part of the book, still have a lot to teach us about our era.

I'm happy to see the two parts of the book in one volume as I originally intended. This work came after I wrote *A Hacker Manifesto* and *Gamer Theory*, and the two parts form a backstory or prequel to those two previous books. After *Leaving the Twentieth Century* I wrote *Molecular Red*, which also tries to find resources for the present world-historical situation in mutant-Marxist practices.

I share only one sectarian impulse with the Situationists—a dislike and distrust of Stalinist, Trotskyist and Maoist theory commissars. Otherwise, I'm more interested than the Situationists ever were in the adjacency of different practices and concepts, hence my books *General Intellects* and *Sensoria*. It's through collaboration across different practices of work and play, not extremist posturing, that one might touch the totality.

I learned from the Situationists that theories are made to die in the tumult of time. The conceptual armature of my earlier work has had to be revised in light of subsequent developments, hence *Capital Is Dead*, which updates my conceptual vocabulary, drawing on the Situationists but also other feral Marxist practices. Critique will move not just against but with its time—or not at all. Meanwhile, my little book *Raving* revisits the possibilities of the *constructed situation*. In short, for twenty years, I've been studying, critiquing, applying and developing the work of this little band of outsiders.

Who could have guessed that when the flood came it would come in slow motion, over forty decades rather than forty nights? As the polar ice sheets unravel and plunge into the waters, those who have so mismanaged the fate of all things cling to their private arks. The animals, one by one, will be saved, if at all, as gene sequences. These are times that try a girl's soul.

The avant-garde never gives up. As the waves wash the beach away, we rifle the ruins of past gestures and recycle the blocks for present purposes. We regroup in that underlit surround, where not yet every pleasure is tracked, captured and extracted. Its whereabouts are no secret—we're just discreet about it. Spare us your moralizing, your pedantry, your debate-club antics. Let the dead bury the dead. Our kind will make the good life wherever we are. This is the story of some lost friends, still with us in the movements of our flesh.

McKenzie Wark
Brooklyn, December 2023

1 Street Ethnography

It is a few years after the end of the Second World War. Europe is in ruins. Out in its colonies, the will and the means come together to start throwing off the yoke. The Russians and the Americans brandish bombs at each other. Meanwhile in Paris, the City of Light, curfews and rationing slowly come to an end. The lights are lit again. The black market fades to gray. It's a time to shoot movies rather than collaborators. Formerly banned pleasures still have a special quality: American jazz, gangster movies and crime novels seem to promise unknown thrills, a sort of cultural correlate of the Marshall Plan for European reconstruction. There is a world to build out of books and mortar.

Existentialism is all the rage. All the papers say so, even if they don't approve. A doctrine that puts such a premium on freedom seems somehow both frightening and delicious. The philosophers credited with creating it—Jean-Paul Sartre, Simone de Beauvoir, Maurice Merleau-Ponty—refuse the label while selectively exploiting the attention. Self-styled existentialists turn up in their Paris neighborhood of Saint-Germain-des-Prés. They hang out in the famous cafés, hoping to rub shoulders with intellectual celebrities. After the cafés shut, it's on to the cellar clubs. The wire-service journalists started this fad. Working odd hours, in need of a drink when all else closes, they end up in the cellars, and so the cellars end up in the news.

The most famous was Le Tabou. As Simone de Beauvoir wrote: "People drank and danced and also brawled a great deal, both inside and out front. The neighborhood declared war … at night, people threw buckets of water on the customers and even on people just passing by."[1] De Beauvoir claimed never to have been there. She did not like the way its front people, Anne-Marie Cazalis and Juliette Gréco, traded on the existentialist fashion. But she was friends with Boris Vian (1920–59), who played the trumpet in the band. Vian was a man of parts. Besides his passion for jazz, he wrote a fake American crime novel to cash in on that craze, and he wrote the *Manual of Saint-Germain-des-Prés* (1949).[2]

The *Manual* is a mock ethnography of the quarter. Saint-Germain has its natives, those who ply respectable trades, pouring cold water on the bohemian effusions they consider beneath them. It has its incursionists, new-money people who doubtless got rich off the black market and came looking for ways to spend it. It has permanent invaders, American and Scandinavian and the occasional English.[3] And it has its *troglodytes*, the nocturnal residents of the cellar clubs. Boris Vian regarded himself and his friends as none of the above. The real Saint-Germain was to him a small coterie of creative individuals.

Here are some of them, with their dates, since time is key to this story: the poet Tristan Tzara (1896–1963), the composer Georges Auric (1899–1983), the writer Jean Cocteau (1889–1963), the writer Jacques Prévert (1900–77), the artist Alberto Giacometti (1901–66), the writer Raymond Queneau (1903–76), the writer Jean-Paul Sartre (1905–80), the writer Simone de Beauvoir (1908–86), the philosopher Maurice Merleau-Ponty (1908–61), the writer Jean Genet (1910–86), the saxophonist Don Byas (1912–72), the actress Simone Signoret (1921–85), and the singer Juliette Gréco (b. 1927). None will feature much in our story—with one exception: the poet Gabriel Pomerand (1925–72).

In her memoir, Simone Signoret describes her initiation into Saint-Germain in 1941. She quit her job on a collaborationist paper and came to hang out at the Café de Flore, hoping to get into the film business. Of the people she met there—"some of them Jewish, many of them Communists or Trotskyites, Italian anti-fascists, Spanish Republicans, bums, jokers, penniless poets, sharers of food ration tickets, ambulatory guitarists, genial jacks of all trades, temporary no-goods"—some would not survive the war.[4] Of those who did, a few would become celebrated figures of a new postwar culture, with Saint-Germain as their symbolic home. Saint-Germain was where the forces for the postwar restoration of the spectacle gathered.

American pop mixed with youthful irreverence was not to everyone's taste. In his *Manual,* Vian takes great exception to the portrayal of Saint-Germain in both the conservative and communist press. Gullible cellar-dwelling troglodytes, he suspects, can be cajoled into saying pretty much anything for the price of a drink. They give the place a bad name. The legend the press starts is that Sartre is the Magus and jazz the Pied Piper of an evil cult. Worse, Simone de Beauvoir's *Second Sex* (1949) ruins the morals of impressionable girls. Vian quotes some choice bits of journalese: "Beginning of the legend: an amateur existentialism of destruction. The whole story: blood, sensuality, death." Poor troglodyte existentialists, mere teenagers, living in cheap hotels they can't afford. They are "unwholesome" and "violent," "intoxicated" by American crime novels (or perhaps by Vian's copies of them). In the clubs they can be found "screaming like banshees." The press has fabulated a *folk devil* here, about which to whip up a *moral panic*.[5]

"These zealots recognize each other through thousands of little items of clothing: cowboy shirts flapping in the breeze, red, yellow and green, plaid shirts that hang open down to the belly button." The troglodyte existentialist belongs to a *subculture*.[6] "The women of the tribe are fond of smocks that come in maybe two or three colors: their hairstyles give them the look of a drowning victim … they are none too fond of soap or hairbrushes, but they dance one hell of a boogie-woogie." The press can't decide if they have too much sex or not enough, but either way their desire is out of line, a threat to bourgeois enjoyment.[7] They gather in Saint-Germain, in the shadows cast by its luminaries, to reinvent themselves, by means both fair and shady. Bohemia's other face is delinquency.

She loved to dance: Vali Myers (1930–2003) left home at fourteen and moved to seamy St Kilda, a waterside neighborhood in Melbourne, Australia. She worked in a hair salon for a while, and as an artist's model, but preferred factory jobs. What money she made went towards study with the Melbourne Modern Ballet. In 1950 she left Australia, aged nineteen, determined to dance in Paris. She found a ruined city, cold in winter; poor all the year round. The war had shattered one way of life, and another had not yet risen from the ashes. Myers dropped ballet and went dancing in the cellars where African drummers played. Tourists threw money at her feet. She learned very little French, but picked up the argot of the streets. This is what she wrote about those times:

> The kids who survived after the war years in our quarter, Saint-Germain des Prés, can be counted on one hand. It was … a world without illusions, without dreams. It had a dark stark beauty like a short Russian story of Gorky that one doesn't forget. They were uprooted kids, old for their years, from all over Europe. Many had no home or parents, no papers (stateless), no money … We lived in the streets and cafés, like a pack of "bastard dogs" and with the strict hierarchy of such a tribe. Students and workers were "outsiders." The few tourists on the lookout for "existentialists" were "game" (for a meal or a drink), but no one sold himself. There was always cheap booze and Algerian hashish to get by on. What we had we shared, even the butt end of a cigarette.[8]

Sometimes she slept in cafés or movie houses; sometimes she slept rough. For a while she had a tiny room at the Hôtel d'Alsace-Lorraine, where the concierge was reputed to have worked for Marcel Proust in his last years. She slept by day, and danced through the night as if consumed by fire. Her whole delinquent "tribe" was nocturnal.[9] There was Kaki, the beauty of the quarter, a former Dior model, the daughter of collaborators who killed themselves after the war. Kaki joined her parents at age nineteen. There was Fred, the big blond Corsican, in and out of prison, who later became a *success*: as an artist, husband, and father. There was Robert the Mexican, said to have killed a man. There was Eliane, who had run away from both home and the reformatory. There was Ralph Rumney, dodging military service in Britain. Vali Myers lived on and off with Pierre Feuillette, who was known as the Chief. Unpredictable, with a walk like a cat, he was not the sort of character it pays to romanticize. He cut her once, in a fight. When she danced, it was he who collected the money the tourists threw. These were the scenes and characters from what she called her "opium years"—which lasted until 1958.

Gabriel Pomerand introduced Myers to opium. He was one of several men of the quarter who made her into a bohemian muse. Pomerand wrote that "she disobeys every last law of conventional beauty," and compared encountering Myers to meeting a "cheetah on a leash." The Dutch photographer Ed van der Elsken gave her the leading role in his book *Love on the Left Bank*. "She danced like a Negress," he said. George Plimpton, the expatriate American, wrote in *Paris Review*: "Her dancing is remarkable—a sinuous shuffling, bent-kneed, her shoulders and hands moving at trembling speed to the drumbeats." Plimpton quotes another admirer: "You saw in her the personalization of something torn and loose and deep-down primitive in all of us." Even the great gay Spanish writer Juan Goytisolo idolized the "solemn, hieratic girl, systematically dressed in black, with her face painted like a mask," who declared that she lived in a "damp cave with mice and called on the most daring to try her one night in a cemetery."[10]

Myers said that for her Saint-Germain was "like a little battlefield." Tired of parrying the glances of so many attentive men, she left Paris for a secluded valley in Italy. She would henceforth prefer the company of animals. The remarkable thing is that she survived her marginal Paris life. One of the press stories Vian disparages contains at least a kernel of truth: "Existentialism has ripened so quickly that it is already divided by class warfare. In fact it is necessary these days to distinguish the rich existentialists from the poor ones." Bohemia is fine for those who enter it voluntarily, and its legend is sustained by those who succeeded through it. For those who aren't rich, aren't men, aren't white, aren't straight, for those from the provinces, for those without a home to go back to, it is no picnic. People like Myers's tribe were doubly dispossessed, too young and too marginal. There was nothing for it but to stick together. As Ralph Rumney put it: "Our social exclusion made us a closed group."[11]

It has become an impertinence to say *we*. The collective pronoun is to be distrusted. Only the voice of the self is authentic. This voice declares itself from endless *status updates*, with whole spiders' nests of self-affirmation: ME! ME! ME! It's a world of free agents vainly attempting to establish themselves on the slender résumé of their own qualities. The twenty-first century is the culmination of two forms of individualism. In the first, individuals are all the same; in the second, they are all different. The first is classically bourgeois, the second distinctively bohemian. But whether different or the same, in the twenty-first century it's the same difference. Bourgeois individualism is now infused with bohemian flourishes. In the 1950s Vali Myers stood out even in Saint-Germain. In the 1970s, when she gave the singer Patti Smith her first tattoo, this might still have been a gesture with a point. Now you can get your tattoos at the mall. It's romanticism for everybody, with a little blood and pain thrown in for the price. The collapse of bourgeois and bohemian individualism into the warm embrace of the commodity is the defining style of the middle-class sensibility of today's disintegrating spectacle.[12]

There are also two kinds of collective belonging. In the first, we belong because we are the same; in the second, we belong because we are not.[13] The most insistent form of collective belonging in Paris after the war was the Communist Party, which was definitely of the first kind, a collective belonging that obliged of its members a certain unity and identity as *proletarians*. Wrapping itself in the scarlet mantle of the Resistance, the Party exerted its gravity upon artists and intellectuals even if they were not members. While directing a withering criticism at the surrealist old guard, Sartre agonized over how to align himself with the Communists, who he still took to be the representatives of the working class.

Saint-Germain offered its own alternative to the collective belonging of communism—the collective belonging of the Letterist movement, led by the charismatic Romanian poet and film-maker Isidore Isou (1925–2007). The rogue surrealist Georges Bataille once described him as a genius who lacked nothing except talent. Sartre hated the Letterists almost as much as he hated Bataille: "Letterism is a substitute product, a flat and conscientious imitation of Dadaist exuberance. One's heart is no longer in it, one feels the application and haste to succeed."[14] Yet not the least merit of the Letterists is that they were one of the few groups who managed to stay outside of both bourgeois postwar French culture and its Stalinist alternative. They managed to make something enduring, by seizing control over their own self-presentation. These were things for which Myers and her tribe lacked the wherewithal.

Romania gave the world Tristan Tzara, the poet of Dada, and it gave the world Isidore Isou, the prophet of Letterism, who first achieved fame in postwar Paris by publicly embarrassing poor old

Tzara, even as he began his own avant-garde practice by appropriating the best Tzara had to offer. Notoriety led to the publication of two of Isou's books by the venerable, if somewhat compromised, house of Gallimard. Saint-Germain was at the time the center of the French publishing world, so it made sense for a provincial gate-crasher like Isou to install himself the cafés there while finding a way to both scandalize and break into one of the quarter's few industries. Its other racket was cinema, drawing the likes of Signoret. Isou would tackle that one too, in his extraordinary film *Treatise on Spit and Eternity* (1951).[15]

While most people approached the postwar years as a time of reconstruction, Isou wanted to push the destruction of culture still further. His trans-historical theory of culture took the will to create as its primary axiom. Not Marxist necessity, not Sartrean freedom, but creation was the highest form of human activity. Creation takes us from the spit of unconsciousness to the eternity of a consciously created history, for while the artist creates within history, the act of creation touches the eternal. All forms—aesthetic and social—move from a stage of *amplification* to one of *decomposition*. In the amplification stage, a form grows to incorporate whole aspects of existence. The amplified form shapes life and makes it meaningful. During the period of decomposition, forms turn on themselves and become self-referential. Forms fall from grace and from history. As the form decomposes, so does the life to which it once gave shape. Form becomes unreal, and language becomes tame: "Tarzan learns in his father's book to call tigers *cats*."[16]

Isou applied this theory to all forms, from art to cinema, but poetry had a central place, for he was interested in both the history of poetry and the poetics of history. In modern French poetry, Victor Hugo took the amplification stage as far as it could go. Its decomposition then advanced, phase by phase, through Baudelaire, Verlaine, Rimbaud, Mallarmé, and Tzara. Dada rendered all existing forms worthless. Dada was conscious decomposition. Isou's self-appointed task was to complete the reduction of the word to the letter, through a deliberate chiseling of poetry down to its bare elements. By creating a new alphabet, a new language would be possible, which would reconstruct, amplify, and retell the story of the world. Isou's mission was to gather disciples for an all-out attack on spent forms, and the creation in their place of a fresh language.

Treatise on Spit and Eternity is almost the masterpiece Isou so confidently proclaimed.[17] It has three movements. In the first, Isou wanders the streets of the quarter in his plaid jacket. "The neighborhood of Saint-Germain-des-Prés is an invention of the author, and represents nothing but the author's calvary." The voice-over recounts his (or rather his fictive double Daniel's) attempt to expound his vision of a new cinema to a hostile audience at a film club who shout him down, usually with stock leftist jibes. Cinema has become obese, he declares. Its images have become too banal, too *artistic*. Cinema is merely "an industry organized in defense of current production." The cinema of classic unities has to be rent asunder. He proposes a *discrepant* cinema, where image and sound are severed from each other. It is time to spit out the old masterpieces. Cinema should aspire to a gangrenous beauty worthy of the Marquis de Sade. "The more the subject matter is spoiled and perverted, the more beautiful it is ... The novelty of creation alone interests the creator. That is why the ugliness of our era preoccupies him: it is new and therefore beautiful."

After wandering about Saint-Germain in the first act, Isou meets up in the second with Eve, a Norwegian beauty. Now he attempts to enact the "Manifesto of Discrepant Cinema" just expounded. Isou thwarts the spectators' expectations: "The author knows that people go to the movies to swallow their weekly Saturday night dose of tenderness. And though they don't give a damn about the story, they retell it in the hope of a deserved success. The author does not care for this type of legend, because these are questions of personal taste. Only systems where form goes beyond story are of interest to him." What he ends up with is a charmless account of his alter-ego Daniel's misogyny.

Still, the second act achieves two insights. Daniel recounts how expulsion from the Communist Party felt like a kind of annihilation: "How astonishing to find oneself alive the next day." The other is an observation voiced by another girlfriend, Denise: "How many corpses in the maze of the dictionary? ... Our vocabulary is full of real corpses, a cemetery of men who died for words." Given the brutality of the history Isou survived as a Romanian Jew, the statement carries a certain gravity. It is no accident either that across stock footage of a church service, Isou has scratched the Star of David and that stock footage of the colonial officer class routinely has the faces and bodies scratched out. For Isou, "the evolution of art has nothing to do with the revolution in society." It is a refuge from it.

All one could say in favor of the film's second act is that it manifests the latent male aggression towards women that is an undercurrent of bohemian sexual practices. "I installed myself in her," he says of Eve, before discarding her. The third act can then devote itself to Letterist poetry, with two great performances by François Dufrêne (1930–82), perhaps the most accomplished of Isou's followers where poetry was concerned. In the third act Isou promotes Letterism against all rival avant-gardes. He dismisses jazz, for instance, as "white-collar primitivism." Eisenstein's *Battleship Potemkin* is just the "*King Kong* of the revolution." Cinema in particular has failed as an art. "The God of cinema is dead," like the God of legend who died while making the universe, leaving it unfinished. Isou sets himself the task of completion. "Actually what interests you is creation, invention, discovery. That's what creation is. An unceasing destruction of surfaces to reach a subterranean pool." The film ends with Daniel's voice-over account of his abandoned girlfriend Eve, wandering Saint-Germain and succumbing to madness, until the police round her up and deport her. An indifferent Daniel, who witnesses her downfall, decides to play pinball with a friend, who wins a free game.

The unnamed friend in the film's last act could well have been Gabriel Pomerand. Like Isou a Romanian Jew, his mother was deported to Auschwitz. He spent the war in Marseilles, in the Resistance, but still found time to read the poetry of Arthur Rimbaud and the Comte de Lautréamont. He came to Paris after the war, meeting Isou in a soup kitchen for Romanian refugees. Pomerand quickly enlisted in the Letterists' shallow ranks. In the early postwar years he was a perpetual scandal in motion. He was a mainstay of the Letterist poetry readings at Le Tabou, and produced the first sustained work of *metagraphic* poetry, which synthesized image and word in a visual language. In it he presents a less flattering portrait of Saint-Germain than that drawn by Vian or even Isou. Pomerand's *Saint Ghetto of the Loans* (1950) is a *grimoire* of the quarter, a book for evoking its damned spirits.[18]

Saint-Germain is a ghetto, he says: its denizens all wear a yellow star. It is a "drowned drunk peacefully floating from one bridge to another." It is where American anarchist millionaires cross paths with swells whose wealth lies in castles built beneath the bridges. There is no Saint-Germain. "There are only spirits who survey the streets, from terrace to terrace, awaiting the occurrence of unique events," or for someone to pick up their tab. It is an "open-air temple," a "bullet-holed beauty spoiling in the sun." It is where language is pounded beyond recognition. "How sweet to subsist in a world that is falling apart." Saint-Germain is a Letterist ground zero.

Pomerand compares Saint-Germain to the imaginary city of Donogoo Tonka, from the novel by Jules Romains (1885–1972).[19] In this novel, a geographer faces professional embarrassment because a city he describes in the Brazilian jungle does not actually exist. So he enlists the help of an adventurer to create it. The adventurer finds some unscrupulous bankers, who provide the backing for the Donogoo Tonka company, which outfits an expedition to the jungle. The expedition thinks it is going to an already thriving city, when actually the men will have to build it themselves. When they arrive they find that others have already started work on building the city, drawn by the publicity campaign of the Donogoo Tonka company. In Saint-Germain as in Donogoo Tonka, the place makes a spectacle of itself. It is where the spectacle pulls itself up again by its own bootstraps.

Pomerand and Isou were younger than Vian's notables, but half a decade older than Vali Myers. She ran with a younger crowd, some of whom were attracted to the Letterists, some of whom had their own ideas. There was Henry de Béarn (1931–1995), who lived in a loft with Ivan Chtcheglov (1933–1998) near the Eiffel Tower. The lights from the tower kept them awake at night, so they planned to blow it up. There was Jean-Michel Mension (1934–2006), fortunate not to be orphaned by the war. First they came for his father, a communist militant. Then they came for his mother, both a communist and a Jew. Like many who washed up in Saint-Germain, Mension was drifting away from family, school, the law. But unlike some he had read his Sartre and his Prévert. Like Pomerand before him, Mension found his way to the poetry of Rimbaud and Lautréamont. After that self-education there was nothing for it but drink and mischief.

Mension spent his eighteenth birthday on the street, drinking and talking to Guy Debord (1931–94). Unlike Mension, Myers, and the tribe, Debord had a student allowance, so it was probably he who bought the wine (red for Mension, white for himself). As Mension recalls it, "we would set the whole world to rights while polishing off a liter or perhaps two liters."[20] Though little interested in his university classes, Debord studied Mension and others like him closely. Debord was a sort of street ethnographer, although his method was more intoxicant peregrination than participant observation. "He had a particular fascination with young people like me," Mension says. "He must have been searching in me for the kind of trigger that causes someone to snap one day and begin living without rules." Debord was researching a people who were neither bourgeois nor proletarian nor bohemian—and decidedly not middle-class.

Cursing is the work of the drinking classes. A short text Mension wrote in the early 1950s called "General Strike" declares "nothingness, perpetually sought, is simply, our life." Debord was in search, not of the organic intellectuals of the working class, but of what one might call the alcoholic intellectuals of the non-working classes. He had read his Louis-Ferdinand Céline (1894–1961), whose coruscating prose was capable of dispelling most illusions, not least about the nobility of labor: "We're workers they say. Work, they call it! That's the crummiest part of the whole business."[21] Mension's strike was not against work but against life, and while it strikes the right note of negativity, it does not quite rise to the level of a critique of delinquency—and this was the least of what Debord had in mind. There are plenty of celebrations of bohemia.[22] What is rare is to turn a critical theory of delinquency into a *delinquent critique*.

The first real statement of what would come to be a properly Situationist writing would come not from Mension but from Ivan Chtcheglov, in his celebrated "Formulary for a New Urbanism" (1953).[23] This is the text that pointed the way to the exit from the twentieth century as we know it. It's the key document of the Letterist International (1952–57), the group Debord cofounded and to which Chtcheglov belonged, forming a breakaway from the older Letterists such as Isou and Pomerand.[24] It would contribute some key ideas and practices to the movement that did not yet bear the name *Situationist*.

The Letterist International was a young people's affair. They discarded Isou's self-referential theories and personality cult, but took with them a certain practice of intellectual seduction and the ambition to chisel modern art down to nothing, to clear the ground for something else. The Letterist International dreamed big. They foresaw the end of the workhouse of modernist form. They discovered a new city via a calculated drifting (*dérive*) through the old. Theirs would be a city of play, love, adventure, made for arousing new passions, a city that might finally justify the conceit that this is a civilization worthy of its predecessors: "Although their builders are gone, a few disturbing pyramids resist the efforts of travel agencies to render them banal."[25] They were the other side to the spectacle of bohemia, its delinquent side, its marginal side. They created out of this marginality a collective being, and rendered that collective being in a low theory specific to it, and as we shall see, in a distinctive kind of practice.

2 No More Temples of the Sun

"We are bored with the city, there is no longer any Temple of the Sun," declares Chtcheglov. It is unclear whether he means the Temple of the Sun in Beijing, the Pyramid of the Sun at Teotihuacan or the Pyramids of Egypt, but he was certainly none too fond of the Obelisk of the Place de la Concorde. Besides being fascinated by pyramids (both Egyptian and pre-Columbian), Georges Bataille also had a thing about this obelisk, which had formerly graced the entrance to the Luxor Temple. Bataille called it a "petrified sunbeam."[1] For Bataille, the Place de la Concorde was the locus from which to announce the death of God, "precisely because the Obelisk is its calmest negation." The obelisk stood for the pharaoh's military power, the pyramid for his union with the eternity of the gods. The removal of the obelisk to Paris turned the Place de la Concorde into a negative sacred site. It gave the finger to what was once the eternal heavens, a gesture to the lost union of earth and sky, the point around which the mundane tumult of the city orbited.

Before the war, Bataille had wanted to create a ritual on this site, to transform its meaning. The idea was to soak a skull in brine until it softened, place it at the base of the obelisk and tell the press that the King's skull had mysteriously returned.[2] This was the place, after all, where Louis XVI had been executed—followed not long after by Danton, Robespierre, Saint-Just and not a few others. Chtcheglov had no interest in that. In any case the death of God had already been announced, and from the pulpit of Notre Dame no less, by a group of Letterists. During a quiet moment of the Easter High Mass in 1950, Michel Mourre (1928–77) ascended the pulpit dressed as a Dominican monk to read a sermon written by the Saint-Germain identity and subsequent Letterist International founding member Serge Berna (b. 1925): "Verily I say unto you: God is dead." The organist quickly pumped out a few chords to drown out the rest. Then all hell broke loose. Mourre and two others were arrested. Pomerand slipped out undetected.[3]

All this anti-clerical stuff was old hat to Chtcheglov. "For we are in the twentieth century, even if few people are aware of it." Now was the time to leave the old avant-garde stunts behind. The failure of the earthly city to renew itself was the problem, not the vanishing heavens. "Everyone wavers between the emotionally still-alive past and the already-dead future." Chtcheglov proposed a quite different approach to the space of the city than Bataille. The problem was how to replace God's stabilizing presence with a new relation between the city and the cosmos; the solution was not to fix a place for a ritual sacrifice, but a new arrangement of movement.

Bataille's view of the city took as its starting point the sacred architecture at this center, which he made the site from which to dethrone God. Chtcheglov's view of the city took as its reference point not its ancient, sacred form, but its modern and seemingly rationalist one. His text is aimed squarely against the *radiant city* of Le Corbusier (1887–1965), which if it had its way would erase even more of the city than wartime bombing and replace it with cross-shaped tower blocks aligned along gun-barrel highways and vast open parks. For Chtcheglov, this was the wrong path along which to imagine the postwar reconstruction. He sought not the rational city but the playful city, not the city of work but the city of adventure. Not the city that conquers nature, but the city that opens towards the flux of the universe.

Le Corbusier was the *bête noire* of the whole Situationist project, but it is worth pausing to consider what the thinking of Le Corbusier and Chtcheglov had in common. Le Corbusier wrote that "architecture, which is a thing of plastic emotion, should, in its domain, also begin at the beginning, and use elements capable of striking our senses, of satisfying our visual desires, and arrange them in such a way that the sight of them clearly affects us through finesse or brutality, tumult or serenity, indifference or interest."[4] This understanding of the city as a totality of sensory and emotional affects, this at least they share. The philosopher Jacques Rancière speaks of a "distribution of the sensible," which "reveals who can have a share in what is common."[5] In these terms Le Corbusier and Chtcheglov are close, for both imagine the whole space of the city as something everyone experiences aesthetically. Yet the Letterist International is already pushing against the limits of Le Corbusier's program. His architecture might be for the people, but it is decidedly not of them or by them.

New forms are needed to express a new ruling order. Le Corbusier's architecture is addressed to the ruling class, which does not quite realize the new kinds of forms it needs. The bourgeois at home seem "sheepish and diminished, like tigers in a cage; one sensed clearly that they were happier at the factory or their bank." The forms he offers them, patterned after bomber planes as much as ancient temples, connect modern technology to a spiritual order. Architecture signals the "trace of an indefinable absolute persisting at the core of our being" and "a unifying management in the universe."[6] If for Bataille the temple of Luxor was a sacrifice to an absent God, to an impossible order, for Le Corbusier the harmony of heaven and earth could be reconstituted— but only through modern versions of Luxor's ancient geometric form, shorn of all ornamental excrescence. Le Corbusier imposed the geometry of the temple onto the entire space of the city, and onto everyday life in its totality.

Le Corbusier's city was not modern: it was already out of date. It was a product of a retrograde culture, lagging behind science. The physical world is no longer understood as an orderly geometry, but culture has yet to catch up. The purpose of technology is not to make a city purified of complexity, a Platonic form gleaming in the sun. Life is earthy, not heavenly; life is movement and form, spirit or idea. Chtcheglov's sources for this way of imagining the city were twofold. One was a certain strain of art and literature that proposed fantastic landscapes, such as the paintings of Giorgio de Chirico, in which could be glimpsed a new conception of space and time.[7] The literature Chtcheglov draws on includes Thomas de Quincey, Edgar Allan Poe's "The Domain of Arnheim," and, most interestingly, a Russian children's book by Lev Kassil.

Chtcheglov's Ukrainian father had been exiled from Russia for his political activities, and had been involved in a taxi drivers' strike in Paris, but it was probably his mother who introduced him to

Kassil. Lev Kassil (1905–70) started out as an avant-garde writer in the orbit of the great futurist poet Vladimir Mayakovsky. He survived the brutal years of the Stalinist era, like more than a few others, by writing children's books. In *The Black Book and Schwambrania,* two brothers find a novel way to escape from the discipline of family and school: "There was no need to run away, to search for a promised land. It was here, somewhere very close at hand. We had only to invent it." This world they call Schwambrania: "Our world was a bay jam-packed with boats. Life was an endless journey, and each given day was a new voyage. It was quite natural, therefore, that every Schwambranian was a sailor."[8]

Adventure is close at hand. It does not require Rimbaud's "derangement of the senses," but rather, an arrangement of the sensible. There is nothing exotic about it. It does not require a surrealist expedition to foreign lands. What James Clifford calls a "Surrealist ethnography" still relies on a notional other, an exoteric to contrast to the esoteric, however much it might trouble or surprise accepted notions of which is which.[9] A Situationist ethnography has its own distinct methods. It emerges out of Debord's close study of Saint-Germain delinquents. It adopts their habits, their *ethnos*, and turns it into method. The Letterist International are ethnographers of their own difference, cartographers of an attitude to life. This life did not lie outside the modern, Western one, but inside, in the fissures of its cities. It did not yearn for a *primitive* life from before history, but rather for one that was to come after it. In the life of the Saint-Germain delinquents' *tribe* could be found particles of the future, not the past, and not from some colonial Donogoo Tonka but from the very epicenter of what history had wrought: the colonization of everyday life at the heart of empire.

Chtcheglov's other source was not previous art or writing, but a certain kind of practice, what he and his friends would call the *dérive*. It's a curious word. A note in the Letterist International's journal *Potlatch* gives some of its resonances.[10] Its Latin root "derivare" means to draw off a stream, to divert a flow. Its English descendants include the word "derive" and also "river." Its whole field of meaning is aquatic, conjuring up flows, channels, eddies, currents, and also drifting, sailing or tacking against the wind. It suggests a space and time of liquid movement, sometimes predictable but sometimes turbulent. The word dérive condenses a whole attitude to life, the sort one might acquire in the backwaters of Saint-Germain-des-Prés.

"Note: a certain Saint-Germain-des-Prés, about which no one has yet written, has been the first group functioning on a historical scale within this ethic of drifting."[11] It is the dérive, writes Michèle Bernstein, "from which we expect to draw educationally conclusive results."[12] Bored with her university studies and her bourgeois background, Bernstein (b. 1932) started hanging around Saint-Germain in 1952 and found herself in the company of the Letterist International. She was the one who, on a rented machine, typed up the articles for *Potlatch*, which mixed news snippets, in-jokes, theoretical texts and notes on the dérive. As her friend Jacqueline de Jong says: "Without her there would not have been any *Potlatch*."[13]

"'Alienation'—I know it is there whenever I sing a love song or recite a poem, whenever I handle a banknote or enter a shop, whenever I glance at a poster or read a newspaper. At the very moment the human is defined as 'having possessions,' I know it is there, dispossessing the human."[14] Henri Lefebvre introduced many French readers to Marx, but to a Marx not quite containable by party orthodoxy. When Lefebvre published his *Critique of Everyday Life* (1947) he was a member of the Party, but—and one can't resist the gesture—he was increasingly alienated from it. The party was an imitation, a thing apart, not an expression of proletarian power. Lefebvre's critique of the abstract and mystified disaffections of the surrealists with everyday life nevertheless implied another critique, of the limits of official Marxist orthodoxy. What he did not yet have was a practice that could produce a knowledge of the relation between the workers' dispossession of the product of their labor during the working day, and the encounter with these same products as potential possessions during leisure hours.

Lefebvre writes of how capital makes the modern city. Capitalism divides time into work time and leisure time. It further divides work time up into equivalent units—workers are usually paid by the hour—and tries to make each unit as productive as possible. Leisure time is free from work, but tends increasingly to be used for consumption. The worker is paid to work in the factory, and pays to spend her free time consuming factory-made products. Such is the standard Marxist view of time. It corresponds to a certain experience of space. There is work space, leisure space, and resting space. The worker works in one space, spends free time in another, and schleps home to sleep in a third.

A graffiti slogan proposed in *Potlatch* for the dormitory suburbs around the factories: "Remember, you are sleeping for the boss!"[15] Unlike the surrealists, the Letterist International put little faith in the dream world. They stay awake nights. They implicitly accept the denunciation mounted from such otherwise incompatible sources as Sartre, Isou and Lefebvre of the futile gestures of surrealism. Rumney: "It was an exquisite corpse that was beginning to give off a bad smell."[16] Their chosen terrain was not the dream, but rather a lucid practice outside of and against the work and leisure diptych. Debord's attack on latterday surrealists was called "The Big Sleep and Its Clients" (1955) which neatly connects the title of a Hollywood movie, the most palpable channel of unconscious desires in postwar France, with the aging surrealist champions of radical desire.[17]

Patrick Straram (1934–88) arrived in Saint-Germain in 1950, but left for Canada in 1958 to avoid national service. In that brief time he hung out in the jazz cellars, drank with the tribe, signed texts by the Letterist International and wrote a novel about it. *The Bottle Reclines* (1953) describes dérives with characters resembling Debord and Chtcheglov in a style somewhere between the surrealists and the Beats: "The wine went to his head. Rambler well led despite himself in a labyrinth of colors and shadowy forms, incapable of assimilating them, distorted interpretation, according to a deformed optic, and however shockingly accurate."[18]

The dérive, with Straram, is a groggy and disorienting affair, continued from night to day:

> It was already dirty and bluish whiteness, something lazily mechanic, the chloroformed ambiance of sprawled-out rays of a staggering, sleepy sunrise. A nearly medical beam of scraped sun on the heavy walls of unhealthy sleepwalking, perpetual surveillance of the city, clinical guards/prisoners. The battle picked up from the point where it was brutally interrupted yesterday, from the heap of bricks and fire, automatic incubator, and from the perverse perforation, certain, of light. The ultimate everyday renaissance.[19]

Straram never finished his novel. Perhaps the novel is not the ideal form for writing about the dérive. Perhaps the dérive could be a practice that leads to quite another project than literature.

While the critical theory of commodified experience of time and space that Lefebvre initiated would become a commonplace in the postwar years, Chtcheglov, Debord, Bernstein, Straram and friends were one of the few groups to imagine a *critical practice*.[20] The dérive cuts across the division of the space of the city into work, rest and leisure zones. By wandering about in the space of the city according to their own sense of time, those undertaking a dérive find other uses for space besides the functional. The time of the dérive is no longer divided between productive time and leisure time. It is a time that plays in between the useful and the gratuitous. Leisure time is often called *free time*, but it is free only in the negative, free from work. But what would it mean to construct a positive freedom within time? That is the challenge of the dérive. The breakaway Letterist International created a new practice, a new way of being in the world, out of which to derive a new kind of practice.[21]

Strikingly, both capital and labor accept the division between work time and leisure time. Capital extends or intensifies the working day; labor struggles to shorten it, and within it to resist speed-ups and other attempts by capital to extract more value from it. Perhaps it is this shared fixation on productive time that will draw both capital and labor towards the middle-class cultural norm.[22] While they are at odds as to its use, both take for granted a certain functional concept of time, and a certain acquisitive and accumulating approach to everyday life that comes with it. The Letterist International sought a quite different concept of time, resolutely based on non-work.

Debord's first major *work*, by his own later accounts, was a simple three-word graffiti that translates as "Never work!"[23] Rather than reduce the working hour, avoid it as much as possible. But if there is no work, then there is no leisure either. It is rather like Nietzsche's annunciation of the death of God which is also the death of a certain understanding of Man, since God and Man form a conceptual couple, each made in the other's image.[24] Debord's "Never work!" frees time from its binary form of work time and leisure time. The dérive then becomes the practice of lived time, time not divided and accorded a function in advance; a time inhabited by neither workers nor consumers.

Chtcheglov's text announced some forthcoming books, including one by his friend Henry de Béarn which provisionally names the people of the dérive and their passion: *The New Nomadism*. This book would never be written, or at least not by de Béarn. In the 1970s, the philosopher Gilles Deleuze (1925–95) would join with the psychiatrist and activist Félix Guattari (1930–92) to write *Anti-Oedipus* (1972) and its sequel, *A Thousand Plateaus* (1980), which among other things would propose a *nomad thought*.[25] They start with a burlesque of psychoanalysis and expand it into a whole worldview based on the productive powers of desire. As they write: "A schizophrenic out for a walk is a better model than a neurotic lying on the analyst's couch."[26] By the time they wrote this, much of what had once been critical thought had laid its weary head on that analyst's couch—depressed, anxious, irritable, neurotic. Obsessed with old wounds. Unable to forget. Unable to get up. At its melancholy end.

Deleuze and Guattari's exemplary walkers were literary characters, but it turns out Chtcheglov was that schizophrenic out for a walk, and he already had a theory of his own nomadism. Years before Deleuze and Guattari, he already saw the dérive as a kind of analysis. "The dérive is certainly a technique, almost a therapeutic one." Unlike psychoanalysis, it did not sever language from the continuum of practices in which it is embedded. "The dérive (with its flow of acts, its gestures, its promenades, its encounters) was to the totality exactly what psychoanalysis (in the best sense) is to language," Chtcheglov writes. The Letterist International refuse the separation of urban space from urban culture, each assigned to their own specialists. They refuse the separation of the external, social space of the city from the internal, private space of subjectivity. The subjective belongs to the city and can be analyzed experimentally, much as the city is subjective and can be reconstructed to expand with our desires.

The dérive was an intervention against geography as much as against psychoanalysis. Academic geography in France arose out of the defeat of the Franco-Prussian war. If the dominant form narrowed its focus to an objective science of landscape existing outside of social practice, there was also a counter-geography, more interested in social practices of landscape-making.[27] Paul-Henry Chombart de Lauwe (1913–98) offered a synthesis of both the objectivity of the former and the attention to social process of the latter. From an aristrocratic family, Chombart was a Catholic, with progressively more leftist leanings throughout the 1940s and '50s. Before the war he studied with Marcel Mauss, from whom he took an organic conception of socialism and a commitment to social science as the study of social problems, with a view to their solution. He crossed the Sahara in 1936 on a tourist flight, as his contribution to Marcel Griaule's legendary ethnographic expeditions.[28] During the war he joined the Resistance, before becoming a fighter pilot for the Free French. His monumental study of Paris and its environs came out in 1952, and would become a critical point of reference for the Situationist theory and practice of *psychogeography*.

Chombart used a range of methods to construct an understanding of the city as both form and process, ranging from aerial surveillance to interviews with workers. Drawing on his wartime experience he became an expert in techniques of aerial surveillance, and these in turn had given Chombart a bird's-eye view of class struggle. He could clearly see in the photographs of Paris a slightly squished version of the concentric rings that the Chicago School claimed defined urban space. These concentric zones, like the rings of Saturn, orbit what the Chicago urbanists christened a *central business district*.[29] (A notion that would have horrified Bataille.) The qualities of the zones are determined by the price of land within them, which is a function of their distance from the center. Or as Chombart might say more directly: class maps onto space.

Chombart came to advocate a participatory approach to town planning, but always with something of an aerial—or what Bataille would call Icarian—view, flying over and detached from the city and its tangle of situations.[30] He represented the best of progressive postwar urban thought: leftist but not Stalinist, sympathetic and engaged with working-class struggles, but viewing these from within orthodox social science as problems to be solved rather than battles to be engaged. He recuperated social geography for the science of landscape. He was all too easily seduced by the idea of housing the working class in Corbusian mega-blocks, for their own good.[31] All this made him a conspicuous target for attack by Debord and friends. Chombart's aerial techniques in particular were to be détourned in the service of a quite different practice—psychogeography.

Psychogeography is a *practice* of the city as at once an objective and subjective space. It is not the city as mere prompt for surrealist reveries. Nor is it a thing apart, to be dissected by social science, no matter how well-meaning. The city of Debord, Chtcheglov and their friends is a complex beast, always in process, with its own rhythms and life cycle, as it is for Chombart. What Chtcheglov and Debord add to this is a certain turbulence. The city simultaneously has subjective qualities that are nevertheless interpersonal. Debord: "From a dérive point of view cities have psychogeographical contours, with constant currents, fixed points and vortexes that strongly discourage entry into or exit from certain zones." The dérive discovers these contours. The city is an aesthetic practice irreducible to the interests of state or market.

The surrealists brought psychoanalysis to the streets, but it was only a detour, on the way back to literature.[32] Chombart brought social science to the streets, but again it was a detour, back to planning from above. The Letterist International invent a new kind of knowledge, a street ethnography, whose primary method is the dérive. What the dérive discovers is psychogeography: the lineaments of intersubjective space. In place of the chance encounters of the surrealists, they create a practice of play and strategy which invents a way of being, outside of commodified time and outside of the separate disciplines of knowledge—including geography. Henceforth the city will not be a site for fieldwork but a playing field, in which to discover intimations of a space and time outside the division of labor. The goal is nothing less than to invent a new civilization which will make a mark on historical time with the grandeur of the Temple of the Sun.

The civilization of play had already existed. Even little Saint-Germain—a handful of city blocks—left a trace. The artist Constant Nieuwenhuys (1920–2005), who will feature in our story further on, had a rather different experience of the place to Vian's bohemians, Vali's tribe or Chtcheglov's renegade Letterists, because he was there with his little boy: "The Parisians are not so nice, that is why they paint abstracts, and that is also why they slam the door when, with Victor holding my hand, I ask for a room. Yes, everything is abstract here ..."—even compassion. And yet writing about it later Constant could not but agree with Chtcheglov: "The atmosphere of this bourgeois quarter of Paris was so profoundly altered by a small group of intellectuals, the so-called existentialists, that it acquired international fame and even became a tourist attraction."[33]

The model, in negative, for a city of play is Las Vegas: a city in the desert, with no harbor, no river, which since 1931 was dedicated—if not consecrated—to wasting time. To Chtcheglov, the ideal setting for a new avant-garde was not the metropolis of commerce or industry, but tourism. Las Vegas would eventually sprout its own pyramid, and take on all the pretensions to immortality that to Bataille already seemed ridiculous, and are perhaps more so in the twenty-first century. In 2003 the United States government issued a warning that if nothing was done, Las Vegas would run out of water by 2025.[34] Much as it fascinated Chtcheglov, Las Vegas was not the prototype of the Situationist city.

In the jungle is a city that moves. When its inhabitants build new districts it is always to the west. Each time they cut the ribbon opening a new quarter, an old one to the east is abandoned, gradually to disappear beneath the overgrowth of tropical vegetation. This is more like it! The moving city would burst the bubble of the *sustainable* city, the fantasy that the city can become one with its environment, a pure homeostasis, outside of history.[35] It would lay bare the process by which the city transforms nature into second nature, in the process making nature appear as a resource for the city's consumption. And besides, the ruins left behind in the east would be perfect terrain for the dérive. Why can such a city not exist? The conceit of private property is that it is something fixed, eternal. Once it comes into existence it remains, passed in an unbroken chain of ownership from one title-holder to the next. Yet in the course of time whole cities really do disappear. We live among the ruins. We later cities know we are mortal. And yet in the name of property we would hold back the very sea.

The village of Siasconset sits atop a bluff on the island of Nantucket, Massachusetts, a prize location for those of means, except for one thing. Erosion, like Marx's old mole, is burrowing away underneath, threatening to topple the palaces perched above.[36] So in 1992 twenty or so owners of such mansions joined together to form a Beach Preservation Fund, which intends to spend at least $25 million of its own money on dredging 2.6 million cubic yards of sand from a site offshore and pumping it onto the beach below the cliff. "They realize that the sand will inevitably wash away, so they are prepared to do much of the work all over again, perhaps as often as every five years." There seems now more merit than ever in the proposal for a city in the jungle, a city that records its own consumption of the terrain. Chtcheglov's intuition of the opening of the city to the temporality of the cosmos was perhaps more profound than he knew. Even the great city of Teotihuacan failed to stop time. "Today much of the city is buried under five towns, one of Mexico's largest military bases, numerous farms, commercial centers and a string of highways."[37]

What the Letterist International intended was not a new kind of urban planning, but a critique of it. "We need to flood the market—even if only for the moment the intellectual market—with a mass of desires whose fulfillment is not beyond humanity's present means of action on the material world, but only beyond the capacity of the old social organization."[38] They had the old Marxist faith that the development of the forces of production, the machinery of industrial capitalism, would yield the means to free us from necessity. Yet as early as 1953 they realized that capital could not go on treating all of space and time as resources for its own quantitative expansion. They had lived through the war as children and knew, at least secondhand, of the destructive power of modern technology. Why could that power not be used to build a different kind of civilization in the ruins? In the twenty-first century we live more and more with the consequences of the failure to make just such a qualitative break.

The Letterist International used the practice of the dérive as a method for creating a kind of knowledge outside of the division of labor, and outside even of the intellectual division of labor between disciplines. They aimed it not only at rival avant-gardes, but at geography, urban studies, sociology—the legitimate knowledges of the city. It was a "subcultural knowledge,"[39] drawing on a delinquent's distrust of social scientists and their questionnaires.

Psychogeography made the city subjective and at the same time drew subjectivity out of its individualistic shell. It is a therapy aimed not at the self but at the city itself. Letterists did not shrink from the aerial surveillance made possible by wartime technical advances, but did not make a fetish of it either.

It may well seem that the moving city is impractical, impossible. But is it any less impossible than holding back the sea? Is it any less impossible than building garden suburbs in the Nevada desert? The Letterist International discovered the power of a kind of *negative action*. They show what cannot be done within the limits of actually existing capitalism. As Debord writes: "The greatest difficulty in any such undertaking is to convey through these apparently extravagant proposals a sufficient degree of serious seduction."[40] As with any seduction, a kind of strategic game is in play, the key move in which is to act as if the new desire already exists. What will emerge out of the dérive, as practiced by the young Letterists, is a quite different concept of space and time, which, like the dérive, would be outside of property. It may only exist in a few interstitial moments out and about in Saint-Germain-des-Prés, but those few moments marked the exit to the twentieth century.

Having failed to take that exit, now we are trapped on an expressway that seems to keep going until the end of the world. There could be worse plans than turning back to look for the last exit, for which the Letterist International thought it saw the signs. Actually, the Letterist International scouted at least two exits. One leads to a small-scale, local and temporary situation, discovered via the dérive. The other points to a larger scale and a longer duration, perhaps to history itself, but grasped by its most tenuous emanations—language, images, the sign.

3 The Torrent of History

A scandal: historian Stephen E. Ambrose admits that he plagiarized many passages of his book *The Wild Blue*. Ambrose's books on General Custer and Richard Nixon also turned out to contain a good few sentences derived from other works. More scandal: the historian Doris Kearns Goodwin admits that she borrowed passages in her book *The Fitzgeralds and the Kennedys* from three works by other authors. Still more scandal: she then concedes that in 1987 her publisher, Simon & Schuster, paid to settle a legal claim by one of them under a confidentiality agreement. She said she confused verbatim notes with her own words.[1] Take pity on our poor authors! Not even they can tell their own words from another's. They are caught between the monotonous consistency of official historical narratives and the demand that the middle-class author have a unique *vision* that is his or her personal property. No wonder they resort to copying one another. Hypocrisy is the hush money that vice pays to virtue. Given the poverty of middle-class history, perhaps what the times require is a double reappropriation: both of the history of Debord and company, and of the mode of historical thinking to which they aspired, and which they occasionally achieved.

The Marquis de Vauvenargues once wrote that "old discoveries belong less to their original inventors than to those who put them to use." So it is with some justice that lines lifted from the soldier-aphorist should show up, with some slight but key corrections, in the *Poésies* (1870) of Isidore Ducasse, the self-styled Comte de Lautréamont (1846–90). The purpose of the *Poésies*, he wrote, was to take the most beautiful poetry and "correct it in the direction of hope." Thus Vauvenargues' maxim "One can be just, if one is human" becomes "One can be just, if one is not human." In a celebrated passage, Lautréamont expands on his distinctive poetics: "Plagiarism is necessary. Progress implies it. It closely grasps an author's sentence, uses his expressions, deletes a false idea, replaces it with the right one. To be well made, a maxim does not call for correction. It calls for development." It's a passage often taken as saying something about poetics, less often as saying something about history. Lautréamont corrects, not back to a lost purity or some ideal form, but forward—to a new possibility.

Lautréamont's best-known work is *The Songs of Maldoror* (1869), a giddy fringe-romantic epic, which includes the murder of children and sex with a shark. A drunken God presides from a throne of gold and shit. The works of Man don't amount to much, either. The pyramids of Egypt are "those anthills reared by stupidity and slavery." It was a surrealist favorite. In a famous line, set to become a cliché, Lautréamont anticipates the surrealist aesthetic: "As beautiful as the chance meeting on a dissecting table of a sewing machine and an umbrella."[2] But there was more to Lautréamont, and the Letterist International would make off with the best of it.

In a beautiful passage, Lautréamont writes:

> Flights of starlings have a way of flying which is theirs alone and seems as governed by uniform and regular tactics as a disciplined regiment would be, obeying a single leader's voice with precision. The starlings obey the voice of instinct, and their instinct leads them to bunch into the center of the squad, while the speed of their flight bears them constantly beyond it; so that this multitude of birds thus united by a common tendency towards the same magnetic point, unceasingly coming and going, circulating and crisscrossing in all directions, forms a sort of agitated whirlpool whose whole mass, without following a fixed course seems to have a general wheeling movement round itself resulting from the particular circulatory motions appropriate to each of its parts, and whose center, perpetually tending to expand but continually compressed, pushed back by the contrary stress of the surrounding lines bearing upon it, is constantly denser than any of those lines, which are themselves the denser the nearer they are to the center.

Lautréamont is here describing his own swarming poetics—only these lines are lifted straight out of the natural history writings of the Comte de Buffon.

In the early 1950s, something of a scandal ensued when it was discovered that Lautréamont had purloined some of *Maldoror*'s most thrillingly poetic passages from text books. The method announced in the *Poésies* had already been practiced in *Maldoror*. Some, like the literary critic Maurice Saillet (1914–1999), felt the need to defend Lautréamont.[3] Saillet was one of the founders of the self-styled College of Pataphysics. He was a noted scholar of the works of Alfred Jarry (1873–1907), to whose memory the College was consecrated. Started in 1948, the College was a playful, armchair version of the avant-garde impulse. Some of its instigators had day jobs. Others, like Jacques Prévert, Raymond Queneau or Boris Vian were well-known writers. While Saillet could defend Lautréamont in the spirit of linguistic play, the Letterist International credited him with the discovery of a more far-reaching method. Their name for it was *détournement*, as in to detour, to hijack, to lead astray, to appropriate. And it was no joke. The task was to systematize it and—more to the point—practice it.

If there was a precedent in avant-garde poetics for détournement, it came not from the Paris surrealists around André Breton (1896–1966) or even the dissidents around Georges Bataille (1897–1962) but from their Belgian contemporary Paul Nougé (1895–1967). It was Nougé who saw in Lautréamont not a prophet of excess but the inventor of a method. There is, he says, "a certain inclination common to a few minds which leads them to find the elements of creation as close as possible to the object to be created; to the extent that the thing to be desired would come into being by the introduction of a single comma in a page of writing; of a picture, complex in its execution, by the animation of a single stroke of black ink."[4] The texts Nougé corrected ranged from a Baudelaire poem to porn. Some were originally published in *Les Lèvres Nues* (1954–1958), a magazine edited by his friend Marcel Mariën. *Les Lèvres Nues* also published the text that gave this method its name: "A User's Guide to Détournement," by Guy Debord and Gil J. Wolman.

Gil Wolman (1929–95) was not entirely of the Saint-Germain tribe. He had a home to go to—and often brought others to crash there. He lived with his mother. His Jewish father, deported during the war, never returned. Unlike Debord he had a real gift for Letterist poetry. Where Isou chiseled it down to the letter, Wolman pushed on to a poetry of pure sounds, and on again, to a performance art of the diaphragm, of the epiglottis, of corporeality itself. He also pushed Letterist cinema past Isou's comfort zone. Isou's *Treatise on Spit and Eternity* deployed stock footage, scratched images, discrepancies between image and sound; Wolman's *L'Anticoncept* (1950) used no images at all. Unlike Isou's macho posturing, the voice-over of Wolman's film evokes in gentle and sensuous terms the experience of wandering the streets and making love where one can: "in the rain we kiss in the parks I caress you through your dress our muscles tense on the grass ..."[5]

Debord and Wolman both pushed Letterism against itself. "Negation is the transitional term to a new period," as Wolman had written in the preface to *L'Anticoncept*. "Negation of the intrinsic, immutable, pre-existing concept, projects this concept outside of matter, reveals it after the fact to an extrinsic reaction, becomes mutable by as many reactions." Which could be a somewhat abstract way of formulating Isou's theory of the poetry of history and the history of poetry, a key point of reference for both Debord and Wolman. For a moment during the mid 1950s Wolman and Debord's projects flowed together, but the smallest differences would end up pulling them apart. For the moment they were comrades in a civil war against a culture intent on settling for some warmed-up leftovers, banalities such as abstract painting, Beat writing, or existential philosophy, as if these would suffice to fill the void opened up by the war itself.

In "Why Letterism?" (1955) Debord and Wolman characterize the first decade after the war as a time of generalized failure to effect change and a retreat into merely formal elaboration. "One knows, moreover, to what laborious phenomenological refinements professors devote themselves, who otherwise do not dance in cellars."[6] Art and thought appear as a dismal mess—albeit a profitable one. "On a spiritual level, the middle class are always in power." It matters little whether the work takes the form of the bourgeois novel, socialist realist art, the literature of commitment, or the (pseudo) avant-garde: each is just a tactic for restoring middle-class sensibility. "It is necessary to finish with this spirit." This is why there was nothing for it but to join the Letterists, who at least unleashed a potentially fatal *inflation* in the arts, with their reduction of all its forms to the elementary particles of the letter. But the Letterists got caught up in their own fame. Isidore Isou and his factotum Maurice Lemaître (b. 1926) happily appear in a light entertainment called *Around the World with Orson Welles*. They don't notice Welles's sly glance to camera, that makes the viewer complicit in silent ridicule.[7]

Letterism at least pushed formalism to the limit, where it collapsed of its own accord. It was proof of the relative independence of formal development within the arts from social and economic determination. In "Why Letterism?" Debord and Wolman steer between Isou's purely formal theory of art and Marxist determinism. Art has a relative autonomy, its forms develop in their own time, only partly coinciding with a wider historical process. Isou's theory of the formal development of art is linear and autonomous. For Debord and Wolman, development might require going back in order to go forward. For instance, the Precocity movement of the seventeenth century might now reveal itself as a great precursor, a critique in advance of capital's separation of living space from work space according to function. Despite the slanders of Molière, Precocity's devotion to strolling, to conversation, its ideas about décor and architecture, are resources for the construction of a whole attitude to life.[8]

"We write so that our works—which are practically nonexistent—remain in history." This is the hint in "Why Letterism?" of the significance of détournement, which Debord and Wolman only begin to grasp one year later in "A User's Guide to Détournement" (1956). The originality of the Letterist International consists in understanding form not as literary form, in terms of genre, style, poetics and so forth, but as material form, as the book, the film, the canvas. Materiality is the key to the lag by which past culture shapes present culture. If the effects in the architectural domain seem mostly negative, there might be some hope in the lag effect of certain texts. But for past works to become resources for the present requires their use in the present in a quite particular way. It requires their appropriation as a collective inheritance, not as private property. All culture is *derivative*.

Rather than chiseling language down to its bare elements, Debord and Wolman propose something else. Not the destruction of the sign, but rather destruction of the *ownership* of the sign. "It is necessary to eliminate all remnants of the notion of personal property in this area." Détournement offers "an ease of production far surpassing in quantity, variety and quality the automatic writing that has bored us for so long." The surrealist appropriation of Lautréamont's *Poésies* took up his cry that "poetry should be made by all" and read it through *Maldoror* as a poetry that bypassed conscious individual intention in the interests of the collective imagination.[9] The Letterist International's version of a poetry made by all meant two quite other things.

One is that it should be made by and for all the senses at once. Thus dérive as method creates psychogeography as a knowledge via which to design whole new poetic ambiances—the *unitary urbanism* anticipated by Chtcheglov. The other sense of a poetry made by all is a poetry made by the communal appropriation of the past in the present. Chombart's aerial surveys of Paris, not to mention his detailed social science on its everyday life, is not to be quoted but appropriated, détourned, for not only understanding but living the city otherwise.

"Clashing head-on with all social and legal conventions," détournement "cannot fail to be a powerful cultural weapon in the service of the real class struggle. The cheapness of its products is the heavy artillery that breaks through the Chinese walls of understanding. It is the real means of proletarian artistic education, the first step towards a literary communism." The text is true to itself. Debord and Wolman took more than a few lines from Saillet's defense of Lautréamont, and corrected, or rather, developed them. Where Saillet spoke of a communism of genius, this becomes a literary communism. The term *genius* still clings a little to the romantic idea of the text as the product of an individual author's unique gift.

A more crucial détournement is from Marx and Engels's famous *Communist Manifesto* (1848):

> The bourgeoisie, by the rapid improvement of all instruments of production, by the immensely facilitated means of communication, draws all, even the most barbarian, nations into civilization. The

> cheap prices of its commodities are the heavy artillery with which it batters down all Chinese walls, with which it forces the barbarians' intensely obstinate hatred of foreigners to capitulate. It compels all nations, on pain of extinction, to adopt the bourgeois mode of production; it compels them to introduce what it calls civilization into their midst, i.e., to become bourgeois themselves. In one word, it creates a world after its own image.[10]

The inflation introduced by détournement, even more than that of Letterism, is the development that undermines bourgeois culture in turn.

Capital produces a culture in its own image, a culture of the work as private property, the author as sole proprietor of a soul as property. Détournement sifts through the material remnants of past and present culture for materials whose untimeliness can be utilized against bourgeois culture. But rather than further elaborate modern poetics, détournement exploits it. The aim is the destruction of all forms of middle-class cultural shopkeeping. As capital spreads outwards, making the world over in its image, at home it finds its own image turns against it.

It's easy to miss the significance of this claim, buried as it is in a text that spends quite a bit of time on the poetics of détournement. Debord and Wolman discuss a metagraphic composition by Debord —a memorial for Kaki—and the way classified ads about bars for sale contribute to the affect of a remembrance for a suicide. "A User's Guide to Détournement" could be reduced, in other words, to a somewhat limited and clinical statement about *intertextuality*. Tom McDonough: "To carry class conflict into the realm of language, to insist upon the central place that realm occupied in the collective construction of the world to be made, to announce the arrival of a 'literary communism'—these were the inseparable aims of Situationist détournement."[11] Quite, but it is all too easy to elide the significance of literary communism, which is not merely something added to modernist poetics. It is its undoing. It brings class struggle both into and out of language.

Détournement is merely a means to an end. Literary communism is a precursor to architectural communism, to the détournement of built form and the ambiences it can generate. A poetry made by all and a poetry made for all the senses unite in a proposal for the "exact reconstruction in one city of an entire neighborhood of another." An idea which, bizarrely, almost happened—although not entirely as Debord and Wolman intended. In 2008, Dubai businessman Saeed Al Ghandi signed a £350m agreement with the French city of Lyon to build a replica of it in Dubai. "He fell in love with Lyon while strolling along the river-bank," according to José Noya, a Lyon bureaucrat. "He wants to recreate Lyon's soul." The idea sprang from a plan to build a university in Dubai, in partnership with the University of Lyon, that would rival Abu Dhabi's version of the Louvre. This second Lyon would cover an area of about 700 acres, about the size of the Latin Quarter of Paris. The reproduction would not include Lyon's sub-Corbusian tower blocks.[12]

Détournement is the opposite of quotation. Like détournement, quotation brings the past into the present, but it does so entirely within a regime of the proper use of proper names. The key to détournement is its challenge to private property. Détournement attacks a kind of fetishism, where the products of collective human labor in the cultural realm can become a mere individual's property. But what is distinctive about this fetishism is that it does not rest directly on the status of the thing as a commodity. It is, rather, a fetishism of memory. It is not so much commodity fetishism as *co-memory fetishism*. In place of collective remembrance, the fetish of the proper name. The name Lyon, for instance: Al Ghandi's project is a merely a quotation, no matter how vast the scale. Détournement restores to the fragment the status of being a recognizable part of the process of the collective production of meaning in the present, through its recombination into a new meaningful ensemble.

Key to any practice of détournement is identifying the fragments upon which it might work. There is no particular size or shape. It could be a single image, a film sequence of any length, a word, a phrase, a paragraph. What matters is the identification of the superior fidelity of the element to the ensemble within which it finds itself. Détournement is in all cases a reciprocal devaluing and revaluing of the element within the development of a unifying meaning. Détournement is the fluid language of anti-ideology, but ideology has absolutely nothing to do with any particular arrangement of signs or images. It has to do with ownership.

Michel Foucault (1926–84) undermines the romantic theory of authorship by speaking of *discourse* as a distribution of author functions.[13] For Foucault, a statement is authorized by a particular form of discourse, a regime of truth, a procedure for assigning truth-value to statements. It's not hard to see why this captivated the minds of academics. It made the procedures in which academics are obsessively drilled the very form of power itself. As if that by which academics are made, the molding of their bodies to desks and texts, that about which they know the most, even more than they know their allotted fields, were the very index of power. Reading Foucault is like taking a master class on how the game of scholarship is to be played, and with the reliable alibi that this knowledge of power, of knowledge as power, is to be used in the interests of *resistance* to something or other. Détournement, on the other hand, turns the tables, upends the game.

The device of détournement restores all the subversive qualities to past critical judgments that have congealed into respectable truths. Détournement makes for a type of communication aware of its inability to enshrine any inherent and definitive certainty. This language is inaccessible in the highest degree to confirmation by any earlier or supra-critical reference point. On the contrary, its internal coherence and its adequacy in respect of the practically possible are what validate the symbolic remnants that it restores. Détournement founds its cause on nothing but its own practice as critique at work in the present. Détournement creates anti-statements. For the Situationists, the very act of *unauthorized* appropriation is the truth content of détournement.

Needless to say, the best lines in this chapter are plagiarized. Or rather, they are détourned. (It hardly counts as plagiarism if the text itself gives notice of the offense—or does it?) Moreover, many of these détourned phrases have been corrected, as Lautréamont would say. Plagiarism upholds private property in thought by trying to hide its thefts. Détournement treats all of culture as common property to begin with, and openly declares its rights. Moreover, it treats it not as a *creative commons*, not as the *wealth of networks*, not as *free culture* or *remix culture*; but as an active place of challenge, agency, strategy and conflict.[14] Détournement dissolves the rituals of knowledge in an active remembering that calls collective being into existence. If all property is theft, then all intellectual property is détournement.

Not surprisingly, official discourse has a hard time with this concept. The decline of critical theory in the postwar years is directly correlated to the refusal to confront détournement as the most consistent approach to a knowledge made by all. The meandering stream that runs from the Letterist International to the Situationist International and beyond is the course not taken, and remains a troubling memory for critical thought. The path not taken poses the difficult question: what if one challenged the organization of knowledge itself? What if, rather than knowledge as a representation of another life, it is that other life?

Meanwhile, détournement has become a social movement in all but name. Here the Situationists stand as a prophetic pointing of the way towards a struggle for the collective reappropriation and modification of cultural material. One that need only become conscious of itself to re-imagine the space of knowledge outside of private property. Every kid with a BitTorrent client is an unconscious Situationist in the making. What remains is the task of closing the gap between a critical theory gone astray, still caught up in the model of knowledge as property, and a popular movement that cannot quite develop its own consciousness of its own power. As Wolman wrote in his preface to *L'Anticoncept*, "there is no negation that does not affirm itself elsewhere." There might be a link between so-called plagiarism and progress after all.

At stake is the viability of history itself. Officially, history is a spiritless chronicle of events, one damned thing after another. It is so unsatisfying that apocalyptic thinking about time has made a big comeback. To some it seems more plausible that they will shake hands with Jesus than that they could have a hand in their own destiny. But there is official history and there are other histories, including a history of the desire not to end history but to partake of it.

The very idea of history as a process of collective self-making has itself been through a few historical stages.[15] Along came Friedrich Engels (1820–95) and his mechanical time, grinding on. Then came György Lukács (1885–1971) and his expressive time, history as totality, the parts reflecting the whole. Then came Louis Althusser

(1918–90) and structural time, differences meshing and permutating. Then, in desperation, some brought back from the dead Walter Benjamin (1892–1940) and his messianic time, which recasts history from the perspective of its redemption.

As the twentieth century flopped from one horror movie to the next, many gave up on history, but what looked to them like defeat was to others the napalm smell of victory. Sure, the Marxists had their history, which developed through its own internal laws of motion from feudalism to capitalism to socialism, but for Walt Rostow (1916–2003) the latter is just a wrong turn, the industrial state gone mad. The real terminus of historical action was American liberal capitalism. Or perhaps there was another stage to come, what the sociologist Daniel Bell (1919–2011) christened the *post-industrial society*.[16] The computer will overcome all the alienating shortcomings of capital. Work itself will become playful and creative. Commodities will not be mass-produced but custom-made. Not socialism with a human face but capitalism with a smiley face.

The cold war was a clash of historical fictions, Marxist versus anti-Marxist. The outcome seemed far from certain. But with the memory of the communist role in the Resistance fading, Moscow's grand narrative seemed less and less appealing. This left fellow-traveling Western artists and intellectuals with few choices. One was to attach themselves to another promised land. For Régis Debray (b. 1940), this was Cuba. For Althusser this was China. The renewal of history would come via the third world's overthrow of imperialism. The revisionists left the destination of socialism intact, just changed its address and the route to get there. Another choice was to go back to the past in search of the turning point where the narrative of history went wrong, and to become, if not the actual, then at least the spiritual inheritor of the October revolution. This was the choice of the Trotskyites. Alternatively one could abandon historical time altogether, like Jean-François Lyotard (1924–98), and announce the postmodern as a time beyond all these choruses of the grand recital of history.[17]

The Situationists will take another tack. They will not abandon historical thought, nor chime in with one or other chorus as the representative of its destination. To them all the capitals of this world, from Washington to Moscow to Beijing, are capitals of the same spectacular society. This tiny band would set themselves against power in its totality. A futile project, perhaps, but powerful in its very futility, in casting the whole century in negative relief. Against the abandonment of historical possibility on the left, and the triumphant declaration that this is the best of all possible worlds on the right, it's time to step back into the current. The other history, the historical practice left unexplored, restores causality but renders it fluid, complex, turbulent. But not for all that arbitrary or formless. History is no machine, no structure, nor does it call for the solace of a merely figurative redemption.

By the mid 1950s Guy Debord achieved some notoriety with his film *Howls for Sade* (1952), and drew around himself the motley collection of drunks, drifters and geniuses known as the Letterist International.[18] He painted its slogan by the banks of the river Seine —"Never work!"—and did his best to live up to it. He discovered that this implied another, even harder discipline, the unwritten slogan: "Make no art!" In later life Debord would turn the milieu from which the Letterist International spawned into a legendary counterpoint to the spectacle, perhaps even more central than the legend of May '68. Yet in 1957 the Letterist world was more of a constraint on its own ambitions for upending the world. The Letterist International too had to die in the war of time. It was no longer adequate to its own discoveries.

The Letterist International passes on to the Situationist International the practice of a negative action, which lays bare the gap between everyday life in twentieth century capitalism, and what it leaves to be desired. What the Letterist International have going for them is the consistency of an everyday life lived as negation. What they do not have is either the depth of experience or the consistency of theoretical invention that might come with it. That will come from the encounter with Asger Jorn.

4 Extreme Aesthetics

Once upon a time there lived a beautiful dancer, whom some called Tintomara, but who went by many names, all derived from novels and plays. Tintomara was very striking, and both men and women could hardly help but be captivated by her. Or by him, for Tintomara had both a male and a female aspect, like one of those eight-limbed beings of Aristophanes, who met all their own desires and lacked for nothing.[1] One day Tintomara the dancer was rehearsing with the ballet master a piece based on some primitivist fantasy or other. Dressed as a Native American savage girl, he was to be pinned to the floor by four of the chief's men, only to break free and turn away from his captors.

Only he did not just break and turn. "Like a rose that does not want to come into bloom, the savage girl had indeed gone noticeably outside the turn ... A movement clearly due neither to forgetfulness nor ineptitude." Was this too part of the drama? "The savage girl's movements were so exquisite, so charming, that only quite exceptional art or simple nature, whilst transgressing the whole sense of the dance, could yet excite the ballet master in so strange a fashion that he, delighted to see it, was unable to intervene and hinder her from committing so gross a breach of the pantomime's design."[2]

This fable comes from an extraordinary novel by Swedish writer Carl Jonas Love Almqvist (1793–1866). Regardless of whether Asger Jorn ever read *Tintomara,* he was fond of Almqvist and shared with him commitments to a distinctive Scandinavian cultural tradition, to a peculiar combination of mystic and materialist thought, and to a radical conception of aesthetics which could combine extremes of romanticism and realism. All are expressed in Tintomara's gesture. Neither male nor female, nature nor culture, flesh nor spirit, form nor feeling, Tintomara is Almqvist's image of an undivided being, irreducible to any form or essence. Tintomara's fate is not a happy one. In the end her lifeless body will be left to twist in the wind. But from Almqvist to Jorn there is a line of thought, of creation, of cultural action that tries to make a world fit for its Tintomaras.

Asger Jorn (1914–73) is admired as an artist. The art historian and former Situationist T. J. Clark calls him "the greatest painter of the fifties."[3] He is less well known as a theorist, and certainly not often acknowledged as a key theorist of the Situationist International. It is possible to extract from Jorn's texts a unique take on the Situationist project, one he was entitled to claim as his own more than most. Jorn the theorist is intimately connected, not just to his art, but also to his extraordinary life. In 1936 Jorn took off for Paris on a motorcycle. He joined the studio of Ferdinand Léger and worked briefly for Le Corbusier. He spent the war years in his native Denmark, secretly printing a monthly Communist journal and working with the Hell-Horse group, whose project fused leftist politics, modernist aesthetics and pan-Scandinavian culture. After the war he returned to Paris. He met Constant Nieuwenhuys at an exhibition of the Catalan surrealist Joan Miró (1893–1983). Jorn and Constant, together with Belgian surrealist poet Christian Dotremont (1922–79) would be central figures in the Cobra movement, which lasted from 1948 to 1952.[4]

Dotremont and Jorn spent much of 1951 in a Danish sanitarium, recovering from tuberculosis. It was here that Jorn found time for an extensive reading of Kierkegaard thanks to a priest at the sanitarium who had the collected works.[5] It was here that Jorn wrote *Luck and Chance*, the first of a series of strange, intense, theoretical works, blueprints of a sort both for his art and for his continued wagers on collaborative forms of action.

The Movement for an Imaginist Bauhaus was Jorn's next bid for collective acton. Started in Italy in 1954, its impetus was Jorn's antipathy to the Swiss artist and designer Max Bill (1908–94). Like Jorn a person of credible anti-fascist credentials, Bill was commissioned to create a curriculum for a design school in Ulm "following Bauhaus principles," according to Bill. He studied at the Bauhaus in Dessau for a year or so before the war, and had developed his own aesthetics and politics out of his close contact with modernist artists and designers of the interwar years. From Theo van Doesburg he took the idea of *concrete design*, which "arises out of its own means and laws, without these having to be derived or borrowed from natural phenomena."

In Bill's aesthetic, beauty both derives from function and is a function. And yet this beauty is Platonic, reductionist, a shearing away of the accidental to arrive at a certain formal purity: "The whole environment created by us, from the spoon to the city, had to be brought into harmony with social conditions, which implied shaping those conditions too." Where the Bauhaus had originally housed both artists and designers, and concerned itself with both the formal and the symbolic, with objective functions and subjective experiences, Bill completely excluded the aesthetic experimental dimension from his postwar restoration of the Bauhaus aesthetic. "We have to guard against the danger of going by appearances and instead attempt to bring all our contemporary powers into a harmonious balance—into what we'd like to call *the good form*." Yet Bill was an artist, albeit one who could claim "we have eliminated every parasite in painting" by which he meant anything figurative, or any hint of the material world at all. Nothing could be further from Jorn's understanding of the legacy and significance of Bauhaus artists such as Paul Klee (1879–1940) than Bill's declaration that "art is an order, a prototype of harmony."[6]

Jorn's antipathy for Bill's new Bauhaus prompted him to revise and elaborate his own writings on form, eventually published by the Situationist International as *For Form*.[7] Jorn is not as optimistic about postwar culture as Bill. "Culture no longer takes place in a situation, because we can only speak of a situation when there is an event, and an act only becomes an event at the moment it is able to trigger sensation." Jorn's own art, like his collective actions, are attempts to reignite sensation through experiments in emergent form. Jorn thinks of movement and matter rather like Lautréamont's starlings, where discernible form emerges out of random movements of definite proportions. "This new view of the whole leads us to the awareness of a new dynamic method in formal and artistic creation. But this also teaches us that we must throw ourselves into the confusion and act directly on the contradictions by creating new ones, if we want to fertilize development."

Aesthetics means experiment, elaboration, not purification. For Jorn, Bill's pronouncements are "doctrines that merely repeat the anti-poetic perspectives of old Platonism ... and more generally the whole of Hellenic idealism." It is ignorant of the complexities and organicism of other traditions of form, in Europe and elsewhere. It has not kept up with developments in the materialist worldview which rediscover these traditions. "Modern science has reached the point where it recognizes that phenomena consisting of a sufficiently large number of separate phenomena acting without causality, nevertheless strictly obey the law of causality in their ensemble." Jorn wants an aesthetics that is abreast of modern understandings of the physical world, rather than one that harks back to a classical mechanics.

The creative act cannot concern itself solely with the beautiful and the functional. "The rationalists seek an absolute symmetry between form, structure and function, while evolution occurs precisely through an increasing dissymmetry among these three elements." The evolution of form is driven by dreams, longings, imaginary aims, the desire for sensation. The ultimate purpose of a new form cannot be known in advance. "Evolution is a perpetual anomaly." Out of such anomalies—ugly, functionless—emerge new sensations, new situations, and sometimes new enduring forms. "Ugliness is no less rare than beauty." Everything else is just a middling boredom.

With the Imaginist Bauhaus Jorn wanted to revive, on a broader footing, the experimental aesthetic practice of Cobra (1948–52). He saw such collaborative aesthetic experiments as an essential component of the Bauhaus legacy. Imaginist Bauhaus would merge with the Letterist International into the Situationist International in 1957, in the process shedding Jorn's contemporary Ettore Sottsass (1917–2007), who would go on to fame as an industrial designer. Where Sottsass introduced a playfulness and openness quite foreign to Bill, and central to the formation of a *postmodern style* in design, neither Bill nor Sottsass really thought critically about the creation of form within the social and natural worlds in the manner to which Jorn aspired.[8]

Jorn was seventeen years older than Debord, who he met in 1954. His intellectual, artistic and activist formation had come earlier. His politics came from arguments on the Scandinavian left. His practical abilities emerged in the communist-aligned cultural resistance to Nazi control of Denmark. His intellectual formation is a more complicated matter. Jorn developed an original and extensive aesthetic and political theory of art, abreast of, but outside, the established avant-garde patterns of the time. If one seeks the precursors to the Situationists, they might more easily be found not at the Parisian epicenter but in the periphery, in Isou's Romania, in Nougé's Belgium, and in the Denmark of Asger Jorn.

The suns around which Jorn's thought orbits are, as for so many others, Darwin, Nietzsche and Marx, although his path was more elliptical than most. The Marxist in Jorn expects capitalism to collapse, but not through class struggle so much as *ontological* struggle. Its inability to grasp its own nature condemns it. For Jorn, "the socialist way of life is the natural way of life."[9] Everything about Jorn's thought and actions can be read through this statement, including his critique of, and eventual break with, Marxism. Class division is original sin, and the struggle on the aesthetic, political and philosophical planes alike is to restore, not a lost unity but a lost process, an open, creative, play of differences in which collective human endeavor transforms nature without imitating it, but without dominating it either. Being is just like Tintomara's dance, where the turn becomes embellished, ornamented, shaped with and by desire.

Marxist aesthetics is in thrall to the classical. Marx and Engels had not thought through the consequences of their discoveries. Their idealized view of classical—particularly Greek—form distorts the whole of Marxist thought and practice. Here Jorn turns to Nietzsche, and his distinction in *The Birth of Tragedy* (1872) between an Apollonian aesthetic of form and the Dionysian aesthetic of process. Jorn views Apollo and Dionysus as a tension between aristocratic and folk life. When the cultural representatives of the ruling classes make war against serpents, dragons, sirens, they are at war with nature, including human nature—our species-being. They are at war, more precisely, with the Dionysian aspect of our species-being that the subordinate classes embody. Jorn: "It is precisely this distaste for the freedom and richness of life, its color and variation, which one calls *good taste*."[10] Expression, like Tintomara's turn, is for Jorn the key to a Dionysian aesthetics. The Apollonian version of classical culture represses creation, process, difference, and leads to a slavish reduction of flux to static and ideal forms, to representation rather than expression. This might apply as much to Greek vase painting as to Plato's eternal forms.

It is not so much that there is a conflict between the Dionysian and the Apollonian, but that they are two different ways of understanding and practicing conflict. For Jorn there are two kinds of dialectic—dualist and monist. The dualist dialectic is an external conflict between irreconcilable differences. The monist dialectic is a more subtle kind of movement. This is key to Jorn's critique of Marxism: "The defective concept of the whole determines the defective grasp of economic wholeness."[11] The Dionysian experiences antagonism as alternation, flux, turbulence, complexity, and Marxism has not quite internalized this. While Jorn still speaks in a Marxist vein of dialectic, he reads the dialectic as flux. Creation emerges out of giving oneself over to the play of alternating and ramifying movement, out of which something new can arise organically. Strangely enough, he sees in Engels's *Anti-Dühring* (1877) a critique of metaphysical thinking that can be extended to a critique of classical conception of form—and turned against itself. Engels's dialectic is not quite as mechanical as it is often taken to be.[12]

Here a space opens up for an *artistic materialism.* Parallel to the Marxist tradition runs an aesthetic one, from Cézanne to Miró and the Bauhaus artist Paul Klee.[13] Crucial to Jorn's reworking of Marxist thought is his radical revision of the locus and significance of the aesthetic. Art belongs to the infrastructure of society, not to the superstructure. Art is a fundamental kind of social production. Marxism breaks with classical tradition by assigning priority to action rather than contemplation, but its error is to consider art only as a form of contemplation. Art is action.

Engels wrote that "the economic structure of society always furnishes the real basis, starting from which we can alone work out the ultimate explanation of the whole superstructure of juridical and political institutions as well as of the religious, philosophical and other ideas of a given historical period."[14] Jorn would agree with this, but with the proviso that aesthetic practice is part of the economic structure, not just one of the "other ideas" within the superstructure. The qualitative practice of art is as much part of the base of the capitalist social formation as its quantitative production process. The ontological failure of capital, its inability to perceive and produce its own reality, stems from the domination of the quantitative over the qualitative process.

Jorn breaks with the privileging of science that he finds particularly in Engels. Jorn distinguishes between what he calls a *worldview* and an *attitude to life*. Both, he insists, can be materialist, but they do not always go together. Even when science has a materialist worldview, it does not necessarily have a materialist attitude to life. It remains Apollonian. It sees matter as reducible to quantitative data, which in turn measure abstract forms and yield eternal laws. In 2009 Australian scientists discovered that bees on cocaine are much more enthusiastic about sources of food they have found.[15] The cocaine for these experiments was kept locked away by the university's ethics department, which released only enough for each experiment, thus ensuring that no cocaine would be consumed by scientists to make them more enthusiastic than otherwise about their data. This surely would qualify as an instance of the materialist worldview at work—scientific procedure, falsifiable results—without the materialist attitude to life. Everything about it is to remain partitioned from the everyday, which continues in its routine form, free from any whiff of the experimental. The materialist attitude to life is precisely materialism which takes the qualitative transformation of matter into life as primary. The limit for Jorn to *scientific* socialism is that it embraces a materialist worldview, but not a materialist attitude to life. His artistic materialism proposes to fill this gap.

Aesthetic experiment is the necessary complement to scientific experiment, but it is not an imitation of science. While science extends knowledge and expands the materialist worldview, art creates a way of life by shaping material characteristics according to desire. If science concerns itself with objective truth, then art will search for subjective truth. "Rather an entangled and chaotic truth than a four-square, beautiful, symmetrical and finely-chiseled lie." But, crucially, Jorn sees subjectivity as non-individualistic. The art that matters is a subjective realism that extends beyond the individual and invokes a collective practice: "art, therefore, is not a representation, a mirror, of nature but a direct transformation of nature."[16] Art is experimental social practice which transforms nature into second nature, but without reducing nature to essence or order.

Aesthetics is prior to ethics. Aesthetics is about desires; ethics is about duty. The capacity that matters in art is that of actualizing desires. What is best in the aesthetic is not the work of art as a representation of phenomena. Rather, the aesthetic has the capacity to become a part of people's habits of life. The aesthetic is a *cultivating* factor, forming and transforming habits of life. As such, the aesthetic is prior to science, which extracts regularities from the aesthetic, but is dependent on a given stage in its development for its materials. The aesthetic is also prior to all the branches of philosophy. It is that within which philosophy is situated. It is that which philosophy begins to think.

Ruling-class art—the Apollonian—represents the world as made in its own image, and assigns a subsidiary role in that representation for that which it fears. What it fears is the alignment of popular power with the forces of nature as an open-ended process, as the capacity to overthrow form, including political form. Dionysian art is folk memory of the social capacity to merge the processes of nature and desire. This is what attracted Jorn to ritual and mysticism. Unlike Bataille, he was not looking for traces of an ineffable absolute, but rather for a form of knowledge of the capacities latent in the social apprehension of the world. Art is a particular kind of knowledge and practice of the possible: "the highest achievement in art must lie in an orchestration of all our senses together in a communal expression."[17] The dérive already struck out on a path comparable to this. Communal expression will become a core program of the Situationist International, at least in its early years.

Art is playful; play is social. Play may take nature as its object, but not as a means to an end: "play is not consciously directed to any goal but is a delight, an identification with things themselves. This is why play develops best in community."[18] To correct a line from Lautréamont, poetry should be played by all. While Jorn aligns himself with the popular against ruling-class art, he does so critically. For a famous series of works called *Modifications* (1957–62), Jorn painted on some amateur pictures he bought in the flea market, but without obscuring the figures and landscapes of the Sunday painters. While Jorn approved of the democratization of art, it fell short of its own power. "The art of naïve adults in our society represents nothing more than the clumsy attempt to master the current forms of classical art."[19] The mistake lay in the imitation of existing forms, which tended also to preserve the idea of art as something separate from life. Popular art risked losing its playful quality. Following the Dutch historian Johan Huizinga (1872–1945), Jorn thought that "if play lacks its vital purpose then ceremony fossilizes into an empty form."[20] The solution was a popular art which did not imitate isolated forms but which applied itself to the transformation of matter. Art can extend the cooperative qualities of nature into social life.

From the Russian anarchist Peter Kropotkin, Jorn takes a sense of nature as cooperation, not as Darwinian struggle. Jornian nature does not really yield an ethical model to imitate. Nature, as Spinoza says, "subjects all things to a certain indifferent will."[21] Nature has no final cause, no end determined for it. Without at this time quite realizing it Jorn is heading away from the historical determinism of his Marxist training. In some respects he anticipates the Spinozism of Gilles Deleuze. Against the conventional image of one organism competing against another of the same kind, Deleuze proposes the image of the wasp and the orchid, two dissimilar organisms which cooperate to reveal and increase each other's powers.[22]

A reading of the natural sciences still has some critical work to do, however. From it Jorn extracts an ontology of nature as flux, difference and also cooperation on the basis of which Jorn asserts that class struggle is an aberration, and that the social Darwinist model of nature as competition is false. For Jorn, "man's nature is just to cultivate and nourish his urges."[23] Our species-being is *homo aestheticus*, close to what Huizinga called *homo ludens*, the playing kind. It is not *homo economicus*, or the war of all against all. This image of nature is merely a distorted image of capitalist society: "there is nothing so unnatural for man as what the bourgeoisie calls naturalness."[24]

It is Engels who leads Jorn down the slippery slope of a dialectics of nature, and like Engels he risks a somewhat vapid generalization of certain figures from scientific literature which, while in some ways different to capitalism's ideological recourse to a self-image as natural, are no less partial. But what distinguishes Jorn from Engels is not just that his readings in scientific literature are more contemporary; they are readings of a different kind. Jorn does not aspire to a materialist worldview, as Engels did, but a materialist attitude to life. He wants not a metaphysics legitimized by science but a *pataphysics* that reads science creatively. Rather than imitate scientific writing, Jorn—like Alfred Jarry—appropriates from scientific writing according to his own desires.[25] Truth for Jorn is subjective, but subjective truth is social. His ontology is true to the collective experience he lived through, of Hell-Horse, Danish socialism, the Resistance. His version of Marx diverges from all the main currents of what would come to be known as Western Marxism.[26] Unlike Lukács he embraces Engels's dialectic of nature; unlike Althusser he distances himself from the scientific worldview.

"All that we know of life is that it is organized movement." It is chaos and complexity: Tintomara's turn. The aesthetic begins by organizing the powers of matter and elaborating them in a way that responds to their complexity. A word for this might be *ornament*, but where ornament is not an exclusively human phenomenon: "we see air currents forming ornaments across the earth." Jorn is drawn to those frilly styles that modernism generally repudiated: Gothic, Rococo, Jugendstil. But the modern moment has its uses, and here Jorn's thinking comes close to Isidore Isou: "The tremendously consistent purge of empty ornamental elements of form is in reality classicism's Pyrrhic victory. It is a *tabula rasa* for what is to come; for an art of the future." That art will return to ornament not as an addition to nature or its representation, but as a process of drawing it out and turning it towards the expansion of the possibilities for social life. At its best, ornament demonstrates a "pact with the universe."[27] Ornament in art extends and distends the line as it is discovered in the social practice of qualitative engagement with matter. Ornament is the aesthetic key to Jorn's monism, the signature of a being that is univocal, and the reminder that history has diverged from coherence in flux.

Jorn's thought is opposed to art as representation, but also to abstraction, both in Max Bill and, more fundamentally, in Le Corbusier. His problem with Le Corbusier is that while he also drew inspiration from nature, he understands nature in Apollonian terms, paring away at complexity—nature's own ornamentation of itself—to get at an eternal geometrical essence. Le Corbusier aligns the aesthetic with a materialist worldview, but not a materialist attitude to life. Perhaps it is no surprise then that Le Corbusier took a top-down approach to building new worlds. Likewise, abstract art became dominant because a new ruling class could tolerate neither the symbols of the old one nor the express desires of the people. But the problem for the development of a popular art is a split between the symbol and the community. The symbols artists can come up with now are diagrams of personal forces, not social ones. This is a problem even for radical artists. Surveying the generation before his, Jorn observes that Klee found symbols, but not popular ones; Mayakovsky became the voice of the people, but at the expense of the symbol.[28]

Jorn took his distance from both socialist realist art and from abstraction, thus dodging the aesthetic fissure of the cold war. He found a way to reconcile them in what is best described as the *diagram*. He shared with Debord an attachment to the beauty of Paris street plans and subway maps, and saw them as part of a larger aesthetic tradition. "A map of the metro is not naturalistic, but it certainly cannot be said that it is unrealistic. We know the same method of working from modern [comic] strips in color magazines as well as from Bronze Age rock-carvings, from Chinese and Egyptian murals, from the drawings of Australian aborigines as well as from the modern art of people like Klee and Miró, and all this is in glaring contrast to the whole classical tradition of composition."[29] The goal must be a pictorial process free and open to the whole of life, a diagram of forces, trajectories, possibilities, rather than a representation of an object, cut from the world as a frozen moment.

Jorn was almost but not entirely seduced by the *primitive*. Natural culture for Jorn does not date from the Paleolithic, which is rather a time of alienation: "Class society arises when an unproductive tribe of hunters, specialized in weaponry, comes to dominate a cultured people and forces them into servile labor." The historical precedent for a natural culture is Neolithic agrarian society, with its experimental transformation of nature via agriculture, and its combination of the division of labor with a rough equality. Here humans "found the key to nature's way of developing."[30] Naturalism for Jorn is not a question of imitation but of qualitative development. Jorn's is a mystical materialism, in that he sees mystery as the intuition of the unity of being, of totality. But the significance of mystery has been betrayed by the course of historical development. "Instead of the materialist's ecstatic love for matter, life, mankind and himself, religions have turned to the non-existent, which is really to be equated with death but which religion calls God."[31] The sense of the univocity of being is lost, and with it the intuition of difference and flux.

Religion emerges because of the deviation from a truly naturalistic and social human development. In class society, religion replaces an open totality with a closed and imaginary one. Most strikingly, Jorn asserts that "communism is much older than all religions."[32] By communism Jorn means both a consistency between the spiritual and the temporal, and a collaborative practice of aesthetic transformation of nature. Originary mysticism is the worship of fertility, the materialistic cult par excellence. A modern reinstatement of mystery can supply a cultural ideology to Marxism which encourages everyone towards cultural activity. Put simply: "Art is cult." Culture is our species' love affair with the earth. This was the idyllic line of thought Jorn proposed in the wake of an era of mass destruction. "We have lost our paradise on earth and what is worse, those who seek to restore this paradise are seen as idiots estranged from life or individuals who are dangerous to society."[33] It is not God that is dead; death is God.

Dualism comes from class society: ruling-class spirit pits itself against subordinate class matter. From his—eccentric—reading of Kierkegaard, Jorn derived class society's three neuroses: art, ethics, and religion. Each produces a worldview of illusory unity in isolation from social processes. Against this, Jorn asserted the vitality of a spontaneous, creative aesthetics and a series of three revolutionary forms from below: anarchist, syndicalist and communist. But Jorn's attachment to the Communist Party waned rapidly after the war. Cobra failed as a movement at least in part because it positioned itself as a communist art form, only to be rejected and vilified by party art commissars.[34] It is not hard to see in his feverish theoretical activities of the 1950s and his various organizations an attempt to create a fourth form of radical monism, one for which Debord would propose the name—Situationist.

One thing that united the two men was Jorn's explicit and Debord's implicit rejection of the dualistic philosophy of Jean-Paul Sartre, in which *situation* figured as a key if somewhat troubling concept. Sartre's wartime classic *Being and Nothingness* (1943) famously makes the category of *freedom* a central one, but in so doing it has a sly recourse also to the category of situation. That which is for-itself, consciousness, presupposes something external to it. "There can be a free for-itself only in a resisting world."[35] It is because of the intractable physicality of things that freedom arises as freedom. If it were enough to conceive of a project for it to be realized, then, like the surrealists, Sartre would be "plunged in a world like that of a dream in which the possible is no longer in any way distinguished from the real," and Sartre could no longer distinguish a fiction from a desire. Once this gap disappears, then freedom disappears too. To be free is not to have what one desires, but to determine oneself to desire. To desire is to act on that desire. To be free is, paradoxically, not a choice. We are "condemned to freedom." Even a decision not to be free presupposes freedom. Freedom exists only in the end it posits, but its existence is not given in that end. "Thus the empirical and practical concept of freedom is wholly negative; it issues from the consideration of a situation and establishes that this situation leaves me free to pursue this or that end."

What then is this situation that leaves Sartre free to pursue this or that end? Writing during wartime, Sartre's example of a situation is telling: "Remove the prohibition to circulate in the streets after curfew, and what meaning can there be for me to have the freedom … to take a walk at night?" Sartre goes out for a walk in the city at night during curfew. The street might look beautiful to him, or it might not, but this is just the street as an object of contemplation. As a situation it is something else. The situation is the common product of its own unknowable facticity and of Sartre's freedom. The situation is an ambiguous phenomenon in which consciousness cannot distinguish in advance the contribution of freedom and the contribution of the in-itself.

The street Sartre wants to walk is the object of his freedom. His freedom selects it. But what his freedom cannot determine is whether it can be walked safely without running into the police. This is part of the brute existence of the street. But the street only reveals its hazards to his walking it when he makes it the object of his desire to walk. He integrates it into the project of walking. He cannot determine in advance what comes from freedom (the for-itself) and what from the in-itself of the street. Sartre: "it is only in and through the free upsurge of a freedom that the world develops and reveals the resistance which can render the projected end realizable." There is no obstacle in an absolute sense. It is Sartre who determines what is a constraint on freedom by positing freedom in the first place. Thus while the curfew appears as a limit to his action, it is his freedom which constitutes the method and the ends of action in relation to which the curfew appears then as a limit.

What meaning can there be in the freedom to walk at night, through the Paris of the mid 1950s, the curfew of the occupation lifted and the curfew of the Algerian war not yet descended? The dérive appears almost as if it is a direct answer to this question. The dérive is the experimental mapping of a situation, the trace of the probabilities of realizing a desire. There is still the police to contend with, and delinquent Letterists and their friends would occasionally end up in jail for the night. But the dérive is more than the no-man's-land between consciousness and facticity, for-itself and in-itself, freedom and constraint. It is rather the flux, the monist dialectic, which produces as one of its effects the experience of the gap between in-itself and for-itself in the first place.

Practices like dérive, détournement and potlatch, which will become the defining practices of the Situationist International, produce among other things the possibility of new concepts outside of Sartrean dualism. The interest is not in consciousness and its freedom, but in the production of new situations as an end in themselves. In the Letterist International, Jorn saw fellow travelers engaged in the critical practice of producing an autonomous space for new practices.

Jorn's amateur Marxist theories from the 1940s and early '50s went largely unpublished at the time and received scant attention. The most influential appropriation of Marxist thought would not be Sartre's but that of Jorn's contemporary, Louis Althusser. They could hardly be more different.[36] Althusser spent the war in a POW camp, not the Resistance. Althusser's thought was in Jorn's terms clearly that of a materialist worldview. It took science rather than aesthetic practice as its model. Althusser stayed within the Communist Party (with Maoist sympathies) rather than break with it. He made Marxism respectable within the space of the academy, rather than attempting to found a new nexus between theory and practice outside of it. Althusser was much more interested in history as objective process than as subjective practice. Where Althusser became a respected academic philosopher, Jorn's academic advisor gently suggested that his thesis was not really the sort of thing that could even be submitted. Like Walter Benjamin's, Jorn's doctoral work is of interest because of its failure of good academic form.

And these are precisely the reasons why Jorn now merits attention, and why his thought deserves development. Jorn points towards the question of practice, outside of, and now after the eclipse of, both the Communist and bourgeois versions of history. If Althusser cements a place within the academy for developing Marxism as a critical postwar discourse, he does so at the expense of aligning it with high theory. Marx is absorbed into the conventions of academic thought, into its spaces of authority, its codes of discipline, its temporality of semesters and sabbaticals. Jorn offers something in addition to all that. His is a development of Marx as a critical postwar discourse that creates its own games, makes its own rules, answers to a quite different time, and belongs to a more marginal but more interesting space, the space not of an institution but of a provisional micro-society, within which the practice of thought might be otherwise.

5 A Provisional Micro-Society

The Situationist International was founded at a meeting of three women and six men in July 1957. All that remains of this fabled event are a series of stirring documents and some photographs, casual but made with an artist's eye, by founding member Ralph Rumney.[1] The Situationist International dissolved itself in 1972. In its fifteen years of existence, only seventy-two people were ever members. It was born out of the fusion of two and a half existing groups, the Movement for an Imaginist Bauhaus, the Letterist International and the London Psychogeographical Society (the last represented by its one and only member, Rumney). Its founding conference took place in Cosio di Arroscia a little Ligurian town where founding member Piero Simondo's family had a small hotel. Or at least that's the official story. Debord writes in a letter to Jorn: "I think it is necessary for us to present the 'Conference at Cosio' as a point of departure for our distinct organized activity."[2] From the beginning, Debord has a fine hand for the tactics of appearances.

Debord the tactician saw the Letterist International as something of a dead end. The dérive could only be taken so far. After he was institutionalized, Chtcheglov would write Debord and Bernstein from the sanatorium explaining that the dérive has its limits, and cannot be practiced continually. "It's a miracle it didn't kill us. Iron infected our blood."[3] To even propose a new architecture for a new way of life took more resources than they possessed. The complete renunciation of what one might now call middle-class life cut them off from vital resources. "To reach this superior cultural creation—that which we call the Situationist game—we now think it necessary to be an active force in the actual terrain of this era's culture (and not on the fringes of it, as we cheerfully were ...)."

Hence the change of policy from the "pure (inactive) extremism" of the Letterist International.[4] Going forward called for taking a few steps back. The project would—temporarily—require some resources to advance its aims. The Situationist game must proceed "by all means, even artistic ones."[5]

Debord skillfully positioned himself as the secretary for a new movement, the Situationist International. Of all the roles Debord chose for himself, not to mention those assigned to him by posterity, the one that receives the least attention is that of secretary. Late in life he was to say: "I have been a good professional—but in what?"[6] While the question was meant to be rhetorical, one not entirely implausible answer would be—as a secretary. Not the least interesting thing about him might be the tactics with which he ran the Situationist International, and the best way to approach them is via his *Correspondence*. Prepared by his widow Alice Becker-Ho (b. 1941) and published posthumously, the *Correspondence* presents a carefully vetted and selected account of Debord the secretary.

The secretary's task, as Debord conceives it, involves the organizing of exhibitions, provocations, occasional publications and, above all, the journal *Internationale Situationniste*. It is, Debord writes, "our 'official organ,' the ideological coherence of which was made my responsibility." Debord will act as secretary with remarkable tenacity and industry. *Internationale Situationniste* would not be a duplicated flyer like the Letterist International's *Potlatch*, but a beautifully edited, illustrated, designed and bound affair. By 1960 the author of "Never work!" would be complaining: "I am overwhelmed with work." Here he is discussing the use of a material called Lumaline for the cover, in a way that will bring a smile to anyone who has ever labored over manufacturing something beautiful: "The effect is obviously superb. But the price is terribly high: 100,000 for the cover (for only 1,600 copies of the journal), but especially 60,000 for supplementary expenses to the printer, representing a lot of work in folding and sewing, entirely by hand— the machines break the Lumaline, which soon tears. And then we will have nearly lost the stock at that stage of assembly (in this process, one loses at least 10 percent due to badly sewn copies)."[7]

Debord labored in the service of producing *Internationale Situationniste* as a collective expression, a document of a provisional micro-society whose practice is to treat all of culture as collective property. "Our editorial committee has a heavy hand (and, as you may imagine, no respect for literary propriety)." Détournement was both a signature Situationist practice and a theory of how culture as a totality works. Debord writes to Straram in Canada: "All the material published by the Situationist International is, in principle, usable by everyone, even without acknowledgment, without the preoccupations of literary property. You can make all the détournements that appear useful to you."[8]

One makes a movement with what one has. The practice of the *exclusion* of members from the Situationist International begins very soon after its founding. As a good secretary, Debord has little tolerance for opportunism or ineptitude. He writes to Walter Olmo, a founding member: "I reproach you for having accepted, in particular circumstances, several ideas that are stupid." Olmo will not last long. Ralph Rumney lasts almost a year. Debord writes to him in March 1958: "you still haven't done any real work with us."[9] To compound Debord's annoyance, Rumney boasts of his Situationist connections to art-world acquaintances.

Rumney's official offense was to submit his psychogeographical report on Venice too late for inclusion in the journal. Between harassment by his mother-in-law, Peggy Guggenheim, and the birth of his son, Rumney had his hands full.[10] Since he was the one at Cosio who advocated zero tolerance towards anyone not fully committed to the cause, his expulsion was fair enough. Rumney's "The Leaning Tower of Venice" went unpublished at the time, but it is not without interest. It took the form of a détournement of the photo-romance strips then particularly popular in Italy, and is an early example of Situationist détournement of narrative graphic art.

Rumney took photographs of the Beat writer Alan Ansen and arranged them as a narrative with captions. "It is our thesis that cities should embody a built-in play factor," reads one. "We are studying here a play-environment relationship." Rumney's photographs follow Ansen on a "trajectory through the zones of psychogeographic interest." Its subject is specifically play, as "play and game are not synonymous." Ansen's gambols are not constrained by formal rules. There is no boundary marking of the space of a game from the space outside it. Play has no conditions for winning or losing, and no end condition determined in advance. Play simply comes to an end when Runmey spots Lawrence Alloway, the English art critic, and in this case spoil-sport.[11]

Becoming a Situationist required a certain rigor. Debord: "I am still with the Situationist International and, as long as I am in it, I will keep a minimum of discipline that excludes all collaboration with uncontrollable elements."[12] To today's middle-class sensibility, submission to a discipline for reasons other than getting paid seems like some kind of perversion, and for that reason membership in the Situationist International seems as unintelligible a sacrifice as the mysteries of religion. A more common model for what remains of the artist in today's disintegrating spectacle is that of the small business proprietor. Take as an example Jeff Koons (b. 1955), who "staked his budding penchant for expensively fabricated art by working as a commodities broker on Wall Street for six years ... Today he has a factory in Chelsea with ninety regular assistants."[13] To be an artist, it seems, has become just another kind of middle-class ambition, the dream of a franchise with your name on it.

The exclusion of members is sometimes taken to reveal some sinister side to Debord's character, so it is interesting to read in the *Correspondence* that "Jorn was the first partisan of the measure of exclusion." Jorn was one of the few Situationists who had ever been a member of an orthodox Communist party. But while the Situationist International is often compared to such a party, the parallel is usually made by people who have never belonged to one. Certainly, to an ear trained by the cold war to protect its precious individualism, the Situationists can sound like invasive body snatchers, as for example in this telegram to an excluded member: "The I without we falls back into the prefabricated mass."[14] What the Situationists were struggling to achieve was a new kind of collective being, unlike both the Communists and previous avant-gardes such as the Letterists.

Situationists were expected to know what was expected of them, and without being told. Debord's policy as secretary was "to place a priori confidence, in all cases, and only until the first proof to the contrary, in a certain number of recognized comrades, based upon objective criteria." The reason for most exclusions is not mysterious. It was a failure to live up to expectations. Members are what they do: "No problem in our collective action can be resolved by goodwill." A certain unsentimental understanding of how friendships form and dissolve, of how character becomes different to itself as it struggles in and against time, underlies the distinctive quality of Situationist subjectivity in which "neither freedom nor intelligence are given once and for all."[15]

Bataille had thought that what binds community together is the experience of death.[16] Under the guidance of the surrealist turned Stalinist Louis Aragon (1897–1982), postwar communist culture created a real cult out of its dead Resistance fighters. The red flag shrouds its martyred dead, whose blood dyes its every fold. The Situationists borrowed at least this much from the communists—that the exclusion of living members meant social death. Given that communist culture really did comprise an entire social world, to be excluded from the party really did mean excommunication. The Situationists had no such power. But they wrestled with the problem of how to make collective belonging meaningful, as something requiring some sacrifice. The possibility of exclusion made participation in the Situationist game meaningful.

Not the least difference between the Situationists and the Communist Party is that the former rarely recruited. "I have no need of fabricating false disciples." Nor was adherence to doctrinal orthodoxy required. "Quite surely, never any doctrine: perspectives. A solidarity around these perspectives." Indeed, doctrinaire postures could be grounds for exclusion. Debord writes to Simondo: "situationism, as a body of doctrine, does not exist and must not exist. What exists is a Situationist experimental attitude"—something like the Jornian materialist attitude to life. This is the paradox of the doctrine of no doctrine. To Pinot Gallizio, who Jorn had recruited for the Imaginist Bauhaus, and who was the key figure among the Italian founders of the Situationist International, Debord writes: "We have always been sure that you are strongly opposed to the metaphysics of which Simondo currently reveals the dogmas."[17] The exclusion of Gallizio would take a while longer than Simondo.

In his letters, Debord often mentions "propaganda" and even "internal propaganda." Both for external and internal purposes, statements were to be formed and made tactically. The Situationist

International formed itself in part out of the material of the art world, but anticipated the overcoming of art as a separate practice. Hard to grasp for the middle-class sensibility of what Debord will call "bourgeois civilization" is that there really might have been a threat to the organization—in the form of the opportunistic exploitation of the potential cachet of the Situationist International, particularly by its artist members. The Situationists were never an *artistic* avant-garde. Debord: "we already have amongst us too many artistically old men who have missed out on their own nineteenth century."[18] Artists were only accepted as members if they appeared ready to move beyond art, in a "brutal evolution"—as Debord said of the ill-fated German artists of the Spur group.

Situationists create new collaborative play-forms out of the old materials of the separate creative practices, of which art was just one. The moments of inclusion and exclusion within the Situationist International are best explored in relation to this strategy, rather than attempting to decode them as banal dramas of personality. "The most urgent problem, tactically, is to firstly balance, then as quickly as possible surpass the number of painters in the Situationist International with the largest possible number of architects, urbanists, sociologists and others." This ambition came with its own dangers. "We can hardly have confidence in 'specialized collaborators' who do not share Situationist experimental positions. If not, we will discover bitterly that the architects, sociologists, urbanists, etc. are as limited as the painters in their defense of the particular prejudices of their separate sectors."[19] The Situationist International was not a collaboration between specialists, but the overcoming of specialization in the name of a new kind of collective activity.

As secretary Debord tacks this way and that, trying to keep the International together. Debord's problems are compounded by the presence of several powerful personalities, all of them his senior. Around the time the Situationist International was founded, Debord was twenty-five, Constant was thirty-seven, Jorn was forty-three, and Gallizio fifty-five. These discrepancies should be borne in mind when reading his letters to each of them. Given his relative youth, the self-confidence of the letters is extraordinary. The tone of Debord's writing fluctuates considerably in his attempts to engage with each of these outsize personalities, even if he does not lack confidence in calling all of them to account. As one of Debord's favorite writers, the Cardinal de Retz, says: "The talent of insinuation is of more service than that of persuasion, because one can insinuate to a hundred where one can barely persuade five."[20]

Giuseppe Gallizio (1902–64), Pinot to his friends, was, by his own account, an "archaeologist, botanist, chemist, parfumer, partisan, king of the gypsies."[21] To which one might add: chancer, amateur, dandy, dilettante. It was he, together with Asger Jorn, who convened the Congress of Free Artists in 1956 in Gallizio's hometown of Alba. This was the event that laid the groundwork for the formation of the Situationist International the following year in Cosio, where he would become a founding member. Gallizio's approach was consistently experimental, and he saw the materials and practices of an experimental comportment as available to everyone: "the masses have understood and already the breathlessness of a new poetic moment is anxiously beating at the doors of people bored by the tired ideals fabricated by the self-righteous incomprehension of the mysterious powerful of the earth."[22] Gallizio called his method *ensemble painting.* His goal was what he called an *anti-patent* process for the sharing and modification of life.

Gallizio's ensembles did not just produce rare and singular works, like other artists. They produced *industrial painting.* These were only very minimally the product of actual machines. The idea was more that painting could be made using mechanisms of repetition and variation to undermine the unique gesture. The result would bring together the creative and singular with the serial and repeated. He invented, in short, a synthesis of the two opposed strands of the avant-garde: surrealism and constructivism, in what Michèle Bernstein called "a shrewd mixture of chance and mechanics." As art historian Mirella Bandini put it, his project was to "unleash inflation everywhere."[23]

Debord pours considerable energy into arranging Gallizio's debut in the French and German art worlds. At first all goes well: "The tumult over your glory grows great, despite the discretion we maintain." But art-world success is Gallizio's downfall within the Situationist International. This is less the fault of the exhibition itself than of the way it is used tactically: "The most serious deficiency was that Pinot, in his practical attitude toward the Parisian public, more or less consciously accepted the role of a very ordinary artist recognized by his peers (by contrast, the exhibition of détourned paintings by Jorn [the *Modifications*] was, I believe, a very rough break with this milieu ...)." The upshot was the exclusion of Gallizio and his son Giors Melanotte for "sickening arrivisme." As Debord would comment much later: "the Situationist International knew how to fight its own glory."[24]

While Debord could recognize, even in retrospect, Gallizio's "virtuosity," he was nevertheless the *right wing* of the Situationist International.[25] Its *left wing* was Constant Nieuwenhuys. He had been a member of the Cobra group with Jorn, but had moved away from painting towards experiments in new kinds of potential urban form. In the "Amsterdam Declaration" of 1958, Debord and Constant called for "the development of complete environments, which must extend to a unitary urbanism" which they saw as "the complex, ongoing activity that consciously recreates man's environment according to the most advanced conceptions in every domain," as the "result of a new type of collective creativity."[26] A poetry played by all; an *all* played by poetry.

It was Gallizio who set Constant on the path to his famous New Babylon project of *unitary urbanism* when the two of them were together in Alba. Gallizio, who was on the local town council, solved the problem of the town's antipathy to visiting Romani, or Gypsies, by making some land he owned available for their camp. It was an idea not without precedent. As Alice Becker-Ho writes, quoting from a 1569 text: "Their sojourns in particular villages are always sanctioned by the local squires or dignitaries."[27] Gallizio commissioned Constant to design a new kind of mobile architecture that might house them. Constant's model was never built, but it set Constant on a new path. He would come to reject art in general, and painting in particular, and like Gallizio posit the machine as the central fact of contemporary creativity, writing: "A free art of the future is an art that would master and use all the new conditioning techniques."[28]

Yet Constant and Gallizio were in many respects quite incompatible figures, and not just as personalities. For Constant, art had come to an end. A unitary urbanism of constructed situations supersedes all of the separate arts. "The artists' task is to invent new techniques and to utilize light, sound, movement and any invention whatsoever which might influence ambience. Without this, the integration of art in the construction of human habitat remains as chimerical as the proposals of [Ivan Chtcheglov]."[29] In principle, Debord agrees. "No painting is defensible from a Situationist point of view." But where Constant insists on the principle, the secretary does not want to get too far ahead of the memberships's level of consciousness. "Yes, any spirit of the 'pictorial' must be hounded and this, though obvious, isn't easy to get everyone to acknowledge."[30]

Debord looks to Constant as a tactical ally, but tries strenuously to keep him from pushing the organization too far too fast. He wants Constant to work on the editorial line for the journal with this in mind: "This will certainly help the really experimental faction in the Situationist International." But Debord is initially reluctant to break with Gallizio or Jorn, both of whom are earning Constant's stern disapproval as *artists*. "I don't have the right—and I do not have the least desire—to try to impose directives on the painters (for instance) in the name of a real movement that is no more advanced than their work."[31] A shrewd move, since for Debord to attempt to direct the painters would only draw him—and the Situationists—deeper into the obsessions of the art world.

The unraveling of Debord's relationship with Constant is the great moment in the early life of the Situationist International, and shapes the whole space of what will be possible for it. Debord is caught between the left and right wings of the movement. And though the artists are excluded one by one, Constant is not appeased and resigns anyway, and the movement, so to speak, moves on. But this is the moment, like the opening scene in a novel or film, where circumstances are fluid, where many things are possible. One discovers in the first three years of the Situationist International many potential versions of it, besides the ones of legend or even historical record. This is perhaps why so many keep returning to them, and to these early years in particular, as the scene of a moment in still-living movement, or in other words, a situation.

Debord's judgments in the *Correspondence*, whether one agrees with them or not, are not purely capricious. Against Constant and the Dutch section, Debord makes two charges, both in many respects perspicacious. The first is that there is a strand in Constant which, despite his denials, is close to the utopian legacy of Saint-Simon and Auguste Comte, particularly in the way it privileges an intellectual class as the only agents for bringing about a new world: "when you only find progressive forces in the 'intellectuals who revolt against cultural poverty,' you yourselves are utopians. What can intellectuals do without liaison with an enterprise that brings global change to social relations?"[32] Liaison, in short, with the proletariat. While Jorn was starting to rethink class in interesting ways, the Situationist International was at something of an impasse, caught in the old dilemma between romantic revolt and class struggle.

The second issue concerns the status of unitary urbanism. Where Constant is focused on the way unitary urbanism realizes and overcomes the more limited achievements of the separate arts, Debord is already looking ahead to realizing and overcoming unitary urbanism: "Our necessary activity is dominated by the question of the totality. Take note of it. Unitary urbanism is not a conception of the totality, must not become one. It is an operational instrument to construct an extended detour."[33] While Debord and Constant are allies in their embrace of technicity (against the rather technophobic Jorn), Debord does not think it enough any more to just break down the arts and combine them in the construction of new ambiences, new terrains of play. Unitary urbanism is much less a positive, constructive modeling and more a negative and critical tactic for opposing the kind of tower-block mentality that characterized postwar reconstruction. The chimerical quality of Chtcheglov's version of unitary urbanism still has a tactical value.

Legend has it that when Debord broke with people he simply cut them dead and moved on. With Constant this was not the case, and for once the correspondence continues on, to the stage of a love gone wrong. "Passion leads you astray," writes Debord to Constant, sounding for all the world like Madame de Merteuil in *Dangerous Liaisons* (1782). Playing Valmont, Constant retorts by telegram: "If passion misleads me, indecision causes you to be lost." Debord resorts to threats: "it is up to you to choose the terrain."[34]

"Staying friends with Constant was quite difficult. He liked to fight," says Jacqueline de Jong. At stake are 200 copies of Constant's book, which Debord feels are owed to him. It may sound like just a pretext, but one of the essential components of the Situationist International was the internal exchange of documents and their *donation* to external parties. As this incident highlights, the group was held together by the gift. The gift enters via the writings of the socialist anthropologist Marcel Mauss (1872–1950), which were taken up and expanded into a theory of the general economy by Georges Bataille. Both drew on anthropological work by Franz Boas (1858–1942) and others working among Native Americans of the Pacific Northwest, and their concept of *potlatch*. This version of the gift linked it closely to reputation. The gift is not selfless charity, nor is it a Christmas present.[35] Rather, it is a very special kind of donation, in which the donor gives away valuable time, matter and energy in order to acquire reputation. The journal of the Letterist International was called *Potlatch*, and despite the meager resources of the group it was given away for free.

The Situationists sold their journal in bookshops, but many were given away and for the same reasons: to exchange time, energy and materials for reputation. The Situationist International was a provisional micro-society founded on its own quite particular economy of donation and reputation. While some of its activities might be supported by selling art to collectors or other banal forms of compensated labor, there is a sense in which the Situationist International was a grand potlatch, consigning to the flames the thought and work of a whole little community, daring the world to match its extravagant consumption of its own time. Hence the donation of copies was no mere pretext in Debord's quarrel with Constant, for if Constant refused to donate them it would constitute a real break in the economy—if that is what it was—of this micro-society. It was a quite paradoxical economy.

The philosopher Jacques Derrida (1930–2004) was Debord's contemporary, although beyond that they had little in common except perhaps rather nuanced notions of the gift. Derrida: "The gift is the gift of giving itself and nothing else."[36] Marcel Mauss had thought of a gift economy as driven by an underlying generosity, the very *mana* of socialism. Debord and in particular Jorn practiced it in much the same spirit, and even saw it as the basis for a break beyond socialist thought and action. But Claude Lévi-Strauss (1908–2009) took thinking about the gift away from the "shop girl's philosophy" of everyday life, and in the direction instead of a structural logic of exchange.[37] This line of thought would flourish in the hands of Roland Barthes (1915–80) and Louis Althusser, where gift exchange reappears as the structural logic of symbolic exchange, and becomes the technique by which the superstructures of capitalist society can be decoded. They wanted a parallel competence to the *marxisant* political economy still thought to explain the workings of the base. Derrida proposes instead that the gift must interrupt the economy. The gift is not supposed to be returned. It is outside circulation and circular time. Giving suspends all calculation. The gift is canceled by any reciprocation, return, debt, countergift or exchange. Derrida departs from anthropology by thinking the gift in its singularity, outside of exchange, to reveal just how troubling it is to any such structural logic.

If the recipient of a gift recognizes it as a gift, then it ceases to be one. "If it presents itself then it no longer presents itself." For Derrida this opens up an intriguing realm of paradox and a way to get payback on his structuralist precursors. For the Situationsts, the very impossibility of the pure gift calls into being a whole terrain of possibility for an art and politics of the impurity of the gift. Every impure donation forces both giver and receiver into the invention of an attitude to life that can accept the donation, but not exchange it. The invention of everyday life could be nothing but the inventive accommodation to donation, to the subtle art of not returning the donation, of giving again in a way that is not circular, that does not simply pass on the debt.

Exchange affirms the identities of givers and receivers, and the value of the thing exchanged. Exchange arises as a way to contain the disturbing capacities of the gift. "The subject and the object are arrested effects of the gift." This might be the last nobility left to life: to give and not receive, receive and not gift, to invent *unreturnable acts* (another name for which might be situations). Not only does Derrida construct a theory of the gift, his writing inserts itself into just such an unreturnable practice, or tries to. The Situationist International composed a whole micro-society on the premise of potlatch, that is, the art and politics of the donation. Potlatch is not really sustainable. It's a game, a challenge. It isn't a circular exchange. The early years of the Situationist International are a game of potlatch, of the donation time, in which the players, in the end, run out of moves. For Debord in particular, the challenge of the gift of time went, in his terms, unmet. It was time to forget and move on.

In the end, the gifted but impetuous left of the movement is no better for Debord's purposes than the *sprezzatura* of the easygoing right. Here, in a couple of sentences addressed to Constant, Debord speaks all at once of a crisis of friendship, of tactics and thought at a crossroads: "I am sure that, here, we have arrived at the point where the Situationist International must immediately choose (or must be abandoned). Because you know well that I have always thought that 'there are moments at which it is necessary to know how to choose'; that you haven't needed to teach this to me; and that, if there has been a certain opportunism in the Situationist International, I have been among those (you, too) who have counter-balanced it."[38] The collapse of the Situationist International into the art world that Debord feared did not happen, at least not yet. The vigorous application of the principle of exclusion —that generously ungenerous act—took care of that.

The Situationist International exercises a continued fascination because its members made a gift of their time that was not returned. They did not really take their place in the exchanges of views between the journals and groups of their time. Their beautiful, expensive journal—with Lumaline covers or not—did not so much circulate as spiral off into the void. Until May '68 appeared, and appeared to many as the return of the gift in spades. But still, something remains of an uncanceled gift.

The early years of the Situationist International are ones in which it may develop itself, elaborate itself, ornament itself—in many possible directions. The movement exercises a lasting fascination on art historians for this reason. All of the major figures of the early years have their favorites, who excise them from the game and hoist them up as their champions. What is perhaps more interesting is to keep these figures in play, to view what passes between them as what matters. And perhaps also what passes unnoticed, undetected in this flux of passions between temperamental men. When Michèle Bernstein writes in her two novels of exactly this remarkable time in which the Situationist International was born, the squabbles that animate the men barely rate a mention. It is just something a character not unlike Debord takes a train to Amsterdam to attend to, before hurrying back to a quite different kind of game. A game in which women not only figure, but which they may even win.

6 Permanent Play

On the subject of love, bourgeois novels are variations on two themes. The first is the couple in love getting together despite all obstacles; the second is how unhappily they live ever after. "Marriage seems to have been invented to reward perversity," the utopian socialist writer Charles Fourier once said.[1] Marriage, says the bourgeois novel, is the worst of institutions for a woman, except for all the others. In the novel, a woman can refuse marriage. She may be drawn towards sexual ecstasy, but that way lies poverty, misery and social exclusion. Proper love is of the sacred domesticated kind, placed in the service of reproducing the heterosexual family and passing on property. Socialist writers, from Fourier to Engels to Alexandra Kollontai had long opposed marriage as a relation which makes women into property, and pointed to the hypocrisy of the bourgeois gentleman who polices the sexual fidelity of his wife yet goes adventuring in bohemia for a bit on the side.

And yet in postwar France, the figure of the monogamous, heterosexual couple became ever more widespread. Kristin Ross: "the construction of the new French couple is not only a class necessity but a national necessity as well, linked to the state-led modernization effort. Called upon to lead France into the future, these couples are the class whose very way of life is based on the wish to make the world futureless and at that price buy security."[2] The couple was a modern alternative to both the more reactionary order of the wartime collaborationist Vichy regime, and the autonomous female sexuality embodied by Saint-Germain figures like Juliette Gréco or Françoise Sagan, and promulgated as a theory in Simone de Beauvoir's *The Second Sex*. The couple refuses both the patriarchal past of Vichy and the feminist future of *The Second Sex*, and secures a private space where the good life of the spectacle can be brought home and domesticated.

In the third issue of *Internationale Situationniste* is a reproduction of the "Map of Tenderness" by the Precocity movement writer Madeleine de Scudéry (1607–1701). This famous drawing was included in her popular multivolume novel *Clélie*. The map charts three possible journeys from the town of New Friendship at the bottom. Friendship could take the paths of Inclination, Esteem or Gratitude to one of three destinations in the center of the map. It could wander off course, and end up in dismal places such as the Lake of Indifference. Or the journey could go too far, into uncharted territory. For de Scudéry, love requires skill and tact if it is not to lurch towards great ecstasy, which also brings great pain.

The goal was not marriage. De Scudéry was more interested in erotic friendship between women. Hers was a Sapphic alternative to Platonic relationships between men, a tenderness that can be sustained, developed, transformed and ornamented, without rupture. De Scudéry initiates a counter-tradition, skeptical of the sacred quality of ecstasy, indifferent to questions of property and outside the heterosexual norm.[3] While acknowledging the power of feeling, it can nevertheless be crafted and directed. It can become the material of play and strategy.

How is a modern woman who lives in a so-called *open relationship* with a man supposed to retain her hold on him, if he starts an affair that has a little more intensity than usual? Affairs are allowed. They are within the rules, but they are not supposed to break with a fundamental agreement between the man and the woman. And if this man is coming too close to breaching that agreement, what stratagems can the woman employ to see that he returns to it? This scenario can be found in what Debord calls Michèle Bernstein's "fake novel" *All the King's Horses*, and its sequel *The Night*.[4] These books, which both describe the same events, concern the lives of three characters who are not unlike Michèle Bernstein, her husband Guy Debord, and his lover Michèle Mochot. Bernstein borrows from socialist, bohemian and aristocratic writings to create an alternative to the middle-class ideal of the married couple. "The personal is political," as feminists would say later in the 1960s, but for Bernstein, writing in the early '60s, the political is very, very personal.[5]

Both novels cover the same events in the lives of Gilles and Geneviève, but from different perspectives and in different styles: *King's Horses* adopts the style of Françoise Sagan (1935–2004); *The Night,* that of Alain Robbe-Grillet (1922–2008). Saint-Germain identity Sagan's racy novels coincided with the arrival of mass paperback publishing in France in the 1950s. Those of Robbe-Grillet were a high-modernist analogue of the new consumerist and technocratic France of those years. Lefebvre called them "pure spectacle." As Maurice Blanchot pointed out at the time, what was once a cultural rhythm to the diffusion of writing had with the arrival of the paperback been replaced by a technical one. The technical purported to solve all problems. "There is no need for political upheaval, and even less for changes in the social structure. It suffices to reproduce works."[6] Even radical works started appearing in paperback. Literature discreetly integrated itself into the spectacle.

Bernstein's strategy was a détournement of the spectacle of the novel, first in its popular form, then its literary form. "There is not much future in the détournement of complete novels," declared Debord and Wolman, "but during the transitional phase there might be a certain number of undertakings of this sort." Elsewhere, Debord sets out the tenets of a Situationist approach to literature in the transitional phase: "In the novel, the fundamental question of time resided more in the liberty of beginning and ending the story at significant points, rather than in the choice of including certain moments and excluding others … I believe it is this form of sovereignty (used derisorily in the novel) that everyday life aims at appropriating."[7] In the absence of the means to construct situations, the détourned novel might at least gesture towards the liberty of beginnings.

Debord met cabaret singer Michèle Mochot in 1955, at a Paris opening for the Belgian surrealist painter Jane Graverol.[8] Bernstein's fictional Gilles meets Carole a few years later, also at an opening of a surrealist painter, only Bernstein's painter is male and Carole is his stepdaughter. In *The Night* we learn of the sexual tension between them. The painter covets his stepdaughter. "Though by her spite she showed that she wanted no part of it, still she encouraged it a little, admitted it was there."[9] With a little prompting from Carole's mother, Gilles and Geneviève whisk Carole away from the old man. Gilles takes her wandering around the streets of Paris, and in the morning finally makes love to her.

In *Horses*, we only hear in general terms about Gilles and his art of wandering. Geneviève goes home to sleep and the story picks up again the next day. *The Night* is structured around the dérive itself.

> They pass beside a column, a streetlight rather, on which is fixed, above their heads, a blue and white sign indicating by an arrow: Cluny Museum. On the same column, another signal, luminous and blinking, is the only one that attracts the glance of the passersby. At regular intervals, for the pedestrians, the permission to go or the order to wait flashes. Gilles and Carole pass near the column without seeing it. Gilles waits, before crossing, for the cars to stop. Carole follows Gilles, who holds her by the nape of the neck. They take the direction indicated by the sign Cluny Museum, and skirt the railings of the garden of the museum.

The dérive is Carole's initiation into the knotted streets of the sleeping city. "I'd like to be in a labyrinth with you," says Carole. "We already are," says Gilles.[10]

A Galton machine is a grid of equally spaced pins, arranged vertically, above which is a single slot that releases balls, and below which is a series of slots that catch them. If the top slot is positioned in the middle and balls are released into the grid of pins, the chances are that most balls will deviate a bit when they hit the pins but will fall in one of the center slots below. A few of the balls will end up bouncing farther off the center line, but overall the device will show a *Gaussian distribution*. It's essentially pinball without the fun. Pinball arrived in Saint-Germain bars such as the Mabillon and the Old Navy after the war, and became a favorite way for quarter people to waste time. Arthur Adamov wrote an absurdist play about it called *Ping-Pong* (1955).[11]

In pinball, the ball is always going to end up passing through the middle between the flippers, but some balls—through luck or skill—will take longer to do so. The Galton machine, or pinball, is Jorn's image of a *situology*, both ludic and analytic, "as a game device, this machine that tilts, can be found in most Paris bistros, and is the possibility of calculated variability."[12] Time and space are not smooth or even. There are tilts, there are eddies, there are zones that attract the balls and zones that repel them. Debord and Wolman had already proposed a détournement of pinball, in which the "play of the lights and the more or less predictable trajectories of the balls would form a metagraphic-spatial composition entitled *Thermal Sensations and Desires of People Passing by the Gates of Cluny Museum Around an Hour After Sunset in November*."[13] They abandoned this idea, for Paris was already a pinball machine. All that remained was to bounce around it like a shiny silver ball, and find its psychogeographic centers of gravity.

The grid at the Galton machine is like a street layout or a telephone network, a flat and even field, a distributed network.[14] A ball could land anywhere; a call could connect any two points. There are infinitesimal eddies and fissures shaping the ball's trajectory, or the call's circuit, or the swerve of someone on a dérive who takes this street rather than that. Actually, some passages are more likely than others, but only by playing the game does this become clear. The city, unlike the Galton machine, may have several vortices of gravity. *The Night* is structured around the passage of Gilles and Carole through the streets of Paris, bouncing from one trajectory to the next. *The Night* subordinates the narrative of the affair to the description of the dérive. *Horses* is rather more conventional, and the dérive there is just a moment. It reverses the relationship between situation and story.

Gilles' affair with Carole causes at least two rifts in the libidinal universe. Carole's girlfriend Béatrice is jealous and possessive. Geneviève's feelings are perhaps more complicated. It is not the first time Gilles has had other lovers, but Geneviève is a little worried about this one. *The Night* can be read as an account of the disturbance the affair causes Geneviève. Her character is in the habit, on waking, of putting the events of the previous day in order, but in *The Night* events refuse to fall into place. The novel jumps from one fragment of time—charged with affect—to another. It is a beginning that doesn't end.

Horses presents a rather more straightforward version of Geneviève's strategies for holding on to Gilles. One tactic is to become Carole's intimate friend, establishing a relationship independent of Gilles between the two women. It is an emotional intimacy—Sapphic, in de Scudéry's sense—that is perhaps greater than the sexual one between Carole and Gilles, if rather one-sided. Carole confides in Geneviève, but not vice versa. It's a tactic on Geneviève's part, to be sure, but not quite as coldly manipulative as the similar move in *Dangerous Liaisons*, a book from which Bernstein freely borrows.[15] Another tactic is to take the same liberties as her husband. Whereas Gilles found Carole at a party hosted by passé old surrealists, Geneviève finds her love interest at the rather more advanced soirée hosted by Ole, an artist perhaps modeled on Asger Jorn (Ole is the name of Jorn's son). There she hooks up with a young man called Bertrand, fucks him in a hotel, throws him out next morning, then telephones Gilles to tell him about it. This tactic doesn't work: it doesn't make Gilles feel as jealous as she feels. Bertrand is handsome enough, but, if anything, bringing him into the picture only gives Gilles more license to love Carole.

Both Carole and Bertrand make bad art. Carole dabbles at painting, merely repeating the clichés current in the art world. Bertrand's poetry is worse, in thrall to experiments that have long since lost their charge. As Debord once wrote to his old Letterist comrade Patrick Straram, "poetry, yes, but in life. No return possible to surrealist or preceding poetical writing."[16] What neither Carole nor Bertrand quite realizes is that they already embody the aesthetic. Neither knows that they are in play in a game of everyday life. Of the two, Carole comes closer, at least when she sings. She has a small repertoire of old French songs. When she sings for Gilles she appropriates their words as her own, détourns them, and reveals a capacity that leads Geneviève to suspect that here might be a rival.

The four of them, Gilles and Carole, Geneviève and Bertrand, go off on vacation. They meet Bertrand's friend Hélène, a slightly older and very sophisticated woman from the literary scene. On returning to Paris, Geneviève discards Bertrand and takes up with Hélène. This gets Gilles' attention. Gilles drops Carole. The trio of Geneviève, Hélène, and Gilles hang out together for a while, but it doesn't last. In the end it is just Geneviève and Gilles again—for now. But the game has changed. *Horses* ends with letters from Carole and Hélène in which it is clear that Carole, although still young, is beginning to appreciate a new way of thinking about life, while Hélène, encrusted with habit, is left to her fate.

In her letter to Bertrand, Hélène dismisses Gilles and Geneviève as "damaged people," but she does not really understand them.[17] Neither Gilles nor Geneviève are really heartless libertines. They appreciate beauty but not just as an object, a thing apart. Their romantic strategies are not about conquest or possession. Gilles really does fall in love, and often. Geneviève's strategies are aimed mainly at sustaining Gilles' love for her, because she cannot help loving him. This love is hardly romantic. Their feelings are genuine, but feelings can be shaped aesthetically, in pursuit of adventures, in the creation of situations, in the river of time.

Love is temporal, an event. There is nothing eternal in it. Timeless Love, like God, like Art, is dead. Eternal love is death itself, the metaphysical principle that plagues romance, that would make the lover one's private property for all time. All that remains is the possibility of constructing situations. Odile Passot: "In Bernstein's universe, there is no transcendence, divine or diabolic; humans are subject to their own negativity, which they cultivate to destabilize their century's received truths."[18] Like the devils in Marcel Carné and Jacques Prévert's film *The Devil's Envoys* (1942), Geneviève and Gilles trouble the sheets of the bourgeois bedchamber by disregarding property and propriety in the name of a quite different ethic of love.[19] For all its *genderfuck* charm, *The Devil's Envoys* still affirms in the end that love is eternal; in Bernstein's world it is not.

As Geneviève says of Gilles: "When I met Gilles three years ago, I realized quickly that he was far from the cool libertine most people took him for. His desires always contain as much passion as he can put into them, and it's this same state that he always pursued in various love stories that you'd be crazy to call unserious. The climate he created everywhere is one of honest feelings and a heightened consciousness of the tragically fleeting aspect of anything to do with love. And the intensity of the adventure was always an inverse function of its duration. Trouble and breakups happened with Gilles before any valid reason appeared: afterward, it was too late. I had been the exception, I was immune."[20] Strategy, as Debord says, "tends to impose at each instant considerations of contradictory necessities."[21] Geneviève's strategies aim at the very least to preserve her immunity, but perhaps she has other ambitions as well. She might surpass her master at his own game.

Geneviève trumps Gilles' desire for Carole when she presents him with her affair with Hélène. While Gilles is intrigued by Carole's now lost love of Béatrice, he is much more attracted to Geneviève's for the elegant Hélène. The reconciliation between Gilles and Geneviève entails not so much a renunciation of their desire for others, but rather a gift of the renunciation of that desire to each other. But while this ending has the appearance of equity, it is really Geneviève who wins the game. She secures her alliance with Gilles and puts her rival in her place, without invoking proprietary rights—but while taking her pleasures with Bertrand and Hélène. She does not insist that Gilles be hers, or that she is his.

Horses highlights the story of Geneviève's triumph. *The Night* puts the story back into the situation of multiple and parallel encounters. While Carole or Bertrand are part of Geneviève's story, she is also part of theirs. The reader glimpses a whole playing field, a veritable arcade of pinball machines. Jorn would later co-author an elaborate mock ethnography of Paris bohemia, which would do for structuralist theories of myth what James Joyce did for the myth of Ulysses. The elaborate kinship diagrams of his imaginary tribes seem baffling at first, until the reader decodes the forest of symbols and realizes that anyone can fuck anyone. It could be a mock-theoretical diagram of the world of *The Night*.[22]

The soundtrack to the lives of these characters, besides the American jazz popularized by Vian, was a distinctively French version of the folk-music revival. The title *All the King's Horses* refers to an old song, "Aux marches du palais." Carole sings it on the night when she and Gilles and Geneviève fall into one another's lives. It is a song about a queen and her lover. One evening, the knight steals into the king's castle and lies with the queen in her bed. Together they make a river that all the king's horses cannot cross. Greil Marcus: "It is as deep and singular an image of revolution as there has ever been, but in *All the King's Horses* so distant an element is barely an image at all."[23] When one is bored with the desire for mere things, there is only the desire for another's desire. Gilles desires Geneviève's desire for Hélène. But what if one could create a desire so strong that it put a river between it and its other? A desire that, like a river, has to keep moving, has always to change, a desire that can play out in time and play in the end into the sea. This then might be what the novel is still good for: that the situation of desire might not pass away all at once, but pass rather into another time.

7 Tin Can Philosophy

Abdelhafid Khatib, a comrade of Debord's from the Letterist International days, wrote a detailed psychogeography of the Les Halles district of Paris, noting with care how its ambiences morph from one place to another, from one time to another. Here the dérive starts to yield definitive results. Particularly appealing to Khatib is the way the carts of the vegetable vendors make temporary barricades in the streets at delivery time, forming a changeable maze. Shifting from psychogeography to the prospect of the construction of situations, Khatib declares that "any solution aimed at creating a new society requires that this space at the center of Paris be preserved for the manifestations of a liberated collective life."[1] It is a model for "perpetually changing labyrinths" constructed consciously for drifting. It hints at a space and time free of necessity, in which a liberated life could be free to create its own necessities, its own games.

Khatib's text came at a time when other necessities imposed themselves. Since it began in 1954, the Algerian war of independence had been met with increasing French repression. Colonial war destabilized the French state, and brought Charles de Gaulle to power in 1958. But rather than strengthen French power in Algeria as some of his supporters wished, de Gaulle began searching for an alternative policy. This led in turn to assassination and coup attempts against de Gaulle. As the war reached its peak, Paris became the scene of bombings and reprisals. A curfew was declared. It would not be healthy for an Arab man like Khatib to be wandering the streets at night, jotting things down in a notebook.

Opposition to the war among French intellectuals generally took one of four positions. One was Catholic, and appealed to conscience. One was republican, and appealed to the rights of man. Another was third-worldist, and put the anti-colonial struggle in place of class struggle as the motor of history. The last was revolutionary, and scripted the line the Communist Party ought to take if it really was the representative of the international proletariat.[2] Situationist thought and action always conceived of itself outside of the conscience-talk of public intellectuals, and was never romantic about underdevelopment. Debord's *Correspondence* of the late 1950s shows instead a skeptical engagement with the would-be Bolsheviks and non-party Marxists of the French left.

The anti-colonial struggle, the crisis of the French state, and the theoretical debates of the time converged to force a more profound articulation of Situationist theory. Initially skeptical of the Socialism or Barbarism group, Debord would gradually warm to their consistent critique not only of capitalism and colonialism, but also of the socialist states. They saw in the wildcat strikes and periodic eruptions of revolt in both Eastern and Western Europe the signs of a new revolutionary movement. Debord would read them together with the leading theorists of what Lenin had once described as the "infantile disorder" of left-wing and workers-council communist thought of a previous era: Lukács, Karl Korsch (1886–1961), Anton Pannekoek (1873–1960).[3] This would culminate in the text that is Debord's masterpiece: *The Society of the Spectacle* (1967), which is above all a détournement of the texts circulating in the radical milieu of the time.[4]

In deciding between the competing Marxist currents, there are many paths not taken. Debord would be close to, then estranged from, the veteran Marxist philosopher Henri Lefebvre. He would also encourage and collaborate for a time with Asger Jorn on the development of a distinctive Marxist project. Jorn's pamphlet *Critique of Political Economy* (1960) was published with a cover to match Debord's *Report on the Construction of Situations* (1957), as if to give it the same status as a statement of Situationist research results. It seems some of the copies were seized by customs agents, so it never achieved the level of circulation intended for it.[5] In this often overlooked text, Jorn tries to draw together his earlier pataphysical rewritings of Marx with the results of the Letterist International's experiments, in a new synthesis which goes beyond the project of the construction of situations to a new theory of value that might embrace them.

The burden of Jorn's critique of political economy is to show that something is left out of Marx's equation of labor with value. It is not labor alone that creates value. On the one hand Jorn restores a role for nature, for materiality. On the other, he insists on the role of another class in the creation of value, even if he does not quite have a language with which to describe it. This other class he occasionally calls the *creative elite*, in contrast to "the delicious name of the power elite."[6] *The Power Elite* by C. Wright Mills (1916–62) is a powerful restatement, in the teeth of the cold war, of the existence in the West of a ruling class, in control of modern means of production and communication.[7] Mills exposes corporate, state and military power as an integrated nexus, in the hands of a ruling caste with a consistent world view. The same people circulate through the commanding heights of all of the institutions at the disposal of the power elite. Democratic governance is a sham. The mass parties no longer control their leaders. One-way communication has usurped the space of civil dialogue.

Jorn's creative elite is something else. It has no power, but its significance is that it can give form to value. It renews the form of things. The term creative elite seems at first ill-chosen, even for Jorn, who has very little time for the elites of the art world. The sources of creation in Jorn are popular. He happily describes himself as a vulgar Marxist—after *vulgus*, of the people.[8] Where Marx identifies himself with another class—the proletariat—and reconstructs the world from its point of view, Jorn sees the world from the point of view of his own class, or at least from his own milieu—the bohemia of Saint-Germain that Bernstein documents and the extensive network of other creative bohemias with which the peripatetic and multilingual Jorn was intimately familiar.

Like William Morris (1834–96), and drawing on his own anthropological studies, Jorn thinks something has come between art and life. Unlike Morris, his response is a socialism that is not utopian, nor is it quite what Marx and Engels would recognize as scientific. Rather, Jorn's socialism is *experimental*. Where Marx begins with a critique of bourgeois economics, Jorn begins with a critique of socialist economics. Unlike most critics of the Stalinist regimes from the left, Jorn sees them not as wrong in implementation, but in essence. The Trotskyites saw them as deformed workers' states. The Socialism or Barbarism group dispensed with this formula, but not (yet) with the socialist ideal. Probably without knowing it, Jorn picks up the critical thread of Marcel Mauss and others who thought the problem with the socialist states was not just a political deformation, but fundamentally economic.[9]

Marx was fascinated by capital, almost seduced by it.[10] He marveled at its astonishing productivity, its vast accumulation of wealth. While denouncing its violence and inequity, Marx could still love capital's productivity, which the revolution would deliver to the proletariat as its rightful inheritance. Jorn sees capital quite differently. He thinks it has not increased but abolished true wealth, which is variability in consumption. In abolishing difference, the wage relation and the commodity form impoverish the world. For Jorn, the bourgeois revolution of 1789 and the proletarian revolution of 1917 were "two sides of the same affair."[11] Jorn makes the astonishing claim that in their effort to abolish poverty, socialism abolishes wealth along with it. Socialism is a permanent politics of devaluation. This was not inevitable. This was the significance of Gallizio's industrial painting: it showed, experimentally at least, that difference was not incompatible with abundance.

For Marx, wealth and value are the same, and value is derived from labor. Jorn sees Marx's writings as a critique only of the capitalist form of value, not of value in general, and certainly not of value-forms to come. Jorn wants a concept of value more in line with the pataphysical writing on natural science he developed in the 1940s and '50s. Marx's theories assume a nature in which form, complexity and difference can be spirited away by the white-hot flame of reductive analysis. Marx's scientific socialism rests on a materialist worldview which reduces the complexity of forms to an underlying essence. Jorn's materialist attitude to life intuits the possibility of a science of forms, and of the centrality of this science of forms in connecting natural science not only to social science, but to an experimental practice. Elements of such an experimental practice persist in modern art, but its roots are ancient. It continues a communism of the collective making and unmaking of forms.

Marx lacks a sense of the materiality of forms. The concept of form is never placed in relation to that of *substance*. Marx thinks instead of form and *content*. A content is what is enclosed in a form. Marx insists that the content of the form of value is always labor. Labor is the truth hidden within the form. In Marx, "The transition from use value to exchange value happens by the devaluation of the article of utility's material actuality." Use value and the article of utility are the same. But, says Jorn, "if we accept that the use value is the commodity's actual substance, then it is impossible to perceive an article of utility as being identical with a natural form. An article of utility is not a natural form but a cultural form."[12] The question of form cannot be discarded like an old tin can.

Use value is the same as the article of utility for Marx. In Jorn, use value is the opposite of article of utility. Use value is the negation of an article of utility, of its form. Use value is the using up, the consumption of an article of utility. Use value is a negation of a quality. This brings us to Jorn's most striking conclusion: "The market value of things is not conditioned by their quality, far less by their amount. It is conditioned by their *differences*, their variability."[13] Form is not a husk to shuck off, revealing some essence that is an independent content, the universal essence that is labor. "The exchange value of two commodities is thus not their equivalence but their dissimilarity." Jorn restores the claim of form, and at two moments in the production process: natural form and the form of the article of use.

Having dispensed with Marx's dialectic of form and content, he does not pursue the complexity of Marx's value theory much further. Rather, he unfolds his own subtle analysis of value. One is tempted to say that Jorn's value is as subtle as Marx's, but that would of course mean in Jornian terms that, being equivalent, it had no value. The point might be rather to stress its incommensurable difference. If Marx discards the question of form, Jorn stresses it. There are many kinds of form in Jorn. Money as pure equivalence is actually valueless, except as a form. It is empty form. The form that matters to Jorn is the form of substance, but there are others, notably container form and cultural form.

Jorn replaces political economy with aesthetic economy. He does not want to reduce the appearances of value as form to the content of labor, and in so doing make the working class the exclusive heart of economy. The working class is present in Jorn. Unlike bourgeois economics, he does not want to hide them away behind the surface-effects of exchange. Rather, he shifts attention away from exchange to production; not to production as quantity, but production as quality, as difference. The key to this is not labor as the universal content of value, but form as difference, as the production of differences. Labor may be the content of value, but creation is its form. There is both a laboring class and a creating class. Capitalism is the alienation of labor from creation.

In short: substance is value, value is process, and process is difference. Substance is something that can't be measured. It is a materiality of differences, without number or dimension. Dimension is the quantity of a particular quality. Value is a particular quantity of qualities undergoing a process or change. Natural form becomes substance in a process that makes not quantity but other kinds of form, or qualities. Substance is the material reality of the change or transformation. Substance is the ornamentation of natural form. Tintomara's turn is the transformation of natural substance into aesthetic substance.

To complicate things somewhat, Jorn proposes seeing substance as having its own form, or rather, that substance is potential for *transformation*. In an article of utility, the volatile form of substance is held in a certain tension with another kind of form, what Jorn calls container form. Jorn reads Marx as seeing all form as container form, a form which, analytically at least, can be opened to reveal a universal and homogenous substance—labor. But not all form is container form. Substance has its own form which is different from container form and works against it. A substance form is volatile; a container form, relatively inert.

"A substance is a possibility of value." But only a possibility. Value is not a state of things, but comes and goes. One cannot own value. Quality is an attribute of matter; value is the dynamics of matter. "The value of a form … thus depends upon the ease with which one can dissolve the form and liberate its latent energies, whilst its character of quality consists in its resistance to this."[14] Form as container is thus only a special case of form, an instance where value can be easily produced, the quality of the thing readily overcome.

Viewed in quantitative terms, container form seems desirable. Containers yield their contents readily. Container form maximizes the amount of value that can be extracted. But for Jorn the failure of socialist economics lies in actually attempting to realize Marx's conceptual separation of value from form as mere container. Socialist economies measure their progress in terms of rising quantities, all the while presiding over a massive devaluation. The extinction of difference, of the qualities of substances, is an impoverishment of the world. Jorn's critique might apply in attenuated form to socialist economies. Now that most of these have ceased to exist, the salience of Jorn's critique for capitalist economies is all the more acute.

Jorn challenges the central tenet of socialist thought: that the worker alone makes value, that value is labor power. He even claims that mechanical and industrial work is without value at all. The equivalence of units of labor time under industrial conditions, for all its efficiency, does not make more value, it abolishes value altogether. It is not labor, but time that is alienated from the worker. "Surplus value is not created in the work but in the variability of the work."[15] Difference is value. Who creates difference? The creative elite. There are two classes that make value. One is exploited by commodity production; the other marginalized. Jorn's is a recognizably romantic critique of the modern world, but what is distinctive is how far into the realm of the economic Jorn is prepared to pursue it.

Jorn's is perhaps a perverse kind of Leninism. It is not the party that brings class consciousness to the workers from without, but bohemia. The nucleus of a radical form of action is not the specialists in political praxis, but the connoisseurs of the free use of time (Gilles and Carole, wandering the labyrinth of the city at night). Theirs is not a politics of work, but an aesthetics of leisure. Both capitalism and socialism make free time over in the image of work. Sounding a theme that will be a major one in Debord's *Society of the Spectacle*, Jorn claims that the industrial worker's life is eventless, as she does not transform or change things. Leisure time has the same quality, or rather lack of quality, as work. Leisure is as much a sham as work.

Both socialist and capitalist societies have parallel ideologies of form: that container form abolishes differences. The container appears to function as a unit, making substance forms equivalent. Differences are—apparently—abolished as the units increase in number. Jorn calls this "tin can philosophy."[16] It equates the abolition of difference with progress. Both socialist and capitalist societies specialize in the efficient delivery in uniform containers of what has no value. In place of this, Jorn wants an ecology of forms.

The article of utility becomes a commodity when the producer has no use for it. It can either be given away as part of a gift economy of rivalry and recognition, the potlatch, or it can be exchanged. Either way, the problem is what to do with the surplus. Jorn's economics, like that of Georges Bataille, is not about economizing or efficiency, but expenditure, or wealth. Not scarcity but abundance is the key to his thinking: "wealth is surplus, abundance, multiplicity."[17] Where he differs from Bataille is in this emphasis not just on quantitative surplus, but a surplus of difference. Bataille sees both capitalist and socialist economies as distinct from all hitherto because they accumulate rather than disperse surplus, thereby reproducing the problem of surplus at ever higher levels. Jorn sees both capitalist and socialist economies as distinctive for their impoverishment of surplus as multiplicity.

The politics Jorn practiced is also about surplus rather than scarcity. Politics is surplus fellowship. For Jorn, the state is an anti-politics. The statesman is the prototype of the *manager*, and whatever else they may be, socialist states are fanatically managerial. In Engels's phrase, in socialism, the administration of men ought to be replaced by the "administration of things." It became the management of men as if they were things, not least during what Henri Lefebvre called "Stalin's assault on the universe." The socialist vision, from Alexander Bogdanov (1873–1928) forward, is for cybernetics to replace politics. "Statistical robots will compute, guided by effective soundings of public opinion, in accordance with the wishes or otherwise of the majority." Socialism abolishes the state only to make it universal, a container for everything. The socialist goal is in opposition to working-class interests, "for bureaucracy is the container system of society."[18] As Debord was increasingly turning towards a political conception of praxis, Jorn was turning away from it. The parting of the ways, this time, would at least be amicable.

If there is a Situationist praxis, it has to take time in a quite different sense to a Marxist one. It is not just that capital quantifies time and cheats the worker of the value of it. Rather, it is that the quantification of time suppresses the qualitative aspect of the transformation of one substance into another. The slogan "live without dead time" comes to mean something quite specific here. It is not that the situation is the spontaneous irruption of a pure event, severing all ties with the past, freeing itself from the grip of technologies, built spaces, all the massive forms of dead labor. As Debord wrote to Jorn: "I am in agreement on the question of time. To put the accent on non-preserved art or all other deliberately 'direct' situationist activity is not—has never been—a choice between amnesia and refusing history."[19] But this leaves open the question of what a *progressive* orientation might be, if it is neither the purely quantitative piling up of wealth, nor the sudden revolutionary break that abolishes the old world in an instant.

For all their differences, Jorn and Marx are in love with a notion of progress, and this is instructive. It is perhaps the key to resisting the slide of critique towards certain kinds of conservatism, not to mention mere resistance. It's a question of redefining what progress might mean. In Jorn, progress is transport; progress is movement. "In order to give possibilities of orientation, progressive movement must be movement collected from within in relation to the surrounding element."[20] Orienting action is like turning the rudder of a boat in a swift and uncertain current. It is not an act of domination, of imposing a will on time. It is an act which works both with and against the current of the times, ornamenting it.

8 The Thing of Things

Henri Lefebvre is swimming in the ocean one sunny day. He is alone, and the waves are choppy. He swims far, far out from the shore. Clouds obscure the sun. Anxiety grips him. He turns back. While swimming hard against the rip, a vision unfolds, born of real danger, and of quite a different order to the spectacle of waves and sun. It becomes "a shifting totality, roaring, buffeting, overwhelming: the sea." He no longer looks at the waves, he is among them, "each new one taking up the terrifying void left by its forerunner." And yet this ocean of danger is not formless void. "The duration of each wave is strictly determined by its objective logic, which leaves us with an indeterminable wealth of contingencies, accidents, appearances, and—I was about to say—ornaments. Logic and splendor. Before me, around me, I have space-time."[1]

Henri Lefebvre (1901–91) was a contemporary of Jacques Lacan (1901–81), but their trajectories could not be more different. In the late twentieth century, Lacan would become the king of secular bourgeois thought, raising the practice of psychoanalysis to a high pitch of Delphic profundity. Meanwhile, Lefebvre would leave the Communist Party by the rarely used leftward exit. Lacan sought to acquire the dignity of the status of philosopher; Lefebvre pushed philosophy out into the streets. And while Lefebvre was at his most influential in the blazing years of the 1960s, Lacan would eclipse him in the long dark decades that followed.

If there is one abiding purpose to psychoanalysis, it is to make bourgeois lives seem fascinating, at least to those who live them. That it is a form of bourgeois thought is attested by the status of *the real* in Lacanian doctrine. The real is always something terrible, formless, lawless, which the *symbolic order* tries to shield from awareness, but which keeps slithering in, unbidden. It is a modern version of the serpents that in Jorn's account Apollonian thought has to slay, again and again. The symbolic preserves for the ruling class, to whom it classically belongs, an order that keeps at bay the self-ornamenting powers of nature and labor, working together, writhing and worming their way into the cracks in Apollonian form.

In Lefebvre the real is the fulcrum of action rather than an apprehension of terror. His vision of it comes to him while swimming against the current, the body acting on raw need to survive. "The real can only be grasped and appreciated via potentiality."[2] It is by attempting to transform everyday life that the contours of the real are encountered. The real is not entirely formless, even if its forms are not an order that reveals itself in the clear light of day. The encounter with the real, because it is active, informs the *imaginary*. From the struggle in and with the real emerges an imagining of what might be possible. The object of study for both Lacan and Lefebvre is in a sense always everyday life, but in Lefebvre study is a stage in the project of transforming it.

From the Landes department, in the western Pyrenees, Lefebvre joined the Communist Party in 1928. He was active in the Resistance during the war in the countryside near where he was born. An unofficial blacklist kept him from returning to teaching after the liberation, so his friend and contemporary Tristan Tzara found him a job working in radio in Toulouse. It was not until 1961 that he became a professor at Strasbourg, before moving in 1965 to a post at Nanterre, on the outskirts of Paris, a suburb of "misery, shanty towns, excavations … housing projects … a desolate and strange landscape," which would become one of the flashpoints of May '68. His was a lively, diverse, but hardly orthodox career.[3]

He was fifty-six when Debord met him in 1957, via Lefebvre's girlfriend (and typist) Evelyne Chastel, who knew Michèle Bernstein. Lefebvre was at the time the most talented philosopher of the French Communist Party, if hardly the most trusted. He left the party in 1959, the year he published *The Sum and the Remainder*, in which he sets out his theory of *moments*. Lefebvre's moment is closely related to Debord's turn towards the situation. Lefebvre starts from the observation that the leading strategists of advanced capitalism recognized the futility of clinging to colonies such as Algeria, and advanced instead a strategy of colonizing everyday life. Formerly outside the sphere of capitalist social relations, everyday life had become a new site of both commodification and its contestation. Out of everyday life, even in its commodified form, crystallizes a series of moments—of work, but also of play, love, rest, justice, contestation—each of which presses towards the absolute realization of a specific possibility. The moment is "the absolute at the heart of the relative."[4]

A welder welding and a weaver weaving perform quite different acts, but Marx had shown in elaborate detail how the qualitative particulars of such concrete labors became the quantifiable substance of abstract labor through the imposition of the wage relation, the commodity form and the *general equivalent* of money. The Situationists wanted to create what one might call the *specific non-equivalent*, and their name for this was the *situation*. But the very word resisted becoming a concept. The relationship between Lefebvre and the Situationists would dissolve before they got very far with their parallel investigations and experiments with it. It was, as Lefebvre later said, "a love story that ended badly, very badly."[5]

Shortly after his encounter with the Situationist International, Lefebvre published two books which invoke them. The second volume of the *Critique of Everyday Life* (1961) opens with Debord, and *Introduction to Modernity* (1962) closes with the Situationist International. The books are as different as day and night. The former is almost a classic of the sociology of culture, as systematic and structured as anything Lefebvre ever wrote. The latter is a wild ride, a romantic medley of genres, mixing memoir, critique, essay, letter, myth and even science fiction. Between them can be found the practical results and problems of the Situationist International raised to the level of method, and comprehended in the long, deep context of the moves and movements that try, in Rimbaud's words, to change life.

The second volume of the *Critique of Everyday Life* was a book for which Lefebvre had high hopes. He wrote to his friend Norbert Guterman: "So, the book of all books comes to an end. Since the beginning of December, 1,600 handwritten pages, 800 typed (Evelyne only charged me 12–15 per page) … Now I can see what will hinder this book from being the book of all books, the total book of this era. I can see the errors and the flaws. I now understand what should have been done. Now it is too late. There is no way of stopping the machine now."[6] *Introduction to Modernity* maps the uncharted coast that the *Critique* had yet to reach.

Lefebvre the sociologist invents hypotheses and images as much as concepts, and nothing in his writing matches the formal beauty of Lacan the psychoanalyst's topological knots. The proof or refutation of Lefebvre's ideas lies not in the elaboration of a coherent discourse, but in *transduction*, in which the practice of encountering the necessities and contingencies of the real elaborates on it in the direction of the possible. "To know the everyday is to want to transform it."[7] Knowledge is a strategy whose tactics are concepts, forged for discovering the options latent within the everyday. Lefebvre's work of this period encompasses at least five concepts, around which others cluster, which respond to and inform the Situationist project: the everyday, totality, moment, spectacle and the total semantic field.

Freedom is not the opposite of necessity in Lefebvre. Freedom is born out of *need*, and the starting point is a theory of needs.[8] Without the experience of need, there can be no being. Needs are few; desires are many. There is no desire without a need at its core. Need can be intense: hunger, thirst, lust. Need without desire, without play, artifice, luxury, superfluity, is no longer human. It is human poverty. Desire abstracted from need loses vitality, spontaneity, and ossifies into the mere accumulation of things. It is abstract and alienating, another kind of poverty. Lefebvre's critique aims to bring together a presentation of needs and a determination of desires to arrive at a theory of situations, as they arise in the everyday.

The *everyday* overlaps with what Martin Heidegger (1899–1976) calls the *ontic*. But rather than bracket it off in favor of a more fundamental ontology, Lefebvre takes the trivial and seemingly superficial aspects of the everyday seriously. "Either philosophy is pointless or it is the starting point from which to undertake the transformation of non-philosophical reality, with all its triviality and its triteness." His project is an overcoming of the internal limitations of both philosophy and the everyday. "The everyday is a philosophical concept and cannot be understood outside philosophy … it is not the product of pure philosophy but comes of philosophical thought directed toward the non-philosophical, and its major achievement is in this self-surpassing."[9] Everyday life might be a concept internal to philosophy, but it directs philosophy to that which it excludes in the interests of a coherence, the achievement of which renders it null and void.

If the *everyday* is a problem for philosophy, so too is *life*. Eugene Thacker: "Every ontology of life thinks of life in terms of something other than life."[10] The thing other than life through which life is thought can take one of three forms. One: life is spirit. It is interiority and exteriority. It is an incorporeal essence that remains the same, or immaterial essence common to all forms and moments of life. Two: life is time. It is affirmation and negation, movement and change. It is dynamic and self-organizing. Three: life is form. It is additive and subtractive. It is boundaries and transgressions. For Jorn life is form, for Lefebvre it is time, and for nobody in the Situationist orbit is it spirit.

If the central question for antiquity was being, and for modernity the death of God, then the central question today is life. And yet the metaphysical problem remains of identifying "an animating principle of the world that is not itself reduced to its own attributes." What Lefebvre's turn to everyday life, like Jorn's to the attitude to life, accomplishes, is an opening towards new fields of practice which do not require a retreat to ancient regimes of the *care of the self*. The fissures within the concept of life yield not just a critique but the seeds for new forms and tempos of living itself, and perhaps also a fourth category of the thing other than life through which life is thought: matter. Life as surplus and scarcity, as need and desire, a way of (thinking about) life not reducible to biology yet completely outside the grasp of theology. Life is *praxis*.[11]

The everyday can be a realm for forms and times of life, if it yields situations for a collective praxis. Praxis here might mean a coming-into-being through the encounter with something other, an encounter which necessitates a moment of both transformation and reflection. Labor is a form of praxis, but not a privileged one. Praxis is the struggle to overcome need, but also the game of creating and satisfying desires, of desires collapsing back towards need, and so on. In modern times the free creation of relations between desire and need has come to an end. Lefebvre: "As Guy Debord so energetically put it, everyday life has literally been 'colonized.'"[12] The imposition of the commodity form on one aspect of everyday life after another breaks the tension between desire and need. Those unable to discover a relation between need and desire are cut off from their own being, alienated from an active encounter with the real. Hence the need for negative concepts, for *negation,* to reveal not just what everyday life is, but what it isn't. It isn't all that praxis can be imagined as becoming.

The everyday is a mediating level. It is where people appropriate for themselves, not nature, but a second nature of already manufactured articles. It is where needs confront goods. It is not just a functional sphere of consumption and the reproduction of labor power. Nor is the everyday a prisoner of any pervasive disciplinary power, of cops and social workers, psychologists and sociologists intent on prying into people's lives. There is always something unformed in the everyday, something that exceeds and escapes both commodity and power. It is a strategic terrain for experimenting with practices and possibilities. "Today," writes Lefebvre, "what is the aim of utopian investigation? The conquest of everyday life, the recreation of the everyday and the recuperation of the forces which have been alienated in aesthetics, scattered through politics, lost in abstraction, severed from what is possible and what is real."[13]

Two kinds of time meet and mingle in the everyday. One is a linear time, the time of credit and investment. The other is a cyclical time, of wages paid and bills due. This is how class makes itself felt in everyday life. Linear temporality is ruling-class time; cyclical temporality is working-class time. The workers spend what they get; the bosses get what they spend. Cyclical time is the time of needs and the struggle to meet them. But it is also the experience of a certain kind of desire, for example in the patient waiting for the festival to return, and with it the gorgeous consumption of goods in the name of desire. Linear time imposes its own distinctive necessities, its booms and recessions, and this is not the least aspect of the colonization of the everyday by the commodity form. It introduces a distinctive kind of desire as well, desire deferred, not until festival time and its potlatch of goods, but in the interests of accumulation.

The everyday also has a third kind of temporality, the time of adventure, which is perhaps a remnant of aristocratic time. A notable characteristic of the Letterist International, which persists in the Situationist International, is a longing for this time of adventure. It is not because they are titled knights and ladies that they expend time freely in search of adventure; it is because they expend time freely that they consider themselves entitled to style themselves with a certain louche nobility. This is not the least aspect of them that would appeal to the Lefebvrian sensibility. "On the horizon of the modern world dawns the black sun of boredom, and the critique of everyday life has a sociology of boredom as part of its agenda."[14] Adventure is nothing if not the practical refutation of boredom.

What could the everyday become? "Could it be some sort of grand game without any precise objective?"[15] The colonization of everyday life by the commodity form diminishes the role of collective experience, yet groups persist. Within groups, individuals have tactics and strategies, as the early years of the Situationist International makes abundantly clear. Groups also have tactics and strategies in relation to other groups. The everyday is the level of tactics; history, that of strategy. Whether or not traditional societies were governed by the gift, as Mauss and Bataille thought, Lefebvre thinks modern societies are governed by the *challenge*. "Challenge is a means of exerting pressure beyond the group, but its actions reverberate within it."[16] The classical bourgeoisie loved a challenge. It overcame feudalism while staving off the challenge of the working class. Postwar technocrats seem challenge-averse. They prefer to manage challenges, rather than confront them. Not the least pleasure of Lefebvre is his sense, won from his own remarkable experience, that history had still more challenges up its sleeve.

Lefebvre sees everyday life as a mix of *agôn* and *aléa*, of contest and chance. "In the beginning was action; in the end action is recognized … Every human life is a progress or a process toward a possibility, the opening up or closing down of what is possible, a calculation and an option based upon random events and the intervention of 'other people.'"[17] As with linear and circular time, there is a class basis to the experience of the everyday as contest or chance. Experiencing life as a contest to which to apply strategies is a view far less available to the individual members of the working class. Only through collective action can the proletariat enter history at the level of strategy. In decline, its forces lose their grasp on the game of history. All that remains are the tactics of the everyday.

If there is a distinctive experience of modern life, it is the *aleatory*. It is rather like pinball, or Gallizio's industrial painting, a mix of necessity and chance. Confronted by the aleatory, people gamble and gambol with their lives, making moves in a game that may be based on tactics and even strategies, but where the variables are not all known, and the outcomes are far from predictable. Few moves in this game could be considered a *rational choice*. This is the lesson Lefebvre takes from game theory and other technocratic attempts to annex the everyday to social science. They reduce the experience of the everyday to signals and calculations. They describe what everyday life is not: a rational totality. Rather: "Everything becomes disjointed, yet everything becomes a totality, everything becomes reified, yet everything starts disintegrating. The aleatory is triumphant."[18]

Johan Huizinga believed that vigorous civilizations have the capacity to elaborate new forms of play. In decadent ones, play becomes codified into more formal games. Lefebvre differs from Huizinga in that he thinks modernity is a time in which play can flourish. "But it is certainly rather surprising that it should be our era, the era of functionalism and technology, which has discovered homo ludens."[19] Writing at the high watermark of rational and functional social science, Lefebvre thinks history is still capable of objective irony, of confounding order and revealing contingency. History is a game in Lefebvre, the rules of which are never clear and in any case keep changing. It is not a machine or a structure, but neither is it random. It is more like the flocking of starlings. Groups play each other with more or less awareness of the local rules of the game, though not of how their moves swarm together and affect the historical stakes.

Within everyday life, groups challenge one another, and not the least part of the challenge is the tactic of appearances. "The secrets of groups, their opacities, which are what give the illusion of substance, are made up of anxieties or audacity with regard to what is possible, of entrenchments or offensives, of retreats and advances in relation to other groups, of courage or of weakness of will in response to problems."[20] Here Lefebvre and the Situationists are very close, and close also to Huizinga, for whom play always has an element of the secret about it. The game within the group ought not to be apparent to the group's rivals.

Play is a misunderstood aspect of praxis. Play "uses appearances and illusions which—for one marvelous moment—become more real than the real."[21] Through the concept of play, Lefebvre manages to bypass two of the great theoretical fetishes of his times: *structure* and *sign*. Structure is just a reified apprehension of play, its fossilized remains. "Structure itself is nothing more than a precarious and momentary success, a win or a loss in a complex gamble."[22] The sign is just one aspect of play, that which a player brandishes, the better to conceal a secret—and to display that a secret is concealed.

The concept of *totality* would become the great boo-word of late twentieth-century thought, linked, through a rather casual association, to the *totalitarian* state of the Soviet Union. Particularly for the so-called new philosophers, totality reeked of the gulag. Some genuine conceptual objections were bent to the service of legitimating the status quo. For Lefebvre, totality has a somewhat different sense. Not totality as an achieved philosophical system, but as an orientation for praxis. "Discourse strives for totality. It must strive for totality, yet it is never more than incomplete." What Lefebvre calls *totalization* is praxis revealing itself in terms of its tendency. Every praxis wills its own totalization. "Every totalization which aspires to achieve totality collapses, but only after it has been explicit about what it considers its inherent virtualities to be." The concept of totality directs research. "If there is no insistence upon totality, theory and practice accept the 'real' just as it is, and 'things' just as they are: fragmentary, divided and disconnected."[23] Totality is a negative concept, it is the gap between what is possible and what is impossible. The critique of everyday life hinges on thinking certain moments within it as far as they will go.

Groups acting within everyday life pursue their strategies as far as they will go. Praxis is at once repetition and creation. Creation emerges out of repetition. Inventiveness is born from the everyday, through the action not of individual genius but of collective play. "Could not inventiveness—or the seeds of inventiveness—be a product of the limited and daring praxis of small-scale groups: sects, secret societies, political parties, elective groups, laboratories, theatrical troupes, etc?"[24] As in Jorn, the sources of creation are popular, but this does not lead to an uncritical celebration of all things popular. The everyday is vital for what it can be, not for what it is.

Praxis has its dangers. What was once a living form of collective self-discovery and self-invention can harden into a thing-like routine. It can, in short, become *alienated*. Lefebvre differs from much of the Hegelian Marxist writing of the time in thinking of alienation as something less than a total, remorseless, one-dimensional and one-directional descent into a nicely equipped hell. Modern life is not all alienation. Rather, it's a game in which certain tactics prove dis-alienating for a time, then fall short of their own totalization, cease to work, forcing groups to either come up with new tactics or lose sight of their self-affirming praxis. Praxis can fail both by falling short in its totalization and by exceeding it. "Beyond a certain limit, the negative becomes a fetish, a vision of nothingness; radical critique becomes hypercritique, and nihilism is established as a truth without that truth having been legitimated."[25] It's a critique that could be applied with some justice to the Situationist International after the exclusion of the artists.

Everyday life is to be transformed according to its own tendencies. When a group discovers a dis-alienating practice in everyday life, it may crystallize into a *moment*. Possible moments might include love, play, rest, knowledge, although nothing prevents the creation of new moments. Philosophy might be nothing other than making contemplation into a moment. The moment emerges out of the cyclical time of repetition, but creates a time of its own. The moment constitutes its own kind of space, and enables the stabilizing of determinable relations with otherness. A moment is constituted in space and time by a decision which singles it out from ambiguity.

The moment weaves itself into and out of the everyday. The moment tries to achieve the total realization of a specific possibility. It exhausts itself in the act of pursuing its own goal to the very end. "It wishes to perceive the possibilities of everyday life and to give human beings a constitution by constituting their powers, if only as guidelines or suggestions."[26] The moment wants to endure. It wants to gather its own temporality. The moment requires a certain amount of ritual and ceremony. It makes for itself a special time and place. It creates its own specific form of memory.

These forms the moment creates run the risk of repeating themselves, of no longer serving the moment but enclosing it. The moment provokes its own specific alienation. The gamer or the lover becomes obsessed. A Korean man expired in 2005 after playing the game *Starcraft* in an internet café for fifty hours, with only brief naps and toilet breaks.[27] The gamer forgets to eat, to sleep, commits everything to beating a level. The lover spends sleepless nights thinking about the object of affection. At this point alienation is complete, and the moment disappears.

Moments may have different scales. *Festival* might be the grandest scale to which the moment can aspire, a historical scale. "Festival only makes sense when its brilliance lights up the sad hinterland of everyday dullness, and when it uses up, in one single moment, all it has patiently and soberly accumulated."[28] Lefebvre thought of the prewar leftist Popular Front—with its mass demonstrations, equal parts celebration and desperation—as festival. At quite a different scale, he writes movingly of a working-class painter from his hometown whose work was shunned even by the provincial museum, but who was a decisive influence on the young Lefebvre. "There are men who are not artists and not philosophers, but who nevertheless emerge above the everyday, in their own everyday lives, because they experience moments: love, work, play, etc."[29] Just as there is a tomb for the unknown soldier, there could be one for the unknown artist, whose moments are unrecognized and fade clean away.

Situation is a persistent concept in philosophy, if usually a marginal one. From Hegel to Kierkegaard to Sartre it designates a zone in which otherwise different elements confront each other.[30] Those elements can be isolated, defined, made into concepts, but the situation within which they meet and mix has a singular quality. Lefebvre's procedure is in some respects the other way around. "The moment is not exactly the same as a situation. The result of a decision or a choice—of an endeavor—the moment creates situations." Thinking aloud in a letter, Debord tries to specify the situation in its difference from Lefebvre's moment: "The difficulty of the 'situationist' moment is … marking the exact end (its reversal? And another), its transformation into a different term of this series of situations that (can?) constitute such a Lefebvrian moment."[31]

Here, in this hesitating language, Debord gropes towards an understanding of the Situationist practice of creating collective experiences of space and time that have their own singular coherence, but neither collapse back into the dead time of routine, nor ossify into mere artifacts. Unlike the moment, the situation "must unify falsely separated categories (love, play, expression, creative thought). And each of these formations—as conscious and calculated as they can be, that is to say, brought into play with superior chances—inevitably move towards their own reversal, because each one is entirely lived in time along with its negation and permanent supersession."[32] For Debord all of the singular moments, of love, play, work, knowledge, can be combined within a situation.

Between writing *Critique of Everyday Life, Volume 2* and *Introduction to Modernity*, Lefebvre appears to lose faith in the possibilities of the moment.

> You used to think that an auto-critique of everyday life through its own transpositions was possible: a critique of the slimy animal by its delicate shell and vice versa—a critique of the everyday by festivals, or of trivial instants by moments, and vice versa—a critique of life by art and of art by life, of the real by its double and its reverse image: dreams, imagination, fiction. The times change. Technology began penetrating everyday life. There were new problems.[33]

Modern life might not give rise to its own critical agent of transformation—what Lefebvre terms *modernity*—and praxis might be foreclosed, and with it being, the engagement with the real. "It is not that God is absent, but something worse: modernity is like a shell to hide the absence of praxis …" Modernity is the "ghost of revolution."[34]

What forecloses the possibility of praxis is what Lefebvre, citing Debord, calls the *spectacle*. The spectacle makes totality visible, but only in fragments, and visible only within the space of the private. It does not make the private social as well. The spectacle is a one-way street, the public privatized. "It is the generalization of private life. At one and the same time the mass media have unified and broadcast the everyday; they have disintegrated it by integrating it with 'world' current events in a way which is both too real and utterly superficial."[35]

Lefebvre calls the spectacle the great pleonasm, the Thing of Things. Thought in terms of its totalizing tendency, "it would be a closed circuit from hell, a perfect circle in which the absence of communication and communication pushed to the point of paroxysm would meet and their identities would merge." What is real is what is known; what is known is what is real. The illusion of permanent novelty occludes the possibility of surprise. It is a world of incessant redundancy. Everything is always the same, only better. It makes the same special offer to everyone, all the time: "the faked orgasms of art and life."[36]

The challenge of the colonization of the everyday by the spectacle calls for a reassessment, not just of tactics but of strategy. Lefebvre takes a step back to the terrain on which the challenge appears, the *total semantic field*, of which the spectacle is an alienated form. Everyday life takes place not just in the streets, but also in the total semantic field. It has three registers: signals, signs and symbols. *Signals* form closed systems of redundant messages which appear mostly in the form of commands. A traffic light is a signal. It commands the driver to stop or go. *Signs* form a region within the semantic field of relatively open networks, a mix of information and redundancy. *Symbols* cannot command and are not particularly legible. They irrupt into the semantic field as noise. Symbols may have faded and gone into hiding, but they can still be glimpsed through the spectacle. The total semantic field is "complex, differentiated, polarized, alive with the fluxes and tensions which come and go from one pole to the other. Language tries to equal this totality, but is never more than one of its parts."[37]

Cybernetic theories totalize the whole of the semantic field as signals, and imagine it can be made self-regulating. Semiotic theories totalize the semantic field as if it were composed entirely of signs and governed by the grammar of their combination. Lefebvre's strategic move is to counter the spectacle's growing reduction of communication to the level of signal and sign by moving onto the terrain of the symbol, or rather by treating the whole semantic field as the space of the challenge: signal, sign and symbol together.

"Communication in depth implies the totality of the semantic field. The more it incorporates that totality, the more aesthetic it becomes."[38]

The legacy on which Lefebvre draws is a certain understanding of *romanticism,* which might be the memory of a series of practices for crystallizing the total semantic field itself into moments. Lefebvre is sometimes thought of as a Hegelian Marxist, but his understanding of romanticism owes more to Stendhal. From Stendhal's *Racine and Shakespeare* (1823), Lefebvre draws out a theory of the romantic as the precursor to a critical modernity, and like it the product of defeated revolutions. Romanticism brings everything into art. Everything classical art excluded is drawn into it, to the point of exhaustion. Romanticism occupies the total semantic field and gravitates particularly to the pole of the symbolic, to stimulate the creation of works of art. The artwork in turn condenses the total semantic field. "Living romanticism reveals a totality."[39]

If there are symbols through which the romantic and its antithesis, the classical, might first be approached, they are the knight and the king. The king stands first and last for order, if also for an unknown range of things in between. The knight is the figure of adventure, driven by a certain goal but of uncertain outcome. The knight submits to a vow and lives his life in the name of an ideal, but one which is constantly challenged by circumstances. The knight's horse raises him above earthly things, but when he falls he comes crashing down into the shit. The knight is a figure of the aleatory, standing for all those who live in an ambiguous or shadowy milieu, which perhaps explains Debord's taste for *Prince Valiant* comics.[40]

The classical assumes a legitimate order, revealed by the light of the sun. God's in his heaven, the king's on his throne, all is right with the world. And what goes wrong can be rectified. Like Le Corbusier's plans, classicism favors the right angle and the straight line. It favors the form of the myth, in which order is destabilized, restored, legitimated. Its privileged medium is architecture. Its method is *imitation*. Everyone imitates the one above them in the social order, just as the king imitates God, and the whole social order imitates nature. Classical humor, from Molière to Sacha Baron Cohen, ridicules failed attempts at imitation. In Molière's satirical attack on the Precious movement, provincial ladies shun some noblemen as beneath them, so these retaliate by having their grooms pretend to be Precious sophisticates. Hilarity ensues, but classical humor serves order.

The romantic is a corrosive fluid that attacks the classical on every front. It is a refusal of obedience. It lurks in the dark, in the mist, within the eclipse. Time is out of joint. It favors the wave, the vibration, the curlicue. It mixes forms, detaches symbols from myths, and puts them in play against all that is legitimate. Its medium of greatest affinity is music. Its method is *creation*, which it claims as a human potential, not a divine attribute. For Lefebvre the romantic intersects with a certain strand of irony. Unlike Jorn he idolizes the achievements of the Greeks, not least Socratic irony, which is the undoing of any order of belief. The subjective irony of Socrates anticipates the objective irony of history, which sweeps order away in its aleatory currents.

Romanticism can be both pre- and post-revolutionary. Lefebvre acknowledges that most notable French romantics sided against the revolution. Its key tension is between the ideal of bourgeois life, and its pallid reality. Romanticism became a bourgeois art in the sense that they were the class that consumed it. This kept romantic artists from pursuing romanticism to its logical conclusion. The romantic lives outside bourgeois society yet within it, "like a maggot in a fruit."[41] Or like the grit within the oyster, forcing it to make the classical pearl. The fate of the romantic gesture is—if not obscurity—to become classical, to calcify into *the good form* (something Jorn identifies in Max Bill, for example).

From the symbolic pantheon, romanticism draws on figures who rarely occupy central and active roles in classical culture: the knight, the prince, the seer, the child, the witch, the devil, the stranger, not to mention some even more strange, like Tintomara. Those who can't find their place in the classical world—the marginal, the minor, the delinquent, the weird—might find it here. But while one aspect of romanticism is otherworldly, an escape from this alien planet to one more hospitable, the symbols drawn from the total semantic field can also be brought back to the everyday. They can be lived. And while isolation might be one practice favored by romanticism, it is also an initiation into deviant or secret groups. Although Lefebvre does not use the term, its homeland is *bohemia*.

Romanticism includes a desire for communion in some kind of lived utopia. A desire which, at the limit, feeds into utopian socialism.

Lefebvre: "The best man of action is one who chooses his moment well ... His decision simplifies the complex situation and the ambiguity, and by the very act of simplifying them, transforms them."[42] If Guy Debord was not that man, it was certainly what he aspired to be, at a time when even the aspiration was becoming rare. The Situationists were not the only group working over the remains of romanticism in postwar Europe. But if there was a dominant strategy, it was to pursue the romantic exploration of the total semantic field only so far, before turning back and setting up a new classicism in the resulting ruins. This was the trajectory of absurdist theatre, modern jazz, Robbe-Grillet's *nouveau roman,* or new wave cinema. What the Situationists acquired from Isou and the Letterists was a commitment to pursuing a certain romantic decomposition to the limit, if not his claim to build a new classicism of entirely new forms on the ruins. What Lefebvre perceives as the open path is to pursue the romantic further, in two directions: further into the semantic field, and further back, not into new art forms like Isou, but into everyday life. "The most brilliant Situationists are exploring and testing out a kind of lived utopianism."[43]

The romantic strategy is not without difficulties: "contradictions are thick-skinned, and their bones are even thicker."[44] Lefebvre identifies contradictions between cosmopolitanism and nationalism, between futurism and the middle ages, between religiosity and revolt, and between subjectivity and the outside world. These all pass through the Situationist International. These contradictions are traceable to a central tension between two worldviews: an anthropological nature and a cosmological nature. The roots of anthropological nature lie in the enlightenment philosophies of eighteenth-century France, articulated by Buffon and others. It is optimistic, it stresses human perfectibility and equality. The worldview of cosmological nature is more German than French. Here nature appears as wildly other, as an inaccessible external world. It enters the French semantic field in force relatively late, with surrealism. Can what is real become rational? Can what is rational become real? Such might be the terms of this irresolvable tension. It infuses the entire scope of possibilities for our species-being.

In playing with the devil of romanticism and its symbols, the Situationist International inherited its contradictions, which would play out through the movement in the splits and fissures of the 1960s. The relationship with Lefebvre was also a casualty of the tensions of the times, both personal and political. And yet not only did he provide the Situationists with the concept of everyday life, he also engaged with them in thinking through the two key concepts of the spectacle (or pleonasm) and the situation (or moment). And while it was not a welcome insight, Lefebvre as seer foresaw the necessity for the formation within the everyday of multiple forms of group action. The monolithic party of labor would not have as its counterpart a single party of play, but rather a number of fractious groups, playing off and against one another, challenging one another. In the twenty-first century, when so many intellectuals seem unhealthily obsessed with the ubiquitous thought of an omniscient power, Lefebvre, even in his less ebullient moments, radiates a sense of possibility. He still swims against the current. The following chapters trace the detours and deviations of the most interesting attempts to appropriate from the early versions of Situationist thought and practice, and open up new possibilities, to recall them and not let their moments pass.

9 Divided We Stand

"Newell Street, London, E14 7HR. £1,250,000: A beautiful Grade 2 listed house formerly headquarters of The British Sailors Society. Built circa 1802 for one of Horatio Nelson's captains, the property retains many naval features including one of London's only Victorian swimming pools, originally built to teach sailors to swim. The property is laid out over three floors and consists: large entrance hallway, drawing room, conservatory, four bedrooms, two bathrooms, studio room, sauna, private garden and two parking spaces. The property has also been used for filming, including *Beginner's Luck* and *Dead Cool* and has been graced by stars such as Rosanna Arquette, Liz Smith, and Julie Delpy."[1]

It's easier to sell a property with a story, but beneath these stories lie others. The ad neglects to mention that the same address formerly housed the homeless, or that it was once disgraced by the anti-celebrities of the Situationist International. In preparation for the 1960 London conference, Debord and Jorn embarked on a dérive of the city looking for a suitable venue. They settled on this hall in the Limehouse district, mythologized by Charles Dickens as a seedy warren of opium dens.[2] With them was Jacqueline de Jong (b. 1939), one of the handful of women who, like Michèle Bernstein, was able not only to put up with men like these, but make vital contributions of her own. "I mean, no washing the dishes and things like that."[3]

De Jong's was a sophisticated family from provincial Holland. Her father's company made seamless stockings for Dior. When the Nazis invaded Holland, two-year-old Jacqueline crossed over the Jura Mountains with her mother, while her father hid out in Amsterdam. After the war de Jong moved to Paris, where her father found a position for her at Dior. She met Jorn in the company of her father, when he bought one of Jorn's pictures. The family collection included works by several Cobra artists, a Franz Kline, and many other fine contemporary works. In 1957 de Jong was in Holland, working as an assistant to Willem Sandberg at the Stedelijk Museum. The Situationists were involved in a somewhat fraught collaboration with the Stedelijk, which brought de Jong into contact with them.[4]

The Spur Group (1957–66) was one of the stronger signs of life in postwar German culture. It formed in 1957 in Munich. De Jong joined Spur in 1959. "Jorn thought very highly of them," she says. He found them a dealer and brought them into the orbit of the Situationists. They would not return the favor. "If you pick a strange baby, don't be surprised if it craps on you!" Or so the artist Roberto Matta advised his friend when Jorn became their champion.[5]

To Spur, art was the last free domain from which to oppose the rationalization of social life. Spur defended art against attempts to rationalize it as well, a last redoubt against administered life. They had read their Theodor Adorno (1903–69), and while the cardinal of critical theory would hardly recognize them, they were his mutant offspring. "We are against truth, against happiness, against satisfaction, against good conscience, against fat stomachs, against HARMONY," their manifesto declares.[6]

Many postwar German artists looked back to the 1920s as a time from which to start building a new German culture, but for Spur the roots of Nazism also lay in the ambiguities of that period. They wanted to make contact with history, but theirs was a détournement of 1920s expressionism, rather than an imitation. There they found the resources to mobilize against both the lingering Nazi presence in postwar Germany and also the amnesia of a modernizing, technocratic state. They cast their lot with Jorn's creative elite rather than Debord's renewed interest in the proletariat.

To escape both the Nazi past and techno-statist future in Germany, Spur tried to occupy a transnational avant-garde space, and this cosmopolitanism was not the least thing about them that caused offense in their homeland. They spurned not only the state and its official culture, but also the proletariat. Where the Communist leadership in the resistance cast an aura over the idea of the French working class, Spur saw their German brothers and sisters as compromised by Nazism and coopted by Social Democracy. Spur took refuge in art as precursor to another kind of labor, a free play in which a psychic surplus could feed back into self-production.

Spur became the German section of the Situationist International in 1959, and found themselves caught in the same tensions as the Italian section around Gallizio. The artists might see their creative efforts as aligned with the Situationist International, but artists need collectors, and to find collectors they need dealers. To the dealer, an artist's adherence to a movement merely gives the work a certain glamor, not to mention some free publicity. To the dealer the actual aims of such a movement are neither here nor there. To the extent that the movement promotes the artist and the artist succeeds, the artist is then pulled out of the orbit of the movement and into that of the art world—dealers, collectors, curators, critics. This would happen to Spur as it did to Gallizio. Vincent Kaufmann: "If a … Situationist art exists, it functions as an invisible model: all representation is treason, including when it is the product of a real … Situationist."[7] Or rather: art could only function tactically, as provisional instances of a total project.

The prevalence of artists tilted the Situationist International towards their particular concerns. So Debord gathered the forces that would enable him to dispense with their nettlesome presence. The Brussels-based writers Attila Kotányi (1924–2004) and Raoul Vaneigem (b. 1934) replaced Constant as the anti-art left wing of the movement.[8] The tensions between the mostly Francophone theorists and the mostly German-speaking artists were papered over at the London conference, where de Jong was both translating and taking the minutes. The French were turning towards the proletariat, just as the Germans were abandoning the idea of its revolutionary force. The conference did manage to unite in support of Alexander Trocchi, facing serious drug charges in New York.

While in London the Situationists made a farcical appearance at the Institute for Contemporary Arts (ICA), something of a replay of Debord and Trocchi's appearance there three years earlier to show Debord's film *Howls for Sade*.[9] De Jong: "The event was just one big joke, snubbing the public." After the London conference, the energetic and able de Jong found herself active on the central council of the Situationist International at twenty-one years of age. After the exclusion of the group around Constant, she effectively was the Dutch section. She proposed to the central council that it needed an English-language journal. The others agreed, and appointed her co-editor with Trocchi. It never appeared—at least not as planned.

She also made a pilgrimage to Alba. "Pinot asked me to come and work with him. He became completely impossible. Anyway, my whole idea was not to stay very long, to make as many meters of industrial painting as I could, then roll them up, take them away and see what I could do with them. He wanted me to leave them. Later, when he made an exhibition with them, he told me that was my payment for my stay! So I do understand Debord, who was pretty well fed up with Pinot. For me it was finished. A week doing this industrial painting and you've had it! It was industry, literally. But the idea of industrial painting was fantastic. Very Beuys-like, although Joseph Beuys was later."

In an extraordinary letter of 1960, Jorn discussed the status of his donation to the movement should he leave it:

> My interest in the situationist movement is purely personal and passionate, in a direct fashion, and, if the inevitable developments of social circumstances necessitate my exclusion from the movement this changes absolutely nothing in my purely economic attitude towards this movement. The economic surplus that my social situation, insofar as I am a painter, gives me is best placed with the situationist movement, even if this movement is obliged to attack me for being in a situation from which I can't escape, but which embarrasses the movement.[10]

Jorn declares himself a strategic ally of the Situationists even if the Situationists turn against him tactically. Jorn left the Situationist International, officially at least, in 1961, and with him went his nimble fencing between aesthetic and theoretical practices. It was time to move on. As Debord wrote to Jorn in 1962: "I only want to work on a 'moving order,' never constructing a doctrine or an institution." Then he détourns Jorn back at himself. It's a question of "creating veritable disequilibria, departure points for all [future] games."[11]

The Reeperbahn district of Hamburg is best known today as the place where the Beatles really learned to play. While a young George Harrison (1943–2001) was probably on stage somewhere, playing with a toilet seat around his neck, Debord, Kotányi and Vaneigem decanted the "Hamburg Theses," although they were not so much hammering out theses as getting hammered. Debord wrote soon after to Vaneigem:

> As a profound theoretical justification of our indolence ... we agreed not to write the "Hamburg Theses," so as to impose all the better the central meaning of our entire project in the future. Thus, the enemy cannot feign to approve it without great difficulty. Moreover, one can certify that this is the height of avant-gardism in the formal presentation of ideas, perhaps opening the way for the explication of Lautréamont's *Poésies* by schoolboys? One adds the most fortunate confusion to all this if one bears in mind that it will be necessary to rank among the authors of this constellation of situationist theses (a very nebulous theoretics, out of reach and imprecise where its frontiers are concerned, but nevertheless bright and shiny) Alex Trocchi, who follows the same path but without being in nor being seen in Hamburg, at least not at the moment.[12]

Nineteenth-century revolutionaries like Louis-Auguste Blanqui plotted in secret. Marx and Engels chose instead to declare their aims to the world. With the "Hamburg Theses," the remaining rump of the Situationist International took the novel path of openly declaring that henceforth they would maintain certain secrets.

Art was now officially anti-Situationist. Spur were expelled. There was no procedure, no consensus. They were out. The timing wasn't brilliant, as Bavarian police had just seized copies of the *Spur* journal and arrested the group. De Jong shared some of Debord's reservations about the quality of Spur's journal, but she resigned from the Situationist International over the high-handed way in which a faction within it had routed them out. The nature of the movement was changing. As de Jong observes in retrospect: "This wanting to have very serious people and also clowns is in the beginning, right from the start,… It's a pity it stopped being like that."

Together with Jorn's brother Jørgen Nash (1920–2004) and Swedish ceramic artist Ansgar Elde (1933–2000), she wrote a protest against Debordian treachery. The letter sets the stage by describing the Paris of 1962 as a "cauldron of political instigations and demonstrations, armored cars in the streets, the bloody shadow of the Algerian war … strikes, police raids, censorship … shootings and reprisals."[13] This is the atmosphere in which they accuse Debord's faction of turning on their own comrades. And yet about all that Spur, de Jong and Nash had in common was a rejection of Debord's style of organization of the Situationist International. De Jong eventually lost patience with the mercurial Nash. She was certainly not pleased to discover him forging paintings by his more famous brother, Asger Jorn.

The Second Situationist International put together by Nash, Elde and other Scandinavian Situationists, whose founding document de Jong also signed, claimed that "now everyone is free to become a Situationist without the need for special formalities." Gone were the structural forms: the sections, the central council, the direct democracy, the vetting of potential members, and above all the principle of exclusion. While this seems in some respects a step forward, something is also lost. The possibility of exclusion binds a member to a group in a quite particular way. The game is not the same.

This founding text, "The Struggle for the Situcratic Society" (1962), was philosophical about the split between what it saw as the French and Scandinavian approaches. While the "First" Situationist International denounced the "Nashists" in harsh terms, the latter did not return fire. They identified Debord's practice as one of *position*, as opposed to the Scandinavians'—one is tempted to say Jorn's—of *mobility*. "In the argument neither side can claim to have a monopoly on the right ideas."[14] The distinction does not seem quite right. Perhaps it is rather one between an analytic conception of mobility in a fixed space, and a ludic conception of mobility in an open and variable space. Here the so-called Second International seems justified in its self-awareness as a fragment of a wider movement. Combining a low theory with a critical practice that might evade, if not avoid, capture by the institutions of art and the academy remains a challenge.

The Second International hung together for a decade or so, producing extraordinary work and one or two interesting situations.[15] They took the practice of art directly into everyday life, to create situations as experiments in ways of behaving and being together. Among them was Jens Jørgen Thorsen (1932–2000). An artist and anarchist, he was also for a time a tabloid journalist, and had a knack for provocations that could puncture the routine of the spectacle. He proposed a relational approach to art, with "the disappearance of the spectator and his replacement by the participator. A communicative art is an art which lives between. In the space between people."[16] With Thorsen's help, the Second Situationist International carried off at least two great feats of communicative art.

Out on an island in Copenhagen harbor sits the iconic statue by Edvard Erikson, the *Little Mermaid*. In 1964, the head mysteriously disappeared.[17] The Second Situationist International put out a press release claiming to know its whereabouts. They invited the media to a beach location. A diver swam towards them from a boat, but paused midway on a reef where in view of the assembled media he dropped a bag, containing a heavy object, into the sea. In 1968, when anarchists picketed the Venice Biennale, Thorsen and friends used fake press passes to get through and occupied a pavilion, complementing the siege without with an occupation within. They issued a statement denouncing the art concentration camp, which concluded with the slogan "divided we stand."[18]

The Second Situationist International set itself up as both a rival and a replacement for what it called the "First" Situationist International. Their sophistication was at the level of participatory experiments. As Thorsen said, "The situationist idea is based on utilization of art and the forces of creativity within art being used directly in the social environment." Nothing in their writing bears comparison to what T. J. Clark once called the "chiliastic serenity" of Debord's key texts.[19] And while the contempt of Debord was a given, they also managed to lose the support of Jorn, who disapproved of Thorsen's antics. While no doubt fun at the time, the *Little Mermaid* and Venice Biennale pranks do not seem to advance much beyond the Notre Dame affair the Letterists pulled off back in 1950.

In a handwritten note about the improper expulsion of the Spur group, de Jong wrote, perhaps addressing Debord: "I'm proud you call us gangsters, nevertheless you are wrong. We are worse: we are Situationists."[20] She goes on to articulate, for the first time, an accurate formula for the impasse into which the Situationists had wandered: "The Situationist International has to be considered either as an avant-garde school which has already produced a series of first-class artists thrown out after having passed through their education, OR as an anti-organization based upon new ideology which is situationist and which has not yet found in details its clear formulations in the fields of science, technique, and art."[21] The Situationist International had indeed functioned as a school for scandal, through which many fabulous (one would not say distinguished) writers and artists passed. But it could not function as an anti-organization.

De Jong adds the first principle of the new anti-organization to come: "Everybody who develops theoretically or practically this new unity is automatically a member of the situationist international and in this perspective the *Situationist Times*."[22] Here de Jong dispenses with the notion of organization altogether. The Situationist International could henceforth be taken as just one player of a collaborative game that could be challenged by another, or triangulated by a third. De Jong: "That was my idea. The important thing is: no interpretation and the freedom for anyone to join in." Perhaps it was more of a détournement of the form of the organized avant-garde than an avant-garde. Here a new kind of relation appears, perhaps with new dangers. If the Situationist International acquired the vices of collective being, anti-organization might be just one step towards the vices of an all too familiar individualism. The *Situationist Times* would head that off for now by documenting a network of related experiments, steps towards what it called the *situcratic society*.

Revenge is a dish best served from a great height. The *Situationist Times* that de Jong edited from 1962 to 1967 is a remarkable set of documents. The early issues were edited jointly with Noël Arnaud (1919–2003). A hospital administrator by profession, he was a member of Dada and surrealist groups, of Cobra and Oulipo, a satrap of the College of Pataphysics, and Boris Vian's biographer.[23] Collaborating with him suggests de Jong's awareness that the Situationists' recuperation of their own immediate avant-garde past was by no means complete. The *Situationist Times* would pointedly include texts by François Dufrêne, who left the Letterist movement in 1964 to start the Second Letterist International with Gil Wolman and others.[24] There is also a text by Piero Simondo (b. 1928) who started a new institute in Turin in 1962 to further the researches begun at Alba. Produced outside of the Situationist International and without Trocchi, the *Situationist Times* turned out to be a somewhat different beast. It was multilingual, and even its English-language texts were written in what one might now call *netlish*—transnational English unapologetically cast as a second language patterned after the writer's first language.[25] The era of French as the lingua franca of the avant-garde was over.

The *Situationist Times* pursued a different course to the experimental practice of the excluded artists and the strategic logics of the Debord faction. It offered resources for thought, action and creation, rather than a consistent line. It was more about suggesting possible connections than pronouncing on fault lines. De Jong was interested in a logic of images, of concepts that might be discovered and presented through visual conjunction. If one took seriously Lautréamont's injunction that "poetry should be made by all," then perhaps a journal—any reproducible media—should distribute both finished art and raw materials with which others could make art. Or perhaps there could be no difference between a raw material and a finished work.

Each issue contained the statement, consistent with established Situationist practice, to the effect that "all reproduction, deformation, modification, derivation, and transformation of the *Situationist Times* are permitted." This was similar to the *copyleft* statement published in *Internationale Situationniste*, and connects Situationist practice with the hacker and pirate practices of twenty-first-century struggles around free culture as a fitfully acknowledged, still barely understood, precursor.

The first issue of the *Situationist Times* defended the Spur group, expelled from the Situationist International at a time when charges were being brought against them for their allegedly licentious publication. In a little dossier of texts is included a strong editorial from

Arnaud, a statement by Debord and others, and some fragments of a comic strip called "Spur: Paintings and Sculptures." It includes a panel with a Situationist last supper, the elements of which include: Bauhaus, shit, violins, birds, beauty, belches, mercilessness, coffee, and kisses. The issue also documents the expulsion of the "Nashists" of the Second Situationist International with a crude détournement of pages from the *Internationale Situationniste* journal.[26] There is a letter in Danish from J. V. Martin, the only Scandinavian to remain loyal to Debord, attacking Nash. Where the *Internationale Situationniste* always aims at a consistent line, the *Situationist Times* is interested in the relationships between players.

Several issues present what remained of *Mutant*, a post–Situationist International collaboration between Jorn and Debord that turned away from the then-current spectacle of the *space age* towards a prescient intervention in the technological transformation of earthbound life.[27] Never set foot in a fallout shelter, *Mutant* advises, for "it is better to die standing with all the cultural heritage of humanity, the perpetual modification of which must remain our task." Nuclear weaponry's main function is to deter not the enemy but the state's own population. Contrary to the Ban the Bomb movement, this position sees not nuclear annihilation as the main threat, but the disarming of critique. The channeling of critical energy into the anti-nuclear cause serves the interests of existing political forces. Hence: "I … pledge myself not to expect the necessary upheavals of society [to be effected] by any of the existing formations of specialized politics." One wonders how much the twenty-first century's obsession with things environmental might likewise play a demobilizing role.

A consistent project in the *Situationist Times* is the investigation of *topology*, in keeping with one of Jorn's abiding interests.[28] The mathematician and surrealist collage artist Max Bucaille (1906–96) contributed a whole series of texts on the subject. Topology is a geometry of transformations, and it exercised a fascination over a number of postwar artists, architects, and writers, including Henri Lefebvre, who were looking for a more modern understanding of space than perspective drawing. Topology seemed to better describe the geometric imagination of folk art, with its knots, rings, spirals and labyrinths, all of which the *Situationist Times* documented with copious photographs from cross-cultural sources. While many were interested in its formal properties, here it points towards a way of diagramming practices in space and time, a *situology* of singular and variable forms. De Jong: "That is the beautiful thing about topology, that everything can be changed at any time."[29]

Following his withdrawal from active participation in the Situationist International, Jorn took on some ambitious new projects. His great interest at the time was in documenting what he took to be a Nordic spatio-temporal folk culture, quite at odds with the formal geometry bequeathed to modern art and science by the Renaissance. For this purpose he created yet another organization, the Scandinavian Institute for Comparative Vandalism (1961–65). According to Jorn's friend and collector Guy Atkins, "the unattractive name was deliberately chosen to put off art lovers."[30] It referred to graffiti found in Normandy churches in which Jorn saw the hand of peoples migrating from the North, leaving their mark, so to speak, on European culture. More generally, *comparative vandalism* named an understanding of popular cultural creation that could appreciate the way it flowed along migration routes, subtly defacing the edifice of every cultural center it encountered. Jorn was interested in the traces left by the dérive of whole peoples over centuries and continents. Jorn thought that the wandering attitude to life of different migrating groups might have produced comparable understandings of space and time, expressed in similar visual iconographies.

Jorn co-authored a book on the church graffiti, but the main part of the project was the documentation of the distinctive symbolic and ornamental forms of the northern world.[31] The project was to culminate in a massive book series—*10,000 Years of Nordic Folk Art*—but little was published at the time. Jorn may have run into difficulties with his academic partners, state officials or his collaborator, the noted photographer Gérard Franceschi (1915–2001). De Jong, who worked closely with Jorn on the project, says that "the trouble started with Franceschi, who wanted more money and more credit." While the project acknowledged traditional archaeological classifications, Jorn was also interested in applying his comparative method to the visual forms, tracing patterns of modification and borrowings across place and time. Jorn: "Through my art I have learned to see and find meaningful relationships where others might not see them."[32] The volumes were to contain articles by specialists, but the meat of them is Jorn's organization of Franceschi's photographs into stunning, elaborate, purely visual essays.

When *10,000 Years of Nordic Folk Art* stalled, Jorn used the Institute for Comparative Vandalism as the vehicle for another extensive publishing project, this time of his own writings. The Institute began issuing his manuscripts as reports: *The Natural Order* (1962), *Value and Economics* (1962, including a revised version of his earlier *Critique of Political Economy* of 1960), *Luck and Chance: Dagger and Guitar* (1963), and *Thing and Polis* (1964). What the Marquis de Sade was to the surrealists and the Comte de Lautréamont to the Situationists, Emanuel Swedenborg (1688–1772) was to the Jorn of the Comparative Vandalism period. From the Swedish mystic Jorn took the principle of correspondences and turned it into the literary technique of *triolectics*, in which he would triangulate any three concepts, and through analogies, puns, transpositions, permutate them in unexpected directions. This procedure for navigating flocks of concepts, arranged in threes, combined a precise discipline with limitless movement. To Jorn it was a topological approach to the concept, a way of thinking concepts via spatial transformation, in a "polydimensional cosmos of the surface." Or as he said elsewhere: "all my outpourings of words are just one long defense of a world to which words have no right of entrance." In these texts, Jorn taught himself to swim atop Lautréamont's old ocean. Peter Shield: "Jorn's texts are a work of art."[33] Works that have yet to find a domain of critical reception.

De Jong made her own use of the extraordinary photographs Jorn collected for his researches on comparative vandalism in the *Situationist Times*. They are a key part of the journal's attempt to gather materials for a situology to come, a critical practice in time and space no longer dependent on the language and forms of art or politics. The Situationist International had surprisingly little to say about actual situations. Drawing on Jorn's extensive researches, the *Situationist Times* would at last attempt a more explicit inquiry. Perhaps the abandonment of the more rigid geometry of the organization, with its static national sections, opened up the possibility of a variable field of collaboration.

"Situation: Life space or part of it conceived in terms of its content (meaning). The life space may consist of one situation or two or more overlapping situations. The term situation refers either to the general life situation or the momentary situation."[34] Situation is (Satrean) a hinge between subject and objective space. "Situation, overlapping: Two or more situations which exist simultaneously and which have a common part. The person is generally located within this common part." Once space and time are thought in terms of situations, then an assessment of the potential of such spaces and times is possible. "Space of free movement: Regions accessible to the person from his present position. The space of free movement is usually a multiply connected region. Its limits are determined mainly by (1) what is forbidden to a person, (2) what is beyond his abilities." Situations and the regions they compose can be not only thought but appropriated according not to boundaries of function or ownership, but relations of contiguity and continuity. "Structure of a region: Refers to (1) degree of differentiation of the region (2) arrangement of its part regions, (3) degree of connection between its parts." The *Situationist Times* is, among other things, elementary research into space and time that can be self-composing.

A situology might be a theory and practice of intervening in the currents of a turbulent time, an art of the event, a politics of the event, but one that seeks out the limits of art and politics. With the irrevocable split between Paris and everyone else, the conditions were not ripe for sharpening such practices and experiments against the blade of critique. Howard Slater writes:

> In many ways the conflicts with Spur and the [Nashists] were to some degree encouraged and used by the First Situationist International to prune itself of contradictions that may have eventually led to a deepening of the theory of the spectacle, a politicization of the practice of art and a productive extension of its notion of class … The problem of creativity—the right to productive socialization as a countervalue—was not resolved, it was polarized.[35]

Or perhaps Debord did everyone a favor by forcing the issue, by choosing paths, rather than allowing the movement to sink, like so many others, beneath the weight of its incoherence.

The contradictions the Situationist International attempted to prune may well be those inherent in romanticism, the strategy that Lefebvre thought was the headwaters of the movement. The Situationist International never worked through the terms of this tension. It relied on the romantic staple of a poetics to bring together an anthropological and a cosmological nature. The tension proved too great. Debord and Constant stuck close to the project of an anthropological nature, indeed Constant made the entire world over in its image. Nash and Spur head in the opposite direction, where a wild and woolly cosmological nature can irrupt into the social.

Only Jorn and de Jong come close to appreciating the necessary tension between an anthropological and a cosmological nature, although in Lefebvre's terms, Jorn's Dionysian proclivities rule out the possibility of superseding the tension between them. Lefebvre: "the Dionysian dance is not always a round." Sometimes it destroys rather than creates. Jorn found a writerly procedure, a spatial or topological logic of the concept, for navigating the difference between reason and nature. Lefebvre really thought that the Situationists had opened a new path, extending romanticism in a new direction. Perhaps he was, and is, right: "The most brilliant Situationists are exploring and testing out a kind of lived utopianism."[36] In the pages of the *Situationist Times* are carefully documented many the irreconcilable elements strewn about by the implosion of the Situationist International, together with not a few innovations contributed by adjacent avant-gardes.

Perhaps it can all be put best allegorically. In the *Situationist Times* No. 5, de Jong reproduces the "Parable of the Three Rings" by Gotthold Lessing (1729–81). Saladin, ruler of Jerusalem, summons Nathan to his court, and asks him which of the three faiths of the city is the true one. Nathan can hardly tell a Muslim ruler that Christianity or his own Judaism is the true faith, and in any case he suspects Saladin's real intention is to milk him for cash. So he answers with a parable. Once upon a time lived a man who possessed a ring which made its bearer beloved by man and God. He had three sons, so he had copies of the ring made, and bequeathed the three rings to his three sons. At once the sons set to fighting over which was the real ring. When the case came before the judge, he observed that all three sons had nothing but enmity for each other, which led him to conclude that none of the rings was the real one, that each was a détournement. Perhaps the father had lost it, and given all the sons copies. Or perhaps the father did not want one ring to dominate the others, and so made copies so exact nobody could tell the difference.

The judge exhorted the three descendants each to live as if he possessed the real ring, thus demonstrating that he would be worthy of it. Saladin was pleased with this tale, and dismissed Nathan. Before taking his leave, Nathan tactfully offered to leave a substantial sum on deposit with his ruler, who after all had the power to judge between the three faiths of Jerusalem and determine their fortunes. It is not immaterial to this story that Jorn was the patron of all of the descendants of the Situationist International, usually through donations of his rather valuable paintings. He supported them all for a time. Nor was this unusual behavior for Jorn, who by hewing to the principles of the gift economy accumulated a remarkable collection of modern art, most of which now constitutes the collection of the Silkeborg Museum, an enduring monument to potlatch.

In *For Form* (1958) Jorn was largely critical of contemporary architecture and design, which he thought had usurped the role of art as a critical and creative practice. Yet the book offered one image by a living architect: an elevation drawing for his submission to the Sydney Opera House competition by his Danish contemporary Jørn Utzon (1918–2008). Utzon at one time wanted to commission some of Jorn's colorful ceramic tiles for the Sydney Opera House. This did not come to pass, but Jorn returned the favor when he asked Utzon to design his museum at Silkeborg. Utzon presented plans and a plaster model for the project in 1964. Bulb-shaped galleries three stories high, buried underground, with crocus-like protrusions above ground, clad in brilliant ceramic, the proposal combined curved shapes with mass-produced components. Visitors would enter the caverns on curling ramps, strolling past hanging artworks lit by natural light filtering in at odd angles from above. While there could be no such thing as a Situationist art museum, Utzon's proposal certainly embodied Jorn's aesthetics of pliable form.[37]

Housing his gift would take more than potlatch. The Utzon plans for Silkeborg never materialized because Jorn couldn't raise the funds. But perhaps there was something premature in even such a fitting mausoleum for Jorn's life and work. Considered as the husk of a once-viable unitary project, Situationist materials may yet have some juice in them that has not been sucked dry in a three-way necrophilia with the museum and with scholarship. But there might be other projects, spun off out of internal tensions with the Situationist International, that also might be considered as materials for a future critical practice. Two such projects exemplify the possibilities and limitations of a practice after art. Both were nurtured within the Situationist International, and both extend beyond it. One is mostly a project for the overcoming of literature, the other for the overcoming of architecture. They are otherwise quite different and are the product of former members who had very little to do with each other. Indeed, both revealed significant differences from the Situationist International.

After literature comes project sigma, whose instigator was Alexander Trocchi (1925–84). After architecture comes New Babylon, the lifework of Constant Nieuwenhuys. Constant and Trocchi were roughly contemporaries. They were both products, among other things, of Saint-Germain. About the only other thing they had in common was that at one time they had earned Guy Debord's respect—and he had earned theirs. Just as Nash and de Jong parted ways with Debord and spun off into their own collaborative practices, so too did Alexander Trocchi. Or at least he gave it a go.

10 An Athlete of Duration

Better known as a novelist, Trocchi tried and failed to form a much more ambitious movement. He called it project sigma, after the mathematical sign that can stand for the sum or the totality. He thought it "free of bothersome semantic accretions." He set out his sigma project in two luminous texts, "The Invisible Insurrection of a Million Minds" and "Sigma: A Tactical Blueprint." "Revolt is understandably unpopular," he writes, and generally conceived in a somewhat backward way. Just as Leon Trotsky knew enough to seize the railways and the power stations while the old guard persisted in defending the offices of the state, "so cultural revolt must seize the grids of expression and the powerhouses of the mind." Rather than a frontal confrontation, Trocchi suggests a more subtle practice of installing the material basis for a new practice of creation. It is no longer a question of a new journal or art movement. "Art can have no existential significance for a civilization which draws a line between life and art and collects artifacts like ancestral bones for reverence."[1] It's a question of new relations of creation.

The key Trocchi finds in a stray quote from his contemporary Raymond Williams (1921–88), a pioneer of cultural materialism and British cultural studies: "The question is not who will patronize the arts, but what forms are possible in which artists will have control of their own means of expression, in such ways that they will have relation to a community rather than to a market or a patron."[2] Williams is best known today for the project of democratizing the practice of critical reading. Here he takes up the production side of the creation of a people's culture. This appealed to Trocchi, who found proletarian culture rather more stifling than did Williams. In what must have been a charming thought to Debord, Trocchi wanted to bypass the brokers of the culture industry—the publisher and art dealers. In an extraordinary mix of the practical and the sublime, he plots the means of creative autonomy within capitalism itself.

Trocchi's project sigma is partly inspired by Black Mountain College (1933–57), the famous North Carolina school, where Franz Kline, Robert Creeley, Merce Cunningham, John Cage and so many other transformative figures of the American avant-garde once taught. Trocchi also conceives of sigma as "a continuous, international, experimental conference."[3] Spaces of free creation, of ongoing and unfolding situations, could be based just outside metropolitan areas, a network of experimental sites in constant communication.

The actually existing university has become a microcosm of spectacular society. It reproduces and reinforces a strictly functional approach to creation. Trocchi mentions a contest at Cambridge University to come up with a use for its neglected chapels. Many are quite beautiful and once functioned as the unitary heart of their respective colleges. The winning suggestion was to turn them into canteens or student housing. Trocchi thought brothels would at least be a more spiritual solution. The postwar university was rapidly becoming a mere functional support for the spectacle, training the mediators who would manage its desires. What was lacking was a point at which to start making situations.

The sigma texts are part manifesto, part manual. The practical side to Trocchi's proposal is the means of funding it. Project sigma is not just a university, it is also an agency for what Jorn called the creative elite. Those who join it become part of an agency controlled by the creators themselves. Sigma lives off residuals, patents, commissions, even what one would now call consultancy fees. Its network of spontaneous universities function as advertisements for themselves. One might almost say that they are brands. Trocchi's solution is a weird kind of Leninist dual power.[4] An autonomous, self-managed, unalienated power of seamless creativity exists alongside the old commodified spectacle until such time as it can subsume it within its new means of creation. It is both science fiction and a business plan, a utopian future and an almost exact description of sophisticated spectacular business in the twenty-first century. It could almost be the model for the Blue Ant agency of Hubertus Bigend (b. 1967), the fictional son of a Situationist in the novels of William Gibson.[5] It is a summation of Trocchi's own extraordinary experience, yet it is also a program he was in no sense fit to carry out in person.

Trocchi survived a genteel-poor upbringing in Glasgow. During the war he sailed on convoy ships taking supplies to the Soviet Union. After a stint at Glasgow University he took advantage of a scholarship to ship off to Paris. He was an editor of the English-language journal *Merlin* (1952–54), which coexisted in friendly rivalry with the *Paris Review* of George Plimpton and friends. In Paris he fell under the spell of Samuel Beckett and managed to get Beckett published, together with Jean Genet and Eugène Ionesco, with Olympia Press, a Paris-based, English-language imprint best known for its porn. Like more than a few expats, Trocchi wrote porn novels for Olympia's charming but deeply dodgy impresario Maurice Girodias.[6]

The best of Trocchi's porn novels is *Helen and Desire* (1954). Growing up in the far north of Australia, Helen is a bored teenager with only her own immediate sensations to amuse her. "I count the sea as my first love … it was an impersonal one." She embarks on the adventure of renouncing her own will, her subjectivity, her interiority. Instead she allows herself a terrible and ungovernable thirst for annihilation. And yet Helen remains a writer. The book purports to be a found manuscript, a diary not of a person but of a process of depersonalization. The body becomes a surface for the replacement of self with sensation: "Riven now at twin poles of delight, my glistening torso slithered under discs, flats, and surfaces, under flanges of containment and protusion, all seeking the weld of female union. My breasts, charged with ambiguous alluvial sensations, slipped to and fro under their counterparts …"[7]

Helen's writing recounts the steps by which the very possibility of authorship is undone. Her diary ends when there is no longer a subject to be writing it: "And gradually the whole desire to commit my experiences to history has been outflanked by the terrible pleasure I experience in approaching the unconscious state of an object … It is indeed doubtful whether I can still usefully use the word 'I.'"[8] Helen gives herself over to the situation, and abolishes the act of writing, the possibility of literature as a separate art, in the process.

Self-destruction seemed preferable to self-construction, to the institutional forces that pinned the self in place. Trocchi wrote about such institutions in a short story for his *Moving Times*, a literary journal that was supposed to appear as posters in subway stations:

> At the third jolt the patient's body was seen to shudder like a tall jelly within the leather harness, and a wisp of blue smoke issued from his nostrils, a reaction generally regarded as a symptom of what, in technical nomenclature, is called "reintegration." The patient reintegrated slowly, the shuddering subsided gradually over a period of two and a half hours, after which he was returned to the deep freeze as a precaution against pong.[9]

The construction of the stable subject requires a huge effort of disciplinary force, but it is not as if there were a natural self which such techniques suppress. Rather, it's a choice between two kinds of process, between the psychiatric techniques of the subject, or the crafty whittling of the body into sensate being within the unstable, unfolding embrace of the situation. As the social and medical sciences claim the body as their own, Trocchi finds resources for the body's self-experiments in writing.

As a writer Trocchi connects Beckett to William Burroughs, and both to Debord. His great, *Cain's Book* (1960) is often considered a Beat classic, but it is rarely read as a Situationist text. Debord was an admirer of Malcolm Lowry (1909–57), author of *Under the Volcano* (1947), with whom Trocchi had at least two things in common. They both produced only one book that was a literary success, and they both preferred to destroy themselves rather than inflict more literature on the world. Lowry was an alcoholic; Trocchi a drug fiend. Both explored in depth the practice of playing with time, with time outside of both labor and leisure. Trocchi's advice to ambitious writers: "Let them dedicate a year to pinball and think again." Both were adepts at what Trocchi called "the chemistry of alienation."[10] Both found the limits to becoming a professional in the art of intoxication.

"Tomorrow is an age of Doctors," Trocchi says prophetically. By 2007 the American Environmental Protection Agency will announce that what it calls the *emerging contaminants* in drinking water come mostly from anti-depressants, painkillers, antibiotics, hormones and blood pressure remedies.[11] It's the effluent of the affluent world of spectacular medicine. The disintegrating spectacle has inadvertently medicated whole populations, not only of humans but of other species too, a whole biosphere rendered comfortably numb. It's a by-product of constantly reintegrating the human body into the uniform time of production and consumption, for a time that repeats the same steady intervals without end; and rendered efficiently, without the blue smoke.

The central character in *Cain's Book* avoids work as best he can, and takes to its extreme the practice of playing with his own life. This play is far from a joyful distraction. It is an immersion in one intensity after another. "To mean everything and for everything to be a confidence trick, tasting power coming into being for others; I had often thought that only through play could one taste that power safely, if dangerously, and that when the spirit of play died there was only murder."[12] From Sartre, Trocchi took the idea of being condemned to freedom. Unlike Sartre, he did not limit himself to discussing banal situations in which one might be confronted by this freedom. Rather, new situations had to be created. For Debord this creation of situations was always a collaborative project, of love and play and boisterous rivalry as a means of effacing bourgeois consciousness. For Trocchi it was a much more grim and solitary business, a lone self-purgation amid the purgatory of other people.

Cain's Book was, for all its brilliance, something of a dead end. It lacks the self-annihilating power of *Helen and Desire*. It allows itself the one masochism the earlier book did its utmost to refuse: that of becoming the plaything of *literature*. Its failure to put an end to literature led the critic James Campbell to declare with smug satisfaction: "The novel didn't die, after all, but, following *Cain*, Trocchi's part in it did."[13] This is not the least reason that Trocchi's post-*Cain* writing calls for a fresh appreciation. He borrowed in part from his friend and contemporary Wallace Berman (1927–76) and his attempt to redefine circuits of communication for poetry and visual art with his homemade journal *Semina* (1955–64). Trocchi shifts attention from form as a question of arranging words on the page to form as the question of the medium and economy by which words are communicated.[14]

While *Cain's Book* is now a captive of its own literary success, the same cannot be said of the *sigma portfolio* (1964). The *portfolio* allowed Trocchi to abandon literature and yet keep writing. It's a project he hatched in New York, but brought back to London with him, "close under his eyelids, an electronic load, an unwritten book, a plan in four dimensions, a shadow one, including time ..." This puckish, punkish project would be self-generating and self-published. "The *sigma portfolio* is an entirely new dimension in publishing, through which the writer reaches his public immediately, outflanking the traditional traps of publishing-house policy, and by means of which the reader gets it, so to speak, 'hot' from the writer's pen, the photographer's lens, etc."[15]

Through a probably deliberate misunderstanding, Trocchi presents the early Letterist movement as being based, not on chipping writing down to the letter in the typographic sense, but on the sending of letters in the postal, or perhaps topographic sense. He borrows from the Letterist International the name *Potlatch*, but to designate what he calls an *interpersonal log*. It is to be an open-ended series of simple typed and duplicated documents. "This gambit, a round robin which includes *n* participants, an interpersonal experiment in expression; a man responding as and when he pleases; copies of his response at once roneo-ed for circulation; individuals chiming in, checking out at any time."[16]

Trocchi calls it a *log* to stress the temporal aspect, the sequence of statement and rejoinder: "it should literally discover many things, including the dialectical process of its own growth." Where the book puts an end to the transformations of the text and sets up a distinction between author and reader, the interpersonal log keeps transforming itself, and makes of its readers writers and of its writers readers. "Essentially ludic, and calling, it seems to me, for a particular kind of gesture, it might be called *potlatch*." It might also be called *blogging*.[17] Trocchi invented a web of logs before there was even an internet.

Or it might be called sigma, that blank, elusive, all-embracing one-word poem that Trocchi put at the heart of the enterprise. "For, sigma is a word referring to something which is quite independent of myself or of any other individual, and if we are correct in our historical analysis, we must regard it as having 'begun' a long time ago."[18] The term sigma stands in for a process, without beginning or end, without subject or goal, and yet which is not a mere abstract force, but something experienced within the lived time of everyday life. This willful and collaborative play within and against creative forces is the thread that becomes lost under the conditions of spectacular society.

And so "it is the object of sigma to bring all informations out into the open." The *sigma portfolio* is a kind of residue of a process, which leaves behind a diagram of the ephemeral forces that make and unmake situations. Passing through the interstitial spaces of spectacular society, not least its literature, the *sigma portfolio* finds light, cheap, temporary means to bypass the spectacular and yet, for all its evanescence, to become an exemplary instance of the new power at work in the world. Sigma is a new power which is at the same time the ancient power of homo ludens, joining in with the ineffable play of the world.

Trocchi quotes Debord: "Everything being connected, it was necessary to change it by a unitary struggle, or nothing." Trocchi's sigma texts abound in tactical maxims: the round robin of Roneoed texts is an outflanking gesture, which exploits a loophole in the technical apparatus of mechanical reproduction. But where Debord's tactics are always elusive, seductive, Trocchi wants to create a center, which he sometimes calls the *box office*, as if it offered tickets to the endgame of the spectacle itself. "The box office will be a primitive micro-model of a possible future." This plan for a consciously constructed environment includes audiovisual media as well as *futiques* (future antiques), objects designed for open-ended play. The resources of all the arts are to be integrated into the conscious construction of situations.

The portfolio includes Trocchi's détourned version of a "Situationist Manifesto." What he adds and subtracts from the *orthodox* Situationist document is instructive. Like Constant, he stresses the role of automation in clearing the way for a ludic world. "Automation, and a general 'socialization' of vital goods will gradually and ineluctably dispense with most of the necessity for 'work': eventually, as near as dammit, the complete liberty of the individual in relation to production will be attained." In place of surplus value, a play value. But play meets resistance. Just as the church resisted the festival, so the authorities seize *Cain's Book*. The unions resist automation and defend work. Sigma has to take place outside of all forms of existing power: "we propose immediate action on the international scale, a self-governing (non-)organization of producers of the new culture beyond, and independent of, all political organizations ..."[19]

No matter how euphoric his theory, Trocchi's practice is modest in scale: "so long as our techniques for the passing on of informations grow with the passage of time more and more effective, etc., our insurrection will snowball of its own momentum."[20] The means of dissemination for sigma was the stencil duplicator, or mimeograph machine. Ironically enough it was a popular medium for the kinds of organization sigma eschews, such as churches, schools and social clubs. It was the original medium for science fiction fanzines. Trocchi found that this low-tech device also afforded a means for making low theory. Duplicating was an easy and cheap means of making copies by the hundreds without recourse to a professional printer. Popular makes included Gestetner and Ditto. Trocchi used another trademark as a verb—to Roneo—although strictly speaking this brand worked by a slightly different process.

Trocchi claims at least some sigma texts were composed directly on the stencil. He would have taken the ribbon out of the typewriter, inserted the stencil and typed away. The stencil was a stiff sheet of card backed with wax, and attached to it a thin sheet of tissue paper. The impact of the keys cuts the letters into the wax, with the residue sticking to the tissue paper. Judging by the *sigma portfolio*, Trocchi was a good stencil cutter: type too hard, and the enclosed spaces within the letters turn to black blobs. Once Trocchi cut the stencil, he removed it from the typewriter and attached it to the drum, which was filled with ink. He would then turn the crank by hand, each rotation drawing a sheet of paper under the drum, through the pressure rollers, copying his text in the process. On most duplicators, it takes a bit of fiddling with various settings to get good copies. Judging by surviving copies, Trocchi and his sigma associates mastered it. Martin Heidegger: "the typewriter makes everyone look the same."[21] Perhaps not, if one looks closely enough.

Trocchi was not exactly master of his own life. Constant: "Freedom is the most difficult way of living that man can lead. For freedom can only be realized in creation and creation means discipline."[22] The quest for extreme situations quickly collapsed into the sheer habit of junkie life. When he was living in Venice Beach, California, hanging out with the Beats, he was visited one day by Irving Rosenthal (b. 1930), who wrote down his impressions of Trocchi's materialist and experimental attitude to life there in his very own Musée Imaginaire:

> Everything functional had been drafted into the service of art, taken apart and reassembled, and many things looked subjected to more than one transformation, as if the lust to create had been so overpowering as to become cannibalistic, or as if each object of art, once created, became as stupid as a lamp or bookend, and had to be destroyed and built anew. The whole room seemed to belong to another world, to whose inhabitants these uncanny furnishings were the beds and chairs of everyday life.

Rosenthal quickly soured on Trocchi and his miniature version of unitary urbanism: "Even the little true beauty I picked up there, to pop in my mouth and suck on, was mixed with a slow-acting poison to make the eyes opaque and dreamless …" It would not be long before the whole place burned to the ground.[23] Trocchi was an addict, and like many addicts, left a wake of casual violence behind him. The poet, artist and jazz musician Jeff Nuttall (1933–2004), who assisted him for a time, left a portrait that has the rare quality of being critical but nonjudgmental: "Trocchi once told me he first took heroin for the sense of inviolability it gave him. If the cool hipster is severed from identificatory processes and thus from other people's pleasure and pain, he is nevertheless an athlete of time. … No user is punctual."[24] This queer athleticism has nothing to do with stopwatches and world records. It is not an athleticism of measurable time. Rather, it is an extreme sporting with duration, with immeasurable time itself.

In his novel *Tainted Love* (2005), Stewart Home (b. 1962) is not so kind.

> Alex liked women, but clearly he preferred getting them fucked up on drugs to any kind of physical intimacy. Trocchi got a kick out of watching a beautiful woman like Lyn spiraling downwards through endless cycles of degradation. And when Lyn did die Alex was mortified, and it seemed to me that he'd been killed either with or before her. Trocchi no longer simply took drugs; he had become heroin. Alex was dead and didn't yet know it. I liked and admired Trocchi, he was a visionary who'd written two brilliant novels, but when it came to his relationship with other people he could be a complete cunt.[25]

This is written from the point of view of a young woman who is herself hustling for heroin, who is the mother of the novel's narrator, and who dies in dubious circumstances. It's a timely reminder that not everyone survives bohemia, and that those who rise to it from delinquency rather than fall into it out of privilege have rather a hard time of it. The romance still clinging to Rosenthal's version is here—almost—expunged.

For someone like Constant, the failure of Trocchi's project sigma had less to do with Trocchi's personal limitations than with objective necessity. The spectacle required a structural transformation which no mere passing of *informations* between disaffected hipsters could ever achieve. New Babylon placed its bets on changing the forms within which everyday life is experienced. Constant: "The culture of New Babylon does not result from isolated activities, from exceptional situations, but from the global activity of the whole world population, every human being engaged in a dynamic relation with his surroundings."[26] In an era that would become absorbed with the permutations of cultural superstructures, Constant's obsession with infrastructure was a rare corrective.

11 New Babylon

> Frankfurt [in 1950] was indescribable. I'd borrowed a studio from a painter who was himself in Paris. I was working there for an exhibition in the Zimmergallerie Frank, and every morning I took my son to school. The walk to the school was across an enormous bomb site. A greap heap of rubble, with here and there some places that had been flattened so you could walk over them like paths. There were some outer walls of houses still standing. A doorway, and some stretches of wall. It was a surreal landscape ... If you walk through a town that lies in ruins, then the first thing you naturally think of is building. And then, as you rebuild such a town, you wonder whether life there will be just the same, or what will be different.[1]

Perhaps for Constant very different.

Constant built a future out of offcut Plexiglas and bicycle spokes. Later he would say that his marvelous models of New Babylon were appreciated in much the same way as African masks were in surrealist times, as interesting forms, but stripped of their significance for everyday life. What is lost from New Babylon is a passion gone from the world, a desire to seize the world itself as the object of desire, to find a form for the whole of life.[2]

Constant had photographs made of New Babylon, and a film. He produced a newspaper for it, and he gave his famous lecture-performances. All to conjure into being a landscape that envisioned what was possible right here and now, but was held back by the fetter of outdated relations of production. It was not a utopia. "I prefer to call it a realistic project, because it distances itself from the present condition which has lost touch with reality, and because it is founded on what is technically feasible, on what is desirable from a human viewpoint, on what is inevitable from a social viewpoint."[3] The question that lingers is not whether New Babylon was merely a dream, but whether actually existing built form is really a nightmare.

Modern architecture, begun with so much promise, had found its default setting in functionalism. It divided the city between the functions of work, transport, leisure and the home. Its ruling passion was *efficiency*. The city was a machine for the free circulation of capital, labor, materials and products. Planners merely accepted existing social relations as given. They accepted the division between public and private. On the one hand, private property, the bourgeois family, and the car. On the other, pathetic little Bantustans of public life, hived off to the margins.

New Babylon is a détournement, not of art or literature, but of modern architecture and town planning. Jorn: "Why are we, free artists, so interested in the doctrines of modern architecture? Because they exclude us." Even more troubling, architects co-opt artists, or claim the role of artist for themselves.[4] If there is a key architect whom New Babylon can be read as détourning, it is Constant's friend, mentor and patron Aldo van Eyck (1918–99). While caught up in the modern movement, van Eyck was critical of architecture as a pseudo-science, and critical of modern built form with its "miles upon miles of organized nowhere."[5] He took his inspiration more from modern art and physics than architecture. Like Jorn and Gallizio, he saw art and science as creative experiments that shattered the last vestiges of a Platonic universe of static order and eternal forms. Once famous for the hundreds of children's playgrounds he built in Amsterdam, he was also an original theorist. He extended the momentum of what he called the "great riot" of modernism into built form.

The key architectural form for van Eyck is the threshold, which he imagines not as dividing one space from another, say public from private, but as connecting one possibility to another. Rather than an efficient division of space by function, he imagines a landscape of place, occasion, threshold, an architecture in which to tarry. As he writes in the *Situationist Times*, "a house is a tiny city, a city is a huge house." The key is to think built form more in terms of time than space, a time that can't be measured. For people who can linger there, the city enables times of full participation and rich experience. The city is when "associative awareness changes and extends perception, rendering it transparent and profound through memory and anticipation." The urban malingerer becomes aware of *duration*. Here time acquires depth and subtlety, and "awareness of duration is as gratifying as awareness of the passing instant is oppressive. The former opens time, renders it transparent, whilst the latter closes time, rendering it impenetrable."[6]

The sensation of duration is the sense of being itself. Architecture should make us at home in duration, not enclose us in space, nor in time measured out as if it were space. Van Eyck does not want to build a dwelling for *being*, but a nexus for a homecoming. Such in-between places, or thresholds, can "resolve the conflicts which exteriorize man from time (thereby closing the door on himself)." The people make places, but not with the space of their own choosing. Van Eyck wants an architecture that can imply the capacity for making meaning, for turning space into places. This is why his playgrounds contain only abstract forms, which play makes meaningful in its own inimitable ways. Constant radicalizes van Eyck's program. He extends the playground over the surface of the earth. The problem, he realizes, is total, and if the architect-planner does not take on the totality of built form, then, as van Eyck says, "people will spread over the globe and be at home nowhere."[7]

While Constant borrows his program from van Eyck, the architectural language that he détourns comes from French utopian architects of the postwar years. There were at least three such utopias. The Architecture Principe group built on the bunker archaeology of Paul Virilio (b. 1932). They proposed massive forms, sloping floors, all to create a conserving architecture that would arrest and congeal the rapid flux of contemporary life. The Utopie group, which included Jean Baudrillard (1929–2007), took the opposite tack, favoring a temporary and playful architecture of inflatable pods (if not of blow-up dog turds). Meanwhile, architects like Yona Friedman (b. 1923) proposed building space-frames in the air, hoisted aloft on pylons. Like Le Corbusier, Friedman thought this form allows for the separation of networks that move different things at different speeds.[8] This was the form Constant favored too, even though he used the elevated space-frame for quite different ends.[9] Of all these seemingly utopian projects, Constant's is the only one for which a transformation in built form can only come out of a transformation of social relations.

Rather than demolish the old world to build a *radiant city*; rather than build a *garden city* on greenfield sites, Constant cantilevers new spaces up above, leaving both city and countryside untouched. Automated factories would be underground, the surface level is for transport, while up above stretches a new landscape for play, a massive superstructure of linked *sectors*, within which everything is malleable, changeable at whim. Considered vertically, as an elevation, New Babylon makes literal Marx's diagram of base and superstructure. Its airy sectors are literally superstructures, made possible by an infrastructure below ground where mechanical reproduction has abolished scarcity and freed all of time from necessity. It is an image of what Constant imagines the development of productive forces has made possible, but which the fetter of existing relations of production prevents from coming into being.

New Babylon responds both to the expansion of material resources and the expansion of population. Like a suburban family that adds a new story when the second kid is born, Constant builds a second deck—for the whole planet. Rather than suburban sprawl inserting itself into any and every terrain, he leaves much of the old world intact—including, interestingly, the classic spaces of the dérive in the heart of the old cities such as Paris and Amsterdam. The Les Halles of which Abdelhafid Khatib was so fond would remain. This is a new world that expands, not horizontally but vertically. It is a "a new skin that covers the earth and multiplies its living space."[10] Not the least charm of New Babylon is that Constant thinks the planet is a robust enough foundation on which to build such a bold addition.

Like many others at the time, Constant was influenced by the *cybernetic* theories of Norbert Wiener (1894–1964), particularly his notion of a second industrial revolution. Wandering the streets of London and Manchester, Friedrich Engels movingly recorded the human misery that resulted from the first one. It confounded modern artists, who felt compelled to either reject industry or embrace it. The alternate utopian visions of William Morris and

Edward Bellamy represented these two seemingly incompatible options.[11] As Lefebvre might say, they détourned the resources of romantic dissent against the rise of capitalism, drawing respectively on its visions of a cosmological and an anthropological order. But this debate was now moot. The first industrial revolution had given way to the second, a revolution in the use of information as a means of control.

Cybernetics might just provide the means of mitigating the damage of the first industrial revolution, while building on its enormous expansion of productive potential. Or it could result in what Wiener called the "fascist ant-state."[12] Constant takes to heart Engels's formula that communism reduces the state to the administration of things. Cybernetics as control is relegated below ground, to the world of administered things. Cybernetics as freedom, as the ability to connect anywhere, anytime, is in play up above. Constant pushes the debate about technicity to both extremes at once: total control and total freedom. By exacerbating the instrumentalizing tendencies of cybernetic control, freedom from necessity appears in the realm of the possible.

Constant was not alone in imagining cybernetic automation to be a transformative development, but he was in rarer company in seeing it in the context of a social revolution. "Well then, how could such far-reaching automation be achieved without social ownership of the means of production?"[13] Automation changes the relations of production, which in turn change social structures. The increase in productivity wrests freedom from necessity, but generates a surplus which needs dissipating somehow. New Babylon addresses the prospect of a new kind of necessity. As Constant says, "automation inevitably confronted us with the question of where human energy would be able to discharge itself if not in productive work."[14] New Babylon addresses a major theme of Georges Bataille: that surplus presents more fundamental problems for human societies than necessity. Where for Bataille the solution tends to involve orgiastic sacrifices to an impossible absolute, for Constant it is more a question of enabling playful and challenging social relations to take place. Constant takes to the limit the Lefebvrian play of need and desire.

Meanwhile, in the twenty-first century we appear to inhabit, automation lives within the old relations of production rather than prompting new ones. Nearly two-thirds of automated machine tools use controllers made by a secretive robotics company called FANUC. This near-monopoly allows FANUC to reap the lion's share of profits from automation. "FANUC's headquarters, a sprawling complex in a forest on the slopes of Mount Fuji, looks like something out of a sci-fi flick … FANUC lore holds that the founder, Seiuemon Inaba, believed yellow 'promotes clear thinking.' Inside the compound's windowless factories an army of (yes, yellow) robots works 24/7." On a factory floor as big as a football field there might be only four workers—also in yellow.[15] FANUC does its business by fax, paranoid about the new digital networks and their roiling seas of piracy. The promise of automation has come down in the twenty-first century to just another kind of monopoly.

Constant's multilevel layout borrows a recognizable figure from modern architecture. The space-frame suspended in the air on pylons appears in the work of Le Corbusier, and becomes an image of utopian form in Yona Friedman. Constant greatly expands its significance. In his hands it becomes the image of a world in which the time of free movement takes priority over the space of private property. Fencing off one space from another as private property is for Constant a "dehumanization of the earth," against which New Babylon presupposes "the socialization of the earth's surface."[16] Rather than lines that make borders, Constant's *experimental geography* proposes lines that make connections. His vast aerial sectors, the size of little cities, link up and spread out over the landscape like reinforced-concrete crabgrass.

Owning property affords someone a house in which to be at home, at the price of being homeless in the world. Dispense with property, dispense with separation, and the feeling of being merely thrown into the world goes with them. Our species-being can give vent to its wanderlust, at home in a house-like world. Constant thought modernity was already accelerating a return to a nomadic existence. New Babylon is nomadic life fully realized. It is an architecture of duration, of thresholds, of collaborative place-making, writ large. Freed from the fixity and uniformity of property, space could again have its qualities. A short trip in New Babylon should offer more variety than the most interminable journeys through the concentrated city of spectacular society. "Life is an endless journey across a world that is changing so rapidly that it seems forever another." The New Babylonians could wander over the whole surface of a world that was in flux. "New Babylon ends nowhere (the earth is round)."[17]

Beneath the ground, the automatic factories; across the surface, endless highways; and up above—a global network of superstructures, within which play takes place. Without borders, without centers, without a state, it snakes and forks all over the map. New Babylon "is organized according to the individual and collective covering of distance, of errancy: a network of units, linked to one another, and so forming chains that can develop, be extended in every direction."[18] And above that, figuratively at least, up in the ether, is another network, of communication. Constant intuits some things about what will turn out to be the internet. "The fluctuating world of the sectors calls on facilities (a transmitting and receiving network) that are both decentralized and public. Given the participation of a large number of people in the transmission and reception of images and sounds, perfected telecommunications become an important factor in ludic social behavior."[19] Interestingly, Constant's vertical arrangement also corresponds to his friend Henri Lefebvre's total semantic field, with cybernetic signaling at the base and symbolic play at the summit.

Through a decentralized network of communication, a nomadic species of play-beings coordinates its frolicking, designs and redesigns its own habitat, and creates a life where "the intensity of each moment destroys the memory that normally paralyses the creative imagination."[20] Constant experiments with a geography for a world beyond spectacle, where dérive and détournement are generalized practices, and indeed become the same practice. Both physical space and the space of information belong to everybody, and are resources for a life without dead time. It's a world not only made for but made by *homo ludens*, whose species-being is play. The only question is whether we are, or could become, such beings. New Babylon may very well be a posthuman critique of the limits of our species as we know it.[21]

Writing in the 1930s, Johan Huizinga offered homo ludens as a way of thinking our species-being that was outside of the *homo economicus* of political-economic discourse. We do not contend with each other to maximize our utility, whatever that means, but for the pleasure of the game, for the renown a good move brings.[22] Huizinga also opposed his figure of homo ludens to the *homo politicus* of Nazi jurist Carl Schmitt. For Schmitt contest cannot be playful, it is to the death. But, says Huizinga, if victory is total, who remains to *recognize* the victor? Constant's contribution is to propose in spatial form the conditions under which contestation can be playful rather than fatal, by distinguishing contest from control of resources, or desire from need. Automated production makes the surplus available for all, not just the victors. A playful dissipation of surplus energy can then become a pure game, its stakes only recognition, not domination.

Huizinga also opposes homo ludens to *homo faber*, the productivist worker-ant of Stalinist discourse. But as Constant discovers—more through aesthetic experiment than textual scholarship—what Marx always had in mind was the reconciliation of quantity and quality, of the substance of labor with the creation of forms. The productive surplus generated by the industrial revolution could restore, at a higher level, the qualitative being of the premodern world. In short, something closer to homo ludens. The struggle of the proletariat reduces the working day, from ten hours to eight, and—why not?—down to six, four, two, zero. As time becomes free, why should not space be freed also? Homo ludens will no longer make art, but will create everyday life, altering the ambience of the world, as easy as programming the jukebox in a Saint-Germain café.

Here is the architecture that Guy Debord and Ivan Chtcheglov only dreamed of as they wandered the streets of Paris: "Every square mile of New Babylon's surface represents an inexhaustible field of new and unknown situations, because nothing will remain and everything is constantly changing." Constant wanders far beyond his erstwhile comrades, if at the risk of an absolute euphoria. For Constant, the Situationist International "did not constitute a real movement. The adherents came and went and the only view they shared was their contempt for the current art practice."[23] He does credit the movement with contemplating the end to culture conceived as scarcity and property, and pursuing this possibility to its conclusions. "Unlike other Situationists, I realized straight away that the theory of unitary urbanism was not primarily concerned with micro-structures or with ambiences. On the contrary, these depend largely on the macro-structure ..."[24] Those who design the future by halves plot their own graves.

In the 1960s, New Babylon came to seem very out of step with the times. "Spontaneous, direct action struck many people as more important than analytical study." Favorite paperback reading included not just Marx but also his anarchist antagonist, Mikhail Bakunin. Constant: "This mentality continued until the mid-60s and achieved its apotheosis, but also its end, in ... Amsterdam with the appearance of Provo, an anarchic movement that took delight in making the establishment look ridiculous and which attracted international attention."[25] In the early 1960s the Provos, like the Second Situationist International, created a style of direct action as performance art, and no matter how much the Situationist International despised them, they embodied a certain spirit that was recognizably their own. While they claimed Constant as an inspiration of sorts, and he contributed to their publications, their projects were different.

"I had given priority to the structural problems of urbanism while the others wanted to stress the content, the play, the 'free creation of everyday life.'"[26] Looking back, peering through the ruins of the disintegrating spectacle, it appears that Constant was right to be skeptical about the political effusions of the sixties. New Babylon is the most thorough negation, not of the world of the late twentieth century, but of a world which is only just now coming into being. It is Constant who seems in touch with the real historical development of the twentieth century, and closer to the possibility of leaving it. He understood the transformative power of the second (cybernetic) industrial revolution, and that its consequences would be a vast reconfiguring of space. In the absence of a social revolution, this transformation of the means of production produced quite the opposite result, New Moloch rather than New Babylon. Welcome, then, to New Moloch, a global division of functions, which banishes the factory to the sites of cheap labor in China and elsewhere, while massively concentrating control over networks in the overdeveloped world. The fascist ant-state has gone global.

New Babylon looks less implausible that many of the landscapes that are now supposed to actually exist. "Her first day on the job,

Min turned seventeen. She took a half day off and walked the streets alone, buying some sweets and eating them by herself. She had no idea what people did for fun."[27] Like a hundred million others, Min came down from the country to find work in one of China's new industrial cities. (Rural labor is cheaper than FANUC's controlled robots.) She came to Dongguan, a city of some ten million people in the Pearl River Delta. She thought it would be fun to work on an assembly line, with people talking and joking, but it was not that way at all. Factory work is noisy, tiring and boring. Factory dorms are full of petty crime, gangs, cliques and doomed romances. All that keeps anyone in touch with anyone is the mobile phone. When she lost her phone she lost her friends. Time is governed by shifts on machines and the global shopping calendar. When the nights are warm and the days are long, Americans think it time to buy sneakers.

Like so many others in China's early-twenty-first-century boom years, Min changes jobs often, but keeps finding much the same thing. It's not so different to the 1960s in Europe, only on a vastly greater scale. Young people weaned away from the provinces, from the farm, become proletarian, and discover that factory life dulls not just the muscles, but the mind. Yet the break has been made. Cast out of the old life, they make up the new as they go along. The difference is that unlike so many of the young people of the '60s, Min has never heard of Chairman Mao. The local museum manages not to mention him. When the boom bust, the Chinese government committed billions to propping up New Moloch with vast projects, aimed at building more of the same. Who would have thought, back in the middle of the twentieth century, that in the early twenty-first century, the fate of global capital might hinge on the prudent stewardship of the Chinese Communist Party?

Perhaps Mao's portrait could come down from Tiananmen Square. Perhaps a more appropriate figurehead would be the great swindler Charles Ponzi. Even the *New York Times* has to admit that these days the disintegrating spectacle looks like a giant Ponzi scam: "We have created a system for growth that depended on our building more and more stores to sell more and more stuff made in more and more factories in China, powered by more and more coal that would cause more and more climate change but earn China more and more dollars to buy more and more US T[reasury]-bills so America would have more and more money to build more and more stores and sell more and more stuff that would employ more and more Chinese."[28] This disintegrating spectacle built no great pyramids: the best it could manage was a great pyramid scheme.

Is it possible to imagine collective human agency as productive of something playful, joyous, communal, even beautiful? "The culture of New Babylon does not result from isolated activities, from exceptional situations, but from the global activity of the whole world population, every human being engaged in a dynamic relation with his surroundings."[29] New Babylon extends the ethos of the dérive to its limit, to world history. It is ultimately a philosophical work. "New Babylon is not a town planning project, but rather a way of thinking, of imagining, of looking at things and at life."[30] It is the disintegrating spectacle in negative. The great abundance really came to pass, only rather than free itself from labor, our species-being decided to labor making more and more things. "The growing presence of excess human energy has started to make itself felt."[31] But rather than outlets for joy—outlet malls. The disintegrating spectacle in which we actually live is the most utopian world of all, because of its savage insistence that it has abolished the very possibility of utopia for all time.

Walter Benjamin once drew a distinction between the fascist tendency to aestheticize politics and the revolutionary potential of a politicized aesthetics.[32] Constant retrieves the formula for an era way past the promise of art. It's a choice between a techno-fascist technologizing of aesthetics and the possibility of an aestheticizing of technology. Constant does not make a fetish of technology, as either saving grace or iron cage. Rather, it's a question of thinking the possibilities of social and technical transformation together.[33] The essence of technology is nothing technical. But could it be something playful? Could it be a way, not of instrumentalizing nature, but of producing a new relation to it, as a totality? Such was the scale of Constant's ambitions, the ambitions really of a whole way of life. One which leaves behind beautiful objects as unreadable as African masks.

12 The Beach Beneath the Street

There is a sixties to suit every taste. It's a truly versatile era. There is a psychedelic sixties, a Provo sixties, a cybernetic sixties, an anti-colonial sixties. There was the Prague Spring. There was the Watts rebellion. August 1965: the Black population rises up. Debord: "But who has defended the rioters of Watts in the terms they deserve?" Before Watts, there was Newark, July that same year. Ronald Porambo (1939–2006) wrote a first-rate book about it, *No Cause for Indictment: An Autopsy of Newark* (1971).[1] In it Porambo takes the hard-boiled American style of journalism to delirious, obsessive lengths, slotting together facts, quotes and anecdotes to create an unrelenting portrait of relentless oppression in a podunk town ruled by what Dashiell Hammett used to call the cops, the crooks and the big rich.

The book was not the hit that Porambo imagined. America in the 1970s preferred the *new journalism*. The ruling tastes ran more to the minutiae of status details than to Porambo's hard-luck stories. But this is where it gets interesting. Like Pierre-François Lacenaire before him, Porambo would have preferred a literary success, but, failing that, chose the infamy of a life of crime. Not just any crime. He robbed drug dealers. A dealer died in an aborted attempt at one such robbery, and a week later someone shot Porambo in the head. Arrested and tried for the murder, Porambo drew a life sentence rather than the Pulitzer Prize. He died in jail. The prison says he choked on an orange. Criminal acts, as Constant says, are "an expression of a frustrated will to power."[2]

The Situationists did not write about Porambo, or Newark, but Debord wrote about Watts. "The Los Angeles revolt was a revolt against the commodity," he said. It was at least partly so.

"The flames of Watts consumed consumption." The spectacle, diffusing itself throughout society, presenting back to it the image of the abundance of things, could only appear as a cruel reminder of inequity to Black America. Just as the spectacle ranks its objects in order of desirability, so too it ranks its subjects. Its Black subjects saw through it: "they demand the egalitarian realization of the American spectacle of everyday life." Some among them negated the commodity through the unwitting gift. They saw the swag on offer—and looted it.

There is a lot that is missing from Debord's account: the thirty dead, the thousand injured, the four thousand arrests. Nor was he aware that here, unlike in France, the context is not the strength but the weakness of the old left, of the Communist Party and its union and popular-front forces. The red purge of the 1950s created a gap that the Black nationalists would fill with a quite different theory and practice. Still, it might have interested the Situationists when later investigations upheld their hunch that while the riots were leaderless, they were not without organization. Impromptu meetings in the park after dark coordinated movements. Safe-conduct hand signals, of gang origin, allowed looters to move outside their home turf. The areas burned and looted correspond to key gang territories. Gerald Horne: "the Watts Uprising was decentralized; it was a mass uprising and not organized in inception and conception."[3] It was a Lefebvrian festival, at least until the police opened fire.

It all happened again in 1992: fifty deaths, sixteen thousand arrests. The strenuous efforts of the state to prevent a recurrence were overturned with gas and a match. One scholar sums it up in a statement of the kind that only those who dream of being close to the policy process could love: "Present policies of selective imprisonment are not only the most expensive solutions but also the most counter-productive in the long run."[4] And it happened again, in Paris, November 2005. The biggest riot in Paris since May '68, the papers said. One dead, three thousand arrests. It spread to over two hundred towns.

The signature Situationist concept for such—recurring—events is *potlatch*. Where Marx compared the transformation of the object of labor into a commodity to a transubstantiation, the Situationists were interested in a kind of reverse miracle, by which the thing lost its status as commodity and became the gift. The looted object is no longer a commodity. But the perversity of the gesture is that its seizure does not break the spell of exchange and return to things their value. Rather, looting takes the spectacle at its word. In the spectacle, what is good appears and what appears is good.[5] The looter jumps the gap between desire and the commodity. The looter takes desires for their necessity, and necessity for their desires, but freeing the commodity from exchange does not expunge exchange from the commodity.

The riot contains a quite contrary movement as well—arson. The arsonist is not the same as the looter. The arsonist's is a negative relation to what appears, particularly to the built environment. The arsonist's actions are marked by the refusal of spectacular form. Constant: "Enormous energy is being withdrawn from the labor process and it finds no other outlet than in aggression prompted by dissatisfaction."[6] In the riot, that aggression turns against two of its sources: against the time of the commodity form; against an alienating urban space.

Looting and arson are recurring events within what René Viénet calls the "overdeveloped world." They are the mark of overdevelopment, of the quantitative expansion of production outstripping the qualitative transformation of everyday life, of desires spinning their wheels, without traction in the elaboration of needs. The proximate causes may vary, and are usually to do with the thuggery of the police and the indifference of the state. What the Situationists point to is the consistency and persistence of what follows, the twin forks of seize it all or burn it down. Sometimes the riot takes a different form, and moves towards rebellion, even towards revolution, or perhaps those in the middle of it think it does. This is why May '68 has a special place in not only the theory but also the mythology of the Situationists. It was more than a riot. It was the fabled *general strike*.[7]

The Situationist account of May '68, *Enragés and Situationists in the Occupation Movement* (1968) was issued under the name of René Viénet, although it was probably something of a collective effort. The son of a dockworker from Le Havre, Viénet (b. 1944) came in contact with Debord in 1961 via an affair with Michèle Bernstein's sister. When he came to Paris to study Chinese, he joined the

Situationists. In 1965 he went to China, and saw the beginnings of the Cultural Revolution before being expelled in 1966. As Debord wrote of him, somewhat prophetically: "René's often fallible turn of mind—resolving problems by trenchant extremism—becomes obviously just and timely when the real conditions are such that it is necessary to envision being truly trenchant."[8] It was probably Viénet who wrote some of the more startling of the famous graffiti of May '68, including: "Beneath the pavement, the beach."

In Viénet's version, the proximate cause of May '68 is the provocation on the Nanterre campus by the Enragés, a group who had already made contact with the Situationist International. Viénet: "The agitation launched at Nanterre by four or five revolutionaries, who would later constitute the Enragés, was to lead in less than five months to the near liquidation of the state."[9] It's a hyperbolic statement, but what is distinctive about Viénet's little book is that it is a subjective account of history, and seen from the point of view of an active subject. Like the *Memoirs* of the Cardinal de Retz—one of its literary models—it preserves and extends the moment of insurrection with a form of memory specific to it.[10]

Nanterre at the time was a bleak spot in the western suburbs of Paris. Viénet: "The scene was perfect: the urbanism of isolation had grafted a university center onto the high-rise flats and the complementary slums. It was a microcosm of the general conditions of oppression, the spirit of a world without spirit." Dominique Lecourt: "The whiff of cordite hung over the desolate campus adjoining the shantytown, far from the Paris elites." Lefebvre called it "a place of damnation."[11] And so it proved: in 2002 Richard Durn opened fire with two Glock pistols at the end of a town hall meeting, killing eight councilors. Durn: "Because I have by my own will become a kind of living-dead, I have decided to end it all by killing a small local elite which is the symbol of, and who are the leaders and decision makers in, a city that I have always detested."[12]

Bernard Stiegler makes of this pointless massacre an emblem for what he calls a loss of *individuation*. To constitute the self requires collective belonging, and what the spectacle erodes is both the collective and the individual, or rather the situations that make both together. "Today we are enduring an enormous suffering of this individuation."[13] The situations that assure individuation are not far removed from the Situationist inventory of the forms of praxis: dérive, détournement, gift, and finally potlatch. The spectacle makes all of time homogenous—*synchronized*, in Stiegler's terms. The spectacle does not require that we think alike, dress alike or act alike, merely that we act within the same time in relation to the same form, the commodity form, which synchronizes our actions. The triumph of the spectacle erases what Stiegler calls the *diachronic*, or what van Eyck called duration, and the Situationists, play. It forecloses the connection of actions through time. May '68 was a critique in advance of the impoverishment of individuation.

Back in 1968, that handful of Nanterre agitators were brought before a disciplinary committee of the University of Paris. By trying to break up the support meeting in the courtyard, the authorities provoked the movement into action. Workers and lumpenproles joined in, daubing slogans on the walls and throwing up barricades. Viénet: "The construction of a system of barricades solidly defending an entire quarter was already an unforgivable step towards the negation of the state." Chlorine gas grenades overcame the barricades. Meanwhile events on the street acquired their inevitable spectacular double. Daniel Cohn-Bendit (b. 1945) became the spokesmodel for the revolt, an honest but limited revolutionary, as the Situationists would characterize him. He was the one who could speak acceptably about the unacceptable.[14]

The movement occupied the Sorbonne and called for a general strike. The Gaullist Prime Minister Georges Pompidou, who was no fool, freed arrested students and withdrew the police. His strategy was patience rather than confrontation. The Sorbonne became the scene of a wide-ranging discussion which attempted to create out of itself some kind of self-organization. The Situationists and the Enragés formed a joint committee. They made posters denouncing the remnants of art, warning against recuperation, and calling for the disinterment of Cardinal Richelieu, which would have warmed the ghost of his sometime antagonist Cardinal de Retz. When it came time for the general assembly to elect delegates, eighteen-year-old Enragé René Reisel gave a rousing speech proclaiming that the struggle was not just about the university, and that sociologists and psychologists were the new cops. It ensured his election to the occupation committee.[15]

Elsewhere, workers seized the opportunity with wildcat strikes and occupations of their factories. The Communist union federation tried to limit this development, and to steer it towards the routine demands of wages and conditions. They did their best to prevent contact between striking workers and students. Meanwhile, the Sorbonne Occupation Committee proved ineffective, or as Viénet says, "showed itself incapable of self-respect." The Situationists, Enragés and friends withdrew, and convened their own uninterrupted general assembly at the National Pedagogical Institute in the rue d'Ulm. They set up standing committees for liaisons, printing, and requisitions, the latter to keep it fueled with money, vehicles, food and wine. It was not just a student group. Among its thirty-odd members were Guy Debord (1931–94), Alice Becker-Ho (b. 1941), René Viénet (b. 1944) and René Reisel (b. 1950).[16]

There is a certain charm to groups such as astronomers and professional footballers declaring themselves for *self-management*. The general air of tolerance made it hard to resist the antics of some other professional groups, such as film-makers and museum directors, who recast the revolt as a pretext for reviving some warmed-over *radical aesthetics*. They preferred changing their métier to the métier of change. What is of genuine interest lay elsewhere: "in the space of a week millions of people had cast off the weight of alienating conditions, the routine of survival, ideological falsifications, and the inverted world of the spectacle."

For Viénet, this is an idyllic situation. "People strolled, dreamed, learned how to live." Time assumes a measureless quality. "For the first time youth really existed. Not the social category invented for the needs of the commodity economy by sociologists and economists, but the only real youth, of life lived without dead time ..."[17] The outpourings of popular creativity showed just how much of what Jorn called surplus fellowship actually existed. Cars now attracted only the match. People modified the landscape to suit themselves—a spontaneous critique of urbanism. Police stations at Odéon and rue Beaubourg were "enthusiastically sacked," as was the stock market. It was as if a blind but determined force was undermining the foundations of Gaullist order. As Viénet says, "the 'old mole' spared nothing."[18]

It was not to last. "The Stalinists began to despair of the survival of Gaullism." The chain reaction of wildcat strikes could not be sustained as a general strike. The unions channeled the inchoate desires of the strikers towards specific demands on wages and conditions. The Trotskyites, the Castroites and the Maoists all wanted to replay one or other revolution they had missed, rather than the one they were in the midst of actually having. They drew their lessons from past defeats.

"The state was ignored for the first time in France." But the odds weren't good. "Everything was to hang on the power relations in the factories between the workers, everywhere isolated and cut off, and the joint power of the state and the trade unions. The movement was dismantled strike by strike, either by negotiations or by force." The movement divided was rapidly conquered. The occupied factories lacked the means to remain in communication with each other. They would not know what to say even if they were. Viénet puts it down to "backwardness of theoretical consciousness," but surely it was more than that.[19] The means were lacking to create social relations of a new kind. The state banned certain leftist organizations while making discreet overtures to the far right.

Theory lags behind the situation that calls for it. These days one wonders if the moment of theoretical consciousness arrives at all, or is short-circuited by brutal acts like Durn's. Hegel's owl of Minerva no longer flies at dusk, because the shotgun of Dick Cheney fired at first light.[20] If Viénet's problem in writing about May '68 was how to remember it, then our problem is how to remember that remembrance. Perhaps one way to start is as Maxim Gorky does, at least on Lukács's reading, or the reading of Vali Myers. Start with supposedly *minor characters*, the Viénets and the Porambos, whose actions are neither famous nor typical, but who in their extremity embody, and are embodied in, the extremes of the situation itself.

With the failure of the revolution, Viénet turned away from the critique of urbanism and towards the other pole of Situationist action—détournement. *Can Dialectics Break Bricks?* (1972) takes a kung fu action film, reorders some scenes, and replaces the subtitles with Viénet's own, making of its narrative a rather more pointed allegory for the co-option of radical desires by the supposedly leftist wing of spectacular power. In one scene, two Stalinist bureaucrats lounge in a hot tub. One says: "It seems their latest discovery is to détourn the mass media." The other replies, "That, old man, is the beginning of the end." And the first concludes: "They are capable of reducing our own wooden language to sawdust." In Viénet's hands, détournement is a Marxist chainsaw. It becomes a tool for remembering what was and forever could be.

It may seem quixotic, in the twenty-first century, to talk about Marx, and certainly much now escapes the contemporary reader—not only about the collective practices of the Situationists but also their theoretical obsessions. But perhaps there is something to be said for a Marxism the memory of which one cannot abandon, just as one cannot abandon the memory of a certain lover, or of one's home town. But one lives on. In place of the memory of that lover, another love. In place of the hometown, an adopted city. In place of that memory of the Marxists, the memory of the Situationists. Fidelity, or rather, the solidarity without faith that is détournement, outlives that with which it stands.[21] Not the least virtue of speaking at length about Situationist détournements of Marxism is that they form a bulwark against the collapse of their legacy into a disciplinary scholarship, into art history for instance, even Marxist art history.[22] Better to tilt at windmills than pawn the lance.

There is a passage by Marx that Lefebvre liked to quote:

> A philosopher produces ideas, a poet poems, a clergyman sermons, a professor compendia and so on. A criminal produces crimes. If we look a little closer at the connection between this latter branch of production and society as a whole, we shall rid ourselves of many prejudices. The criminal produces not only crimes but also criminal law, and with this also the professor who gives lectures on criminal law and in addition to this the inevitable compendium in which the same professor throws his lectures onto the general market as "commodities." This brings with it the augmentation of national wealth.[23]

Marx goes on to show how the criminal produces the police, the judiciary, a whole division of labor, "creating new needs and new ways of satisfying them."

Who says crime doesn't pay? Crime also produces technological improvement: "Torture alone has given rise to the most ingenious mechanical inventions." The criminal produces new necessities: criminology and even criminal law itself. The criminal produces new desires: popular entertainments such as novels and TV shows, from Balzac to Gorky to Vian to *The Wire*. Marx: "The criminal breaks into the monotonous yet secure everyday life of the bourgeoisie, provoking it out of stagnation. The illicit desire for the criminal life gives rise to that uneasy tension and agility without which even the spur of competition would get blunted."

The same could be said of delinquents, radicals, and perhaps especially radical delinquents such as the Situationist International, who keep a veritable industry alive, including the book you hold in your hands. Reduced to the logic of *productivity*, the activities of the Situationist International "augment national wealth" with the best of them. And if mere delinquent radicals can *produce* all this, what then of the social crime of a failed revolution? May '68 did not induce the revolution so much as a whole industry of commentary. Violence is the midwife of history publishing. Enough books entered the market to rebuild all the barricades many times over.

The trick might be to recall this legacy otherwise, to stimulate a quite different kind of production. Not just to quote it or imitate it, for quotation and imitation are classical forms of connecting past to present, here to there, this to that. Let's be done with nostalgia for '68 and all it represents. If there's a consistent lesson in the Situationist approach to history, it is to expect surprises. No doubt Prince Charles was surprised when his limo lost its escort one day in 2010 and he found himself surrounded by protesters angry about the privatizing of British higher education. Somebody shot it with paintballs. Comrades, the time of life is short, and if we live, we live to tread on kings![24] But in these spectacular times, when royalty is hardly royal, it might do to startle a prince, pink-faced and blinking, in the presence of cameras. The moment of surprise, when power ceases its phantom existence even for just a moment, is not limited to May '68. It recurs on all kinds of scales, all the time. Historical thought has the task of preparing the active subject for the emergence of promising situations within lived time. The art of détournement is a training ground for the appropriation of historical time itself.

In the novel *2666,* Roberto Bolaño (1953–2003) describes the phantom novelist Benno von Archimboldi (b. 1920): a possible candidate for the Nobel Prize, a "veteran, a World War II deserter still on the run, a reminder of the past for Europe in troubled times. A writer on the left whom even the Situationists respected. A person who didn't pretend to reconcile the irreconcilable, as was the fashion these days."[25] In literature and art, the Situationists are sometimes invoked as if to bestow a certain blessing on the proceedings, as if making a genuflection to the dangerous saints could preserve art and literature as they go about business as usual. Scholars search out the Situationists like the elusive Archimboldi, to finally pay back the gift, to be done with the unseemly *generosity* of what they offer, their unbidden donations of thought in action. This gnawingly unaccountable quality is the very thing with which to try to settle accounts.

"Philosophy," says Simon Critchley, "begins in disappointment." After the death of God, the end of Art, the failure of the Revolution, there's nothing left but philosophy, the moment of contemplation of the ruins. For Jacques Rancière, it is not that literature arises out of failed revolutions, but that revolutions are failed literature.[26] Certainly the high theory of the post-'68 era was born of the disappointments, not just of May but of the *red decade* of 1966–76, of which May was the high water mark. If other failed revolutions gave us Hegel and Stendhal, Marx and Baudelaire, this one gave us Foucault and Deleuze, Derrida and Lyotard. Whatever interest such thoughts may once have held, they are now no more than the routine spasms of an era out of love with itself.

Low theory returns in moments, not of disappointment, but of boredom. We are bored with these burnt offerings, these warmed-up leftovers. High theory cedes too much to the existing organization of knowledge and art. It is nothing more than the spectacle of disintegration extending into knowledge itself. Rather a negative theory that reveals the gap between this world and its promises. Rather a negative action that reveals the void between what can be done and what is to be done. Rather a spirited invention of genuine forms within the space of everyday life, than the relentless genuflection to the hidden God that is *power*.[27] For such experiments the Situationist legacy stands ripe for a détournement that has no respect for those who claim proprietary rights over it. There is still plenty of fruit to be gleaned from the vine.

Viénet: "Nothing is too beautiful for the Blacks of Watts."[28] That is why low theory pushes critique away from the relentless quotation and commentary on itself. Low theory takes critique gently by the neck and leads it outwards, towards the labyrinth that is the production of situations, including the production of new forms for critique itself. It is not too embarrassed to turn up as shopgirl philosophy or on delinquent mixtapes: "Our ideas are on everybody's mind." Even before May '68, Viénet wanted critique to détourn new forms, including comics, chick lit, cinema, pirate radio, porn. He thought every Situationist should be able to make films. One could translate that today to mean that the low theorist should know not only how to détourn some Hegel but also some code, or should at least be able to throw up a decent website or viral video, but without making a fetish of such media practices.

"Up till now our subversion has mainly drawn on the forms and genres inherited from past revolutionary struggles, primarily those of the last hundred years. I propose that we supplement our forms of agitation with methods that dispense with any reference to the past," says a twenty-three-year-old Viénet. Ah, youth! Or perhaps: use the past as a reservoir of tactics, not to imitate, but from which to learn the tactical arts, and not least how all tactics fail in the end. The Situationist project, as an instance of low theory at work, made some rare moves. Among other things, it advanced a new romantic agenda on the least likely terrain, that of architecture, the most steadfastly classical of forms. As Lefebvre shows, many of the tactics that worked, if only for a time, were themselves détournements of romantic game plans.

Here are some techniques for discovering the way into the total semantic field that they détourned, alone or in combination: alcohol (Debord), opium (Trocchi), psychosis (Chtcheglov), mania (Spur), synaesthesia (de Jong), fatigue (the dérive), obsession (Constant), love (Bernstein), revolution (May '68), solitude (late Debord). Many of the tributaries into which the Situationist project flowed found one or other of the alibis that Lefebvre identified for avoiding the question of how to supersede aesthetics and ethics in praxis: aestheticism (Jorn, de Jong, Spur); technicism (New Babylon);

moralism (the Situationist International sans artists), nihilism (Trocchi again). Every spent tactic is a lesson in how to make new ones. And unlike the romantics, the Situationists made the fateful leap beyond subjective revolt to class struggle. They were not content to play merely within the total semantic field, within the economy of tolerable middle-class dissent. Détournement challenges that very economy.[29]

It's still a fine slogan: Never work! Perhaps we could add: Never play! For play is becoming as co-opted as work, a mere support for the commodity form.[30] Just as the Situationists adjusted romantic tactics to suit new situations, so too Situationist tactics can be adapted at will. To the dérive, psychogeography and unitary urbanism, what could one add but the question of scale? Where now does the space of the city end?[31] Détournement is now a whole social movement in all but name, able to sample anything and everything but unable to know its own provenance. With the commodity form extending even into *social networks*, what could be more pressing than Jorn's contemplation of an extreme aesthetics, an invention of forms as something other than mere containers? With the end of the Situationist International as an organization, its fantasy of being the vanguard of organized form died with it, but not perhaps the experiment with social form. Let a thousand internationals bloom! Each with their own provisional rules of labor and donation, inclusion and exclusion, initiations, rituals, forms of remembrance.[32]

Shorn of its chemical romances, project sigma is still a signal instance of creating a counter-network. New Babylon, for all its supposedly utopian grandeur, looks a whole lot more endurable than the new Moloch that was actually built in its stead. The *Situationist Times* is still a remarkable precedent in creating an intercourse between languages, and between languages and different visual practices, within which to propose a new kind of knowledge and practice of form. Speaking of forms, Jorn opens up novel ways of thinking about the severing of the production of quantities from the production of qualities as a class division.[33] Supposedly superseded by the structural turn in both philosophy and urban thought, Lefebvre's body of work seems far richer than either its fans or detractors credit. Perhaps everyday life offers ways of escaping the prison house of *biopower*.[34]

In an age which still worships eternal love—albeit with a frenzy that belies a still unacknowledged waning of belief—what could be more telling than Bernstein's amorous tactics? And speaking of tactics, was not Debord brilliant at the tactics of knowing when things should end? When to split from Isou, when to break up the Letterist International, when to be done with the artists in the Situationist International: he knew when to move on. The terrain changes, the disposition of force changes, and so the tactics change. Just as Debord, with the founding of the Situationist International, accepted the tactic of positioning the movement within rather than against the art world, perhaps today one might take up a defensive position within higher education rather than against it. The Situationists are often taken as offering dogmas when really they practiced something else: tactical mobility combined with the ruthless criticism of all that exists. There's a constant non-identity of tactics and theory. Extremist theory, put directly into practice, leads to quietism; provisional tactics, translated directly into theory, aren't theory at all. The difference is the thing.

The world has only changed philosophy. The point, however, is to interpret it. Is philosophy that domain to which the project of transforming the world retreats? Or is it rather premised, as Critchley says, on disappointment with this world and what it lacks? If the latter, then perhaps critical theory needs to chart another path through the aftermath of May '68, one that does not take one or other royal road back to philosophy. The archive too is a space for dérive. There are turning points where the monuments of the critical theory canon intersect with more interesting back alleys: take the streets named Lefebvre, not Lacan; Jorn, rather than Althusser; Debord, not Foucault. Or: praxis, not therapy; form, not structure; situation, not power. The renewal of critical theory as critical practice might take these or other alternate pathways through the twentieth century, if it is to find its way back to the labyrinth rather than end up on the steps to the Panthéon.

The contributions of Situationists and ex-Situationists by no means ended with May 1968. The organization disbanded in 1972, but there were other projects, other adventures. Writing about those will have to wait for another moment. What continues unabated, regardless of what anyone writes, is the détournement of the

Situationist project. Beneath the pavement, the beach. Wherever the boredom with given forms of art, politics, thought, everyday life jackhammers through the carapace of mindless form, the beach emerges, where form is ground down to particles, to the ruin of ruins. There lies what the old mole is always busy making: the materials for the construction of situations. These too might be recuperated into mere art or writing some day, and sooner rather than later, but not before their glorious time. Our species-being is as builders of worlds. Should we consent to inhabit this given one as our resting place, we're dead already. There may be no dignified exits left to the twenty-first century, the century of the flying inflatable turd, but there might at least be some paths to adventure. The unexamined life is not worth living, but the unlived life doesn't bear thinking about.

13 The Critique of Everyday Life

What good is knowledge if it isn't practiced? These days real knowledge lies in knowing how to live.

Baltasar Gracián

Henri Lefebvre started this line of thought with his 1947 book *The Critique of Everyday Life Volume 1* and raised it to a fine pitch with that book's second volume in 1961. But the group who really pushed it to its limit was the Situationist International, a movement which lasted from 1957 until 1972, and which its leading light Guy Debord would later describe as "this obscure conspiracy of limitless demands."[1]

While their project was one of "leaving the twentieth century," in the twenty-first century they have become something of an intellectual curio.[2] They stand in for all that up-to-date intellectual types think they have outgrown, and yet somehow the Situationists refuse to be left behind. They keep coming back as the bad conscience of the worlds of writing, art, cinema and architecture that claim the glamour of critical friction yet lack the nerve to actually rub it in. Now that critical theory has become hypocritical theory, the Situationist International keeps washing up on these shores like shipwrecked luggage. Are the Situationists derided so much because they were wrong or because they are right?

Consider how their legacy is isolated and managed. The early phase of the Situationist project, roughly from 1957 to 1961, is safety consigned to the world of art and architecture. Its leading lights, such as Pinot Gallizio, Asger Jorn, Michèle Bernstein and Constant Nieuwenhuys, all have books and articles dedicated to managing their memory.[3] The period from 1961 to 1972 is considered the political phase, and its memory is kept by various leftist sects who reprint the writings of Raoul Vaneigem, Guy Debord and René Viénet, and are mostly concerned with the critique of each other.[4] Of more interest to us now perhaps is Post-Situationist literature, in which former members or associates, including T. J. Clark, Gianfranco Sanguinetti and Alice Becker-Ho, restate or revise the theses of the movement, which runs more or less from 1972 to Debord's death in 1994.

The life and work of Guy Debord, the one consistent presence in the movement, is fodder for all kinds of recuperations. For biographers he is a grand grotesque, or a revolutionary idol, the hipster's Che Guevara. Certain enterprising critics have turned him into a master of French prose.[5] By recuperating fragments of the Situationist project within the intellectual division of labor, its bracing critique of everyday life as a totality, not to mention the project of constructing an alternative, tends to disappear into the footnotes.

In 2009 the French Minister of Culture, Christine Albanel, declared the archive of Guy Debord a *national treasure*. The archive, in the possession of Debord's widow, Alice Becker-Ho, contains a holograph of *Society of the Spectacle*, reading notes, notebooks in which Debord recorded his dreams, his entire correspondence, and the manuscript of a last, unfinished book, previously believed to have been destroyed. Yale University had already expressed interest in acquiring the archive, prompting the Bibliothèque Nationale, or French National Library, to make securing the Debord archive a priority.

The fund-raising arm of the Library holds an annual gala dinner to hit up its big benefactors for cash, and its 2009 event displayed Debord notebooks to tempt donors. Present were several board members, including Pierre Bergé (co-founder of Yves Saint Laurent) and Nahed Ojjeh (widow of the arms dealer Akram Ojjeh). Only €180,000 was raised, a fraction of what the Library had to find for Becker-Ho. "This evening depends upon the spectacular society," fund-raising chief Jean-Claude Meyer admitted in his speech. "It's ironic and, at the same time, a great homage." But if the Library could make an archive out of the Marquis de Sade, then anything is possible. The gala dinner took place in the Library's Hall of Globes, a monument to the presidency of François Mitterrand, who Debord particularly detested.[6]

The gulf that separates the present times from the time of the Situationist International passes through that troubled legacy of the failed revolution of 1968 and 1969 in France and Italy, in which Situationists were direct participants. There was no beach beneath the street. Whether such a revolution was possible or even desirable at that moment is a question best left aside. The installation of necessity as desire in the disintegrating spectacle is a consequence of a revolution that either could not or would not take place.

Even if a revolution could not take place in the late twentieth century, in the early twenty-first century it seems simply unimaginable.[7] It is hard not to suspect that the over-developed world has simply become untenable, and yet it is incapable of proposing any alternative to itself but more of the same. These are times in which the famous slogan from '68—"be realistic, demand the impossible"—does indeed seem more realist than surrealist.

And yet these are times with a very uneasy relation to the legacy of such intellectual realists. Debord in particular is at once slighted and envied, as he was even in his own time. He was, by his own admission, "a remarkable example of what this era did not want."[8] He seemed to live a rather charmed life while doing nothing to deserve it. Debord: "I do not know why I am called 'a third rate Mephistopheles' by people who are incapable of figuring out that they have been serving a third rate society and have received in return third rate rewards ... Or is it perhaps precisely because of that they say such things?"[9]

Not the least problem with Debord is that of all the adjutants of 1968 he was the one who compromised least on the ambitions of that moment in his later life. "So I have had the pleasures of exile as others have had the pains of submission."[10] Unlike Daniel "Danny the Red" Cohn-Bendit, he did not become a member of the European Parliament. As Debord wrote in 1985, looking back on the life and times of the Situationists: "It is beautiful to contribute to the ruination of this world. What other success did we have?" The key to the Situationist project of transforming everyday life is the injunction "to be at war with the whole world lightheartedly."[11] This unlikely conjuncture of levity with lucidity, of élan with totality, has rarely been matched.

It's not as if there aren't enough studies of the Situationist International and its epigones. While written in another context, these lines from Becker-Ho seem to apply: "Time and again in all the works dealing with the same subjects and sharing the same sources, one finds the same bits of information paraphrased more or less successfully, often with the same words endlessly repeated. Other people's findings, acknowledged in underhand fashion, re-emerge as so many new discoveries, stripped of quotation marks and references, and more often than not adding nothing to what is already known on the subject. But what this does is allow the whole field of information going unchallenged to be enlarged quantitatively, and on the cheap..."[12]

Culture is nothing if not what the Situationists called *détournement*: the plagiarizing, hijacking, seducing, detouring, of past texts, images, forms, practices, into others. The trick is to realize in the process the undermining of the whole idea of the author as owner, of culture as property, that détournement always implies.[13] Thus this study makes no claims to originality. Rather, in its act of inflating the whole field of information on the cheap, it seeks only to encourage others in this far from fine art of cultural inflation. The Situationist archive is there to be plundered. Unlike Becker-Ho, *The Spectacle of Disintegration* makes no proprietary claims, but it does set out to be a version of these materials of use to us *now*.[14] It's the past we need for the critique of this present.

Situationist thought is often imagined as a species of Marxism, particularly of the Hegelian variety. Sometimes it is regarded as the inheritor of the fringe romantic poetry of Arthur Rimbaud and the Comte de Lautréamont. Sometimes its project is imagined to be that of superseding the avant-garde movements of Dada and Surrealism, and presenting a spirited rival to contemporary movements as diverse as Fluxus, Oulipo or the Beats. Sometimes it is recalled as a precursor to punk rebellion, anarchist dumpster-diving or postmodern fabulousness.[15] That the Situationists took on the whole world does seem to align it with the more obstreperous of all these currents. What the Situationists fought against, much more vigorously than any of these movements, was their own success. The aim was to preserve something that could escape recuperation as mere art or theory. As Debord writes, "nothing has ever interested me beyond a certain practice of life. (It is precisely this that has kept me back from being an artist, in the current sense of the word and, I hope, a theoretician of aesthetics.)"[16]

The Situationists could be insolent, recalcitrant, insubordinate, but at their best their project of transforming everyday life had a playful quality. Everything is at stake, but the world is still a game. This attunement to life connects the Situationists to a quite different legacy. Michèle Bernstein, Gianfranco Sanguinetti and in particular Guy Debord were fond of quoting quite different sources which point toward different ancestors: Niccolò Machiavelli, Baltasar Gracián, Carl von Clausewitz and the Cardinal de Retz were, in their different ways, writers who tried to put into words the lessons of their own actions or the actions of others upon their time. Situationist writing thus belongs to that tradition of inquiries upon everyday life that ask: how is one to live? And that posit answers that are more than a critical theory, but form the tenets of a *critical practice*.

Debord was particularly fond of the *Mémoires* of the Cardinal de Retz (1613–79). A leader of the Fronde, that last aristocratic resistance to the imposition of absolutist monarchy in France, Retz contributes a quite particular orientation to everyday life that Situationist thought and action observes in its finest hours and neglects in its lesser moments. Writing a hundred years before Rousseau, Retz was not concerned with an armchair analysis of his inner life. He was crafting a public self, styling himself as a being in action. His *Mémoires* are an account of his successes and failures, but an account further perfected. A key quality with which Retz imbues his life is disinterestedness. His conduct of his affairs is something like a work of art or a well-played game. The chief aesthetic quality is being worthy of the events that befall him. He is versatile rather than a specialist. Often he acts from behind the scenes, an unseen power. The prevailing style is a certain appropriateness and consistency.

There is a certain aggrandizement to Retz, as there is to the Situationists, particularly Debord. Events are presented as if he was at the center of them. But what undercuts this seeming self-importance is a sense of the ridiculous quality of power in this world. Neither Retz nor Debord suffers fools gladly. Above all, this appreciation for human comedy relieves the writing of the bitterness of defeat. As Debord writes, in a style that is a modernized Retz: "I have succeeded in universally displeasing, and in a way that was always new."[17] To take this world seriously would be comic; to see the comedy of it is perfectly serious. What the Situationists share with Retz is a comic approach to life as a game which commits one to the cause of the world. Or to quote Debord, quoting Retz: "In bad times, I did not abandon the city; in good times, I had no private interests; in desperate times, I feared nothing."[18]

Like everything else, the Situationists got caught up in the spectacle. They became a mere image of themselves. Critical reception of them finds itself led by the nose into accepting a spectacular version, in which the whole project is reduced to Debord's personality, which is in turn reduced to a certain fanaticism.[19] Alain Badiou reduces Debord to psychoanalytic terms, as posing an image of the real against the symbolic and imaginary. Simon Critchley sees him as a religious rather than an ethical thinker. Jacques Rancière sees only aesthetic project.[20] Such readings take certain tactics at face value. Debord is not a modern Pascal, but a modern Retz; it is not faith but the game that is at stake.

"Of all modern writers," Debord said, quoting the eighteenth-century writer François-René Chateaubriand, "I am the only one whose life is true to his works."[21] Perhaps the most enviable thing about his life is that he managed to avoid wage labor. He did not work for the university or the media. And yet he produced several films, edited a journal, ran an international organization, and wrote a few slim books. Debord: "I have written much less than most people who write, but I have drunk much more than most people who drink."[22]

The drinking did him in. Peripheral neuritis is one of the more painful conditions from which a hard drinker can suffer. As a good Stoic, Debord put his affairs in order. He collaborated on a television documentary with Brigitte Cornand. He prepared his correspondence for publication with Alice Becker-Ho. He may (or may not) have burned certain documents. Then he shot himself in the heart. In the words of Louis-Ferdinand Céline, one of Debord's favorite writers: "When the grave lies open before us, let's not try to be witty, but on the other hand, let's not forget, but make it our business to record the worst of human viciousness we've seen without changing one word. When that's done, we can curl up our toes and sink into the pit. That's work enough for a lifetime."[23]

Debord was not by any means the only member of the Situationist International to leave her or his mark, and if other members did not exactly dazzle their century, they may yet have their chance to inform ours. The wager of this book is that critical practice needs to take three steps backwards in order to take four steps forward. First step back: the early, so-called *artistic* phase of the Situationists is richer than is usually imagined, and not so easily recuperated as mere art or architecture as is often supposed. Second step back: the political thought in action of the Situationists in the sixties is not well understood, and much of what transpired in this period still speaks to us today, if it is seen more broadly than May '68. An early book, *The Beach Beneath the Street,* set itself the challenge of retracing these two steps.

The Spectacle of Disintegration concerns itself with a third step back: that the defeat of May '68 did not mark the end of the Situationist project, even if the organization dissolved itself shortly afterwards. This book begins again with the story in the seventies, via the work not only of Debord but also his collaborations with his last comrade in the Situationist International, Giancarlo Sanguinetti, with Debord's second wife, Alice Becker-Ho, with his patron and film producer Gérard Lebovici, with professional filmmaker Martine Barraqué, with video documentarian Brigitte Cornand, and in the independent work of three former members of the Situationist International: T. J. Clark, Raoul Vaneigem and René Viénet. It is a disparate body of work through which we can read the last quarter of the twentieth century. They still dare us to outwit them, outmatch them. They dare us to stake something. There is more honor in failing that challenge than in refusing it.

This book is not a biography of Guy Debord. It is not a history of the Situationists. It is not literary criticism or art appreciation. Out of what is living and what is dead in the Situationist legacy it concerns itself mostly with what is living. If the Situationist slogan LIVE WITHOUT DEAD TIME is to be understood at all, it can only be in writing which treats its own archive as something other than dead time. The project is to connect Situationist theory and practice with everyday life today, rather than with contemporary art or theory. Hence the presence of certain anecdotes, cut from their journalistic context and taken on a journey, a detour, relieved of their fragmentary context and connected to a theoretical itinerary which treats them as moments of a lost totality. As the Situationists said: "One need only begin to decode the news such as it appears at any moment in the mainstream media in order to obtain an everyday x-ray of Situationist reality."[24]

Debord, like Retz and so many others, failed to transform the world of his own time, but this failure is the basis of a certain kind of knowledge. Right thinking in this tradition depends on the confrontation of thought with the world. History's winners are confirmed in their illusions; the defeated know *otherwise*. Debord: "But theories are made only to die in the war of time."[25] At least the Situationists found strategies for confronting their own time, to challenge it, negate it, and push it, however slightly, toward its end, toward leaving the twentieth century.

As impossible as that task was, leaving the twenty-first century may not be so easy. It is hard to know how to even imagine it. Perhaps a place to start, then, is by returning to some situations where it seemed possible to leave previous centuries. One of the virtues of writing in a Situationist vein is that it opened up the question of an activist reading of past revolutions. In our opening two chapters, we look back over the seventies writings of Clark and Vaneigem, but through their eyes look back again over the whole series of French revolutions and restorations. Then, we turn our attention to the rather critical accounts Sanguinetti and Viénet offered, from firsthand experience, of the Italian Autonomists and the Chinese Cultural Revolution, moments which, strangely, are back again, in a rather spectacular fashion, as touchstones for twenty-first-century political thought. After that, we pursue the tactics of Debord and Becker-Ho for keeping alive the spirit of contesting the totality as the era of the disintegrating spectacle was dawning.

14 Liberty Guiding the People

To follow the times is to lead them.
Baltasar Gracián

Suppose a team of archaeologists from an alien civilization came upon the ruins of the disintegrating spectacle, but all they had with which to understand it, besides some blasted fragments, was one or two books by T. J. Clark. What sort of sense would they make of it? Of course, we are already ourselves those very aliens. Much of what we now think of as what was once modern comes down to us in bits and pieces, as inscrutable as ancient Egyptian funeral art. But Clark's books might be singularly useful for this unearthed modern, since certain of his books quite consciously read the art of the nineteenth century as intimations for the twentieth century. As Clark reflects in *The Sight of Death*: "The advantage of the historical allegories in my previous books was that, if I was lucky, a point occurred at which the politics of the present was discovered in the histories—the distant histories—generated out of the object in hand."[1] These allegories might have further resonance in our own times.

One way to grasp the genesis of the disintegrating spectacle might be to rewind it, back before it sped up, before it flung apart. What Situationist writing might have going for it in this task is that, as Clark puts it: "It was the 'art' dimension, to put it crudely—the continual pressure put on the question of representational forms in politics and everyday life, and the refusal to foreclose on the issue of representation versus agency—that made their politics the deadly weapon it was for a while."[2] Clark can help us to formulate the problem of thinking aesthetics and politics together, within the vicissitudes of historical time.

Clark was, however briefly, a member of the Situationist International, and while his books are by no means a mere pendant to that fact, they respond to it; and respond, more particularly, to the stresses of a certain kind of political time through which Clark has lived. His writing was for him "a place to shelter from the storm. Doing art history—being an academic—was a compromise. It was as much as I had the nerve to do."[3] (An aside: And who am I, and who are you, dear reader, to ask of anyone anything more? Only those who throw stones can begrudge us our glass houses.)

Clark recalls standing on the edge of a demonstration in the late sixties, on the steps of the National Gallery in London, "discussing the (sad) necessity of iconoclasm in a revolutionary situation with my friend John Barrell, and agreeing that if ever we found ourselves part of a mob storming through the portico we ought to have a clear idea of which picture had to go the way of all flesh; and obviously it had to be the picture we would most miss."[4] Which picture would Clark choose? We shall find out later. Suffice now to say that it did not come to that, and perhaps just as well.

It is sometimes lost on readers familiar only with the opening overture of Debord's infamous book that the spectacle is not just some vast and totalizing shell that secretes itself out of the commodity form and envelopes all around it. While it may be the dominant form of social life, it is not the only one. Clark: "The spectacle is never an image mounted securely and firmly in place; it is always an account of the world competing with others, and meeting the resistance of different, sometimes tenacious forms of social practice."[5] Clark enlarges and refines the sense of the struggle over social form, and the role within the struggle played by the making of images. For while society may have become in part disciplinary, it has never ceased to be spectacular in its totality.[6]

If there is a limit to Clark—evident particularly in the later texts—it is in the way the auras of certain images start to become stand-ins for a contest of forces, struggling not just over what images can mean but also over what they can do. Clark: "If I cannot have the proletariat as my chosen people any longer, at least capitalism remains my Satan."[7] A Satan which art alone is not up to the task of confronting.

There are times when aesthetics and politics appear as discrete and free-standing categories. At other moments they can't help but fall over each other, which in the French context at least might be telegraphed by the following dates, and from the events that spill forth from them and evaporate into history: 1789, 1830, 1848, 1871, 1945, 1968; from the first *successful* French revolution, via the Paris Commune and the Liberation, to the last failed one. While Clark will have quite a bit to say about epochs of restoration, where art and politics interact only tangentially, of particular interest is the kind of time where they fuse. "Such an age needs explaining, perhaps even defending."[8]

Modernity is all about beginnings, and it might as well be said to begin with *The Death of Marat* (1793) by Jacques-Louis David (1748–1825). David shows Marat dead in his bath, clutching the letter written to him by his murderer. It's an image of a secular martyr, but not exactly a secular image. It was first shown at a ritual occasion, contrived by David. Quite a struggle went on over the meaning and ownership of the cult of Marat. While Marat was close to the Jacobin faction, the Enragés—the most radical expression of the most radical class, the sans-culottes—claimed him as one of their own. The image of Marat hovered for a moment, caught between the role of martyr to the state on the one hand, and friend to the sans-culottes and their demand for a thoroughly social revolution on the other.

"Surely never before had the powers-that-be in a state been obliged to improvise a sign language whose very effectiveness depended on its seeming to the People a language they had made up, and that therefore represented their interests."[9] The Jacobins had a tenuous grasp on state power. They relied on the sans-culottes for direct action against their enemies to the right, but having moved against the right, the Jacobins turned instead against their erstwhile allies to their left. The sans-culotte passion for direct democracy was a hindrance to the Jacobin claim to the state at a time of war.

The Death of Marat is a remnant of a historical event: the people's entry into history. For Clark, this is the cause of modernism itself, even if it doesn't usually know it. Robespierre and the Jacobins claimed to represent a pure and united people, forever to be purged of traitors, but this double act of representation, at once political and aesthetic, required vigilance. As for the people, as Clark put it with a chilling phrase: "It had to be killed in order to be represented, or represented in order to be killed."[10] Marat dead stood for the people, but the body was not up to the task. Representation as a whole isn't up to the task, but doesn't see it. The obsession with the false during the revolution did not lead to a questioning of representation in general.

Not the least extraordinary thing about David's version of Marat is that the whole top half of the portrait is a vast, blank space, a tissue of empty brushwork. It signals, in part, Marat's self-sacrificing austerity. For Clark, it is something more. Marat could hardly embody a revolution when nobody could confidently claim possession of its spirit. David's portrait could not quite work the old magic of the religious image, but nobody was quite ready to let the spiritual charm of images die. "Art had come out (been dragged out) of the Palais de Fontainebleau. That did not mean it was ready to understand its place in the disenchantment of the world. The whole history of modernism could be written in terms of its coming, painfully, to such an understanding."[11]

The blank wall behind Marat is "the endless, meaningless objectivity produced by paint not quite finding its objects, symbolic or otherwise, and therefore making do with its own procedures."[12] The revolution put in place a regime of the image in which for the first time the state was the representative of the people, but the people themselves could hardly be represented. The Jacobin notion of the people was empty, pure opposition to the parasites of the aristocracy. It was a problem that would take a century to resolve, and the name of that solution is the spectacle, but in solving the problem, the spectacle dissolves the people into itself—then itself dissolves.

The people appear on the historical stage in *Liberty Guiding the People* (1831), by Eugène Delacroix (1798–1863). It is an image of the myth of a revolution in which the bourgeoisie believed, if only for a little while. In 1830 the bourgeoisie has defeated tyranny and gained a constitution, all in three glorious days at the barricades. Delacroix's painting both restates and rephrases this myth. It repeats the forms of the popular lithographers, in that the barricade has become a stage, with characters propped on it rather than cowering behind it. Delacroix's Liberty is a woman, but not quite the conventional symbol. What unadorned Liberty reveals a little too much is the naked power of popular revolt. Delacroix's contemporary Honoré de Balzac saw in her eyes only "the flames of insurrection."[13] This is not exactly the liberty the bourgeois revolutionary bargained for.

Who exactly is Liberty guiding? The bourgeois in his top hat is surrounded by the rabble. If revolution is the door through which the people enter history, then it makes a troubling figure for bourgeois thought. Outnumbered, it might only be a matter of time before the rabble turns against their allies of the moment. And they did: By the time Delacroix's picture was hanging in the Salon of 1831, a new class war was on in earnest. The people didn't particularly want a constitution; they wanted bread and work and wages. They wanted a social revolution. The picture was an anachronism. It was quickly spirited out of sight, not to be seen again until the next revolution. What the bourgeoisie wants to remember henceforth is not revolution, but restoration. The revolution through which the people enter history is the revolving door that also spirits them back out if it again.

Delacroix's picture resurfaced in 1848, but he was not the painter of that revolution. Clark assigns that honor to Gustave Courbet (1817–77). By the 1840s, when Courbet came into his own as an artist, bourgeois power was an established fact. An insecure one, to be sure, but established, and artists could not but wonder "whether bourgeois existence was heroic, or degraded, or somehow conveniently both."[14] What would come to be known as the artistic and literary *avant-garde* was already an established part of cultural life, the antechamber of success. Also already in play was the avant-garde gambit of attacking the *forms* of the dominant order, whilst offering that order, knowingly or not, new forms.

The avant-garde rubs shoulders with, but is not the same as, *bohemia*. In mid-nineteenth-century Paris, bohemia was not yet a fantasy spun out of the *Scenes from Bohemian Life* of Henri Murger as *La Bohème* of Giacomo Puccini, let alone *Rent* by Jonathan Larson.[15] It was a genuine social class, outside of the ruling order, closer to the dangerous classes than the intellectuals. Clark calls them "the first debris of industrialism."[16] What bohemia lacked in aesthetic sophistication it made up for in recalcitrance. It was the genuine unassimilated force: "the real history of the *avant-garde* is the history of those who bypassed, ignored, or rejected it; a history of secrecy and isolation; a history of escape from the *avant-garde* and even from Paris itself."[17] Or in short, the only avant-garde worthy of mention is that which was unacceptable even to the avant-garde. Bohemia contains at least some element of the inassimilable waste product of spectacular society, what it pushes on ahead of itself, rather than what it leaves behind.

Clark identifies the bohemian's game as what Slavoj Žižek would later call over-identification. Clark: "the Bohemian caricatured the claims of bourgeois society. He took the slogans at face-value; if the city was a playground he would play; if individual freedom was sacrosanct then he would celebrate the cult twenty-four hours a day; laissez-faire meant what it said. The Bohemian was the dandy stood on his head."[18] Such a strategy had its limits. By the 1840s it offered little more than a shopworn romanticism, turned more toward nostalgia for the past that to present exigencies.

For Henri Lefebvre, romanticism is a viable strategy for advancing onto the symbolic terrain within what he calls the total semantic field.[19] It digs into the past to find the figures that still trouble the present. For Clark this is a temptation to be resisted. The promise of transforming everyday life has to be rooted in the materiality of everyday life itself. For Courbet, bohemia nevertheless offered a space within which to make a break with the expectations of the art world. His break from bohemia and its tired romanticism, in turn, would come via a return to his provincial roots.

From the bourgeois point of view, February 1848 was the beautiful revolution, but soon the bloom faded. Karl Marx: "The June revolution is the ugly revolution, the repulsive revolution, because realities have taken the place of words, because the republic has uncovered the head of the monster itself by striking aside the protective, concealing crown."[20] February was a bourgeois struggle to make again a constitution and secure its own power, with some few concessions made to popular power to secure its support. June was the uprising against bourgeois power when concessions proved not to concede enough. The avant-garde was for the revolution in February but against it in June; bohemia was not so biddable.

With the suppression of the popular forces, Courbet retreated to Ornan, and discovered, in the countryside, the missing element, something bohemian life couldn't supply—everyday life: "Courbet saw that the commonplace was not the life of other people, but his own life."[21] For Clark, the *Burial at Ornans* (1851) is one of Courbet's greatest achievements. It is an image of a religious ceremony, but it is not a religious image. It dissociates ritual from belief. It is not explicitly anti-clerical, which makes it all the more effective. Courbet pictures a kind of collective distraction, at once religious and secular, comic and tragic, sentimental and grotesque.

More challenging still is that it pictures the rural bourgeois. It confounds the myth of the unitary character of rural life, and at a time when the bourgeois replaced the aristocrat as the locus of peasant hatred. Courbet pictures the countryside at a time when power within it shifts toward the rural towns, and the countryside as a whole is absorbed within capital. Courbet at his best limns the relation between forces that animate the scene. His is a realism that thwarts art's supposed mission to imagine the *ideal*. The working of the canvas doesn't purify appearances, revealing an essence, but neither is it a fidelity to them.

With the defeat of the Parisian proletariat in June 1848, the role of Paris as center of political contest was for the moment eclipsed. What emerged in the shadow of Red Paris was Red France. The French peasantry had its own issues: land hunger, debts, rights to the commons. In 1848 the French peasantry arrives on the political stage as an actor in its own right. In 2010 the Thai peasantry did the same. After a populist prime minister was deposed in a judicial coup, the so-called Red Shirt movement came down from the countryside to Bangkok to try to force the end to a quasi-feudal political regime in which the monarchy presided over a state and army that represented only shifting compromises among business interests.

Early in March 2010 the Thai army reported the theft of six thousand assault rifles, but who stole them? Was it what the government called *terrorist elements* in the Red Shirt movement? Or did the army steal them from itself, so it could blame any violence in a coming confrontation on the opposition? When the Red Shirt demonstrations came later that same month, they were the biggest in Thai history, and largely peaceful, apart from a few grenade explosions in which nobody was killed. The Red Shirts poured what they claimed was their own blood on Parliament and called for elections to end the undemocratic rule—of the Democrat Party. Not getting what they wanted, they expanded their occupation from the Phan Fah Bridge to the Rajprasong intersection in the heart of Bangkok's tourist and commercial zone, and then into the nearby shopping district.

As part of a crackdown on Red Shirt–aligned media, including websites and radio stations, the army tried to shut down a TV station sympathetic to them. The Red Shirts stormed the station and occupied it, restoring broadcasts, at least temporarily. The army tried to retake Phan Fah bridge without success, killing two dozen people. The Red Shirts built bamboo barricades in the Rajprasong district, and held up a train coming from the Northeast carrying military vehicles.

A Red Shirt leader declared at this point that "we do not condone but we cannot control. There is no more control among the followers." Attempts at a ceasefire negotiation failed. Red Shirts forced their way into Chulanongkorn hospital near their Rajprasong barricades searching for troops, but they did not find any. The government added US$8 million to the Bangkok police budget. Khattiya Sawasdipol, a former army officer advising the Red Shirts, was shot in the head by a sniper while being interviewed by the *New York Times*.

In May, helicopters dropped leaflets on the demonstrators urging them to decamp, while they fired back with homemade rockets. Their encampment was surrounded, and the army launched an assault with armored cars. There were occasions of mutiny among the government forces, shooting at the army instead of the Red Shirts, but the government prevailed. Red Shirt leaders surrendered in an attempt to prevent further violence, only to be jeered at by an unrepentant rank and file. The stock exchange, banks and shopping centers went up in flames.[22] Whether or not one takes 1848 to be the moment when the peasantry enters history, in its own right, with its own demands, let's not pretend it ever left it.

The French peasantry in 1848 did not have websites or broadcast stations, but it did have its own forms of expression: songs, pictures, almanacs, secret societies meeting in the woods. The urban left would take some time grasping how to ally itself with all this. The party of order was quicker off the mark, casting the ethereal chains of religious devotion over the populace, while enacting laws to suppress traffic in popular almanacs.

This folk art was not as dangerous as it seemed. Far from being a pure expression of autonomous peasant consciousness, popular art had for a long time imitated that of the ruling classes. By the middle of the nineteenth century, it was a strange amalgam. Popular images included Napoleon and the Wandering Jew, Charles Fourier and the saints. Popular art carries new information but is full of reversals, distortions, exaggerations. Courbet appropriated this system of changes and inversions to make images for a dual public and with doubled meanings. "He exploits the area in which men still think and make images with materials long since falsified by history."[23]

Courbet's method, Clark claims, is what the Situationists call *détournement*: "Instead of reverence, a brutal manipulation of one's sources. Instead of pastiche, confidence in dealing with the past: seizing the essentials ... discarding the details, combining very different styles within a single image, knowing what to imitate, what to paraphrase, what to invent."[24] That there is a traffic between high and low art in Courbet is not all that original or notable. What matters is the direction: "Instead of exploiting popular art to revive official culture and titillate its special, isolated audience, Courbet did the exact opposite. He exploited high art—its techniques, its size, and something of its sophistication—in order to revive popular art."[25] Here is the key Situationist tactic *avant la lettre*.

Courbet confounded the expectations of both left and right: the left wanted a glorification of simple rural life; the right wanted the preservation of the myth of rural harmony. He addressed the possibility of a public that knew itself to be in a state of displacement. "Courbet's public was exactly this labyrinth, this confusion, this lack of firm outlines and allegiances. It was industrial society in the making, still composed of raw and explosive human materials."[26] His achievement was to appropriate from both high and low culture the means to give expression to the possibility not just of a popular art, but of a popular power with one foot in peasant rebellion and the other in the radical traditions of the urban tradesmen, bohemia and the dispossessed.

Courbet is the artist who both grappled with the most pressing problems of representation in his time and got the furthest with them: "In the middle of the nineteenth century both bourgeois and popular culture were in dissolution: the one shaken and fearful, trying to grapple with the fact of revolution; the other swollen with new themes and threatened by mass production. What might have happened—what Courbet for a while tried to make happen—was a fusion of the two."[27] But it was not to be. The vicissitudes of the art market made themselves felt soon enough, but far from being a failure of Courbet alone, this was a general failure.

The failure of a public, political art sets the stage for the more agreeable avant-garde of Impressionism, which discovers what can be achieved in the restricted space that remains. Impressionism is the art of the moment in which "the circumstances of modernism were not modern, and only became so by being given the form called 'spectacle.'"[28] In short, Impressionism was the art that traced the consequences for representation of the colonization of everyday life by the commodity form, even if it did not quite know it.

Impressionism knew itself to be the art of a Paris transformed by the urban planning of Baron Haussmann, and the moral panics that ensued from it. It was a vague but widespread feeling: "Something had gone from the streets; a set of differences, some density of life, a presence, a use."[29] Part of this feeling mapped a real transformation. Haussmann tried to evict the working class from its old quarters, leaving a Paris divided geographically by class. Bourgeois Paris would be in the west and working class in the north and east. The whole space of the city would be opened up to traffic. The political city, the city of the barricade, gives way to the city of circulation. The city as horizon of collective action has to be erased, but so too the city of distinct quarters, each a microcosm of trade and manufacture. Industry became a city-wide affair, with bigger markets, bigger players, tighter margins. In place of the small shop, the big department store, and with it the deskilling of retail. The shop assistant became a whole social category. One kind of capitalism supersedes another.

It was capital that changed things, but popular discourse blamed the city. In the 1860s people believed Paris was disappearing and being replaced by something unreal. Everyday life is becoming a matter of consumption rather than industry. "Paris was in some sense being put to death, and the ground prepared for the *consumer society.*"[30] The unitary world of the quarter, where everyone knows everyone and everyone can measure their social distance from each other directly, was disappearing.

What was so troubling was the anomie of everyday life, the interactions with so many anonymous strangers, who were not always what they seemed. Everyone seemed to be passing as what they were not. To navigate such a city takes maps, catalogues, field guides. The citizens of such a city can only interact with each other via representations that make its strange and fluctuating appearances legible. The city becomes spectacle, a city made to be looked at—for those on the make.

Not that this was to everybody's liking. In 1871, the Paris Commune would attempt to divert history onto another path. For the first time, the proletariat had its own revolution. While the representatives of the state retreated to Versailles, the communards became authors of their own history, if not at the level of government, then in everyday life. That the Commune had no real leaders might not be a weakness, and at least it had the wit to arm the people. It may not have understood power, but it understood the city, and intervened in its space. As Marx said, it suffered from too many trying to refight the old revolutions to grasp the originality of its situation. Or as the Situationists put it: "The Paris Commune succumbed less to the force of arms than the force of habit."[31]

"In our opinion, the Parisian insurrection of 1871 was the grand and highest attempt of the city to stand as the measure and norm of human reality," writes Henri Lefebvre.[32] Product of unique circumstances, and doomed from the start, when the ruling *Versaillese* return, the Commune closes a whole era of revolutionary politics, and perhaps not just politics. Clark: "After Courbet, is there any more 'revolutionary art'? After the Commune, and what Courbet did in that particular revolution, is there the possibility of any such thing?"[33] Charged with instigating the destruction of the Vendôme column during the Commune, Courbet faced imprisonment and exile, and became an enduring hero to the left.

The new city becomes the site for the painter who stays with the truth of appearances. But this imagining of the city is a kind of fetishism, an inability to see capital at work. Those workings are too spectral. Clark: "Capitalism was assuredly visible from time to time, in a street of new factories or the theatricals of the bourse; but it was only in the form of the city that it appeared as what it was, a shaping spirit, a force remaking things with ineluctable logic—the argument of freight statistics and double entry book keeping. The city was the sign of capital: it was there one saw the commodity take on flesh—and take up and eviscerate the varieties of social practice, and give them back with ventriloqual precision."[34] The city becomes the figure that both reveals and mystifies capital at work. Modern art becomes the art of this city, and, unknowingly, the keeper of at least a few capital secrets.

15 The Spectacle of Modern Life

Things have their seasons, and even certain kinds of eminence go out of style.

Baltasar Gracián

Modern art is good at symptoms. It is good at recording the perceptual effects of a certain kind of transformation of sensation, but not always so good at the diagram of forces that animates those appearances. Modern art invents a whole city of images of the city as images. Clark: "This, I should say, is the essential myth of modern life: that the city has become a free field of signs and exhibits, a marketable mass of images, an area in which the old separations have broken down for good. The modern, to repeat the myth once more, is the marginal; it is ambiguity, it is mixture of classes and classifications, it is anomie and improvisation, it is the reign of generalized illusion."[1] The separation of public and private life, and the invasion of both by the commodity form, is coming but is not yet perfected. The artist who worked this seam most assiduously was close to the Impressionists, but borrowed much from Courbet: Édouard Manet (1832–83).

The late nineteenth century is the time of the construction of the *middle class* as an entity separate from the proletariat. Manet shows with extraordinary clarity the sites in which it was produced: pop culture, the leisure industry, and suburbia. Three pictures, and three women's bodies, encapsulate this emerging spectacular regime, starting with Manet's *Olympia* (1863). By the 1860s, the bourgeoisie was used to the idea of an avant-garde. It had decided to be ironical about it. Manet still managed to find the weak point in bourgeois indifference.

The problem was not that *Olympia* was an image of a prostitute. It was not unusual for Salon pictures to be of prostitutes, but the acceptable image of the prostitute was the courtesan. The courtesan was what could be represented of prostitution. Money and sex could meet in private, in the brothel, or in the spectacle, in the representation of the courtesan. But the prostitute could not be made public. The courtesan is the acceptable image of modern desire. She was supposed to play at not being a prostitute. She was supposed to be the false coin in the realm of sexual purity. She was supposed to almost but not quite *pass* for respectable. She was what in twenty-first-century parlance offered something more than a mere hooker's hand-job. She is the ancestress of the *girlfriend experience*.[2]

The girlfriend experience was the invention of a pimp by the name of Jason Itzler. Other escort services offered the porn-star experience, where the client was supposed to receive something like the most perfectly commodified sex for his money. Itzler spotted a gap in the market for something else: "I told my girls … we have to provide the clients with the greatest single experience ever, a Kodak moment to treasure for the rest of their lives. Spreading happiness, positive energy, and love, that's what being the best means to me. Call me a dreamer, but that's the NY Confidential credo." The women who worked for his NY Confidential were supposed to repeat a mantra to themselves before meeting their client, to the effect that he was actually her boyfriend of six months standing, whom she had not seen for three weeks.

Itzler found the perfect vehicle for such a service in 2004: Natalia McLennan, a former Canadian tap-dance champion. "I'm a little money making machine, that's what I am," recalls McLennan. "Yes, he sold the shit out of me, but he sold me as myself, someone anyone can be comfortable with, someone who really likes sex. Because the truth is, I do. I loved my job, totally." But, says Itzler, "If she ever did it with anyone for free, it would have broken my heart."

Both Itzler and McLennan seem conflicted about the nature of their business. McLennan: "Maybe it sounds crazy, but I never felt I was in it for the money." Itzler: "I thought I could save the world if I could bring together the truly elite people." Itzler even tried to turn NY Confidential into a reality TV show.[3] While hardly worthy of comparison to a Manet—and these days what is?—like *Olympia* the *NY Confidential* TV pilot blurred the boundaries of public and private, sex and love, money and gift. Itzler went to prison as much for a category mistake as a crime.

The name, for a start, is a joke: Olympia was a popular trade name for prostitutes. The brothel, like the Salon, put desire under the rubric of a classical goddess. *Olympia* undoes the category of the courtesan, or tries to. She is not a courtesan passing as a lady, but a hooker passing as a courtesan. Or rather, "she" is an artist, and artist's model—Victorine Meurent—passing as a hooker, passing as a courtesan.[4] This *Olympia* challenges the playful relation of money and desire. On its long road to disenchantment, the bourgeois lost faith in God, but it still believes in desire.

If even the image of prostitution escaped from the spectacle it would be an embarrassment. It implies that money has cuckolded even desire. "The fear of invasion amounted to this: that money was somehow remaking the world completely ... Such an image of capital could still not quite be stomached."[5] At least not in 1860; by 1960, things would be different, the frontier of what could not be stomached would be elsewhere, but was likely still being played out across women's bodies.

The official nude was supposed to be about something other than the naked body of desire. *Olympia* pictures also the disintegration of a genre. "If there was a specifically bourgeois unhappiness, it centered on how to represent sexuality, not how to organize or suppress it."[6] The nude became embarrassing. *Olympia* gave female sexuality a particular body, rather than an idealized and abstract one. It gave female sexuality not just a body to look at, but one that returned the viewer's gaze, and in returning it, created a space for a self reserved from the purchaser's look. The look it confounded was the look of both the art lover and the john.[7]

Argenteuil is about twelve kilometers from the heart of Paris, and by the early twenty-first century was one of its most populous suburbs, easily reached via the Transilien railway line. In the late nineteenth century it was still partly farmland, given over to grapes and the white asparagus named after it. The railway came in 1851. The market gardens gave way to factories, which were extensively bombed during the war, leading to a vast urban development plan in the postwar years, then suburban sprawl, and even a little gentrification in the prettier parts with a view of the city.

That this was Argenteuil's fate was not entirely clear in the late nineteenth century. It was a liminal space, to which the railway brought both factories and tourists, work and leisure, and sooner or later one had to yield to the other. For a while, it seemed destined to be a playground, a spectacular version of nature, made of parks and leisure zones. It framed the city with a more or less woody border. For the artists of the avant-garde, the suburb is a special zone, where the modern mix might be detected. "A landscape which assumed only as much form as the juxtaposition of production and distraction (factories and regattas)."[8]

Manet's *Argenteuil, les canotiers* (1874) is a big picture, made for the Salon. A couple sit by the riverside, boats behind them, and in the background, the factories on the other shore of the river. (The river, a vivid blue, is not quite as nature painted it. The color came from indigo dumped by a chemical factory upstream.) He looks at her; she stares into nothingness. Bored, perhaps, or indifferent, or blandly masking feelings for which there is no longer any public form or language. She is fashionably dressed, but the dress does not become her. She is uneasy.

Clark makes much of the disjointed quality of the picture. "Manet found flatness rather than invented it."[9] Her straw hat really is flat, a disc pinned at the back into a cone. "It is a simple surface; and onto that surface is spread that wild twist of tulle, piped onto the oval like cream on a cake, smeared on like a great flourishing brush mark, blown up to impossible size. It is a great metaphor, that tulle, and it is, yes, a metaphor of painting."[10] It is the brushy top half of *The Death of Marat*—domesticated.

Leisure can be a key site where the abstract workings of capital present themselves to the realm of sensation. "The subcultures of leisure and their representation are part … of a process of spectacular reorganization of the city which was in turn a reworking of the whole field of commodity production."[11] The landscape of leisure emerges as the symbolic field for the conflicts of a spectacular identity. At stake are the forms of freedom, of accomplishment, naturalness, individuality.

These were traditionally bourgeois attributes, but the new

middle class claimed them as their own. *Canotiers* is an image of leisure that doesn't quite prove leisurely. The woman in her boating outfit and hat does not quite seem at ease. Leisure is not quite the free time it is supposed to be. Capital is already producing its own specific disappointments. In 2006 Anousheh Ansari, a successful telecommunications entrepreneur, spent A$20 million on a tourist trip—into space. But all she could think to do when she got there was look at the view and eat chocolate.[12]

Leisure becomes a site of tension, just like work. It is work. Manet's last painting, *A Bar at the Folies-Bergère* (1882), stocks all the ambiguities of the new, spectacular version of the popular. It's a scene from a café-concert, or what now might be called a nightclub. But in the late nineteenth century it was still something of a novelty, with its fake marble under electric light, its singers in ostentatious gowns, singing simple pop songs that are poor in melody but rich in inflection. Clark's claim for it is that the "café-concert produced the popular."[13] The café-concert generalized the instability of class. It made class contingent, a matter of passing, and called forth an art of mixture, transgression, ambiguity, in which the new middle class are the heroes, always angling for a way to exploit its edges.

This new middle class was creating a new class consciousness, which stressed what separated it from the proletariat, even if that claim struck the bourgeoisie, and its cultural functionaries, as ridiculous: "their probity was awful, their gentility insufferable, their snobbery outright comic."[14] And yet the avant-garde painters loved them, in their way. Their very ambiguity made them the perfect figure for the times. Modernist art tried to take its distance from the middle class and its entertainments, but artists are paradoxically fascinated by them. This usually served bourgeois interests. A characteristic of Situationist aesthetics and politics, with a nod back to Courbet, is to borrow modernism's contempt for the middle class, but for proletarian purposes.

Clark: "The middle class of the later nineteenth century, and even in the early years of the twentieth, had not yet invented an imagery of its own fate, though in due course it would do so with deadly effectiveness: the world would be filled with soap operas, situation comedies, and other small dramas involving the magic power of commodities...," not to mention the pilot for the *NY Confidential* reality TV show. "But for the time being it was obliged to feed on the values and idioms of those classes it wished to dominate; and doing so involved it in making the idioms part of a further system in which the popular was expropriated from those who produced it—made over into a separate realm of images which were given back, duly refurbished, to the *people* thus safely defined."[15] This inchoate spectacle learns to feed on, and transform, popular expression, extracting and selecting images. Hence the utility of modernism as a counter-project based on contempt for the result. But it is not as if there is a pure popular art that pre-exists its spectacular fate. The Situationist move is not to discard inauthentic pop in favor of an authentic popular, rather it is to appropriate the modernist critique of the popular as the basis for a new aesthetic and political project.

Clark: "It is above all collectivity that the popular exists to prevent, and doing so means treading a dangerous line."[16] It's the same line that threads through *The Death of Marat* and *Liberty Guiding the People*. The representation has to engage the real desires, frustrations, boredoms of its public. Yet it has to arrest these affects and make of them nothing more than spectacle. "Those who possess the means of symbolic production in our societies have become expert in outflanking any strategy which seeks to obtain such effects consistently; but they cannot control the detail of performance, and cannot afford to exorcise the ghost of totality once and for all from the popular machine."[17]

Armed with the techniques of the avant-garde, one can follow in Courbet's footsteps and re-appropriate the appropriators. The middle class are specialists of the image. "Popular culture provided the petit bourgeois aficionado with two forms of illusory 'class': an identity with those below him, or at least with certain images of their life; and a difference from them which hinged on his skill—his privileged place—as consumer of those same images."[18] This is the power of the middle class over the proletariat, its marking itself off both by its distance from the popular, and its possession of the power to mark that very distance. Hence the popularity in the early twenty-first century of reality shows in which workaday proles compete to become designers or chefs.[19] Becoming middle class means command of the surfaces of what now constitutes the popular, from a well-plated dish to kitchen renovations.

The middle class may be exempt from the rigors of manual labor, but it nonetheless encounters new kinds of labor, affective labor, cultural labor, for which it is hard to sustain much enthusiasm. Manet's *A Bar at the Folies-Bergère* shows a woman working behind a bar, fashionably made up. "The face she wears is the face of the popular ... but also of a fierce, imperfect resistance to any such ascription."[20] It might also be the face of someone whose feet ache. The other's leisure is her labor. It can't but provoke a certain boredom. Behind her is a mirror, which famously does not quite reflect the scene we see in front of it. The effect is cinematic. The mirror shows a moment before or after the one we see in front of it. There are two alternating moments, the act of serving, and waiting to serve. Which comes first? It doesn't matter. The picture is an alternation of these two moments, of working and waiting, and neither with any pleasure. She is, in a word, a *waitress*.

Once upon a time New York nightclubs catered to the aristocracy of the fabulous, to those with the looks, the style, or the connections to gain admittance to the world of the night.[21] That all changed with the invention of bottle service. Buy a table for some astronomical sum, and mere money will admit you to this world which once excluded the bridge-and-tunnel crowd, with their real jobs and neat suits. Sucking the credit cards out of their wallets became the main game, and the nightclubs became big business. Nightclubs ceased producing their own special kind of celebrity, and became dependent on attracting the sports and entertainment stars of their day. The nightclub became, in other words, just an enterprise dependent upon the spectacular, rather than one of its prime engines of efflorescence.

The game became one of attracting celebrities, who might in turn attract the bankers and hedge fund men for the VIP rooms. The general admission crowd down on the dance floor would be largely for decoration. The kinds of mixing of the classes that both troubled and thrilled Manet's contemporaries will now be carefully vetted. Managing such intercourse calls into being new kinds of labor. Rachel Uchitel was a VIP concierge director. She was an ambassador of client desire, making sure the big names and big spenders came to her club and kept on coming. "People say 'Oh Rachel, she's such a star fucker,' that I only hang out with celebs. No. I hang out with successful people. I hang out with people who matter, and I'm honored to." Uchitel became famous in her own right for fifteen seconds in connection with a famous sporting identity. The attention was not exactly welcome. Uchitel: "I have big breasts, yes. But I'm really offended by the notion that I used my sexuality."

Or anybody else's. For one of the roles of a VIP concierge director is to introduce people who matter to women they may find attractive. "It's not our job to get anybody laid," Uchitel insists.[22] But it was her job to populate the VIP rooms with women as attractive as they are discreet. Models, perhaps. Or almost-models. And it is the job of club promoters to bring these almost-models in. The contemporary nightclub, in other words, is a sophisticated machine for the highly selective mingling of money and sex. Or perhaps just the promise of sex, and sometimes just the promise of money. Whether the girls put out or the boys shell out is none of the club's concern.

The nightclub is now a long way from the café-concert, with its only partially organized traffic between money's desires and desire's money. Manet glimpses the beginnings of a spectacular industry that has since been perfected. Now that the threat of the dangerous classes seems half a world away, at least from a New York nightclub, the danger to guard against is not that the rabble might reject the desires on offer, but that it might rather embrace them with too much gusto. Leisure, sex and suburbia are no longer marginal sites within which new kinds of spectacular economy grow. They are the very center and essence of that spectacular economy.

16 Anarchies of Perception

There are occupations that enjoy universal acclaim, and others that matter more but are barely visible.

Baltasar Gracián

Camille Pissarro (1830–1903) offers a different kind of leisure in *Two Young Peasant Women* (1892). It is a painting of the end of the French peasantry, the fixing of something passing. Not that being a peasant was all that pleasant. It was hard work, but still, shot through with utopian promise.

Valuing peasant life was a way of resisting the disenchantment of the world, but Pissarro's painting is not an idealization of the image of the peasant as a remnant of the past. It is something more specific. Pissarro paints *idleness* as a moment within the field of work, as the peasant's ability to choose the moment to be idle. He found a way of looking at the people without being disciplinary or sentimental. There are certain things Pissarro's peasant women are not asked to be: figures of sympathy, for one. Clark rightly stresses the rarity of this as an achievement. Unlike Manet's women, they are indifferent to the gaze.

Pissarro's way of seeing is, in effect, *anarchist*. Not in the sense of painting a doctrine, but rather in working, through the act of making art, to a certain understanding of the social world. Anarchism is the theory of a freedom compatible with order. "It is the anarchist temper—vengeful, self-doubting, and serene—out of which *Two Young Peasant Women* comes."[1] Pissarro arrived at it through the materiality of painting itself. In this canvas, the singular and universal are no longer in opposition. It's something Pissarro wrestled with in trying to absorb the influence of Georges

Seurat, in whose distinctive paintings all dots are equal, but not the same.

For Pissarro, paintings are a way of thinking, of investigating vision and rendering it thinkable. The danger, as in Seurat, is that "Every act of submission to one's experience could turn into a system." But one could struggle against it, by immersion in a practice, of painting or something else, to get at the singular structure of sensation as one experiences it. Art is not an Idea cast into a few signs. It is more a matter of a singular sensation calling objects into being in its own way, with its own "folding of parts into wholes."[2] The anarchist critic Félix Fénéon, on Pissarro: "Finally a master of forms, he bathes them forever in a translucent atmosphere, and immortalizes, by means of the benign and flexible hieraticism he has just invented, their exalted interweave."[3]

Pissarro matters for Clark because of a need to recover a version of the history of socialism independent of either the social democracy of the Second International (1889–1916) or the Leninism of the Third International (1919–43). The First International (1864–76), for all its squabbles, was one in which anarchism was alive and well. Socialists pay a high price for suppressing their anarchist side, first with the capitulation to militarism of the Second International, and then by the authoritarianism of the Third.[4] In Pissarro's time, the anarchists at least resisted militarism, and stood apart from the nascent bureaucratic tendencies of the organized labor movement. For Clark what matters is always the internal difference within revolutionary movements, between a people and its representatives. This was already the case with the sans-culottes and David, the proletarians and Delacroix.

Socialist culture and politics, of which anarchism was then a component, were at the height of their power at the end of the nineteenth century. But socialism "had still to devise a set of forms in which the developing nature of bourgeois society—the cultural order of capitalism as well as the economic and political ones—could be described and resisted. Anarchism possessed some of the elements needed. In closing against anarchism, socialism deprived itself of far more than fire. It deprived itself of an imagination adequate to the horror confronting it, and the worse to come."[5]

The anarchists were geographers of the peasant condition. Pissarro certainly responded to the anti-urban strand in anarchism, its refusal to be seduced by labor and the machine. It was possible to read *The Conquest of Bread* by Peter Kropotkin together with Marx, to imagine agriculture as another route to praxis. "But at least anarchists knew already in the 1890s that fighting the state meant thinking geographically and biologically."[6] They counted among their number Elisée Reclus, veteran of the Paris Commune, acute critic of what was becoming of Marxisant socialism, and the founder of social geography. This is the space toward which Clark's viewing of *Two Young Peasant Women* opens.

David's *The Death of Marat* is a canvas that contains in embryo the two tendencies in modern representation. The top half points toward art's recognition of the disenchantment of the sign. In place of its magic, art will turn inward, and succeed by representing its own failure to represent anything else. The bottom half is something else. Here art struggles, and fails, to make a claim to enact a truth that is at once political and aesthetic: Marat's blood on the traitor's letter. But is the failure of the bottom half aesthetic or political? Perhaps it is not art that fails in this instance, or not art alone. Perhaps the failure is in calling on art to represent a people *in absentia*.

One could see Delacroix, Courbet, Manet and Pissarro as attempts to make some kind of painting work in the place of the dead Marat. Delacroix tries to affirm the presence of the people, and fails. What Courbet bequeaths to Manet is the possibility of a realism that finds the gap between appearances and the ruling ideas of their time. What Pissarro offers is the possibility of picturing an actual site in which some other life could be sensed. In their successes and failures is a legacy from which to thieve in the unending struggle of peoples to present themselves to history rather than be represented by the state or the commodity. In short, from the détournement of these formative moments of the nascent spectacle can come resources for a counter-practice to the spectacle in its current form.

Or so, perhaps, was Clark's proposition in his earlier books, up until *The Painting of Modern Life* (1985). In his later writing, particularly in *Farewell to an Idea* (1999), it's the works that descend from the top half of *The Death of Marat* that interest him, by Paul Cezanne, Pablo Picasso and Jackson Pollock. This is where modern art becomes the site of a certain kind of melancholia, the place where the impossibility of the projects launched by the bare half of *The Death of Marat* is registered. This is an art that becomes enclosed within the spectacle, gesturing crazily to what it can't picture, what it can't sense, what it can't know. Modernism is the spectacle in negative.[7] But it is still spectacle.

Debord dates the modern spectacle from the 1920s: "the society of the spectacle continues to advance. It moves quickly, for in 1967 it had barely 40 years behind it; though it had used them to the full."[8] This periodization is no mystery. The key incidents are the Bolsheviks' suppression of the Kronstadt rebellion against the Soviet state (1921) and German Social Democrats' acquiescence to the suppression of the German revolution by the far right (1919). Debord: "The same historical moment, when Bolshevism triumphed for itself in Russia and social democracy fought victoriously for the old world, also marks the definitive inauguration of an order of things that lies at the core of the modern spectacle's rule: this was the moment when an image of the working class arose in radical opposition to the working class itself."[9]

What Debord calls the concentrated spectacle has its roots in David and Delacroix; the diffuse spectacle arises out of the contradictory materials Manet and Pissarro explore. The concentrated spectacle merged elements of both. But what separates the spectacle proper from its nascent state is the incorporation, not of an amorphous people, but of the working class, and not as individuals but via the representation of class power. The disintegrating spectacle resembles the nascent state. Organized labor gradually ceases even to be its own image.

Clark's excavation of the nascent spectacle may well provide resources for thinking about its disintegrating remnants, and what he describes as "a terrible, interminable contest over how best to debauch and eviscerate the last memory—the last trace—of political aspiration."[10] For Clark, as for Debord, there's not much to mourn about the collapse of the Soviet Union and its client states, of what Debord called the concentrated spectacle. Debord rather presciently anticipates that its eclipse casts its western counterpart adrift, that it would be lost without its nemesis. The presence of even a false alternative obliged the masters of the diffuse spectacle to think historically. With its victory, the diffuse spectacle integrated into itself the practices of state secrecy of its rival, to the point where it deceived even itself.

Clark opposes a deep attention to the image as a foil to both the absence of historical thought, and—paradoxically—as a challenge to the apparently image-drenched world of the disintegrating spectacle. "Sure, I count myself an enemy of the present regime of the image: not out of some nostalgic *logocentricity*, but because I see our image machine as flooding the world with words—with words (blurbs, jingles, catchphrases, ten thousand quick tickets to meaning) given just enough visual cladding."[11] Clark himself contributes to the critique of the disintegrating spectacle as one of the members of the group Retort, whose text *Afflicted Powers*, while by no means Situationist, nevertheless can be read as drawing in part upon Clark's earlier work.

Retort's signal date is 2003, when some eight hundred cities hosted anti-war demonstrations. "It was a world-historical moment. Never before had such masses of people assembled, against the wishes of parties and states, to attempt to stop a war before it began." What appeared is "a digital multitude, an image of refusal," but set to become just one more image, "another image-moment in a world of mirages."[12] In 2003 the anti-militarist strain of popular revolt reappeared—and again failed to stop the wars.

Where Clark values Pissarro's anarchist vision as a small token of a worker's movement that eschewed a vanguard, Retort extends this critique to the vanguard form of the anti-western jihadists. While it might tempt some on the left to welcome attacks on the empire, Retort is quick to show that the limits and dangers of this kind of vanguard are the same as the Jacobin one and its Leninist inheritors. The fatal flaw hinges on usurping the political and setting oneself up as its armed image.

As for the 9/11 bombers: "They were exponents of the idea (brilliant exponents, but this only reveals the idea's fundamental heartlessness) that control over the image is now the key to social power." Spectacular power is vulnerable to a raising of the stakes, to being beaten at its own game. Or so it appears: "But the present madness is singular: the dimension of spectacle has never before interfered so palpably, so insistently, with the business of keeping one's satrapies in order."[13]

The colonization of everyday life proceeds apace, an "invasion and sterilizing of so many unoccupied areas of human species-being." What is somewhat blandly referred to as *globalization* turns in on itself, "mapping and enclosing the hinterland of the social."[14] What the disintegrating spectacle leaves in its swirling wake is a world of loosely attached consumer subjects, and a weak form of citizenship which the ramping up of nationalist rhetoric does its best to mask. Weakly attached citizens-consumers still need to heed the call up, from time to time, to make *sacrifices* to preserve the state. Neither the popular forces nor even the state itself seems to manage any form of historical thought. The state comes to believe its own disinformation.

The Situationist project is often dismissed as if it were a claim to penetrate the veils of false consciousness and reveal the essential truth it masks. What Clark's dilation on the history of revolution and representation affords is a more subtle view, in no way reducible to such ideology critique. As Clark writes: "supposing we take Debord's writing as directed not to anathemizing representation in general (as everyone has it) but to proposing certain tests for truth and falsity in representation and, above all, for truth and falsity in representational *regimes*."[15]

A first test would hinge, as in his examples from David and Delacroix to Courbet, Manet and Pissarro, on the materiality of the encounter. A second test might turn on the social form of the relation within which an image is produced. The dilemma of modernity is the split in the results it achieves in these two tests. The avant-gardes of modern art end up channeled into a preoccupation with the materiality of the encounter, even while modern experience is rife with popular social movements that express desires that escape from the regime of representation and produce other kinds of relation. The spectacle emerges not least as the means of absorbing the expression of both desires back into the representation of the commodity. And yet the very persistence of the spectacle indicates that desire still exceeds it, and on at least these two fronts.

What matters is the remaking of counter-strategies that do not necessarily reveal the real behind the symbolic curtain, but rather attempt to produce a different kind of social practice for expressing the encounter of desire and necessity, outside of power as representation and desire as the commodity form. Clark: "Why should a regime of representation not be built on the principle that images are, or ought to be, transformable (as opposed to exchangeable)— meaning disposable through and through, and yet utterly material and contingent; sharable, imaginable, coming up constantly in their negativity, their non-identity, and for that reason promoted and dismantled at will?"[16] In short, why should détournement not be the practice by which the encounter with the world is discovered and produced?

For Debord, the spectacle emerges out of a key moment, when the Second and Third Internationals come to stand in the place of proletarian power, when the proletariat has to be killed in order to be represented, and represented in order to be killed. Clark extends the historical frame back to the nineteenth century, to show that the spectacle emerges out of not this one but a whole series of encounters between the expression of popular power and the power of representation. From there, perhaps it's a question of extending forward as well. It is not as if the social democratic and Stalinist forms of usurpation of popular power are the last.

One of the most salient points of departure for critical thought and action in the early twenty-first century may well be the account rendered by former Situationists of the failure of the popular movements of their time. This might at least forestall the curious nostalgia that animates contemporary leftism, which is so often so indiscriminately fascinated by the *red decade* in France from 1966 to 1976, by the various forms of neo-Maoist philosophy that linger in its wake, and by the Italian Autonomist movement, which arose with a vengeance around 1977 to take up the banner of waning militancy in France.

Situationists and Post-Situationists were consistently hostile to such currents, which might provide a certain useful counterweight to an ahistorical nostalgia for the remnants of such thought. But before turning to the seventies, there is another path that passes from the French Revolution, through its consequences, to the

Situationist International and beyond. If Clark restores to view the life of the image and an anarchist vision, then Raoul Vaneigem brings back to our attention the poetry of utopia, and of that moment in modernism for which Clark has so little sympathy: the Surrealists.

17 The Revolution of Everyday Life

Comrades whom you have offended make the bitterest enemies.
Baltasar Gracián

It was the start, if not of a beautiful friendship, then of a harmonious one, at least for a time. Raoul Vaneigem and Guy Debord met in 1960. Henri Lefebvre introduced them. They sealed their friendship Situationist style. Vaneigem: "My psychogeographic dérives with Guy Debord in Paris, Barcelona, Brussels, Beersel and Antwerp were exceptional moments, combining theoretical speculation, sentient intelligence, the critical analysis of beings and places, and the pleasure of cheerful drinking. Our homeports were pleasant bistros with a warm atmosphere; havens where one was oneself because one felt in the air something of the authentic life, however fragile and short lived. It was an identical mood that guided our wanderings through the streets, the lanes and the alleys, through the meanderings of a pleasure that our every step helped us gauge in terms of what it might take to expand and refine it just a little further…"[1]

Among other things, they discussed the books they would write. Debord was nothing if not encouraging. He wrote to Vaneigem in 1965 that his manuscript is "perhaps the first appearance, in book form, of the tone, the level of critique, of those revolutionaries called 'utopian', that is to say, of the basic propositions for the overthrow of the totality of society."[2] Vaneigem's book got into print a little sooner than Debord's *Society of the Spectacle*. Famous in English as *The Revolution of Everyday Life*, it was at first rejected by various publishers, including Gallimard. Then an article appeared in the press that claimed the Situationists were an influence on the Provo agitations then rocking Amsterdam. Raymond Queneau asked Vaneigem to resubmit it to Gallimard, and so it ended up with one of the most prestigious houses in France. If there was an author who anticipated the mood of May '68, it was Vaneigem with his "lucidity grounded in my own desires."[3]

In contrast to Clark's melancholia, Vaneigem thinks of May '68 as the revolution that never ended, a "genuine decanting, from the kind of revolution which revolutionaries make against themselves, of that permanent revolution which is destined to usher in the sovereignty of life."[4] Its significance lay less in the confrontation with the state than in the transformation of everyday life. It would not be a revolution within the economy, but a revolution against the economy. It would germinate in the pores of the old world and burst through the dead skin of politics. "One day, though, we'll have to admit that May 1968 marked a complete break with the majority of patriarchal values…"[5]

All of which was finally too much for Debord and some of the others in the Situationist International, who retained a rather more Jacobin idea of revolution. After an exchange of not particularly edifying diatribes, Vaneigem resigned in 1970: "How did what was exciting in the consciousness of a collective project manage to become a sense of unease at being in one another's company?" He wrote to his former comrades that he had no desire to see them again until after the revolution, much like Hölderlin's Hyperion, who would not trouble himself with friendships that are mere fragments of a new life yet to dawn.[6]

Vaneigem left the Situationist International, which dissolved two years later. He did not stop writing. Often deploying pseudonyms, over the ensuing decades he periodically issued manifestos restating a small number of themes. Some of his best books were on heresies, as they brought together his unique talents.[7] He studied Romance philology at the Free University of Brussels from 1952 to 1956. Then he taught at the École Normale in Nivelles, a small town in the Walloon region of Belgium, from 1956 to 1964, where a liaison with a student got him fired. He survived on editorial and hack writing jobs thereafter.

If Debord's debut book of 1967 was a détournement of Hegel, Marx and the Marxisant writings of the moment, then Vaneigem's reaches back to one of Marx's precursors, Charles Fourier.[8] Marx and Engels had an ambivalent relation to Fourier. Henri Lefebvre: "Like Fourier, Marx desired and projected the new life." But they kept him at a distance, grouping him with utopian writers with whom he had little in common. They admired him chiefly as a satirist. And yet "Marx owes much more to Fourier than is generally admitted."[9] In drawing up his list of theoretical topics to deal with without pedantry or delay, Vaneigem listed an homage to Fourier, something he never quite carried out, unless one considers his whole life to be such.[10]

Charles Fourier (1772–1837) and G. W. F. Hegel (1770–1831) were both writers shaped by the French Revolution. Hegel perhaps had more enduring impact, for while Fourier had a number of disciples, most were more like Judas than the Apostles. They betrayed his larger vision. He was somewhat selectively read as a socialist prophet. His French followers joined forces with the Jacobin left in 1848 and went down with them. A statue in bronze of Fourier by Émile Derré went up at the Place de Clichy in 1899, but his influence was decidedly on the wane by that time.

André Breton's *Ode to Charles Fourier* (1947) opens with the author reminiscing about the day ten years earlier when he noticed that someone had placed a flower at the foot of Fourier's statue. In 1941 the Germans melted down the statue and used the copper for the manufacture of munitions. Breton: "They've preferred the good old method." Gone is "the immortal pose of the thorn-extractor."[11]

Breton, like his contemporary Theodor Adorno, was exiled by the war in America. Unlike Adorno, Breton did not think the concentration camps obliged him to forswear the poetic, but rather to delve even deeper into it, via Fourier's "extreme tact in extravagance." Caught between the futility of art for its own sake and the utility of art to Stalinism, what remained of the Surrealist movement turned to Fourier in the bleak years of the war and the fragile promise of the peace that followed. Breton: "Fourier they've scoffed but one day they'll have to try your remedy whether they like it or not." Breton revived interest in Fourier not so much as a socialist prophet of associative labor, but as the poet of liberated desire.

In March '69, Pierre Lepetit, a teacher at the École des Beaux Arts, joined forces with some friends of the Situationists and restored Fourier's statue on the Place de Clichy, or at least a plaster replica.[12] René Riesel, René Viénet and Alice Becker-Ho witnessed the installation. Lepetit's statue bore the legend: "In homage to Charles Fourier from those who manned the barricades on the rue Gay-Lussac," the spot where the Situationists took their stand against the police in May '68.

The Fourier of liberated desire was somewhat at odds with the militant asceticism of the French postwar left. Roland Barthes mentions a study group on Fourier formed at the occupied Sorbonne in 1968 that was denounced as *bourgeois* by the militants. Fourier's revolution was always in a minor rather than a major key, a revolution of everyday life rather than of the state. Barthes: "Marxism and Fourierism are like two nets with meshes of different sizes."[13]

Fourier, with his weird fetishes and manic obsessions, is an easy prey for the new priests of psychoanalysis.[14] Barthes rescued him from travesty by drawing attention to Fourier as a writer. He famously characterizes Fourier as a *logothete,* an inventor of a language. He anatomizes Fourier's technique, which isolates itself from everyday language, articulates new rules for its assemblage and regulates the production of text, resulting in the fantastic repetition that characterizes his writing, which like that of the Marquis de Sade contains scene after scene with variations on the same game.

Raymond Queneau thought Fourier's calculus of the passions was more sophisticated than Hegel's dialectical logic. Walter Benjamin saw something machine-like in the meshings of his utopia. Italo Calvino imagined him, and not unkindly, as writing a vast computer program.[15] Roland Barthes' Fourier is the designer of wilder systems, which can never quite complete themselves and yet thrive on the very attempt. Time and again writers find ways to connect Fourier to their own passions. He has been successively a socialist prophet, a free-love utopian and then a writer's writer.

A useful corrective to these Fouriers is that of Fredric Jameson, who finds instead an ontological Fourier, in which a new cultivation of the passions (superstructure) organizes freely associating labor (infrastructure). Jameson reconnects the older, socialist reading of Fourier as prophet of free labor with the surrealist reading of Fourier on liberated desire, while still paying attention to writing as a formal procedure which structures the relation of one to the other as an open-ended practice of systematizing without a system.

As Jameson reads Fourier, that which can be desired is the very basis of social structure, and not just of social structure, but of nature itself. Fourier is the most vigorous resister to the thought that something of desire has to be forsaken, that the condition of life is the tragic one of sacrificing desire on the altar of the real. Fourier is no moralist. Jameson: "The ethical or moralizing habit is above all what resists the great thought of immanence, what hankers after the luxury of picking and choosing among existents..."[16]

Where Debord perfected a style of almost absolute negation, Vaneigem learns from Fourier how to affirm the world: "I first read the selected texts, published by the Editions Sociales, in the early 1960s. I then read the version of the *Nouveau monde amoureux* edited by Simone Debout. One of the things that made Fourier a genius was that he revolutionized the world and the perception we have of it without labeling himself as a revolutionary. He expressed no judgments made on a moral basis. He acknowledges a world of domination. He takes the society as it is—with its desires and hidden passions. He creates the conditions that would lead to their harmonization and refinement. Thus, what in a logic of civilization would be a frenetic race for success (upward social mobility) and behaviors focusing on producing exclusion, is replaced, in a logic of harmony, by ludic imitation."[17]

What Fourier and Vaneigem have in common is their refusal of necessity. Fourier: "The passions are proportionate to the destinies." Vaneigem: "Love is the science of pleasures that organizes destinies."[18] Fourierist writing connects the totality of nature to the events of everyday life via the ubiquity of the passions. While there is always something outside the system, Fourier keeps extending the system sideways to include it, even if, in the process, something else falls out of its reach. The passion that drives Fourier to systematize is always reaching toward what it excludes with fresh gestures of welcome. This is his capricious and capacious beauty.

The limit to the Jamesonian reading is that while it frees Fourier from partial readings via labor, desire or language, the Fourier who spent his days trying to change the world is absent. Vaneigem has the merit at least of attempting to synthesize Fourier on the association of labor, on free love, and as visionary poet, with the praxis of everyday life. Vaneigem: "If cybernetics was taken from its masters, it might be able to free human groups from labor and from social alienation. This was precisely the project of Charles Fourier in an age when utopia was still possible."[19] It is not that Fourier is like a machine or a computer. Quite the reverse: the machinic and the algorithmic could be fragments of a Fourierist playground ready for *self-assembly*.

For Vaneigem it is a question of how poetry can be an activist mode in the world: "Poetry is an act which engenders new realities."[20] Far more than the other Situationists, Vaneigem takes seriously the latent potentials of the Surrealist project: "Surrealism's failure was an honorable one."[21] Vaneigem's roots are more in the revolutionary Surrealism of his native Belgium than the Letterist movement Debord encountered in Paris. Via Vaneigem's détournement of the Surrealists and the Surrealists' of Fourier, a neglected strand for Situationist thought and action emerges. While Debord and Vaneigem were fellow travelers in their Situationist wanderings, in the end they belong to different camps. The nets through which they strained to understand—and change—modern history use meshes of different dimensions.

In the century after the French Revolution, and particularly after the emergence of the art market in the 1850s, the bourgeoisie tried to build a new transcendent myth out of the ruins of religion, an autonomous sphere of Art as redoubt from economy. The struggle for new mythological forms can be traced from David's *The Death of Marat* to Manet's *Olympia*. Vaneigem: "The 'spectacle' is all that remains of the myth that perished along with unitary society: an ideological organization whereby the actions of history upon individuals themselves seeking, whether in their own name or collectively, to act upon history, are reflected, corrupted and transformed into their opposite—into the autonomous life of the non-lived."[22] Where Clark traced the tactics of realist painters in and against the spectacle, Vaneigem records those of the romantic and Surrealist writers.

Three strategies confront the challenge of the bourgeois world's autonomous art. One was a radicalizing of aesthetics from within: Stendhal, Nerval, Baudelaire. A second was the struggle to abolish art as a separate world and realize it in everyday life: Hölderlin, Lautréamont. The third was a systematic critique of aesthetics from that world from which it separated: Fourier and Marx. Dada came closest to a synthesis of the available strategies, but the defeat of the German revolution of 1919 doomed it to failure, too. Dada offered an absolute but abstract break with bourgeois art and life. Surrealism, at its worst, was a kind of reformist version of Dada, obscuring its negativity, restoring partial forms of revolt.

The Surrealists struggled against, and eventually collapsed into, the autonomous sphere of art. Vaneigem: "Hence Surrealism became the spectacularization of everything in the cultural past that refused separations, sought transcendence, or struggled against ideologies and the organization of the spectacle."[23] And yet, not least through Breton's intelligence and discretion, "the Surrealists made a promise which they kept: to be the capricious consciousness of a time without consciousness."[24] Vaneigem appreciates Breton's expulsions of unworthy members, even as he slyly notes "his tendency to choose people's aperitifs for them."[25]

At their best, the Surrealists resisted both specialized art and politics, and hewed close to the discovery of the potentials of everyday life. While some capitulated to the art market, Benjamin Peret, Antonin Artaud, André Breton and Jacques Prévert waged a campaign against Surrealism as ideology. They extracted themselves from the allure of the Communist Party, whose deadly policies Peret saw firsthand as a volunteer in republican Spain. Vaneigem: "The foundering of this project under the helmsmanship of Stalinism and its attendant leftisms was to reduce Surrealism to a mere generator of what might be called the special effects of the human."[26]

Still, they pioneered a psychoanalysis freed from therapeutic pretensions. They remained guardians of dreams, even if they could not quite bring themselves to call for their realization in everyday life. From early on, René Crevel documented the persistence of non-life in the totality of human affairs: "All our life we circle around the suicide that legislators have condemned so that the earth might not be deserted."[27] Crevel took his own life in 1935. His suicide note said simply, "disgust." When they turned away from Stalinism, Breton and friends were left with nowhere to go except the rewriting of everyday alienation as cosmic mental theater, either on the epic scale of Artaud, or as Crevel's chamber pieces.

Vaneigem gives the Surrealists more credit than does Debord for what they preserved through the dark times of the late thirties. They kept alive fragments of a project of emancipation, the trace of a theory of passionate moments, moments of love, encounter, subjectivity. Yet they turned such moments into an absolute, an illusory totality. They fell for the cult of woman, and for a hierarchy of spiritual over carnal love. Breton in particular failed to live up to Fourier's lack of judgment about homosexuality, or so-called deviance in general.

The Surrealists constructed a new canon: the atheist priest Jean Meslier, the romantic extremist Comte de Lautréamont, the criminal poet Pierre-François Lacenaire, and the desiring machinery of Charles Fourier, among others. But they abandoned Dada's quest for collective poetry and total negation in favor of the specialized domains of avant-garde politics and art. Vaneigem: "The discovery of Fourier might perhaps have underpinned an overall recasting of the movement, but Breton would always prefer Fourier the visionary, Fourier the poet of analogy, to Fourier the theorist of a radically new society."[28] At war's end there was not much left of Surrealism as a radical project. "They were Don Quixotes tilting against housing projects."[29]

Vaneigem finds the backbone of the movement in its poets, not its artists, who were usually to the right and quickly absorbed into the art market. They offered, moreover, not particularly interesting détournements of previous modernist advances: Joan Miró redid Paul Klee; Max Ernst redid Giorgio De Chirico. Even the best Surrealist writing on the everyday—Michel Leiris—descended into a sort of queer empiricism.[30] "Never opting firmly either for a poetry made by all or for the venality of the ruling system, Surrealism took something of both and produced an impoverished cultural hodgepodge."[31] One suspects Clark would not entirely disagree.

The Situationist program was a rectification of the Surrealist one. The poetry of everyday life had to be brought in contact with the critique of political economy, where each extended the other. The Situationists wanted to abolish both the *separation* of labor from desire and the *spectacle* in which all that could be desired returned in the form of mere images of commodities. To spectacle and separation, Vaneigem offered a third object of critique: *sacrifice*. If Debord's critique was of political economy in the era of the reign of the image, then Vaneigem's was a critique of *general economy*—of mythical as well as real exchanges—in the era of a generalized political economy. Sacrifice is a key transaction between the finite and infinite realms.

Fourier is quite uncompromising about the new myths of the bourgeois order, not least its emerging political economy: "According to this science all industries are useful as long as they create legions of starving men who sell themselves at bargain prices to conquerors and shop bosses."[32] Its one advance was to reverse the ban on luxury and wealth propagated by the moralists. "It is true that the economists permit us to love wealth, but they don't make us wealthy."[33]

The sacrifice that is labor is not rewarded with anything equivalent to it, as Marx might say, but moreover, it can never be. On the contrary: "They encourage us to submit passively to civilization, with its system of incoherent and loathsome work."[34] Work which, more often than not, does not make wealth for the worker, and sometimes not even for the boss: "There are over a hundred different kinds of bankruptcy: such is the perfection of reason under modern philosophy."[35]

The infirmity that is work has the deformity of leisure for company: Fourier: "And so on Sunday they go to cafes and places of amusement to enjoy a few moments of the sort of carefreeness that is vainly sought by so many rich men who are themselves pursued by anxiety."[36] The worker seeks the playful idleness of the weekend bourgeois, but cannot really afford it. The bourgeois can afford it, but is hardly in a playful mood with the hundred kinds of bankruptcy buzzing around his head. Such might be Fourier's reading of the faces of Manet's café-concert scenes. The workers sacrifice their bodies; the bourgeois their souls. Or so it may at first appear in the bourgeois theology of labor.

To everything there is a place and to everything there is a time under heaven. There is a time and a place to be born, to die; to build, to destroy; to weep, to laugh; to get, to lose; to give, to take; to buy, to sell; to work, to rest—and to sacrifice. Each is particular and separate, fragmenting time and space into disparate, disconnected moments. There is a time and a place for every particular thing. But what of *everything* in the sense of the totality, the unity of time and space—what is the time and place for that? Paradoxically, the totality too has its separate time and space, that of the sacred. The sacred is a separate time and space with the odd quality of being that of the whole. It is the separate moment for what is not separate. The sacred is the place and time for a very particular kind of sacrifice, for the giving up of something of this world of particular things to the world of the totality, imagined as that which is universal and eternal. If once the place of the sacred was the church, now it was the café, or the art Salon.

For the errant Surrealists Michel Leiris and Georges Bataille, the sacred persists as a problem for the modern world, which has lost its contact with this other realm of totality and no longer knows how to offer itself. For Vaneigem, it's more a question of discovering what kinds of gift could be freely given that might break with the whole logic of sacrifice. "The urge to play is incompatible with self sacrifice," and once the rules of the game become the rites of a ritual, it becomes an offering in exchange for something else.[37] Vaneigem extends the Marxist critique of exchange from the secular to the spiritual economy.

For Marx, an exchange between owners and non-owners of property cannot be an equal exchange. With nothing to exchange but labor power, the non-owner of property does not get the full value of labor returned in the form of wages. For Vaneigem, the labor of the non-owner is also a sacrifice, a real giving up of time, effort, not to mention a renunciation of desires. In exchange for this material sacrifice, the owners of property offer imaginary ones. "To the sacrifice of the nonowner … the owner replies by appearing to sacrifice his nature as owner and exploiter; he excludes himself mythically, he puts himself at the service of everyone and of myth."[38]

Fourier had a rather complicated picture of the succession of historical stages. Vaneigem boils it down to what one might call three modes of sacrifice: ancient slavery, medieval feudalism and modern capitalism. Rather than modes of production, they are perhaps modes of destruction, general economies of the immolation of human happiness. Vaneigem is not interested in the social product; he is interested in what is destroyed in its making. He is not interested in the objects extruding from an economy; he is interested in the subjective potential sacrificed to it. His three modes differ in how the sacrifice of free agency is extracted.

In the slave mode of sacrifice, the labor of the non-owner has in the last resort to be compelled by force. The slave sacrifices everything and the owner nothing. In the face of slave revolts, Christianity proffered an ingenious solution that would be crucial to the feudal mode of sacrifice. It created a reason for the non-owner to offer a voluntary sacrifice. The sacrifice of particular labors and desires in the temporal world could be returned in the form of eternal salvation. But wait! There's more! As if that offer wasn't enough, Christianity throws in a free set of steak knives: at the end of times the just will be resurrected and the golden age return. The non-owner will be the closest to God—eventually.

For the moment, however, the non-owner is furthest from God, at the bottom of a hierarchy, underneath the priests and overseers, who in turn are underneath the lords and cardinals, who in turn are underneath the kings and popes. The non-owner makes a modest, particular sacrifice of time and effort. The owner—whether of temporal or spiritual power—makes a symbolic sacrifice to the totality itself. The non-owner is given over to the particular task; the owner is given over to that which orders all particular labors. We all have to make sacrifices, but some sacrifices are more equal than others.

One of the signs of the declension from critical theory to hypocritical theory is the repudiation of Marx's atheism and a credulous respect for all things biblical. Some even go so far as to venerate Saint Paul! Marx, the old mole, who wrote his dissertation on Epicurus and Democritus, would probably grumble and quake from the underworld if it existed. Vaneigem too takes his distance from atheism: "Without God, suffering became 'natural', inherent in human nature, it would be overcome, but only after more suffering..."[39] But he at least charts a path through those heresies of the ancient and feudal world that refused or resisted the sacrifices that the Christian church institutionalized.

Heresies can have quite different relations to sacrifice. One strand to heresy exposes the false sacrifices of the non-owner, but calls in their place for real ones. This is the path that extends from the religious ascetics to the revolutionary militants. Or, heresies can refuse the language of sacrifice altogether. As Vaneigem shows in his studies of heresy, this is the path of Simon of Samaria in the ancient world and of the Movement of the Free Spirit in the feudal world. It is also the path of Fourier: "Duty is man's creation; attraction comes from God."[40] He too is a heretic rather than an atheist.

The Surrealists wavered between modernizing sacrifice and abandoning it. Crevel: "The man who stutters with pleasure will soon seek divine laws, laws greater than those adopted for the petty economy of this expectant globe."[41] Leiris: "Asceticism in fornication, unselfishness in possession, sacrifice in pleasure, these were also the ideals whose antinomian appearance exalted me."[42] Vaneigem continues Crevel in this rather than Leiris.

Fourier and Vaneigem point out a path between the return to the clutches of the church on the one hand and an atheism that collapses into the bourgeois dogmas of sacrificial labor on the other. Vaneigem: "From the ruins of heaven, man fell into the ruins of his own world."[43] Fourier and Vaneigem treat atheism as a failed project, one that did not break the spell of sacrifice, but rather detached sacrifice from the spiritual and attached it to the profane realm. Labor becomes a universal sacrifice to what is supposedly the common wealth, but where the non-owner makes the concrete sacrifice of labor and the owner makes an imaginary sacrifice to the totality of the economy.

One of the manifestations of this imaginary sacrifice is patronage, whether of the church or of art. One of the virtues of Fourier is that he was not arrested at the intermediate stage where art replaced religion as the separate sacred space for sacrifice to the totality. Fourier intuits that the economy itself becomes the sacred whole. In Vaneigem's reading, Fourier is a kind of secular heresy against this "mercantile totalitarianism."[44] Fourier: "We must love work say our sages. Well! How can we? What is loveable about work in civilization? For nine-tenths of all men work procures nothing but profitless boredom."[45] Fourier refuses the "martyrdom of attraction." Desire is not to be sacrificed to work any more than it was to God, and Art is no more compensation than faith. As Vaneigem intuits, Fourier's critique is a powerful one, whose uses if anything multiply in our mercantile times.

18 Détournement as Utopia

Far better the jobs we don't grow bored with, where variety combines with salience and refreshes our taste.

Baltasar Gracián

Perhaps it was because Fourier's is a kind of self-taught *low theory* that he was not tempted into the compensatory realm of art or literature or philosophy, but rather directly attacked the relation of aesthetic experience of everyday life to the totality of nature. Fourier came from the provincial center of Besançon, a town dominated by the church, the army and local government. He was raised in the somewhat Balzacian world of a prosperous merchant family that expected him to take his place in the business. He had as good an education as a small town could offer, and won school prizes for everything (except obedience). His pious mother feared too much education might make him another Luther or Voltaire, and she was not entirely wrong. Fourier became a class traitor. He took seriously that to which his class paid lip service, he inverted its cherished beliefs, and he betrayed its venal secrets. He claimed that at the age of nine he swore an oath against trade just as Hannibal swore to destroy Rome.

If Besançon was Fourier's education in the ways of the merchant class, Lyon introduced him to late-eighteenth-century class conflict. The silk industry was in decline, sharpening the struggles between the weavers and the silk merchants. He was in Lyon when the French Revolution came. For a brief moment Fourier shared in its illusions: liberty, equality and fraternity and all that. The revolution destroyed his attempt to set himself up in business. His cotton bales were requisitioned and used as barricades. Drafted by counter-revolutionary forces, he nearly lost his life in the defense of Lyon. He barely managed to escape revolutionary justice. Conscripted again, this time he soldiered for the other side.

The revolution he experienced wasn't glorious. All he saw was speculation and graft, hunger and death, boredom and arbitrary justice. The revolution may have been made in the name of the people, it may even have mobilized the people, but in the end it was business as usual. Vaneigem: "All struggles for freedom obey a law of business expansion."[1] Whatever sacred mysteries are imputed to the revolution as *event* by latter-day pseudo-Jacobins, this is its quotidian consequence.

Situationists and bourgeois liberals are in uncommon agreement that the red terror is a refutation of Leninism. Only Vaneigem is consistent in seeing the Jacobin terror as a refutation of the bourgeois philosophers as well. This is his fidelity to Fourier, or more properly speaking his *solidarity* with him. Bourgeois thought is convicted by the violence it refuses even to acknowledge as its own. Fourier: "Agitators promise to make people happy, rich and idle; but once they have gained power, they oppress the multitude and reduce it to a more complete state of servitude in order to consolidate their own position as idlers or as managers of those who work."[2] The new Sparta had, like the old one, turned out to be a slave state. What grows out of the barrel of a gun, besides corpses, is investment opportunities.

Fourier was hardly alone in this repugnance, of course, but unlike so many writers of his generation he did not take refuge in the past. In refusing to bow down at the altar of labor subordinated to capital, he did not return to the altar under the tortured Jesus. These are the same thing, modes of sacrifice, and sacrifice itself is the thing to repudiate. Fourier: "If they wanted to attack the Catholic religion, they should have opposed it by one which provided contrary excesses: it sanctifies hardship, so they should have sanctified sensual pleasure."[3] His was a heresy that broke with the imperative to sacrifice of both Christian and bourgeois thought, and he points to the way out of many of the aporias the Surrealists found themselves in by attempting to modernize sacrifice rather than abolish it.

Bourgeois liberalism at its most mindless insists that utopias lead to bloody revolutions, and of course they have this, as usual, completely backwards. It was the miserable experience of the bourgeois revolution that led to Fourier's utopia. The simultaneous devaluing of all values, old and new, created the opening for a recasting of the cosmos out of whole cloth. Not the least of Fourier's cunning is his ability to find value in the damaged intellectual goods left from the chaos of revolution. His writings are an extraordinarily skillful détournement of exactly this intellectual inheritance. Fourier's thought proceeds by way of what Vaneigem, following Bertolt Brecht, calls a reversal of perspective.[4] In place of reasons of faith and faith in reason, Fourier based his doctrine on the passions.

As much as he denounced Rousseau, Fourier took freely from him, but mostly from *Émile*, *The Confessions* and *New Heloise*. Like Lautréamont after him, he read Buffon and other naturalists, but his roots were more in the neoclassical seventeenth century, in Molière and La Fontaine. These were his pawns in a game against logics of sacrifice, both new and old. Vaneigem: "détournement is an all-embracing reinsertion of things into play. It is the act whereby play grasps and reunites beings and things hitherto frozen solid in a hierarchy of fragments."[5] Vaneigem sets some of the pieces Fourier deployed in motion again against the sacrificial order of the late twentieth century. Perhaps confronting the even more terrible and total logic of sacrifice that persists in this next millennia will take a détournement that draws from them both.

In the early twenty-first century the idea gained force that pretty much everything can be sacrificed to the disintegrating spectacle, from which nothing much should be expected in return. Far from the care and management of the *biopower* of its subject populations, the state's role is rather to sacrifice the health and education of present and future populations by cutting taxes on finance capital and freeing the latter for yet more speculative investments, from which not much should be expected beyond a few menial jobs. Nor should the state invest in infrastructure for future industrial expansion. No Haussmanns are to re-engineer American cities to absorb surplus labor and capital and build platforms for new forms of accumulation. Even the ground under American feet could be sacrificed to powerful blasts of chemical-infused water to extract natural gas with few safeguards. The failure of past sacrifices to the spectacle calls forth a cargo cult of unprecedented dimensions, in which everything left is to be fed to the maw of Moloch, simply because it is unimaginable that there could be any other course of action but to offer still more gifts to appease these bored Gods. Such is the end game of all civilizations, as Fourier well knew.

Eric Santner: "Why does the beast need to be starved? Why does the 'flesh' of the body politic need to be reduced, reduced, reduced? The answer we hear over and over again is: for the sake of the 'Job Creators.' The one Creator God has effectively been dispersed into a pantheon of new idols, those to whom we must all sacrifice so that they may show favor on us and create new worlds of economic possibility. Job creation has become the new form of grace or gratuitousness otherwise reserved for divinity. Our duty is to make sacrifices and above all to be vigilant about not calling forth the wrath of the Job Creators lest they abandon us and elect others as their chosen people (other nations who make bigger and better sacrifices). The old culture wars concerning hot-button social issues have simply assumed new guise. Tax increases have come to be regarded as a sort of job abortion, the killing of unborn economic life."[6]

What would it take to imagine a life free from such sacrifice? Fourier's writing is intensely visual. His imaginal architecture, the phalanstery, has all the symmetry and serene poise of a Nicolas Poussin landscape, and yet also the fantastical qualities of a Claude Lorrain.[7] The Harmonians who occupy these spaces seem to relish their time like the gallant youth of Antoine Watteau. A visit to Paris in 1789 gave Fourier tangible models for the architecture of his new world, not least the fairy palace that is the Palais Royale and the covered galleries of the Louvre. Fourier's tastes tended toward the classical, to the dominance of form over movement.

Fourier took a measuring stick with him when he wandered the streets, charting urban improvement plans of mathematical proportion. According to Vaneigem, he and Debord took ether instead, for more measureless encounters with a labile space and time. Vaneigem dissolves Fourierist order into romantic arabesques. Perhaps a more contemporary détournement of both Fourier and Vaneigem might revisit the question of form and dynamics, paying more attention to the play of Fourier's systematic writings, but without dissolving that play into Vaneigemesque gestures. Fourier is a contemporary of the romanticism that effloresced in Germany and England, but is not quite of it. Perhaps this very untimeliness points toward new approaches to the problem of form.

Barthes emphasizes the solitary character of Fourier's writing, but this is misleading. In the years in which he consolidated his ideas Fourier was far from a loner. He seems to have had both lasting friendships and passing affairs. Later, he would discover the company of lesbians, which allowed him to have enduring platonic relationships with women. At work, he donned the mask of the reliable, punctual businessman. He was no nay-saying Bartleby; he was a model employee.[8] He was easily bored, so the life of a commercial traveler suited him well. Travel informed his passion for geography, and he loved to meet new people, learn their stories, share the intimacies of the road, and move on. From his travels he knew first hand the real poverty of Europe. Unlike many of the writers of his time, his work was based on conversations with people from many occupations and regions. His utopia is informed by an ethnography.

Fourier had a gift for confidences. He admits his desire to Désirée Veret, a young feminist, but acknowledges that the attentions of an old man could be of no interest to her. In exchange for such frankness, she writes of her experiences to him. Of sex with the English, she notes: "They make love like they make machines."[9] It is not hard to imagine Fourier alone in his garret, scribbling his sexual utopias with a hard-on in his hand. One wonders if there are stains on the manuscript pages. And yet there is a certain understanding of the desires of others that could only come from fieldwork, or perhaps participant observation.

Fourier's world is a pantheist universe of plural passions. If all cosmologies are analogical, then his is built on a harmony that is at once planetary, mathematical and musical. By denying divine providence, the Enlightenment sent civilization on a course of political revolution that did not result in a harmony below to match the—now abolished—heaven above. Vaneigem: "God has been abolished but the pillars which supported him still rise towards an empty sky."[10] From what he knew of the everyday life of desire, Fourier reconstructs the fabric of the cosmic order.

Fourier takes Newton's celestial mechanics to be the only major scientific discovery, and boldly offers to fill in what it lacks. In the absence of a science of energy, growth and life, he adds to Newton a poetics of that which the science of his time was incapable of systematically thinking.[11] For Fourier the planets themselves are animate. Like humans, they have twelve passions, and communicate with twelve aromas. Planets, like humans, can have one or more dominant passions. Some are monogynes (one dominant passion), some are digynes (two dominant passions), and so on. The universe is dynamic and alive. There is "copulation between the planets."[12] Unlike humans (or perhaps not so unlike), planets each have a male north pole and a female south pole. They are androgynous and bisexual. Fourier's whole universe is queer.

The universe is bound together by planetary passions, and so too could be the earth, if humans did not play so crudely on the twelve-tone system of planetary harmony. "The creatures of various degrees of the polyversal keyboard all have use of the twelve radical passions, but they differ in their exercise of them."[13] Like the planets, the being of humans is relational rather than atomistic, each swings in the gravity of the others. The universal gravity of social life is not reason but the twelve passions. Five of the passions are derived from the senses: sight, sound, touch, taste and smell. Then there are four spiritual passions: ambition, friendship, love and family. The penultimate passions are social ones: the composite, the cabalist and the butterfly.

The composite passion is a kind of vertical axis and the cabalist a horizontal one. The composite passion connects enthusiasms of the most material kind to more rarified sensations, and vice versa. Food, for example, becomes the vehicle for Fourierist *gastrosophy*, an elaborate tending to both sensation and meaning. The cabalist passion is horizontal and connective. Jameson: "Nothing is more remarkable, among the multitudinous slogans this Utopia floats from its banner-head, than this positioning of the conspiratorial schemer as the heroic center of social construction itself; nothing better illustrates the sublime indifference of Fourier to conventional moral judgments (and not only the sexual ones)."[14]

Politics in the cabalistic sense is usually at best a necessary evil for radical thought, something to be endured in order to articulate one demand to another. Or, politics is doubled with a fantasy category of "the political" and recoded as a sort of spiritual Jacobinism of the moment of pure revolt. Fourier affirms the game of politics as a pleasure in its own right, and one that cuts across the liberal distinction between public and private realms.

The butterfly passion seeks variety. Fourier is particularly attentive to the question of boredom. Both bourgeois and radical thought tends to privilege the spectacle of the monogyne who pursues one mania relentlessly, writing book after book, for example. Fourier's world has room for varying and combining the passions. In one of their rare statements on the Communist good life, Marx and Engels draw on Fourier's account of the butterfly passion in action. Why not go fishing in the morning, write philosophy 'til dusk, and party 'til midnight?

Unityism, or harmony, is not so much a thirteenth passion as the sum and totality of them all. It is "unlimited philanthropy." God's method is the association of the passions. Morality, whether of the Christian or Enlightenment kind, is a futile struggle against the passions. "It is erroneous to believe that nature is sparing of talent; she is prodigal beyond all our desires and needs."[15] Fourier's divine order calls for no sacrifices, real or imagined. The coordination of the passions unleashes natural abundance.

The *equality of man* is the most enduring bit of bric-a-brac to descend from the revolutionary period. Becker-Ho: "In the process of its formation as a social class, an ideology of equality between men was of great use to the bourgeoisie. Nevertheless, it is the law of the strongest that prevails everywhere: by force of arms, money, sex, as well as intelligence. Only the dangerous classes dare proclaim it loud and clear though: for where there is in fact no equality or justice among men, then by the same token there can be none between the sexes."[16] As we shall see later, Becker-Ho steps outside of bourgeois legality, to find leverage against it in its margins. Fourier détourned this tenet of bourgeois thought in the most direct manner. He simply reversed it.

Fourier's social universe is based on difference rather than equality. He considers bourgeois philosophers to be the utopians, imagining they can wish away the differences among the passions.

Fourier is completely at odds with the neo-Jacobin thinking of Alain Badiou or Jacques Rancière, for whom equality is a founding political principle. Fourier's thought is anchored to a quite opposite idea: that of the series. Everything in the natural and the social world comes in a series. A series of horticulturalists, for example, growers of tulips, of roses, of chrysanthemums, bound together by affinity, but also by rivalry and contrast. Social organization is not premised on a universalizing abstraction, but rather on enumerating and linking particular practices.

The bourgeois philosophers promise the wealth of nations, but not their happiness. Civilization proceeds by political revolution, but seems still to make very slow progress. Take the centuries it took to abolish slavery. "Like a sloth, civilization moves forward with an inconceivable sluggishness through political storms and revolutions. The new social theories put forward by each generation only serve, like brambles, to draw blood from the people who seize upon them."[17] Social theory either denies the passions or, in acknowledging them, seeks only to contain them.

While Fourier did not believe in equality, he believed in the abolition of unnecessary suffering and poverty. His *phalanstery* offered not only a right to agreeable work and sustenance for all, it also offered a certain minimum of sensual gratification: "society should grant a minimum of satisfaction to the two senses of taste and touch." Or in other words, nobody should go without food and sex.

"While the sense of taste goes into open rebellion, the sense of touch protests silently. But if the ravages it causes are less obvious, they are no less real."[18] The source of revolution is hunger; the source of everyday discontent is sensual hunger. The satisfaction of these basic needs is only a first step. His project for the development of a life beyond so-called civilization has three stages: First, material plenty for all, and the enrichment of the five senses. Second, liberty for the four group passions. And finally, justice for the passions of the series. Relationships should be the major preoccupation of life.

Fourier is famously acute in his critique of the bourgeois family, which he sees as essentially a business. "Prohibition and contraband are inseparable in love, as in merchandise." The bourgeois family leads not to duplicity but to *quaduplicity*, where husband and wife deceive not only each other but also their respective lovers. That the married couple consider each other's passions their property is only the beginning of the family's perversity. The property relation then extends as well to the children. What one might call the family spectacle arises from its foundations in a property relation, not least that of parents over children: "Poor in pleasure, they want to be rich in illusion. They claim for themselves rights of property upon the affections of the weakest."[19]

For Clark, utopia is "the invention of early modern civil servants."[20] But what he finds in Pissarro, Vaneigem finds in Fourier: that passion and order are not opposed. If civilization has discontents, then so much the worse for civilization. Fourier: "All repressed passion produces its counter-passion."[21] De Sade is the ultimate product of manifold repressions. But it is not a question of a simple liberation from repression into freedom. Of the four spiritual passions (ambition and friendship, love and family) civilization puts too much stress on the fourth alone as the pillar of order. Putting an end to civilization means a refinement of the associative potentials of the other passions. From there, the passions of the series can also lead to further enhancements of being.

The passions of the series were known to so-called primitive society, but not to civilization. "This is the secret of lost happiness that must be recovered."[22] The three social passions, the composite, the cabalist and the butterfly, produce only libertines and eccentrics in this world, not to mention Situationists. The twelve passions are common to all, but they are not equally present in all. Fourierist social organization is a geometry based on a probability. Given a unit of social life big enough to have all the types represented, mutuality can then be composed out of them.

Fourier's followers tended to concentrate on this as a geometry of labor, where each could pursue their various passions and yet the sum that resulted would be a prosperous and productive one. The disintegrating spectacle has no interest in labor. Labor is in exile, behind Chinese walls, real or imagined. The Fourier one might counterpose to it is perhaps the Fourier of the passions. This Fourier frees the passions from their sacrificial relation to the commodity form. What Vaneigem takes from Fourier, and what in the age of the disintegrating spectacle one might take from both, is a systematic reversal of perspective, a heretical détournement of spectacular commonplaces, which imagines both labor and everyday life outside the logic of sacrifice, even of Lenin-worshiping neo-Jacobin kinds.

19 Charles Fourier's Queer Theory

To turn sorrows into pleasures is to know how to live.
Baltasar Gracián

If most civilized philosophies are just castles in the air, then why do they not at least have orgies going on inside them? There are not a few pedants who prostrate themselves before this or that philosopher's airy erection, who admire its *rigor*, who have slaved so hard to peer into its many rooms that they cannot but defend its *stature*, even if it means they have to explain away said castle's torture gardens. Fourier too may be a castle in the air, but he takes pains to equip his with parade grounds and covered walkways. He even keeps the noisy spaces for kids away from the quiet ones for grown ups. Violence, for Fourier, is a failure of *design*, of both built space and social relations.

Rural life with his nieces in Talissieu at first seemed designed to please Fourier, but in the end proved to be somewhat trying. It is hard to know how much of a good time his nieces were really having with the dashing young officers who came so often to call. Fourier claimed to have stumbled upon a young officer with a hand up one young lady's skirt while his other niece watched them. Fourier felt they should be free to fuck whomsoever they wanted, but their hypocrisy galled him. When he confronted them they feigned to be offended by the mere suggestion of anything improper. He also suspected the young officers were not as gallant as they claimed and would abandon the young women when they proved inconvenient.

In any case, it all went badly in the end. These circumstances did inform the writing of what may well be Fourier's impossible masterpiece, the *New Amorous World*. It would not see the light of day until 1967. Perhaps it can be read then as a sort of belated Situationist classic. Vaneigem: "I was so fascinated by it that I re-printed some fragments of it (with an introduction) while at Payot's."[1] Those efforts not withstanding, it is still a little-known queer theory classic.

Fourier's fragrant mix of elaborate social imagination and porn was something of an embarrassment to his later followers. It was not without precedent, however. Fourier sets his new sexual order on Cnidus (or Knidos), the Greek city famous for Praxiteles' statue of Aphrodite removing her clothes. It was where Newton discovered a fine statue of Demeter, and also the setting for a work by Montesquieu on chaste and sincere love. The courtly love tradition had imagined ideal household constitutions for the romantic life. Something like it can be found also in Rabelais. Both Restif de la Bretonne and the Marquis de Sade imagined universes arranged around sexual pleasure and, like Freud after them, saw sexual passion as the antithesis of the social.[2] What is distinctive about Fourier is that he imagines the social as entirely composed out of the passions. He refused the erotic Jacobinism of universal monogamy (still to be found in Badiou, for instance). His passionate social order is not one of a universal but singular love, but rather one of the diversity and difference of the passions.

Vaneigem: "Sensual intelligence will bring about the classless society."[3] This is a Fourierist sentiment. At heart Fourier wants to be an erotic umpire of passionate games, not a political economist. His most beautiful writings, on the *New Amorous World*, are a unique kind of philosophy of the orgy, or systems-theory porn. As a pornographer Fourier is interested in the tableaux, the staging, the ritual, rather than the actual fucking.

The world of Harmony satisfies a sexual minimum for all. Every monogyne can get his or her rocks off. Fourier is no egalitarian. He is barely interested in describing such paltry pleasures. It's the baroque world of the omnigynes that attract him, with their polymorphous play on the whole twelve passions. Fourier considered himself an omnigyne, and hence his porn had to arouse all twelve of the passions, not just the passion for "touch-rut."

Philosophy is too concerned with ambitious or major politics, and not enough with amorous or minor politics. If Marx plumbs the limits of political philosophy in political economy, Fourier finds it in an amorous economy, but one where amour is neither private nor at odds with the world. Vaneigem attempts a curious synthesis of these two critical filters, but one where the Fourierist mesh is the finer. In modern civilization, "the space-time of private life was harmonized in the space-time of myth. Fourier's harmony responds to this perverted harmony. As soon as myth no longer encompasses the individual and the partial in a totality dominated by the sacred, each fragment sets itself up as a totality ... In the dissociated space-time that constitutes private life—made absolute in the form of abstract freedom, the freedom of the spectacle—consolidates by its very dissociation the spatial absolute of private life, its isolation, its constriction."[4] In place of which Fourier imagines a new harmonization of desire and the social, and a new built form, the phalanstery, in which public and private are no longer spatially separated and no longer need a phantasmal mediation via the spectacle.

Why is love the passion the philosophers want to admit the fewest possible bonds, when one is supposed to love one's brother, be a citizen of the world, and so on? *Sexual politics* means something quite specific in Fourier's world. There's hardly any point in politics in its civilized senses. In a decentralized world of plenty, there's nothing to fight over, no point to empire. Capital, labor and talent cooperate rather than struggle against each other. Politics is the domain of the cabalist passion, of intrigues and factions, rivalry and collaboration, but the stakes are largely symbolic. Some are richer than others in Harmony, but here social stratification is not a mere mask for class. The real contest is for prestige and renown.[5] Sexual politics is a game of sensual largesse. Its currency is attraction, but the point of the game is not to hoard and covet, but to dispense and distribute the favors of the favored.

The *quadrille* is a dance that requires a refined coordination of the dancers. Fourier imagines an erotic quadrille of sixteen persons. For this quadrille "orgies are prepared by the minister and female pontiff who arrange delightful reunions and cumulative sympathies that heighten each other."[6] Pleasures accumulate and ramify in memory, ours and others. It is an economy of reputation, where liaisons are structured to produce harmonious results. The quadrille heightens all the particular passions through their combination, added to which is the pleasure of unityism, which heightens all the other passions as well.

Rather than random encounters, the new amorous world is one of "harmonic polygamy."[7] Fourier: "The result is very brilliant orgies that furnish charming illusions and precious and durable souvenirs."[8] Participation is not a sacrifice, but a heightening of pleasure. As in the quadrille as a dance, each adjusts to each other, pleasures the other, only some will distinguish themselves more than others. "All men and women who have worn a cross in the court of love advance in steps proportionate to the number of foci they have formed."[9] Its perfection would be the omnigyne quadrille, composed of thirty-two persons whose distribution of passions is the same as the thirty-two planets.

Fourier is a little coy about revealing how the quadrille really works to readers shackled by civilized morality. It's clear that what he calls pederasty and lesbianism are included as expressions of the passions. But perhaps what's more interesting is that he understands difference in desires not so much along the straight/curious/gay continuum, as within a more complicated space of possibilities. It's more about which, and how many, of the passions are dominant.

For instance, a pentagyne straight woman, who has five dominant passions, might require encounters with five monogyne men, each of which corresponds in his dominant passion to one of hers. Of course monogynes rank low in the scale of erotic reputation in the quadrilles. The omnigynes, fully alive to all twelve of the passions, are most likely the ones in demand, acquiring reputation, and eventually playing the roles of conductors of the dance. Fourier upends the moral judgments of civilization. In the erotic quadrille, the sluts rule.

Civilization treats sexual space as a hierarchy of values, with straight monogamy at the top and random fucks at the bottom. The realm of sanctioned sexual practice is a hot topic, but it is really just about where to draw the line. Serial monogamy might be okay for some, a period of random dating among the young before they *settle down*, perhaps. Maybe it's okay for people to have sex outside marriage once the kids are out of the house. Maybe one incident of *cheating* can be forgiven, but not if it's a habit.[10] Maybe gay people can be allowed in the hierarchy of sanctioned sex if they form monogamous relationships like everyone else. And so on. In civilization, the realm of the acceptable distinguishes itself from two things. At one end is the prude, who denies and represses sexuality. At the other end is the slut. If virginity is not as prized by the civilized as it once was, fucking around is still not acceptable, particularly for women. It's random, infectious, a threat to civilized order.

Fourier dispenses with this whole stigmatizing of the space of sexual possibilities. There are no straight-gay, prude-slut or order-random axes to his sexual universe. There are only the twelve passions, and variability as to which and how many of the passions are active. Harmony is the game of combining the passions. It's true that his world is hierarchical, and it is tempting to say that the sluts are on top, but that isn't quite it. Omnigynes are favored in Harmonian sexual politics, but all sexuality is played out in the form of elaborate games. What's valued is the richness of passionate attraction, and the philanthropy with which talent is dispensed.

The most extraordinary sentences, a porn of the relation, not of the act, follow from this, viz.: "The two foci first elect the four cardinal sub-foci of the quadrille; these are the four who are loved in title of favoritism and unityism. Then each one elects, from fourteen loved ones, seven that are pivotal in high scale and seven in low scale. Next are elected four ambiguous in low scale; the surplus from the twelve major and the twelve minor keys, of which seven are pivotal in each octave."[11] This is what is truly remarkable about Fourier: the ability to imagine a relational pornography, where all social contacts are pleasurable and engage as many of the passions as possible. It is a heretical reversal of perspective of liberalism. Rather than sacrifice the body to labor in order to sustain a survival in which some modest pleasure might be endured at the margin, the whole social field can engage all of the passions all of the time.

Something like it happens every other Saturday in a dungeon in Brooklyn. They are men, women, and some unclassifiable. They are black and white, and some none of the above. They are gay and straight, and some neither. They are young and old, beautiful and ugly. They are not the same, but they all have passions, and they all gather and remove their clothes before venturing into a darkened labyrinth. Here a man whips another with a switch. There a woman fucks a man up the ass with a dildo. In the back room is a group scene, too dark to tell of genders or preferences. A cry of pleasure draws five men, cocks in hand, to watch from the shadows, some in the hope of joining in, others simply to watch and come in their own hands, making an offering, if only they knew, to Barbelo, reigning Goddess of one of Vaneigem's favorite heresies.[12] It is hardly what Fourier had in mind. It's not far removed from the seraglios that he knew were the necessary other side to bourgeois morality. Fourier was most likely a solitary wanker. But he might have appreciated the emergence, in such spaces, of tacit rules that enable the meshing of the passions. Readings in decadent literature led him to suspect an erotic charge even—or especially—to the "the secret bambocciades of respectable women."[13]

Harmonian sex is highly regulated. The court of love meets every night. A high pontiff presides, and arrayed beneath her are various other ranks, who enforce the amorous code of conduct. Not infidelity but insincerity is the chief failing that concerns them. Membership is voluntary, so there is nobody to coerce, but recognition in this world is not easily achieved. The main currency of this hierarchy is sexual philanthropy. Saintly rank is bestowed upon those who share their sexual favors with those most in need.

Besides the arranging of the sexual encounters within the court's jurisdiction, the pontiff and her associates have to arrange for the entertainment of travelers. Fourier imagines a host of wanderers and knights-errant, searching the world for rare pleasures. Those with particularly rare fetishes may travel far to join gatherings of their kind. Fourier foresaw a federating globally of the partisans of each branch of passion, with sects devoted to each particular sexual mania. A global association of heel-scratching fetishists might travel the world in search of ardent supplicants willing to offer their heels. Roland Barthes: "For Fourier, and this is his victory, there is no normality."[14]

Everyone wears insignia to mark their whims, although these may of course change.[15] The officers of the court of love, mostly older women, would conduct interviews to determine who wants what and who might best provide it. The court would jot it all down on a card index system. Strangely enough, indexing is one of the few things characteristic of the post-revolutionary era which

Fourier regards favorably. His phalansteries are also all equipped with the telegraph, and form a distributed network, each in communication with each other. Between the card index database and the telegraph network, Fourier imagines Harmony within a dense space of communication—a world wide web.

The *New Amorous World* is a reversal of perspective of the hierarchies and cultic practices of the Catholic Church. In Fourier, its *indulgences* are likewise bestowed by an ecclesiastical order, only one devoted to satisfying pleasures rather than repressing them. The tithes required of members would be more of the order of handjobs for the elderly than a grain requisition. The saints would be paragons of a new kind of virtue, bestowing mercy fucks on the sick and infirm. Excommunication remains the ultimate sanction. Membership in any court is voluntary on both sides.

Fourier thought that if everyone had their minimum sexual needs meet without unnecessary anxiety, it would prompt desires for new kinds of platonic love. Young people in Fourier's world could choose to be bacchantes, or they could choose to be vestals. While the vestals withhold their bodies, it isn't as a sacrifice. In any case, certain lapses are permitted, and it is temporary anyway. One of Fourier's more refined passions is the composite, which laminates sensual and social passions together. The vestal becomes an object of adoration and longing through the delay in choosing whom to fuck.

Fourier's is an amorous order for women, the elderly and perverts—all those scorned by civilization. It honors sexual philanthropy and amorous nobility. Its highest ranks in Harmony are open only to those attracted to both sexes. In Harmony, love is an affair of state. The Situationists were fond of quoting Saint-Just: "Happiness is a new idea in Europe." For Vaneigem at least, what this meant was something more like Fourier than the Committee of Public Safety. Affairs of state would be amorous affairs. War would be more like a game, a war of position in which rival courts would take prisoners for the prisoners' gratification rather than their own.

Fourierist sex takes place in broad daylight, preferably in public, preferably in the context of a carefully directed orgy. What civilization treats as something furtive and nocturnal will be brought into the light. A celestial mirror in the sky will reveal any secret lovers hiding out in the woods. Stendhal's *On Love*, written around the same time, circles relentlessly around the emotional stress of unrequited desire.[16] Fourier's solution is practical. A whole class of officers of the court of love will offer themselves to those not otherwise favored.

Fourier's world may seem impossible, ridiculous. But is it more so than this world that actually claims to exist? Charles Beecher: "It is not given to all of us to imagine a world populated by anti-lions and anti-crocodiles. Nor is it given to all of us to see as clearly as Fourier saw into the contradictions, the wasted opportunities and the hidden possibilities of our own lives."[17] At the very least one can read the symptomatology of civilization in Fourier in negative. Fourier: "civilized social order is an absurd mechanism, the parts of which are in conflict with the whole."[18]

This brings us back to Vaneigem's most famous line, about those who "without understanding what is subversive about love and what is positive in the refusal of constraints, such people have a corpse in their mouth."[19] Here Vaneigem brings Fourier to bear as a critique of the militant asceticism of the Leninist strains of the French postwar left. Lenin too had his utopia: vigorous, ascetic, and drawn from Nikolai Chernyshevsky's *What Is to Be Done?*[20]

Fourier's utopian thought had its absurdist side and, most notoriously the *archibras*, the human tail with a hand and eye at its end. Genetic engineering has not exactly made that possible, and even our pornographers have neglected to explore its theoretical possibilities. On the other hand, Fourier has a strange predictive power. His analogical method enabled him to develop possible permutations on the given in language which bypassed the rhetorical centers of gravity of his time, and not a few of which illuminate, in their own strange light, the spectacle of disintegration.

The seas did not turn to lemonade, but as Fourier predicted, the planet is surely warming. Species dangerous to humans are quickly becoming extinct. For better or worse, more amenable ones have indeed been engineered. Elements of Fourier's sexual universe came to pass, from the global conclaves of fetishists to the hook-up culture of young vestals and bacchantes. This disintegrating civilization refuses to award a social and sexual minimum, and is if anything reversing the progress in that direction that the labor movement, feminism and the counter-culture had, in their contradictory ways, advanced.

And yet, for its treasured hirelings, the disintegrating spectacle has had to deploy Fourierist techniques to stimulate the passions as a way of extracting useful labor. The full-service *campus* for top technical and creative employees would put the marble-encrusted workshops of the phalanstery to shame. The movement toward so called *game-ification* tries to mobilize the cabalistic passion for rivalry as a productivity tool.[21] This is the world that the failure of the revolution of May '68 has led to.

Vaneigem: "The evening that we left the National Institute for Pedagogy, which we had occupied in May 1968, I proposed to the gang to go bar-hopping along the left side of the street where we wandered. It seemed to me that we were following on the footsteps of the combatants of the Paris Commune. The farther we dérived into the mists of a frozen drunkenness, the more we felt the ephemeral and faltering sympathy, given to us by the bar owners, turn into hatred … We had frustrated in them that same hope we were supposed to fulfill. Had it been at the time when the Versaillese patrolled, we would have been put up against a wall and executed, so as to soothe their thoughtlessness. I was then able to measure the extent to which the disenchantment of a promise of life, when not held, could turn into a reflex of death and destruction."[22]

May '68 launched two critiques of the society of the spectacle.[23] Whether knowingly or not, these two critiques had their roots in Marx and Fourier respectively. They were never effectively combined, and both were recuperated in their own fashion. Wage labor was bought off in the usual fashion, with more of the same, at least while it retained the power to demand it. The more Fourierist critique of the alienation of everyday civilized life was met with more subtle attempts to enmesh the passions in the maintenance of the spectacular order. Perhaps the real failure of May '68 was the inability to combine these two critiques in practical ways. Here is where the Situationist International still leaves a useful legacy, for while Debord and Vaneigem took the double critique in quite different and perhaps in the end incompatible directions, the space mapped out by what one might call Post-Situationist practices is rich with productive variations on this double theme.

Fourier thought that social progress and the ends of eras took place accordingly as women progress toward freedom. Engels agreed, as did Vaneigem, as might modern feminism. So too might the Post-Situationist writers of the journal *Tiqqun,* whose oblique debt to Fourier resides in their program "to embrace a form of life … more faithful to our penchants than our predicates."[24] The disintegrating spectacle certainly offers boundless images of women, or rather not of women, but of a certain iconic double, of and for women—let's call her The Girl. If Manet tried to picture particular women caught in the tensions of an emerging spectacle, then The Girl is the image on their reverse side. She is not what is caught in the spectacle; she is the concentrated image of the spectacle itself. And now she is everywhere. You can find her in any magazine. The disintegrating spectacle is not presided over by the Law of the Father but by the figure of The Girl.

The Girl is a new kind of asceticism, a sacrifice of a kind unknown to Fourier. She doesn't deny or repress sex. Rather, she makes it something abstract: not sex but sexuality. *Tiqqun*: "The present sexual misery in no way resembles that of the past, because these are now bodies without desire, burning up inside because they can't satisfy these desires they don't have."[25] In the disintegrating spectacle, sexuality is everywhere, a hollowed-out form that connects not bodies to bodies but bodies to commodities. On the other hand, love is nowhere. It becomes privatized; it is what is supposed to found couples outside of the spectacle, but only so that they might build the storage space within which to accumulate its decorative veneers.

Contrary to appearances, feminism has succeeded far less than a certain *femitude*. Women were not freed from the domestic; the domestic expanded to encompass the whole of everyday life outside the home. Contrary to appearances, there was no sexual liberation. Sexuality was not freed from repression. Sexuality was freed from sex. Whole new kinds of preventable sexual misery reign, beyond those anatomized by Fourier. Sex is sacrificed to sexuality; love to privatization. And yet, while Fourier's diagnosis of the sacrifices entailed in civilization may be a little out of date, his concept of sacrifice and his critical-poetic mapping of other possibilities are alive and well, as Vaneigem has been so good as to remind us. Vaneigem: "He drew from his own subjectivity the project of a society capable of furthering the desires of each and harmonizing them. He does not content himself, like the philosophers, to dress the old world in new clothes. His solitude was peopled by a multitude of beings that prefigure the new global society, one whom the servile masters and slaves of the arrogant old world persist in not seeing before their eyes that she is born."[26]

Vaneigem finds Fourier a convenient foil against both the asceticism of supposedly militant practice and against the game leaders who in the sphere of play might presume to organize everyone's fun for them. The problem of a critical practice might be "to enter the collective project with the calculated innocence of Fourier's phalansterian players, rivaling each other (composite passion), varying their activities (butterfly passion), and striving for the most advanced radicality (cabalist passion). But lightheartedness must be based on conscious, 'heavy' relationships. It implies lucidity regarding everyone's abilities."[27]

This might be particularly so within transformative situations. Vaneigem: "One of Fourier's great merits is to have shown the necessity of creating immediately—and for us this means from the inception of generalized insurrection—the objective conditions for individual liberation. For everyone the beginning of the revolutionary moment must mark an immediate rise in the pleasure of living—a consciously experienced entry into the totality."[28] Against the holy family of Jacobin-Leninist-Maoist political nostalgia, wedded to the pomp and circumstance of high theory within the academy, one might, in the name of Vaneigem and Fourier, go looking for low theories, practiced in the thrall of everyday life, and not shy about inventing critical practices out of any and every situation, for the hell of it.

Voyage to Oarystis (2005) is Vaneigem's own utopia, his textual city, designed for seven thousand inhabitants. Visitors must first stay at a sumptuous hotel on its borders, a place so grand that a mature curiosity is required to move on to Oarystis itself. The city is traversed by aerial and aquatic passageways, as well as terrestrial ones. Function and folly entangle in all its forms. It is a fungible landscape, fashioned after the tastes of a people who confront the last struggle—with boredom. They frequently change their names to suit their moods.

The centerpiece is Fourier Place, bisected by the Grand Canal, fed by Lake Montaigne. A statue to Freud is both honored and despised, and Hegel Street appears to be a dead end. Art is erratic in Oarystis, always being changed or replaced. Every surface is covered by poems, art or philosophical theses. The toilets are named after dictators such as Napoleon and Mao, and are public, so their infamies can be discussed during elimination.

Waste and recycling functions are all below ground, where everyone works three hours per week on essential tasks. Everyone except the Friends of Paul Lafargue, who are engaged in the even more difficult effort of not working at all.[29] Most Oarystians feel the need for the alternating rhythms, the fast pace of work below and the slow strolling up above, as what Fourier called the butterfly passion is common among them.

The Oarystians don't tell lies—unless they are amusing. They are free to exercise their desires, so long as they do not oppress others. Not every matter is settled. The vegetarians campaign to outlaw consuming meat by putting it to a vote in Fourier Place. Various leagues, factions and phalanxes petition the city with their common passions. Screens display the various motions and votes, as well as all information about the stocks of goods available in the city at a given moment.

Oarystis, with its escalators and rolling walkways, is a labyrinth for a great game, where each must navigate within the chaos of their own desires and aversions. Oarystis decomposes the hierarchy of public and private selves, the defensive need for an interiority. Here, "what is tangible, what is invisible, the shadow of our dreams, the tentacles of a forgotten desire, the suppuration of an ancient memory, and quite simply, hence, everything that is in me, everything that is not in me, everything that could or should have been in me, what I would or would not want to experience, all this forms an inextricable terminal of nervous and organic filaments that is called reality."[30]

No system of knowledge, no matter how arcane, is useless in Oarystis. It's just a matter of weaving them into the patterns of desires. In the Quarter of the Illuminati are the makers of delirious systems, impossible geometries, infinite virtualities. Here are the builders of invisible palaces, the technicians of immortality, the vivisectors of desire, the manufacturers of parallel universes, the gatherers of storms. The last survivor of the city's founders is a climate architect, and he spends his time in the Climate Variation Dome, experimenting with different arrangements of the seasons.

Visits to Oarystis can last no more than fifteen days, and Vaneigem's guests must return to their—to this—world just as they are beginning to become oriented in the city. Their mission, and ours, is to build Oarystis where we are.

Even in Oarystis, Vaneigem never quite manages to reconcile the Fourierist critique of the sacrificial labor of militant practice with a Marxist critique of the society of the spectacle. It was René Viénet who came closest to their synthesis, which he turned into a powerful counter to the lingering fascination with Leninist asceticism in the west. Viénet says goodbye to the politics of sacrifice, at the same time as he negates separation and spectacle.

20 The Ass Dreams of China Pop

Those who are first are entitled to fame, and the children who follow are left to file lawsuits for their daily bread.

Baltasar Gracián

René Viénet (b. 1944) was a docker's son from Le Havre. He came to Paris to study Chinese, but he was curious also about the Situationists. As Debord writes in a letter to him: "The simplest manner of approaching all the questions enumerated in your letter to the S[ituationist] I[nternational] is to come see for yourself. We can lodge you, feed you, even offer you a shower, for about eight days at the following address."[1] He became a member of the Situationist International in 1961.

He went to China in 1965, the year France opened diplomatic relations with the People's Republic. He wrote letters to Debord on his impressions, making the Situationists one of the few groups of the time whose views on Maoism were informed by direct reports. He was expelled from China in 1966. He had a somewhat stormy career as a Sinologist on his return, not least because of his virulent opposition to the apologists for Mao.

Enragés and Situationists in the Occupation Movement (1968), the more or less official account of Situationist involvement in May '68, was published under his name. Viénet's text is particularly clear on the role of the movement's would-be recuperators, the Stalinoid apparatchiks of the various factions who wanted to install themselves as its representatives. This text, in spite of its obvious merits, was but a warm-up for a series of remarkable films Viénet made in the seventies, where questions of politics and representation find their most telling answer in the practice of détournement.

Can Dialectics Break Bricks (1973) uses as its raw material a kung fu movie by Tu Guangqi (1914–80) called *The Crush* (1972) and recasts its struggle between vicious warlords and oppressed villagers as a struggle within the left between Stalinists and Situationists by dubbing in new dialogue in French. Meaghan Morris: "Tu came after World War Two from Shanghai to Hong Kong, where he made cultural nationalist Mandarin language films; a right-winger who worked for the Asian Film Company, established in 1953 with American money, Tu helped remake and reinterpret—indeed *détourner*—successful left-wing dramas and themes from a right-wing nationalist perspective. If that is so, there is definite poetic justice in the French fate of *Crush*."[2]

Crush is set in Korea under Japanese occupation, while the hero who appears on the scene looking for a relative is Chinese, and hence naturally has superior martial arts skills. Both China and Korea were occupied by the Japanese at one time, and both had Communist regimes at the time *Crush* was made. The film is already an allegory about Communism as an occupation. What Viénet does is divert the allegory from the service of Nationalist struggle against Maoism to that of a Situationist critique of the Stalinist and Maoist wannabes of the red decade in France.

Viénet's détournement seems at first sight to work by the simple expedient of changing the dialogue, but he has also moved some scenes around, subtly making the moving images serve his own purposes.[3] While in *Crush* the hero's position is never in doubt, Viénet makes him a more ambiguous figure, caught between desires. He does this by changing the role of the central female character in a way that makes her more interesting.

Dialectics opens with the villagers practicing their martial arts on a chilly morning, in a place "where the ideology is particularly cold." A student arriving late gives the password: "live without dead time!" This contrasts with the slogan of the dreaded bureaucrats, a litany of sacrifices: "work, family, fatherland!" The bureaucrats arrive to break up the morning kung fu practice of the revolutionaries and warn them of what is to come: "I don't want to hear any more about class struggle. If not I'll send in my sociologists! And if necessary my psychiatrists! My urban planners! My architects! My Foucaults! My Lacans! And if that's not enough, I'll even send my structuralists!" The structuralists were generally indifferent to the events of May 1968. Lacan looked on in bemused silence. Foucault was out of town. Althusser, the structural Marxist, stuck to the official Communist Party line, even if expressed in his own theoretical language: don't do it, comrades, the conjuncture is not ripe![4] For all the prestige they accumulated in the seventies, these thinkers were outflanked by events. "Mediation is their game," as Viénet puts it. Their language games open as a cul-de-sac in compensation for the loss of the streets.

Like the original it détourns, *Dialectics* hinges on a character of superlative kung fu skills. He seems to waver between rival forms of power. In Viénet's version those forces are the Stalinists and the Situationists. The favors bestowed upon the Stalinist recuperators seem tempting. The decisive event is perhaps the hero's meeting with the courtesan. In *Crush* this character is a *good girl*, but Viénet creates a different impression in the spectator with some small changes. His female lead is a courtesan in the service of the bureaucrats, but she is not one of them. "They offer crumbs," she says. "We want it all!" The glittering prizes for cooperation are not what they seem: "A bit more pay is a bit more poverty." Like many veterans of 1968 adrift in the 1970s, she is in mourning for what did not come to pass, and is looking for solace elsewhere: "The only thing I have left is the experience of love."

The only thing left in the twenty-first century appears to be the crumbs. A sparkler lights the way as a large and expensive order of booze finds its way to the table, making it easy for the models or near-models to find their way to the men whose largesse this is. The sparkler and the bottles are held high by the *bottle girl*, whose job it is not just to serve the table, but to reel in big-spending clients and keep up a steady friction on their credit cards. Says Kim, a twenty-six-year-old graduate of a fine liberal arts college: "you're a bottle waitress, and that means you're half a stripper and half a pimp. If you don't book a client, you're fired. Most places I worked, I had to sign a confidentiality agreement about celebrities." Her services have certain boundaries: "I do have to flirt with them, booty-dance with them, call them, hang out with them, occasionally procure girls and party favors for them, all the while in teeny outfits. So I suppose it's a form of social prostitution." But then what's a girl to do? "I figured: I'm cute, I'm young, I can make a shitload of money, so fuck it!"

Kim is not exactly an innocent player of this game: "Last Spring I went to meet R at the Oak Room at the Plaza Hotel, he was already slurring and three martinis in when we found this sweet young girl in a Jackie O dress reading Baudelaire at the bar." This Jackie O was straight out of an Ivy League school and new to the city. "R started to tell her how he went to Princeton (he did not) and I suggested she join us for a drink, then dinner at Daniel, then more drinks downtown, then a table at a club in the [Meat Packing] district where I could get commission for bringing R. I knew how to deal with him, she did not." When he tries to kiss Kim, she slaps him down a bit. When he tries to kiss the Jackie O girl, she does not know how to fend him off. "He of course pushed farther reaching down her dress. I was just happy it wasn't me tonight and demanded he give me more money for blow. She tried to get me to protect her, he alluded to her being a lesbian and wanting to sleep with me. I played along and ordered another bottle of champagne. She was slurring and wobbling more and more, he was pretty much holding her up as he pawed at her." Kim ditches them both and goes off to trawl for new clients. "I never heard from or saw her again, though I found her Baudelaire book at the bottom of my purse."[5] Such night life would not have surprised Baudelaire, although the absence of a recalcitrant urban proletariat ready to greet these characters of the night the next morning might.

Viénet's films recall a moment when history appeared on a different path than that toward sparkly spectacles. For Viénet the stakes are high. "Whatever is lost in partial confrontation becomes part of the repressive function of the old world." But it is not simply a question of the unfulfilled desires of May '68, and as we shall see Viénet has good reason to stress this: "the falsifiers sang socialism above all the charnel houses."[6] The slogan "those who make the revolution by halves dig their own graves" is not mere overblown sixties rhetoric. It is quite literally true.

Under the big kung fu fight scene, Viénet offers this title: "For this sequence, consult *Enragés and Situs in the Occupation Movement*, Gallimard edition pages 2–7 and 231." These pages point specifically to the problem of recuperation: that the struggle was as much against the left as the right; that if the revolution can't be made consistently then it ought not to be made at all. Viénet's vision is of a mass of popular desire that is constantly wearing away at the old world, but which is captured and channeled into mere innovations in oppressive technique. Under the big chase scene, this subtitle: "On this wall a slogan was just erased: 'Run comrade, the old world is behind you.'" Against the right, Viénet turns the Marxist filter; against the left, the Fourierist one.

Viénet had been to China, had seen the Cultural Revolution begin, and was well aware of the costs of failed revolutions. Latter-day apologists for the Cultural Revolution prefer to speak grandly of the Political as a concept rather than the messy business of politics, and they prefer the terrain of great leaders coming into being as subjects on some astral plane to the everyday life on the backs of which this was built. Rey Chow: "My most vivid childhood memories of the Cultural Revolution were the daily reports in 1966 and 1967 of corpses from China floating down into the Pearl River delta and down into Hong Kong harbor ... There are also memories of people risking their lives swimming across the border into Hong Kong and of people visiting China with the 'little red book' but also with supplies of food and clothing. This was a period of phenomenal starvation in China."[7]

In Tu's film, the Koreans prevail with the help of the superior fighting prowess of the Chinese hero, but at a great cost of life. *Crush* is an imaginary defeat of what to the Nationalists was a real enemy. Viénet underscores the purely spectacular nature of this victory. *Dialectics* also ends with a massacre, but his voice actors break character to declare they are "sick of dubbing dialogue tracks so they're pretending to be dead. It's hard work, it seems, and doesn't even pay the cab fare." Unlike Debord's détourned films, Viénet's always have an undercurrent of earthy laughter.

Hard work indeed, although it did not stop Viénet making a second détourned film, technically simpler, but formally more ambitious. *The Girls of Kamare* détourns Norifumi Suzuki's *Terrifying Girls' High School* (1973), with a bit of Teruo Ishii's *Female Yatuza Tale: Inquisition and Torture* (1973) thrown in, plus a few cutaway shots made especially. Both of the détourned films are examples of the *pinky violence* genre films that became popular in Japan from the sixties onwards.[8] These low-budget films mixed sex and sadism but stayed within Japan's quirky censorship laws. They were a response to declining cinema attendance during the rise of television. Viénet's détournement of the dialogue is much simpler this time: he simply added French subtitles.

If *Dialectics* mourns the moment of 1968, then *Kamare* recalls the moment of 1961: "People of France you knew it already, and it doesn't take a Japanese film, to speak to you about the Algerians thrown in the Seine in October, 1961."[9] This happened during the ugly endgame of the struggle to free Algeria from French colonial rule. The National Liberation Front had been bombing police stations in Paris before it decided to stage a big demonstration for Algerian independence. The police responded by beating demonstrators senseless and throwing them in the river. The colonial war brought home to the streets of Paris is the context for the political turn of the Situationist International. Those who protest the Situationists' abandonment of art in the sixties forget that France was in a state of civil war at the time.

The Situationists were hardly starry-eyed about Algerian independence. "[Ahmed] Ben Bella fell as he had reigned, in solitude and conspiracy, by a palace revolution. He was ushered out by the same forces that ushered him in: [Houari] Boumédienne's army, which had opened the road to Algiers to him in September 1962."[10] This revolution had always been at one and the same time the attempt by the masses to achieve self-management and that of the bourgeoisie to create the conditions of a capitalist economy, if necessary via the state.

Put crudely, the Situationist line was that Fanon, Castro and Guevara are the false consciousness through which the peasants carry out the task of overcoming colonial leftovers. Ben Bella, Nasser, Tito and Mao are the ideologues of the takeover of these movements by petit-bourgeois or military and urban strata. The bureaucracy assumes the function of an absent bourgeois class. Once it achieves state power, the bureaucracy can shed its more political wing, leaving the military or technocrats in power, as in Algeria. The post-colonial revolution is an ambiguous phenomenon at best, even if the "only people who are really underdeveloped are those who see a positive value in the power of their masters."[11]

The kinky eroticism of Japanese reform-school girls supposedly water-boarding one of their number takes on a strange resonance against the background of ongoing colonial war. Viénet: "we learned torture during the colonial wars. The enemy within would do well to remember that." In 2002 Bruce Jessen and Jim Mitchell, retired air force officers and psychologists, were looking for a new business opportunity. They found a great client, the CIA, for whom they designed an interrogation program that culminated in water-boarding. Jessen and Mitchell boasted of receiving up to two thousand dollars a day to supervise the use of their techniques at a secret interrogation site in Thailand. The two psychologists had previously trained American pilots to survive behind enemy lines and to resist interrogation if captured. It transpired that neither had any interrogation experience, nor were they qualified to declare the procedure medically safe. They still managed to rake in millions of dollars in consultancy fees for their services.[12] Once again, the talents learned in colonial wars have an afterlife, this time as a business opportunity.

To the names insulted in *Dialectics*, *Kamare* adds Roland Barthes, Louis Althusser and Simone de Beauvoir. Unlike *Dialectics*, *Kamare* borders on incoherence. Unlike the straightforward narrative of *Crush*, *Horror High School Women* barely makes sense. It does provide the raw material for one fabulous Vaneigemesque set piece. To a scene in which two schoolgirls fuck in a toilet, Viénet appends his manifesto for the cinema, which one reads off the subtitles to the sound of fake squeals of pleasure and seventies soundtrack-funk: "What there is of lived experience in this film I have no intention of making apprehensible to spectators who do not honestly prepare themselves to relive it. I await its becoming lost, then found again in a general shift of consciousness. Just as I flatter myself that current conditions will be effaced from the memory of men. The cinema must be remade. All the production and distribution specialists will not prevent this."

Viénet's school girls, like Pissarro's peasant women, make awkward stand-ins for the desires that reside in the everyday. Women's bodies do the work not only of being the screens on which the spectacle projects the passing show of all that can be legitimately desired. They have to function also as the locus of hidden desires as well. Pissarro shows that, alongside the desire that the peasant woman be some locus of rustic charm, she also indicates the moment of idleness within the labor that, unlike the industrial worker, she controls for herself. The women in the films Viénet détourns possess a certain fantastic castrating power. But what he would rather have them point to is the capacity to order their own passions. The delinquent now takes the place of the peasant as the one in possession of the body's own powers, but it is still a woman's body.

Kamare brings to the surface something rather less obvious in *Dialectics*. Namely, that the source of the capacity for détournement, the distance that enables the appropriation of these cinematic trifles to quite other purposes, is Viénet's own lived experience. This is what separates détournement from so much of the cut-up, remix and mash-up culture that superficially looks so much like it. It's the enduring significance, not just of May '68, but of the moment of negation in general. Where remix bows down before the power of recuperated desire and merely makes a fetish of it, détournement has no such reverence. But nor is it a brute iconoclasm of the kind Clark imagined on the steps of the National Gallery, where he contemplates the destruction of a work by Nicolas Poussin.[13]

Rather, it is like a kung fu move that uses the power of spectacle against itself, leveraging it over into the service of autonomous desire. Or as Viénet says: "One escapes banality only by manipulating it, by détourning it, by delivering it up to the delights of subjectivity. I did more than my share in playing out my subjectivity, but no one should give me any grief about it before having considered what the objective conditions, that the world brings into existence each day, make possible in favor of subjectivity." As always Viénet balances the bravado of his manifesto with sly humor. In films so devoted to the negation of the commodity he nevertheless pauses to plug books from the publisher he works for—even if he advocates stealing them.

Viénet moved the scenes around in *Dialectics*, but with *Kamare* he adds a little as well. This is perhaps another kind of détournement, not one of eliminating the inessential from the détourned element, but adding that which completes its line of thought. The pinky violence films stop short of the sex act itself, and they stop short of connecting their violence to historical situations. While sex and violence will become key dialects of the disintegrating spectacle, sex is always to be disassociated from the politics of desire, and violence is always to be disassociated from the desire for politics. *Kamare* joins the dots, in brief flashes of bodies fucking atop volumes of Red Guard writings from China's Cultural Revolution, writings which embody all the tensions between popular revolt and its co-option by state power. The title of the anthology, *Révo. cul. dans la Chine Pop* (1974), in which Viénet had a hand, could be read as *The Ass Dreams of China Pop*.[14]

21 Mao by Mao

Always speak well of the enemy.
Baltasar Gracián

As if his talents as a Situationist writer, filmmaker and trouble maker were not enough to recommend him to posterity, René Viénet was also a student of Chinese. Expelled from China in 1966, he edited the Chinese Library for Editions Champ Libre, and in that capacity published a famous book by Pierre Ryckmans called *The Emperor's New Clothes*. Ryckmans was a Belgian sinologist who taught for many years in Australia, where one of his former students would even go on to become prime minister. Writing as Simon Leys, he became the Orwell of the east, the first westerner with a real working knowledge of Chinese society to publicize the violence and terror of the Maoist state.

For there is another sixties, the sixties of anti-colonial struggle. While the Situationists had been committed to the anti-colonial cause ever since Debord and Bernstein signed the "Manifesto of the 121," they were hardly starry-eyed about the prospects. The collapse of the international Communist movement, so evident in the split between China and Russia, was actually welcomed by the Situationists. The east's concentrated spectacle was the "pseudo-negation and real support" of the diffuse spectacle of the west, and as it broke up into warring factions, the path to a real transformation of the diffuse spectacle was revealed. Debord predicted the triumph of the diffuse spectacle in 1967, some twenty-odd years before the fall of the Berlin wall, but it was Viénet who had the telling critique of the most influential version of the concentrated spectacle, based on his knowledge of Mandarin, his brief but firsthand experience in China, and his grasp of Situationist theory and practice.

As Viénet wrote in his introduction to the 1971 Champ Libre edition of *The Emperor's New Clothes*: "The plaster statues of Mao will perhaps make less noise when crumbling down than the steel bust of Stalin thrown to the ground in Budapest in 1956 and, because of the distance, perhaps one might only collect the fine, white powder that the eastern winds will deposit on the heads of western Maoists. There, again, a theoretical calculation permits us to get to know the nature of these consequences even before they are gathered for analysis: Chairman Mao's thought is *biodegradable*."[1] How strangely right he would turn out to be.

While many were seduced by the visage of Mao in the sixties and early seventies, the Situationists saw it as the face of the "accelerating disintegration of bureaucratic ideology." The concentrated spectacle was proletarian society turned on its head. The essential thesis, shared by Viénet and Debord, was that the Cultural Revolution was a symptom of a split within the Chinese ruling class over economic policy. Deposed by his rivals for the failure of the Great Leap Forward, Mao staged a comeback through control of the ideological apparatus. The conflict was one between the Maoist faction, "masters of absolute ideology," and the fragile, underdeveloped economic base. Mao mobilized the Red Guards to fight his faction wars, but authentic class struggle arose unbidden, when workers started acting for themselves, mounting strikes, seizing arms and staging anti-Maoist demonstrations.[2] The result was a "confused civil war." The Situationist theses on China were quite classically Marxist, and basically right, even if, when first formulated in 1967, the end was not quite in sight.

Viénet returned to something like the Situationist position on China, and to the cinema of détournement, with two 1977 films. *Mao by Mao* is a short work he co-produced, in which the life of the then recently deceased Great Helmsman is told in his own words, using quotes culled from various Red Guard publications.[3] It is best watched as a warm-up for Viénet's *One More Effort, Chinese, If You Want to be Revolutionaries!*[4] The two titles of this film, pinched from the Marquis de Sade and the Marx Brothers respectively, neatly sum up Viénet's tastes, and even his philosophy. The fake film company that produced it is the Despair of Billancourt, the site of the biggest factory in France, the Renault car plant, whose striking workers held the fortunes of May '68 in their hands. The film is dedicated to Li Yi Zhe, the nominal author of a famous Democracy Wall critique of the Maoist state.

In *Mao by Mao*, the rise to power of the film's namesake appears as the inevitable outcome of a dialectical logic. Or so the voice-over might lead one to believe. If the usual practice of détourned films is for the soundtrack to undermine the image, here the reverse occasionally takes place. The images critique Mao's words. They show that which, even in the official visual record of the times, the narrative elides. The effect is subtle and requires at least a passing acquaintance with Chinese politics to work. *Duck Soup* offers no such delicacies. It has all the qualities Debord once attributed to Viénet: "one feels the assurance of the revolutionary, and also the pedantry of the specialist. In short, that is Viénet, when he happens to write. There is humor and also naiveté that would like to be cynicism."[5] While hardly generous, Debord is here quite perceptive.

Duck Soup opens with a florid sequence in which Chinese Communist Party leaders appear like movie stars in a trailer for some Hollywood A-movie, a neat analogy in which the Chinese version of the concentrated spectacle appears as a low-tech version of its western counterpart. Viénet will later compare the Red Guards to television, agents of enforced passivity sent into every home, not via radio waves but with heavy footsteps. Viénet has the cheek to include a shot of himself waving to the crowd, only the volume he is holding is certainly not Mao's *Little Red Book*.

Before leaping into its bloody saga of modern Chinese power, *Duck Soup* presents old newsreel images of working people from the colonial and civil war periods, to the soundtrack of popular sentimental songs. The songs chosen were mostly banned by the Communists. While the proletariat becomes the official hero of the spectacle after the Maoist seizure of power, what is expunged is the affect of the old songs, their sadness, their longings.

Crucial to Viénet's version of the story is Harold Isaacs' contention in his—Trotskyist, but still serviceable—*The Tragedy of the Chinese Revolution* that the Chinese proletarian revolution was defeated in 1927, when Stalin ordered the party to collaborate with the

Nationalists, and the Nationalists destroyed them. "Stalin made some mistakes," notes Mao himself, in *Mao by Mao*, with world-historical understatement. Mao came to power by deposing those who followed Stalin's line, and his peasant army triumphed in 1949 by winning a civil war, not a revolution. The party was nevertheless thoroughly Stalinist, "even though Stalin has never done them any favors." Sino-Soviet relations were, in a word, colonial.

While "assholes like Sartre" were making apologies for the Soviet Union, the proletariat of Budapest rose up in 1956 against the Hungarian branch office of the Stalinist regime. Mao was sufficiently unnerved to launch the Hundred Flowers campaign, soliciting criticism of the regime in order to defuse it. But the torrent of discontent was not the fealty he expected, and his critics were quickly silenced in the following Anti-Rightist Campaign.

Repression only gets you so far. Mao counted on Russian aid to get the economy moving, and this was not particularly forthcoming. The 1958 Great Leap Forward, famous for its backyard furnaces where peasants were urged to smelt their own hand tools into useless iron, was a desperate attempt to make up the shortfall from Moscow. The failure and famine of the Great Leap Forward led to Mao's demotion.[6] Liu Shaoqi and Deng Xiaoping were in charge, but Mao did manage to install Lin Biao as Minister of Defense. Mao bided his time in luxury resort hotels, plotting his comeback.

Duck Soup has a contrapuntal structure, oscillating between the power struggle at the top and everyday life, as if sifting both coarse and fine-grained history. In this it differs somewhat from Debord's cinema, which does contain privileged moments of everyday affect but lacks Viénet's palpable empathy for everyday popular life. Viénet characterizes the dense net of social control practiced by the Maoist regime by juxtaposing pictures of Chinese youth, a syrupy Serge Gainsbourg make-out tune, and court documents in which a twenty-six-year-old teacher who "promoted a bourgeois lifestyle based on pleasure" is condemned to death. The sequence includes a still of a young woman which one cannot help thinking of as having an undeclared resonance for Viénet. Debord, as we shall see, also included snapshots of loved ones in his films.

Mao's counter-attack, when it comes, issues from his stronghold in Shanghai and seizes the ideological high ground. The official language of the concentrated spectacle is Maoist, and even his opponents present themselves within this language, and this leaves ample room for Mao to turn the tables. With Liu Shaoqi in Pakistan, Mao and Lin Biao arrest their other rivals. Mao swims the Yangtze River to show that he still has it, even if, as Viénet claims, it took four frogmen to keep him afloat. It still makes for terrific newsreel footage. Liu is demoted, but hangs onto power. But when Mao mobilizes the Red Guards, the leadership are confronted with a million of them massed in and around Tiananmen Square.

The Red Guards are literally *mobilized*, traveling the country on the Exchange of Revolutionary Experiences and unaware of the extent to which they are a "choreographed rebellion." Following the general line of the Situationists on such matters, *Duck Soup* characterizes the Red Guards unequivocally as a fascist movement. Fascism and Stalinism are the decadence of the worker's movement. They are the detachment of the representation from that which it represents, its becoming a power over the represented.

Viénet is not so concerned about the Red Guards' destruction of monuments. These are relics of past oppression, and the people always have the right to let their rulers know that one day all oppression may be just a memory. Rather, it is the working over of independent intellectuals by the Red Guards that is the tragedy. They attack China's equivalents to critical Bolsheviks like Victor Serge.[7] The Red Guards quickly descended into pogroms and factional feuding. Viénet's approach is not without its nuance, however. That they were so readily mobilized speaks at one and the same time to the effectiveness of the Maoist state but also to the depth of dissatisfaction within it. While manipulated as tools of Mao's factional war, they were a dangerous weapon. "Mao knows, even if they don't, that there was always a chance they might turn to open rebellion."

Strikingly, both Mao and his opponents within the state apparatus used variations on the same ideological language in their struggles with each other. Even as the state descended into civil war, the ideological façade did not crack. The "proprietors of ideology (Mao and his sidekicks) wanted to re-appropriate the economy. All of the bureaucrats wanted absolute and exclusive control of ideology. For ideology, as everyone knows, is the lever of power." So nobody really wanted to question that ideology. The party still traded in the "myth of an undying comradeship forged in revolutionary struggle." Viénet spends some time debunking this myth, retailing the folklore of the bitter fights among rival leaders, setting the stage so that when some very high-ranking bureaucrats later turn up dead one's mind immediately turns to conspiracy theories.

Events come to a head when what will later be known as the Gang of Four, acting in Mao's name, attack the venerable Communist leader Zhao Enlai. This was over-reaching, for Zhao was a consummate political player, with many allies in the army. Zhao forges an alliance against Mao, Lin Biao and the Gang of Four. The military seizes control of factories. Anti–Red Guard militias are mobilized. The Red Guards are packed off to the countryside.

The film's contrapuntal break returns to the everyday with a free translation of "On Socialist Democracy and the Legal System," by Li Yi Zhe. This was the pen name of four activists whose critique of the Cultural Revolution appeared as a wall poster in Guangzhou in 1974. The text provides a mordant critique of the days when Mao's Red Guards "put politics in command," as the phrase had it. Li Yi Zhe: "Politics was the watch word in every sphere. A word designed to reward apathy and punish enthusiasm." A time when everyone was supposed to be studying the revolutionary thought of the Chairman. "Study? It was more like telling the rosary." A time when everyone was supposed to aspire to revolutionary glory. "And all the talk of the revolution exploding in the depths of the soul. Not so much an explosion as a wet fart." A time when delirium was used as a tool of power, and everything "plunged into a pea soup of religiosity. Until everything began to stink of God." The three principal members of Li Yi Zhe went to the labor camps in 1977.[8]

Outflanked by Zhao and the army, Mao cut his old "comrade in arms" Lin Biao loose. He dies in a plane crash. Things are turning against Mao. He is down, but not out. Mao will be there to greet Richard Nixon when he arrives in 1972, and to show him the ballet version of the *Red Detachment of Women* (1964), one of the eight model plays his wife and Gang of Four member Jiang Qing has inflicted on Chinese culture. But behind the scenes the old possessors of economic power are aligning against him.

Viénet tells the old joke about three prisoners asking each other the reason for their imprisonment. "I was for Deng Xiaoping," says the first. "I was against Deng Xiaoping," say the second. "Oh, it's different for me," says the third. "I *am* Deng Xiaoping." Deng will return to the scene in 1973 and begin his rise to power over the Chinese state.

Zhao Enlai lasts until 1976. Viénet wonders whether he was poisoned, a wild conspiracy theory, lent credence by the extraordinary ways some of his comrades died. The passing of Zhao is the pretext for vast demonstrations. He was known for occasional acts of compassion, and was the least irrational and most refined of the party's overlords. All the same it is not really Zhao that people are mourning, but their own lives. Mao's death in 1976 finally leads to the end of the Gang of Four in what for Viénet is essentially a military coup. Mao's portrait still presides. The concentrated spectacle lives on in his name, only his official portrait is slightly different. A wart appears on his chin.

In twenty-first-century China one can find citizens who are not even sure who Mao Zedong was, even though the Chinese Communist Party boasts some seventy million members.[9] Perhaps this is the time for a different kind of story. Zhang Yuchen (b. 1947) was a toddler at the time of the Liberation; he was born in Shangdong province. His older brother got a job in a state factory in Beijing, so the whole family moved to the capital, and Zhang attended school there. He was a teenager when the Cultural Revolution started, and had what would turn out to be the great good fortune of joining, not the Red Guards, but a construction brigade. Like a character in *The Sims*, he rises from construction brigade worker to brigade leader.

After the Cultural Revolution he was able to study—the universities are returning to some semblance of life—and with his degree go on to become an official in the Beijing construction bureau, which has oversight of all major building projects in the city. He rose through the ranks of the bureau before going into business in 1991 with a wealthy partner from the south who wanted to break into Beijing real estate.

His first major project, Baixan villas, was built on farmland to the north of the city. He sold five hundred of the California-style bungalows. After the success of his Baixan villas development, Zhang came up with the even more ambitious Chateau Zhang Lafitte. This palace on the outskirts of Beijing is copied from François Mansart's Chateau Maisons-Lafitte, twelve minutes out of Paris, but with two additional wings, copied from the royal apartments at Fontainebleau, and a garden modeled on Versailles—buildings that would have prompted Charles Fourier to take out his measuring stick with glee. Zhang: "It cost me $50 million, but that is because I made so many improvements compared to the original." Beijing's *high net worth individuals* can rent rooms there, which might persuade them to buy homes on the grounds. "Buyers want the right environment so they feel they are fully realizing their identity." An environment protected by private security in period livery.

The eight hundred farmers of Yangge village used to cultivate this thousand acres as a collective until Zhang *persuaded* Changping district officials to let him develop it. First, the officials converted it to a *green zone*, then they leased it to Zhang at an annual rent of $300 per acre. Zhang: "The whole project is exactly in line with Beijing's policy to maintain the land as green space." Officials granted Zhang easements to build the Chateau and a thousand luxury homes on 170 acres of it, in exchange for nearly ten million dollars. As part of the deal he pays the elderly villagers a stipend, and the younger ones can apply to work on his grounds, waterways, golf course and vineyard.

The new industries that the money was supposed to start never materialized, and villagers insist that this latter-day enclosure of their land is in breach of contract over many issues. Still, Zhang is nothing if not well connected. Politburo member Jia Qingling, fourth-ranked leader in the whole of China at the time, came to visit. Giant color photos of him inspecting the vineyard grace the wine bar. "Today's leaders have exactly the right kind of thinking," enthuses Zhang.[10] Not surprisingly, Zhang is himself a party member. This was the real destiny of Mao's party, one perhaps not entirely predictable from Viénet's 1977 films, but one that is legible there all the same. In them, détournement at least does its job of negating power's capture of the available signs and the rendering of them as historically mute.

All of Viénet's films embody the qualities that Clark thinks of as those most critical to détournement. In place of reverence, Viénet manipulates his sources with a wry insouciance. The result is not a pleasing pastiche, but a confident assertion of historical consciousness. He cuts between the key instances, and discards that which is of scholarly interest only. Elements of very different styles come together, like in Viénet's recipe for dialectical eggs, where the yolk and white are cooked separately before being combined in one dish.[11]

The whole effect is to cut a template for what it might mean to become the author of historical time itself, while being careful not to have the work stand in for such an authoring, which could only be collective, collaborative, and far removed from the space and time of cinema. Viénet's anti-cinema is not as well known or well regarded as Debord's, and this is a pity, for Viénet's earthy humor and genuine sympathy for popular affect are a useful counterpoint to the more astringent beauties of Debordian cinema, and help us disentangle the elements of personal style in Debord's films from their conceptual advances.

Aside from his merits as a filmmaker, Viénet tried valiantly to put an end to the romance of the Cultural Revolution within the western political imaginary. But Maoist China is only one version of the historical nostalgia that has seized the imagination of leftist intellectuals in the twenty-first century. The other is surely the Autonomist movement in Italy, from 1969 through the seventies and beyond. This is a different story, and its central actors are often not far removed, in theory and practice, from Situationist positions. Yet at the risk of factionalism, certain Situationist or Post-Situationist works might offer a critical distance, a historical reframing, of those events as well.

22 The Occulted State

Know how to wait … Stroll through the open spaces of time to the center of opportunity.

Baltasar Gracián

A woman with two small children tries to board a plane at Ronald Reagan airport. Security officers stop her when they discover that the child's sippy cup contains more than the permissible three ounces of liquid. At once, uniformed agents gather, superiors are notified. The boarding halts. The child's sippy cup becomes an object of extreme suspicion. It is as if the greatest power ever to bestride the world could be brought low by the most modest formula.[1] As Gianfranco Sanguinetti once wrote: "cowardice becomes, for the first time in history, a sublime quality, fear is always justified."[2]

What happens next is obscure, even on the security tape. Perhaps the woman throws the contents of the sippy cup on the ground. Perhaps they accidentally spill. Uniformed goons encircle her and make her get down on her hands and knees and clean up the spilled liquid—twice. (The first time she missed a bit.) Shortly after, the authorities revoke the ban on liquids, describing it as an ineffective piece of *security theater*. It is all in the name of the *war on terror*. A war that, as Vice President Dick Cheney once casually said, can never end.

"War, in a word, is modernity incarnate," as Clark and the Retort group write.[3] Given that these were times when, during a hunting expedition, Cheney shot a friend in the face, and it was *the friend* who thought he should apologize, then naked displays of pure power legitimated by nothing much more than their own balls-out bareness were the norm. The state of emergency, or the state of exception, was revealed once again to be merely the normal state of affairs. Retort again: "Ultimately, the spectacle comes out of the barrel of a gun."[4]

That the state is founded on something other than justice, law or the social contract would hardly surprise the Situationists. As Debord writes to fellow founding member Pinot Gallizio in 1958: "Yesterday the police interrogated me for a long time concerning the journal and the Situationist organization. This is only the beginning. One of the threatening principles that appeared quite quickly to me in this discussion: the police want to consider the Situationist International as an association dedicated to bringing disorder to France."[5] Ever since he moved to Paris in his youth, Debord came into contact with the state mostly via its police. He did not work for any state media or cultural agency. He was not involved in the folderol of its political parties. As Debord would later quip: "It is known that I was a professional, but of what?"[6] Of making trouble. In his experience, the state was the police.

After the assassination of his friend and patron Gérard Lebovici in 1984, journalists took a certain relish in claiming to have been privy to certain details of secret police files on Debord. They claimed that he had been under surveillance for some time. This led him to remark: "What a strange and unfortunate land, where one is informed of the work of an author more quickly and confidently through police archives than through the literary criticisms of a free press or through academics who make a profession out of knowing the issues at hand."[7] Debord specified, in a literary testament like that of the vagabond poet François Villon, that statements he had made to the police should not be included in his collected works. Not because any statements he made there would cause him any embarrassment, but because of literary "scruples about the form."[8]

Debord admitted to using false names and documents in Italy in the seventies, but he had his reasons. This was a time of the *strategy of tension*, in which a rising tide of working-class militancy was diverted by a shadowy game of bombings and other terrorist acts by secretive groups, followed by repressions and reprisals from police agencies of the state. Things reached a peak in 1978 when the

Red Brigades kidnapped Aldo Moro, who had twice been prime minister and was the architect of the so-called *historic compromise* which was supposed to bring the left into the government. Moro was found dead in a parked car. Debord: "It was a mythological opera with great machinations, where terrorist heroes by transformation become foxes so as to ensnare their prey, then lions so as to fear nothing and no-one so long as they retain it, and stool-pigeons so as not to draw from this blow the smallest harmful thing to the regime they aspire to defy."[9] The right blamed the Communists for the Red Brigades. The Communists blamed the far-left Autonomists. The Autonomists blamed each other.

Debord thought he saw the hand of the state in these murky events. He encouraged his young friend Gianfranco Sanguinetti to expose it: "I have known a man who spent his time among the *party girls* of Florence and who loved to keep bad company with all of the hard-drinkers of the bad neighborhoods. But he comprehended everything that went on. He demonstrated his comprehension once. One knows that he will do it again. He is, today, considered by some to be the most dangerous man in Italy."[10] Sanguinetti had, with Debord's assistance, pulled off a brilliant hoax in 1975, and Debord encouraged him to action again. Sanguinetti's response to the Moro kidnapping was even more paranoid than Debord's. On hearing the news, he retreated to his country house and made sure he was seen by the local people, to generate possible alibis in case he was suspected of involvement in the Moro affair. Sure enough, his house was searched by the police, who of course found nothing.[11]

Sanguinetti did not initially credit Debord's theory of secret police involvement in the Moro affair, but he came around to it. He published a short book called *On Terrorism and the State* in which he wrote that: "It is its own secret services which organize and pull the strings of terrorism. Is this not, then, the main secret of the Italian State?"[12] This was an extraordinary thesis at the time, and it got Sanguinetti into even more trouble.

It retrospect it doesn't seem all that far fetched. A war on terror—led by a general no less—aided the consolidation of a state in crisis. The big losers, in Sanguinetti's account, were the Autonomist left. Both the state and its official enemy, the Communist Party, were united in condemning the Autonomists for sympathy, if not complicity, with the armed struggle, pushing the Autonomists onto the defensive. Sanguinetti: "The poor Autonomists, who, for their part, never had much of a clue either about terrorism or about revolution, have thus ended up, like a coveted prey, in the game-bag of the Stalinists and the judiciary."[13]

The most famous of the Autonomists, Antonio Negri (b. 1933), was arrested in 1979 and charged with being a leader of the Red Brigades and for involvement in the kidnapping of Aldo Moro. In exile in France from 1983, he built on his political writings a sustained philosophical critique. He returned to Italy and to prison voluntarily in 1997, in part to honor the hundreds of other political militants still in jail, often on trumped-up charges. He was released in 2003. With Michael Hardt he co-authored a series of original post-Marxist works, starting with *Empire* (2000). His work would become one of the most influential leftist currents of the early twenty-first century.

Not the least merit of the 1970s texts of Sanguinetti is that they provide an alternate window into the hothouse of Italian political economic life in which the Autonomist strain of thought was formed and to which it remains, for better or worse, inextricably linked.[14] And while in the pages of *Tiqqun* Debord is described as "an execrable middleman for all that was explosive in the Italian situation," the analyses he sponsored might still have something to say to those who would make of Italy a sacred memory.[15] Debord and Sanguinetti's critique of the Italian left pleases no one, and that alone may be its sole merit.

From a wealthy Tuscan family with leftist pretensions, Sanguinetti joined a newly formed Italian section of the Situationist International in 1969. He was around twenty years old. The Italian section took part in the struggles of 1969, which like those in France combined elements of a general strike, an insurrection, perhaps even a nascent civil war. Sanguinetti then lived underground in Paris until his expulsion from France back to Italy in 1971. When in 1972 Debord published *The Veritable Split in the International,* his texts on the dissolution of the Situationists, he made Sanguinetti the co-author as a tribute to a friend and comrade. Sanguinetti was arrested in 1975 and spent a few months in prison, and was turned back at the French border in 1976 when he attempted to leave the country again. His experience of the state, even more than Debord's, was mainly of its policing function.

Sanguinetti's analysis of terrorism, while salutary, is nevertheless somewhat unsatisfactory. His identification of terror directly with the state feeds into a conspiratorial approach to thinking about state power, as if by uncovering the secret machinations of the state one could somehow apprehend its truth. Something like this was the aim of the five hundred people who gathered at the Embassy Suites hotel in Chicago for a combination trade show and political convention for the 9/11 Truth movement. Given that Zogby polls show 42 percent of Americans doubting the conclusions of *The 9/11 Commission Report*, and 49 percent of New Yorkers believing that some leaders "knew in advance" about the 2001 attacks on the World Trade Center and the Pentagon, they are not alone. The Truthers are out there.

The talk at Embassy Suites compared 9/11 to the Reichstag fire, the Tonkin Bay incident, the assassinations of President Kennedy and Martin Luther King, Jr. In his keynote address, syndicated radio host Alex Jones rehearsed the main argument of the movement, that on September 11, 2001, a "controlled demolition" brought down the towers of the World Trade Center in New York City, not the impact of hijacked passenger jets.[16] This is the central tenet of the 9/11 Truth ideology. To them it seems more plausible than imagining that, where 9/11 is concerned, the state has nothing to hide.

Sanguinetti distinguishes between offensive terrorism by non-state actors and defensive terrorism by the state. He judged Italian terrorism of the period to be defensive terrorism on the part of the state. This refreshing claim can be turned aside from the path of conspiracy theory and used for new tactics in thinking through the inscrutable surface effects of power at work. Perhaps the origins of terrorism are not so easily decided. Perhaps the origins are not even all that relevant. Perhaps the state can make use of what appears to be offensive terrorism, coming from a non-state actor, as a way to consolidate power and pre-empt social movements. The state that makes a spectacle of responding to a need for security need not answer to any other desires. As the rather more sanguine Debord remarks: "Such a perfect democracy constructs its own inconceivable foe, terrorism. It wishes to be judged by its enemies rather than by its results."[17]

In the disintegrating spectacle of the twenty-first century, truth is as strange as fiction. In his 2007 novel *Spook Country,* William Gibson writes of a *cold civil war,* all but invisible, waged within a state of Byzantine complexity and obscurity.[18] His elaborate spy plot includes the usual agents and counter-agents, but curiously enough mixes in the owner of an advertising agency with the improbable name of Hubertus Bigend (b. 1967). The son of a minor Situationist, Bigend has grasped that the secret is to the spectacle as art once was to culture. The secret is not the truth of the spectacle, it is the aesthetic form of the spectacle. Gibson intuits something central here to Situationist experience, if not its theory: that the spectacle of appearances has another side. That which is good appears; that which is concealed *is better.* And for no other reason than that it is concealed.

The secret is not the truth of the spectacle. The division between the spectacle of appearances and the secrecy of non-appearances is itself an aspect of the falsification of the whole that the spectacle affects. While the spectacle renders all that appears equivalent, the division between the secret and the spectacular implies a hierarchy—the main game of power. Appearances are exchangeable for appearances; secrets exchangeable only for secrets. For Debord and Sanguinetti, it is not knowledge which is power, but secrecy.

A counter-power is then not so much a counter-knowledge as a strategy that is capable both of revealing secrets when it is tactically advantageous, but also of fabricating them. Against the power of the secret as the founding power of the state, Situationists and Post-Situationists alike pose the glamour of the clandestine as a kind of counter-power. The refusal to appear within the spectacle is also a refusal of the division between the spectacular and its secret. Which in turn makes the Situationists (and certain Post-Situationists) appear as dangerous to the state. The paradox is that this apparent danger, while only apparent, becomes in spectacular society a real danger.[19]

Another Hotel Room: this time the Budapest Hilton, and this time the organizer is the International Republican Institute, a nongovernmental group which may or may not be in receipt of US government money. Retired Army Colonel Robert Helvey leads a seminar on the techniques of nonviolent resistance attended by about twenty leaders of Otpor, the Serbian opposition movement. Helvey's approach is based on that of Gene Sharp, author of *From Dictatorship to Democracy* and other works, which in turn draw on the insight of Montaigne's friend Etienne de La Boétie.[20]

The key to de La Boétie's thought is that if people withdraw their obedience to the state, the state cannot stand. Or as Debord says in the same vein: "This is how, little by little, a new epoch of fires has been set alight, which none of us alive at the moment will see the end of: obedience is dead." And yet the outcome is far from certain. The withdrawal of consent from one state may just as easily serve another. Debord: "Yet the highest ambition of the integrated spectacle is still to turn secret agents into revolutionaries, and revolutionaries into secret agents."[21] An exchange of one clandestine form for another.

All the disintegrated spectacle might add to this transaction is that they might not even know it. There might be two ways of becoming an agent of the state. One is to be knowingly co-opted; the other is by descending into the spectacle of violence. Whether the Italian Red Brigades were manipulated by the first method or not, they certainly became agents of the state via the second. Regardless of their allegiances and ideologies, both the secret agent and the armed revolutionary use the same forms of organization: the form of hierarchy and secrecy. Sanguinetti: "All secret terrorist groupuscles are organized and directed by a clandestine hierarchy of the very militants of clandestinity, which reflects perfectly the division of labor and roles proper to this social organization: above it is decided and below it is carried out."[22]

Given that agents of the state invariably have much greater resources at their disposal, it is no accident who gets to infiltrate and manipulate who. But in the disintegrating spectacle, this may not even be necessary. Regardless of the inconvenience, a terrorist attack on the state provides the very pretext the state needs to consolidate its power, and in more recent times, perhaps, to go on the offensive, preempting popular self-organization in advance.

Nothing succeeds as well as a terrorist attack in making the people feel as though they have a common enemy with the state. In the disintegrating spectacle, the state offers nothing but the spectacle of its own necessity. Debord: "Until 1968 modern society was convinced it was loved. It has since had to abandon these dreams; it prefers to be feared."[23]

The spectacle incorporates within itself images of its own overcoming. Debord: "It is known that this society signs a sort of pact with its most avowed enemies, when it allots them a space in the spectacle."[24] It is personified by certain kinds of anti-celebrity, images of the integral action that would further disintegrate the spectacle, but which actually sustain it to the extent that they are mere images.

Anti-celebrities appear as dangerous to the spectacle in spite of being useful for it because the spectacle does not control them. They do its work for their own reasons. Since no other reasons besides the logic of spectacle are supposed to exist, their very existence is both useful and troubling. After the assassination in 1984 of his friend Gérard Lebovici, Debord found himself becoming cast as just such an anti-celebrity, who must be dangerous precisely because of his refusal of service to the spectacle.

The enemy that the spectacle can recognize is, once again, as in certain times past, the terrorist—the *spectacular* negation of the middle-class ideal. An act of terror aims above all at the production of the image. It is the spectacle for those who do not own their own news network or movie studio. It is a hijacking of the vehicle of the image itself. While terrorists appear as, and may even believe themselves to be, enemies of the state, their role is quite different. They are the—apparently—external principle of necessity for the state. They provide it with its reason to exist. They may act of their own volition. They may be agents of another state. They may be agents of the very state they are attacking, or merely its dupes. It doesn't actually matter. They provide the state with a reason to exist, and can usually be assured of its full attention. The state is more concerned with threats to itself than to its subjects.

"The top secret world ... has become so large, so unwieldy and so secretive that no one knows how much money it costs, how many people it employs, how many programs exist within it or exactly how many agencies do the same work." In the United States alone there are at least 1,271 organizations and 1,931 companies at 10,000 locations employing 854,000 people who produce 50,000 intelligence reports per year. As one of the few super-users with security clearance enough to know something about all of it says: "I'm not going to live long enough to be briefed on everything ... The complexity of this system defies description." A certain James Clapper declares: "There's only one entity in the entire universe that has visibility [over it all] and that's God." And he is the Director of National Intelligence.[25]

By 2011 the United States Department of Homeland Security had the third largest state workforce, after Defense and Veteran's Affairs. It is getting a new $3.4 billion dollar complex in Anacostia, the largest government complex built since the Pentagon. Some of the new buildings for the expanding universe of the security state are "on the order of the pyramids" says a contractor who worked on them. Most of these *intel factories* are staffed with analysts making $40–65k per year, some straight out of college, often with little training or language competence, who churn out reports, most of which use the same intelligence and arrive at the same conclusions. It is rather like graduate school. Debord: "It is in these circumstances that we can speak of domination's falling rate of profit, as it spreads to almost the whole of social space and consequently increases both its personnel and its means. For now each means aspires, and labors, to become an end. Surveillance spies on itself, and plots against itself."[26]

In the disintegrating spectacle, the state even renders spectacular the production of its own secrets. As Sanguinetti saw as early as the seventies, when it loses its grip on historical thought, the spectacular state succumbs to the spectacular economy whose depredations it was supposed to at once enable yet guard against. Capital missed the last chance to save itself from itself. The disintegrating spectacle originates in that moment when capital defeats not just the proletariat but also its image, be it Social Democrat, Leninist or Maoist. It is reduced to the security theater of opposing images of images. It frees itself from all impediments to its total war against the earth itself.

23 The Last Chance to Save Capitalism

Don't turn one foolish act into two. Often we commit four blunders to correct one.

Baltasar Gracián

There is a certain vanity in thinking that every aspect of our everyday life is of intimate concern to power. Certain states are less and less concerned with the well being and productivity of their subjects—their so-called *biopower*.[1] The state of the disintegrating spectacle reveals itself as concerned mostly with its own sovereignty. What if power, too, was not much more than a spectacle of appearances? Sanguinetti's greatest work did not just make an argument about the nature of power as appearance, it acted as the means by which power exposed itself in a less than flattering light.

In 1975 Sanguinetti sent out a curious document to a hundred or so prominent people in Italian public life, under the pseudonym Censor. The text contained the Machiavellian argument to the effect that creating the appearance of the Communist Party joining the government does not negate the rule of bourgeois power, but could actually enhance it. The text apparently addressed itself to the real power elite—the ruling class—and took a distinctive form: "One reason we chose the ancient form of expression, the pamphlet, rather than a more systematic text, is that we do not want to renounce the pleasure of speaking with swords drawn."[2]

Censor called for the ruling class to at least attempt to be truthful amongst itself. It ought not to be duped by the specter of the power of the Communists. This was merely a phantom, which the ruling class had itself invoked to strengthen the state during the cold war. But there was no need for power to believe in a phantom that was largely its own creation. The real danger was elsewhere, but before examining it, Censor expounded on the distinctive features of Italian capitalism of the seventies, features not unlike those Debord identified as the *integrated spectacle*.

As a consequence of its own development, capitalism expanded state power, which took on a nominally democratic form, but in the context of expanded secrecy and disinformation. The perimeter of the state may have become more democratic, but only so that its core may become more clandestine. Its principal means of dealing with conflict was to incorporate it at the margin. Censor: "The state is the palladium of commercial society, which converts even its enemies into proprietors."[3] Like the wooden image of Pallas Athena, whom the Romans called Minerva, that the Greeks took from Troy and which Aeneas brought to Rome, the state is that ancient thing that protects capital from the enemies of its own making, the forces which its very development casts before it.

Development had one aspect that troubled Censor, namely that it made the economy an autonomous sphere. He offered a critique of it apparently from the right. Left to its own devices, the autonomous development of the economy might generate the forces capable of overthrowing the state. Censor called for the ruling class to think and act historically and politically rather than to believe in its own ideology of a self-regulating economy.

The organized labor movement—or at least its titular head, the Communist Party—was no longer the enemy. The project of postwar reconstruction had already incorporated it in a subordinate and peripheral role of maintaining labor discipline, in the name of building a modern, democratic economy and society. Certain forces within the Communist Party had threatened insurrection in 1948, but the party itself put down this revolt, thus confirming its allegiance to the bourgeois state. Censor: "The Trojan horse should not be feared, except when there are well-armed Archean troops inside."[4] Much more damaging to the state was the behavior of the Christian Democrats. Censor saw them principally as the party of the middle classes who aligned their interests with the bourgeoisie. The party was riddled with private interests who treated the various organs of the state as so many personal fiefdoms.

The main danger to the state came from neither the apparent strength of the Communists nor the unreliability of the Christian Democrats, but from a new kind of worker's movement. The working class had defected from its own party, the party that in Debord's estimation had become a spectacular representation of the proletariat already in the 1920s. After May '68 the working class could no longer be co-opted via its representative. The workers' response is as the courtesan says in Viénet's *Dialectics*: "They offer crumbs. We want it all!" The workers did not know what they were fighting for, but what they wanted was to fight. They had started to question private property itself—the one thing crucial to the state. Censor: "Private property thus constitutes the fortress wall of society, and all other rights and privileges are the advanced defense."

The internal weakness of the state made this movement particularly dangerous: "on high reigns apathy, boredom and immobility; below on the contrary, political life begins to manifest feverish symptoms." One such symptom was the Autonomist left, outside the Communist Party. But for Censor this was just the fever. The spontaneous action of the working class was the real disease. This was causing something of a panic among the ruling classes: "The bourgeoisie is afraid of being right, and afraid of being afraid. It soon perceived that it was right to be afraid."[5]

Censor stressed the usefulness of the Communist Party in imposing discipline on the working class and keeping refractory elements in line. But this view was not shared by the ruling class, deluded by their own fiction that cast the Communists as the leadership of the working class against the state rather than as the police agent of the state against the working class. The ruling class thought the price the Communists demanded for their services outweighed the guarantees they could offer of their own effectiveness. And perhaps rightly so, as the Communists quite underestimated the danger to themselves of rebel workers who no longer saw the unions and the party as their representatives. And so, from 1968 on into the seventies, Italy descended into an undeclared civil war, in which "the only things still functioning in Italy were the unions and the police."[6]

The hot year of 1969 was the time when the possibility of a general insurrection seemed genuinely close. What averted it was a wave of bombings, variously attributed to anarchists or fascists, but behind at least some of which was the hand of the secret services of the state. Against this, not only the Communists but also much of the Autonomist left felt the need to rally around opposition to clandestine violence. But for Censor, the continued use of the terror tactic was dangerous. If the complicity of agencies of the state were to come to light, this risked alienating the very people that the strategy had neutralized, and re-establishing the conditions for worker's revolt. As Censor wryly observes, in the spirit of Gracián: "If no good policies have ever been founded on truth, the worst policies are founded on the improbable."[7]

Re-founding ruling class power on firmer ground meant a less disingenuous policy. The state had to reinstate legality or disappear. But the state couldn't count on anything but its secret services, and the continual use of force was weakening the state. Alluding to Machiavelli's *Prince*, Censor argued that a state that used force too much and too often did not appear stronger for it, but weaker. And in any case, terrorism was less of a threat to the state than the mutiny of the working class.

The real threat was not bombs but, as La Boétie would say, disobedience. The ruling class had discounted the threat of the working class because the new movement lacked leadership and organization. Organized labor and Communist leadership was co-optable; *disorganized labor* was not. This was much more dangerous: "all revolutions in history began without leaders, and when they had them, they were finished."[8] From their analysis of the Paris Commune onwards, this is the first and last axiom of Situationist politics.

The state had to stop its short-term defensive tactics. As Clausewitz had already shown, the relation between offense and defense is asymmetrical. Censor: "our state, continually defending itself against phantom enemies—red or black according to the mood of the moment, all poorly constructed—never wanted to confront the problems posed by the real enemy."[9] The army was not going to defend the state; it was as useless as the postal service. The secret service risked losing its secrecy, and thus its power. The murder, or rather *theatrical killing*, of the leftist publisher Feltrinelli, for example, was a dangerous move. As Gracián might say, it was not wise policy to cover up a foolish act with a dozen more.

The real threat remained disorganized labor: "this crisis is total because, intensively, it is life itself ... that has succumbed to the contagion." It is not a crisis *in* the economy but a crisis *of* the economy. The workers gained wage rises but were disenchanted with the flimflam that was all these wages could buy. Censor: "we poisoned the world, and we gave the people a special reason to revolt against us every instant of their everyday life: we poisoned life itself."[10]

It might still be possible to head off the danger from disorganized labor by bringing organized labor—the Communist Party—into the outer perimeter of the state. This was the policy of the historic compromise, although as Censor points out it was neither historic nor a compromise. There is nothing historic about a merely expedient tactic that could later be reversed. There is no compromise when only one side—the Communists—gives anything up.

On the international plane, the cold war had subsided into a period of *peaceful coexistence* between Moscow and Washington, between the diffuse and concentrated variants of the spectacle. For Censor this too was a mere tactic. Both sides faced troubling dissent internally. In the West, most clearly in France and Italy; in the east, the Czechs and Poles were creating their own forms of spontaneous withdrawal of obedience. This was the backdrop to Censor's proposal for a fuller incorporation of the Communists into a Western state. The integrated spectacle would replace the diffuse form, drawing organized labor not just within the orbit of the spectacle, but completely inside the state, or at least appearing to do so, while the core of the state's functions became occulted and withdrawn.

Censor called the ruling class to action. Power could not be delegated to others any longer. The maintenance of the state could not be entrusted to the secret police alone. As for the utility of the army, those who think it better to govern with rifles than with Communists overestimate how many of their soldiers are good shots. Power could not be entrusted to the Christian Democrats, who were content to squabble over the spoils of each particular office and leave the state as a whole to its ruin. Power could not be left in the hands of managers, who were no better than overpaid wage earners, unable to grasp the historic process. Nor was it acceptable to cash out and become mere rentiers, passing on the mess to whoever is cashed up. (The Saudis at the time, then Japan, then Chinese sovereign wealth funds.) The diffuse spectacle was undermining the very authority of the class that had created it, and was in as much trouble as the concentrated spectacle in the east. The ruling class risked being overcome by its own creation.

It simply had to be faced that capitalism did not deliver on its promises. The manufacture of abundance had led only to an abundance of boredom. The ruling class lost sight of anything of real value. Far from securing power, abundance threatened it. Censor: "We have thoughtlessly dispersed so much false luxury and comfort that the entire population is quite rightly dissatisfied."

While the ruling class struggles against disorganized labor and its negation of property and the state, it had also the positive historical task of affirming something of value outside of mere abundance. This may be an even bigger challenge. Censor: "this abundance of fabricated objects requires the demarcation of an elite more than ever—an elite that is sheltered by this abundance and takes what is really precious: otherwise, there will soon be no place on earth with anything precious left in it."[11] Prophetic words. Has not the ruling class of the disintegrating spectacle been thoroughly corrupted by the spectacle itself? Even those powers it withdrew into a clandestine core became corrupted by the high-end trade of the spectacle's exclusive other currency—the secret.

In Lampedusa's classic historical novel *The Leopard* (1958), the aristocrat Tancredi justifies going over to the side of Garibaldi's bourgeois revolution in these terms: "Unless we ourselves take a hand now, they'll foist a republic on us. If we want things to stay as they are, things will have to change."[12] Censor pointed the way to the seizure of initiative by the ruling class as the seventies gave way to the eighties. Sanguinetti's pamphlet received creditable coverage in the news media, including much speculation about its author. It was thought to be either the work of some kind of modern-day Tancredi who still retained the patina of classical knowledge, or perhaps of some junior state functionary who had actually learned something at a modern university. When Sanguinetti revealed the hoax, scandal followed, but one aspect of the affair is often overlooked. Sanguinetti produced the aura of authenticity for his document by making it appear as if it were a secret that had been revealed. The secret quality of the document was what made it appear as if it had, not truth, but power.

Sanguinetti's *Real Report* still works as an allegory for the relation between power and the secret in the age of the disintegrating spectacle. Unlike Censor's Christian Democrats, the US members of Congress of the early twenty-first century cannot be bought; one rents them by the hour. They squabble over the particulars while the state as the guarantor of the property interests of the ruling class as a totality becomes nobody's business. Terror still forms a convenient alibi, if not always a terribly effective one. And yet there are major differences between the integrated spectacle of the seventies and the disintegrated spectacle of the early twenty-first century. For one thing, what is left of organized labor is thoroughly integrated into the state.

Perhaps these days one could call this *disorganizing labor*: Emmalee Bauer, using work time to sit at her desk and write about not working. Or Steven Slater, a Jetblue flight attendant who became a working-class hero with a spectacular exit from the workplace. After an altercation with a passenger, who hit him in the head with the lid of the overhead storage bin, he told the passenger off over the intercom, grabbed some beer, activated the emergency chute and slid to the tarmac. Slater made it all the way out through airport security and all the way home before police caught up with him. They found him in bed with his boyfriend. Slater then found himself before the judge on charges of criminal mischief, reckless endangerment and trespassing. Jetblue suspended him, but a fan base sprang up on social networking sites to raise money for his defense. Psychologist Alan Hilfer says, "Despite the celebrity he is enjoying, he will not easily find a new job unless his new job is being a celebrity."[13] A job he held as long as such things last.

In the twenty-first century, the state as the centralized power over the double form of spectacle and secret gave way to a disorganized and decentralized distribution of such powers. Debord: "the liars have lied to themselves."[14] The diffuse spectacle of the postwar years merely incorporated the image of that which would negate it, the image of organized labor and its bureaucratic sock puppets. The outbreak of a fresh form of negation, that of disorganized labor, led to the full incorporation of the organization of labor into the integrated spectacle. With the failure of disorganized labor to turn local and sporadic expressions of boredom into a strategy for dismantling spectacle power, the integrated spectacle emerges triumphant.

It is not as if workers are thus magically rendered content with their poisoned world. Workers respond with boredom, indifference, absenteeism, petty theft on the job, and now and then by popping the escape chute. In the absence of the great game of struggling against that which refuses it, the integrated spectacle begins to disintegrate of its own accord. It becomes the marvel of none other than its own deliquescence. Its motto: That which appears is all there is; all there is, is that which appears. The tricky qualities of appearances, however, are the domain of the ineradicable stain on spectacular perfection, of what one might call the devil's party.

24 Anti-Cinema

Do, but also seem. Things do not pass for what they are, but what they seem.

Baltasar Gracián

There is a strange amnesia about the seventies. The sixties are a subject of persistent nostalgia. Everyone of a certain age claims to have *been there*. Nobody much makes such claims about the seventies. In the seventies, the acid test gave way to the heroin epidemic. Politics as street festival became bombing and kidnapping. The notorious slogan of the Watts uprising (1965), "burn, baby burn," became a lyric to the dance number "Disco Inferno" (1976). If you remember the sixties, you weren't there; if you forgot the seventies, maybe you have something to hide.

The Situationist International dissolved itself in 1972. It cannot be brandished as yet another example of what was wrong with the times.[1] The great break into lived time of May '68 had come and gone. For Debord, Paris lost its charms. He would spend much of this decade, and the next, in voluntary exile from Paris, circulating between Florence, Arles, Seville and the Auvergne. These were quietly productive times. He found new cities, each with their own field of possibilities. He even found something to do in the countryside.[2] He found some sterling collaborators, whose witting and unwitting contributions to thinking a way out of these times has not yet received its due. And he made some remarkable films. Debord had made films before, but these seventies films stand out as both conceptual elaborations of the problem of living in the lackluster light of the society of the spectacle, and practical demonstrations of how to move in and against it.

Debord's films were always ahead of their time. They anticipate, and in many respects exceed, the achievements of materialist cinema. They manage a synthesis in advance of a politics of form and a politics of content. They draw attention to their mode of production but don't make a fetish of this gesture or expect miracles of it. His is a cinema that you have in the absence of certain more important things to do, which will interrupt your program presently. Debord's films, and the Letterist cinema from which they emerged, were widely plagiarized. Tom Levin: "An inordinate amount of Debord's concerns reappear in later works by Godard ... One even encounters the same 'stars': years before she became the leading actress in numerous films by Godard as well as his wife, Anna Karina appeared as the actress in a Monsavon commercial détourned by Debord."[3]

If the key to Viénet's films is insouciance, then *insolence* is the key to Debord's three mature films of the seventies, an insolent disregard for the proper handling of images. Nothing about their provenance is to be respected; not their context, their ownership, their genre. This insolence is not an indifference to what images mean. Debord is not interested in setting them free to frolic in some *postmodern* indeterminacy. Nor is he interested in subjecting them to endless *interrogations*, ferreting out secret codes of significance. Both of these attitudes are too respectful. In and of themselves, images sublimate neither poetry nor power. Rather, he starts with a casual disregard for the value that professional makers or owners or interpreters claim of them. Images are merely moves in a game, tactics in a strategy, the goal of which is the critique and overturning of a world in which images are just objects of contemplation. The people make meaning, but not with the media of their own choosing. The task is a social production of recovered meaning or fresh-minted meaning, with what images one can beg, borrow or steal.

Images themselves are not the enemy. Writing is as much a part of the spectacle as cinema, and the same problems attend to both.[4] How can a text, a film, a representation take sides against itself? Rather than making representations of what is wrong with this world, or of what a better world of the imagination might be like, how can representation be a partisan for another kind of world-making? Could this be an anti-cinema that hastens cinema toward its end? A purely individual and moral choice to not make cinema would be of no consequence, for cinema has not yet exhausted its potential.

The time of cinema is not yet over. But perhaps it can be hastened to its end, and that is what Debord almost succeeded in achieving. In the wild, viral, endless world of the cutting, mixing, mutating, mutilating of cinema in the disintegrating spectacle, Debord's anticipation of the dissolution of cinema is partly realized. And partly not. There is still an extraordinary gift in his films which points to how much further the ebb tide has to go.[5]

Who says the spectator is always a passive receptacle of spectacle? At a 2008 Christmas day screening of *The Curious Case of Benjamin Button,* James Cialella got so enraged at a father and son who would not shut up that he took out a .38 caliber gun and shot the man. "It's truly frightening when you see something like this evolve into such violence," said police spokesman Lt. Frank Vanore.[6] One only regrets that Cialella injured a fellow spectator for obscuring his enjoyment of the spectacle, rather than taking aim at the screen for obscuring his life with his fellow spectators.

In the passing show of images that populate Debord's late films, very little is ever explained to the spectator. In *Society of the Spectacle* (1973) in particular, the images flit by in a seemingly absurd order. Occasionally they seem to correspond to Debord's voice-over, but often the link is obscure. They certainly don't make much immediate sense in relation to each other. It is not as if there is a complete disconnect between sound and image of the kind advocated by Isidore Isou as *discrepant cinema.*[7] Rather, Debord has taken Isou's initial break between sound and image and conceived of a way to reconnect them in a different way. The crisp rhythms of the edits accumulate as the film progresses. Clusters of images that together don't make much sense reveal themselves in the light of later ones. Surprising complexity and consistency emerges if one accepts a central premise: that the spectacle attempts to negate the possibility of making history, but history remains as a residue within the spectacle in fragmented form.

Martine Barraqué edited *Society of the Spectacle* (1973) and its sequel, *Refutation of All Judgments* (1975). They are best treated as one work rather than two. As Barraqué notes, "*Refutation* was entirely made out of footage that had not been included in the *Society of the Spectacle*."[8] *Refutation* is an extraordinary precursor to the answer-video of the kind that pop up like wildfire on the internet in the early twenty-first century. In appending it to *Society of the Spectacle*, Debord makes a complete work that subsumes not only the actual reactions to the film but any possible reaction into the work itself, in advance.

Barraqué came to Debord via the patron Debord acquired in the seventies, Gérard Lebovici (1932–84), the publisher, film producer and film agent, about whom there will be more to say later. Barraqué was already working as an assistant editor for François Truffaut (1932–84) and makes two brief uncredited appearances in Truffaut's *Day for Night* (1973), playing a film editor. Among others, she would go on to edit *The Green Room* (1978) and *The Last Metro* (1980) for Truffaut, but Debord's *Society of the Spectacle* was her first credit as an editor. Of Truffaut and Debord she says: "they were both (I was in the middle of them) curious about one another." Perhaps it is time to be a little curious about Martine Barraqué, too.

Her significance in realizing Debord's films is honored in the credits. She gets a whole title card to herself. It would be amusing to compare her Debords and Truffauts to see if Barraqué left a comparable stylistic signature on them. While Barraqué also lent a hand to Debord's later film, *In Girum Imus Nocte et Consumimur Igni* (1978), it was edited by her former assistant Stéphanie Granel, and it has a rather different pace and structure to it. While both Barraqué and Granel doubtless worked under Debord's direction, highlighting the contribution of his editors might be a modest attempt to prevent the subsumption of Debord under the usual *auteurist* view of cinema production as Truffaut and other *masters*.

Society of the Spectacle uses selected text from Debord's 1967 book of the same name, read by Debord himself in an even tone quite at odds with the tradition of voice-over delivery for the cinema. The soundtrack was recorded in Debord's apartment. The images were cut to the soundtrack. The images come mostly from four sources: stills from popular magazines, newsreel documentation of current events, advertisements, and extracts from classic feature films.

As Barraqué explains the process: "We had lists of documents that we had to search for, keep and file once found, and that we would use in future work. The documents could be old news, we had a lot of still images that he cut-off from magazines (that his wife must have read, and that he used to cut images from), that he kept and that I had filmed in order to have them in the film as 24 frames per second images. It was a very detailed work. He could come to the editing room at 2 p.m. and by then I already had the images sorted so that he would look at them. We went through the images together, and then he decided the order in which they would be presented. Afterwards, we would look for the paragraph that would be juxtaposed to the images."

The relationship between image and text in Debord's late films is not representational. The images do not usually illustrate the text, nor does the text explain or refer to what is onscreen. The relation between the two is critical. Cinema's limitations can be turned to advantage. It is something like a jujitsu move, using the weight and power of the enemy against itself. The spectacle tries to abolish the qualitative space and irreversible time of history. In its place it offers mere representations of time and space, images that have a formal equivalence, any of which can be exchanged for another. The worth of any image is measurable in other images, but only in other images. Any image can follow any other. Time loses its irreversible, historical quality and becomes as homogeneous as the TV schedule—a sitcom followed by a movie, or a movie then a sitcom.

By freeing images from these constraints, Debord does not want to further reduce them to meaninglessness. His approach is quite the opposite. It is to take the images of the spectacle as a true representation of a falsified world. A fine example would be his proposition in *Refutation* that spectators do not get what they desire; they desire what they get. An English television ad shows a man going to a tailor to be measured for a tailor-made cigarette. Once the customer decides on the exact length that suits him, the tailor offers him a Senior Service cigarette which, it turns out, his desire exactly matches. To commit a historical act a people needs its desires, but to merely watch the spectacle act in one's place one merely desires the needs it is offered.

The spectacle classifies the world by genre and organizes it by narrative. All images, sounds and stories are formally equivalent in the spectacle. Any element of it can be measured in the currency of another. A Marilyn Monroe image might be worth four Mao Zedongs or twenty anonymous pin-up pictures. All the elements of the spectacle can be arranged in a hierarchy of value, and the spectator is encouraged to make distinctions between them.

This is the essence of middle-class café or dinner party conversations, not to mention a certain kind of college education about aesthetics: Is Welles a greater filmmaker than Truffaut?—discuss. In *Day for Night* (1973) Truffaut imagines his younger self stealing lobby cards of Welles' *Citizen Kane* (1941) from a cinema. For Debord that might be as good an emblem as any of spectacular value. Truffaut steals Welles to create his own personal values and market value. Debord, as we shall see, will use Welles for quite different reasons.

From the archives of the spectacle itself, Barraqué built an archive specifically designed to catalog images for Debord's purposes. "I had a very, very long list of documents that I had selected, classified and archived by (say) group: history, fashion, scoops, decoration, (what else?), politics, and speeches. So, whenever he would ask 'Do you remember this? Could you find this again for me?' My assistant and I, knowing where we had classified them, would be able to fetch them very quickly." Using this archive, Debord cuts the image away from both narrative and genre, but not to make it just a free-floating sign. Rather, it is to produce, out of the tension between the senses it brings with it from its previous context and the senses Debord imposes by embedding the image in a critical context, a new ensemble of significance.

In *Refutation* another ad shows the American south before the civil war and declares that nothing remains of this civilization but its iced tea. Advertising appropriates the residue of what was once historical time and hitches the thought that arises from it to the commodity. In this case, the idea of the passing into history of a whole way of life. Debord's procedure here is simply to strip the pitch from the idea and insert it into a new context. His wager is against the spectacle's confidence in its ability to subsume qualitative action to the commodity form. While the spectacle has to subsume history always and forever, history has to erupt into the spectacle and destroy it only once.

What separates Debord's seventies films from his earlier ones is the sophistication with which images produce critical friction through their relation to each other independently of their relation to the voice-over. This is where the crisp rhythms of the editing of *Spectacle* and *Refutation* really stand out. For instance, in *Spectacle*, Barraqué cuts together images of women on the beach with images of an iceberg as seen through the periscope of a nuclear submarine, followed by images of that submarine, then of Cuban leader Fidel Castro in a TV studio, then Castro haranguing a crowd. The logic of the images connects what it is that is to be desired within the spectacle, the power that maintains the spectacle, the counter-power of another form of the spectacle. For Debord the cold war clash between the concentrated spectacle of the socialist east and the diffuse spectacle of the capitalist West masks a commonality of interest in maintaining spectacular domination. One side gets half-naked women to look at; the other gets a charismatic demagogue—which have more in common than might at first appear.

Not that the diffuse spectacle of the West is without its own pin-ups of power. Barraqué cuts images of The Girl next to a political leader (Pompidou), a car show, more of The Girl. Here the rostrum camera pans along a series of bikini-clad women several times, as if there were an endless succession of them, just as there is an endless succession of factory-made images, cars, leaders. Henri Lefebvre: "Everything happens as though the image (myth, ideology, utopia, or what you will) of the total woman had replaced the image or the idea of the total man after the latter had collapsed."[9] That women's bodies become the surface of desire, the mediators between the commodity and fetishizing, will become a whole genre of critique. What is interesting is the way Debord connects this to a broader critique of the spectacle. Clark discovers something already beginning in Manet: that pictures of The Girl become a privileged kind of image in the spectacle.[10]

Scenes of industrial waste, a car driving past mountains of garbage, a smoggy panorama of a contemporary city, are then linked to scenes from the 1965 Watts riots. A black woman is manhandled; a bloodied black man lies on the ground. Here Barraqué co-joins the two *externalities* of spectacular society. On the one hand, pollution; on the other, the proletariat. This is followed by riot police rehearsing against a fake street riot, which they easily defeat, then scenes from May '68, then Mao Zedong meeting President Richard Nixon and his Secretary of State Henry Kissinger. The link is between the police function of the state and the spectacular function of the leader. Nixon's pact with Mao isolated their mutual enemy, Russia. But for Debord, the real struggle was between the state of spectacular society—both east and west—and their respective peoples. The spectacle's overcoming of history is spectacular, but history's overcoming of the spectacle will be historical.

Some poignant images of Marilyn Monroe alternate with French socialist politician François Mitterrand, leaflets thrown to a crowd, the Nazi rise to power, more riot police, the Vietnam War, the Nazi rally at Nuremberg, Soviet leader Leonid Brezhnev at a Moscow May Day parade, tanks, traffic, industrial food. The range of available celebrities model the range of available desires, be they sexual or political. Either way they propose an end to historical time, which nevertheless leaves behind fragments of its furtive, fugitive existence. In both east and west, spectacular political power is built on the ruins of failed attempts to seize it. Whether fascist, communist or capitalist, the spectacular falsification is in some respects the same, and should be treated with the same insolence.

A cake factory, motor racing, Mao Zedong and Lin Biao, Josef Stalin, Hungarians destroying a statue of Stalin in the 1956 uprising, a pin-up girl, a box factory: One of these things is not like the others. As the film progresses, its rhythm changes, and more and more images of the subjective moment in history, the seizure of historical time, appear. But the spectacle erases history, turning it into mere images, the significance of which fades.

Perhaps Mao's face is still well known only because Andy Warhol made a portrait of it. But who remembers Lin Biao? The general who led the People's Liberation Army into Beijing in 1949 became Mao's second in command and designated successor during the Cultural Revolution, before he died in that mysterious plane crash. Lin Biao was most likely assassinated in the power struggles of the time, but it is characteristic of the occulted state that nobody who knows would speak of it, and anyone who speaks of it does not know. Debord's *Society of the Spectacle* was made at a time when Mao exercised an extraordinary fascination over the French left.[11]

In Debord's films Mao, Castro, the Soviets are all versions of the concentrated spectacle, and as such images of domination.

Pre-war Shanghai divided by colonial concessions is followed by tourists on a bus and a boat. The city becomes an image of itself. Pleasure boats and seaside apartments follow the riot police who guard against outbreaks of history that might render such spectacular distractions moot. The subjective moment in history can only be represented within the spectacle, and these representations appear as isolated moments, contained within narratives that neutralize them. Debord retrieves them from these constraints, whether documentary or fictional, and puts them together.

Rather than moments of historical time neutralized by spectacular narrative and isolated by genre—here comes everybody! Cavalry charges, the storming of the winter palace, the Spanish civil war: situations of irreversible action in time. Spread throughout the film is the particular sequence of moments in which historical time accelerates, and the conflict of forces pushes it toward new qualities: Paris 1871, St. Petersburg 1917, Barcelona 1935, Watts 1965, Paris again, 1968. The sequence continues in *Refutation* with the *carnation revolution* in Lisbon, 1974.[12] It is a sign of the further progress of the spectacular erasure of historical time that one could be forgiven for not knowing that some of these events even happened, just as attempts to leave the twenty-first century, in Thailand or Greece or Tunisia or Egypt, run the risk of erasure from history.

American Phantom jets on an aircraft carrier; The Girl again—a refrain of the earlier moment where Barraqué links The Girl with a nuclear submarine. Again, these images appear with a picture of Alice Becker-Ho, to whom Debord was married in 1972. *Society of the Spectacle* begins with love and ends with friendship. Dissolved in 1972, the Situationist International no longer exists, so it is back to the forms of discreet sociality out of which it in part emerged. Here two series confront each other. One series is spectacle/spectator. The other is a little harder to define, but is composed of history as the collective and subjective being in an irreversible time, and being in discreet relations of friendship or love which also entail irreversible moments.

Barraqué interrupts the rhythmic succession of clusters of images at key moments for fragments of scenes from movies, complete with their original dialogue and music. While the newsreel footage was simply purchased from archives, getting hold of feature films involved a certain amount of deception and secrecy. Barraqué: "And it was lots of fun! Going, calling, telling people that the director I worked for and the film were very important, but that he was currently scouting for locations in Italy (and then in America, etc.). So that we didn't know the exact date that he could come in to watch the films, and so that I needed them for—at least—three days: the time it took for me to insert the rigs in the copy, have an inter-negative made, wait for the results, then removing the rigs from the copy, and then give it back to the distributor. Still, I was able to obtain all that was needed. We therefore stole—without paying any copyrights (not a dime to any of them)."

The feature films are détourned to a different effect to the newsreels. As Debord writes, these stolen films are deployed for the "rectification of the 'artistic inversion of life.'"[13] They are like blocks of affect, of potential feeling that can be retrieved from the cinematic inversion and "put back on their feet," as the vehicles via which to make one's own meaning, one's own sense. Debord and Barraqué use Nicholas Ray's *Johnny Guitar* (1954) for its ambivalent, tender yet fraught memories of love; *The Shanghai Gesture* (1941) for the confused and excited sensation of adventure; John Ford's *Rio Grande* (1950) for the giddy élan of historical action; Orson Welles' *Mr. Arkadin* (1955) for the pathos of authentic friendship; Sergei Eisenstein's *Battleship Potemkin* (1925) for the moment of collective decision. In each case an insolent disregard for narrative and genre frees the fragment for redeployment.

Cinema, like the novel, was of interest to Debord to the extent that it posed a certain problem with time. His interest in cinematic time is in its historical and affective dimensions, not the conceptual and ontological time of the philosopher Gilles Deleuze. As Debord wrote in a 1959 letter after some remarks on the novel: "It seems to me that the question of time is posed in an analogous manner by the cinema, which is another form of the representation of the temporal flow of things. Here, as there, what's interesting lies in those moments at which the alienated satisfactions of the spectacle can, at the same time, be rough sketches (in negative) of a planned development of affective life, that is to say, of the affective events inseparable from thought and action."[14]

Many of the fragments Debord détourned from various films have a particular quality, a distinctive emotional tone that corresponds to a situation in which an irreversible action is beginning. Johnny and his old flame Vienna warily reunite in very different times. A general commits troops to battle just as he learns that the enemy knows of the attack, dooming it from the start. Sailors gather under threat of a firing squad and in an instant coalesce in mutiny. But where cinema under both the concentrated and diffuse spectacle seeks to neutralize these moments, strapping them down to predictable narrative arcs and the expectations borne of genre conventions, for Debord they can serve as proxies for a quite different kind of sense. This is not to be confused with the idea that spectators make their own meaning, that their viewing is active, subversive of dominant codes and so on. It is not that people make new meaning, but that they could make new social relations. The appropriated images are still only proxies, blocks of sense mobilized to open up a possibility outside of themselves.

It's the Russian civil war. A Red partisan with a machine gun fires on an advancing infantry formation of the White army. She keeps firing, but they keep coming, a look of desperation in her close-up. "Some cinematic value might be acknowledged in this film if the present rhythm were to continue, but it will not."[15] The film is the Vasilyev Brothers' *Chapayev* (1934), one of the classics, if there is such a thing, of Stalinist cinema.[16] In this image, the woman is the active subject, a reprise of Delacroix's *Liberty Leading the People* with updated weaponry. It is an image that is not without its problems, caught as it is in hierarchies of gender, and can only have tactical value. Debord uses it for what it is worth, expends it, and moves on.

Debord's insolence toward cinema does not devalue all of it. Rather, he claims his desire to make of it what is needed. It doesn't always matter which war or which love is portrayed. It's the diagram of forces, the picturing of the game of time, that matters. But cinema, like any art, represents the world too well. Lived time disappears in art, and art at best can only mourn its passing. Cinema is a kind of memory, an abstract memory, not of particular events, particular people, but a memory of the possibility of life before it becomes mere representation. A life about which cinema can say nothing, show nothing, which cinema can acknowledge only in passing. Johnny Guitar asks his lost love, Vienna: "How many men have you forgotten?" And in this game, Vienna gives as good as she gets: "As many women as you've remembered."

The Dancing Kid tosses a coin to decide whether to kill Johnny or let him play Vienna a song on his guitar. She catches the coin in mid-air. Johnny's song for Vienna puts her into a reverie, but she catches herself: "Play something else," she commands. Those times are gone and cannot be relived. Cinema cannot bring life itself back to life. It's the same with historical time on a grand scale. General Sheridan orders John Wayne to catch and kill the Indians, even if he has to cross the border with Mexico to do it. If he is caught he will be court-martialed. If he is court-martialed, Sheridan will have him judged by others who were with them both at Shenandoah.

This prompts Sheridan's reverie: "I wonder what history will say about Shenandoah?" They might say of this civil war event that, with its scorched-earth destruction of the South's economic power, it signaled the beginning of modern warfare. To the practice of which Sheridan later added his genocidal campaigns against the Indians. But for Debord there's something else as well. The experience of lived time, irreversible time, on a small or a grand scale, is that which escapes the spectacle, and hence remains a resource against it. And yet the spectacle cannot help itself. It is drawn again and again to the memory of that which it erases.

Those who experienced lived time together are bound thereafter by it. They may no longer be lovers, comrades, or even friends, but something remains, something unsaid, something unspeakable. Orson Welles as Mr. Arkadin tells a parable about a graveyard where the dates recorded on the tombstones are not the lifespan of the deceased but the length of time the dead kept a friend. He then proposes a toast: "To friendship!" The friendships commemorated on the tombstones may be as brief as many of the memberships in the Situationist International. Raoul Vaneigem joined in 1961 and resigned in 1970. T. J. Clark joined in 1966 and was excluded in 1967. René Viénet joined in 1966 and resigned in 1971. Gianfranco Sanguinetti joined in 1969 and was the last remaining member with

Debord when the Situationist International was dissolved in 1972. These things have their time, and the memory of lived time is a resource against the dead time of representation. Friendships, like montage, both connect and sever.

Mr. Arkadin recounts a second Aesopean parable, in which the scorpion asks the frog to carry him across the river.[17] "But you will sting me and kill me!" says the frog. "Why would I do that? I would drown if I did that," says the scorpion. So the frog carries the scorpion into the river. Half way across, the scorpion stings the frog. "But why? Now we will both die," says the frog. "It's in my character!" says the scorpion. Mr. Arkadin offers a toast: "To character!"

As Barraqué remarks, "Especially with *Mr. Arkadin,* when he is telling the tale of the scorpion—you can see how it completely follows his line of thought, the plan of transforming this *Society of the Spectacle* from the book into a film." The scorpion is the practice of détournement, which stings the image as much as the word, as it crosses the river that separates the sign from its interpretation. "It's in my character!" says détournement.

Johnny rides through the desert and finds Vienna's saloon. When he enters, he finds it empty, the barman and croupiers standing ready. A man shows Gene Tierney around a crowded casino. "The other place is like kindergarten compared to this," she says. "Anything could happen at any moment!" Barraqué adroitly joins scenes from different films which both present the moment a situation opens, with its finite but barely known field of possibilities. Of course, in cinema, only one possibility can occur. The narrative moves on, and cinema is usually impatient to move it on. Barraqué finds the exact bounds of the event in the relentless mechanic time of the cinema. Interpretation can open the situation again, open toward an infinite realm of possibilities. But this is not what interests Debord. Rather, his attention to the situation is to the finite and specific options for action any given situation contains.

Power can't be seized the old way. The revolutionary movement is over. Some might think it dies in Paris in '68. For Debord it died in Barcelona in 1935, when the Communists defeated the revolutionary movement in the name of winning the civil war, which was lost anyway to Franco and his Nazi backers.[18] A civil war general, on learning that Franco's forces know about their attack already:

"Too late. That means we're done for. This time we fail. Too bad. Yes, too bad." The failure of the workers' revolutions is that they relied on the same thought, the same methods, as the successful bourgeois revolutions before them. The fruit of bourgeois enlightenment, from its specialized forms of knowledge to its hierarchical forms of organization, cannot be turned against it.

In *Spectacle,* Debord shows an etching by Jacques-Louis David of *The Tennis Court Oath* (1791), signal event of the French Revolution. The image is designed to draw the eye to Robespierre in the middle, one hand raised, the other on his heart as he takes the oath. David was close to Robespierre, and a powerful figure in the arts during the Revolution. Imprisoned upon Robespierre's fall from power, he would later ingratiate himself with Napoleon I and create for the latter his *empire style*. Debord shows Robespierre, then in close-up the political specialists beneath him, making their little deals on the quiet. Then he cuts to a woman and child in a window above, spectators at the making of history. It is the very form of bourgeois power which now has to be opposed, just as it is the form of its cinema that must be opposed. *Society of the Spectacle* and *Refutation of All Judgments* are about not just the clamor of images but also the silence of power, a silence which, since the seventies, has become deafening.

25 The Devil's Party

Fortune against envy; fame against oblivion.
Baltasar Gracián

"Shipwreckers have their name writ only on water."[1] Debord takes it to be Shelley's epitaph, but it is also Debord's. His last film, *In Girum Imus Nocte et Consumimur Igni* (1978), perhaps his masterpiece, has an aquatic mood. The eddies and currents of the river as it flows into the sea are so many situations that form and disperse on its surface, to be replaced by others, and still others. *In Girum* has a slower rhythm, a more somber mood than *Society of the Spectacle*. The emphasis shifts toward a more fine-grained denunciation of the colonization of everyday life by spectacular images of the commodified world.

Against this, Debord can only posit the remembrance of lost friends and the implacable onrush of a historical time, which will return no matter how much the spectacle denies its existence. Martine Barraqué: "And oddly, while working on the last film (what I am telling you is quite harsh, right?) I had the impression of working with a veteran of war. That he could not write anything else that was new—that everything kept turning round and round in the usual ways because he had already said it all."

In girum imus nocte et consumimur igni. The palindrome of the title means something like: We go into the circle by night; we are consumed by fire. If water is a figure for a particular quality of time, fire is another. The momentary conflagration, the clash of forces, the cavalry charge, or the fatal bullet which, Debord once noted, killed an uncommon number of his friends.[2] Fire is the other elemental time, and if we all are borne along by a liquid current, there are those few, those happy few, who are the friends of fire; the devil's party, orbiting the flame, like moths to enlightenment. By the time of *In Girum*, the party of fire is a diminished band, the everyday situation no longer seems quite so resonant with a wider historical current. In the disintegrating spectacle negation no longer works against it from without. All that remains is the spark of a memory, to be recalled, over and over, until it torches time again.

In Girum détourns scenes from movies as *Spectacle* does, and sometimes the same films, but to different effect. *Shanghai Gesture* appears again, but this time Debord chooses not Gene Tierney but Victor Mature playing Doctor Omar, who describes himself as "a doctor of nothing ... it sounds important and hurts no one, unlike most doctors." Doctor Omar even has the temerity to steal a line from the Roman playwright Terence: "I am a thoroughbred mongrel. I am related to all the earth and nothing human is foreign to me."[3]

He is the first of a series of characters appearing in *In Girum* who might be described as being of the devil's party, agents of deception and division. While Robin Hood and Zorro make appearances as rather more straightforward fantasies of redemption from within the spectacle, Debord is drawn to the more ambivalent and dangerous trickster figure. Robin Hood and Zorro uphold the true society against the false one. Like Censor's tract, the devil's party undermines the true and the false order alike by appearing to be in possession of the secret of the relation between them.

Most of the films détourned in Debord's seventies films are from his youth. A certain veiled autobiographical quality resides in them. Two seem to have particular resonance in this regard. Director Marcel Carné (1906–96) and screen-writer Jacques Prévert (1900–77) collaborated on two great films during the occupation, *Les Visiteurs du soir* (1942) and *Children of Paradise* (1945). Carné and Prévert were leftists before the war. Drawing from Surrealism and popular cultural forms, they were leading exponents of a style sometimes called poetic realism.[4] Their wartime films were big productions, sanctioned by the pro-Nazi film apparatus, but were neither Nazi propaganda nor simply coded resistance allegories. These films and their makers fell rapidly out of favor with postwar audiences and taste-makers alike. It didn't help that Arletty, who stars in both, was accused of collaboration. (Arletty: "My heart belongs to France, but my ass belongs to the world.") These films later became a particular foil for new-wave filmmakers such as François Truffaut. That Debord would borrow scenes from them in 1978 comes with more than a few layers of significance.

Debord ignores the narratives and discards most of the major characters. He concentrates on the character of the Devil from *Visiteurs* and of Lacenaire from *Paradise*. "I come from far away. Forgotten in his own country, unknown elsewhere, such is the fate of the traveler," says the Devil. He is the principle of division, the agent of historical time. Of the comrades of his youth, Debord will say they were "people quite sincerely ready to set the world on fire just to give it more brilliance."[5] Or as the Devil says, "I dearly love fire! And it loves me." In *Visiteurs*, the Devil sends his emissaries, Dominique and Gilles, into the world to create division through a little gender-queer sexual intrigue. As Gilles sings: "sad lost children, we wander in the night." Or as Dominique explains the game: "Other people love us, and they suffer for us. We watch them and then we go away. A fine journey, with the Devil paying the expenses."

"I declared war on society long ago." From *Paradise* Debord takes mostly the character of Pierre François Lacenaire (1800–36), a real historical figure, the criminal-poet-philosopher, who was the model for Raskolnikov and fascinated many writers from Stendhal to André Breton. In his *Memoirs*, Lacenaire wrote, "I come to preach the religion of Fear to the rich, for the religion of Love has no power over them."[6] The Lacenaire of *Paradise* says to some uncomprehending bourgeois: "It takes all kinds to make a world—or to *unmake* it." Later he will pronounce his own panegyric: "I've become famous. I've pulled off a few little crimes and created quite a sensation." Like the real-life Lacenaire, he would have preferred a literary success, but will settle for lasting infamy. "I have no vanity. I have only pride," he says. If, as Adorno says, "every work of art is an uncommitted crime," then to Lacenaire every crime is an act of commitment. Or as Vaneigem says of Lacenaire: "Intrinsic to the logic of an unlivable society, murder, thus conceived, can only appear as the concave form of the gift."[7]

In Girum concerns itself with the world after a series of failed revolutions: France 1968, Italy 1969, Portugal 1974, Italy again in 1977. The flaming moment has passed. The camera holds steady on still pictures of everyday life invaded by the commodity. Debordian insolence is replaced by contempt. But if anything the pathos of the power of memory as the half-life of life itself, the distillate of lived time, is all the stronger. The small-mesh interpersonal aspect of such a project has its stand-ins, such as Doctor Omar, Lacenaire and the Devil.

The large-scale historical moment has its stand-ins as well. From the otherwise appalling *Charge of the Light Brigade* (1936), Debord selects the famous scenes director Michael Curtiz made of the charge itself. From *They Died with Their Boots On* (1941), Raoul Walsh's truly fantastic version of the life of George Custer—another film much used in *Spectacle*—Debord takes the scene of Custer's last stand at Little Big Horn. The cavalry charge is a particle of the combustible moment of historical action. The charge is to coarse-grained events what Omar, the Devil and Lacenaire are to finer ones.

"History advances with its bad side first," as Debord détourns Marx and Engels from the *Holy Family*.[8] Representations—whether art or literature, cinema or song—are where the situation of lived time goes to die. They are the backwash of exhausted forces, which, in exhausting themselves, make the times otherwise. The seventies are a time in which all such forces appear spent. The charge is over, and it is not so much that the good guys lost, as that the fulcrum of conflict, the principle of division, disappears.

The eighties will be a time when the ruling class goes on the offensive again. But its victory is its undoing. Pursued to its limit, the spectacle undoes itself, and in so doing will create the conditions under which the party of fire might appear again, and the critique of the society of the spectacle in acts will reappear, dragging its theoretical understanding along, belatedly, behind it. It is as memory that failed moments of historical action have their other power. Cinema, and the spectacle in general, does a good job of subsuming and defusing the qualitative. It cannot abolish it. The spectacle is haunted by what negates it. Or so Debord seemed to think at the time. In the nineties his mood grew darker.

The police found his friend dead at the wheel of his car in an underground parking lot, with four bullet wounds in the back of his head. No money was taken, only his identification papers. In his pocket was a scrap of paper with the name 'François.' Gérard Lebovici was an agent and producer in the French movie business. The Nazis killed his mother in the camps. When his father died, he had to give up his ambition to be an actor. In 1960 he founded his own management agency. He was radicalized by 1968 and by his wife Floriana, née Valentin. In 1969 he founded the publishing house Champ Libre, which republished Debord's *Society of the Spectacle* in 1971.

Debord denied having any editorial role at Champ Libre, but as his relationship to Lebovici became close, it did start to produce something like a Debordian canon, which grew to include editions of Carl von Clausewitz, Baltasar Gracián, George Orwell, Karl Korsch, and Debord's own translations of the poetry of Jorge Manrique. The filmmaker Olivier Assayas, for whom Champ Libre was something of an education, best captures its qualities: "I remember, I was twenty when the Champ Libre reissue of the *Internationale Situationiste* bulletins came out in 1975. I was discovering Paris ... In Champ Libre's catalogue, even if Debord denies it—there resides something that emanates from his thought ... The unique feature of Champ Libre's editorial project was to have provided an extension of Debord's ongoing dialogue with the works of the past, with the nebulous mass of intellectual and poetic affinities that he increasingly expanded, conjuring in his texts and in his films the shades of writers who, from across the centuries, were his intimates, on the same level as his brawling and drinking companions ... At a time of fearsome ideological puritanism, Champ Libre published classics of political science, but also works that nobody had read for ages ... I have never managed to consider Champ Libre as anything but an extension of Debord's work, publishing as discourse, not only because of what was published there, but also for the juxtaposition of texts that produced another meaning, legible to those who could and wanted to read it."[9]

Lebovici's assassination—there is no other word for it—in March 1984 set off an extraordinary wave of speculation in the French media. Debord documented this with a small book, in which he writes: "We know now what a modern society can do with a parking lot." *Considerations on the Assassination of Gérard Lebovici* (1985) was in part a tribute to his friend: "This century does not like truth, generosity or greatness. Therefore it did not like Gérard Lebovici..."[10] But it had more to say about Debord himself and his curious relation to the spectacle. The occasion was the insinuation by more than one media mouthpiece that he was in some way connected to Lebovici's death. Journalists identified themselves with the assassin, not the victim, and sought with considerable ingenuity to justify the killing. A recurring accusation, which Debord documents in his book, was that it was his friendship with Debord that somehow got Lebovici killed.

"Each epoch uses a particular vocabulary to exorcise the demons that plague it."[11] The eighties were perhaps transitional in this regard. Where one paper accused Debord of accepting "Moscow Gold," another connected him to his mother-in-law's Chinese restaurant, an alleged haven for Moscow's nemesis, the Chinese Communists. These were the old figures of the traitor, from a time when the diffuse and concentrated spectacles confronted each other, across the cold war divide, each internalizing the image of the other as its official enemy. Debord was also attacked variously as a guru, a mentor, a loner, a fanatic, an eccentric, an ideologue, a nihilist, an idealist, a demon, a pope and a terrorist.

Here a more recognizably contemporary figure of the traitor emerges. In the time of the disintegrating spectacle, the global commodity economy relies on Russian energy. The flow of cheap commodities is in the hands of the Chinese Communist Party. New enemies of the people are required. Enemies like Julian Assange, the hacker-journalist-cypherpunk, publishing secret documents on the internet which reveal what those in the know already knew anyway. This was enough to get him labeled a terrorist and—worse—for the *New York Times* to question his personal hygiene.[12]

In the news stories he fulsomely quotes, Debord appears as a shadowy and clandestine figure. He points out that it has become a crime to withdraw from the spectacle when it seeks one out. To remain indeterminate, unnamable, this would be the essential move of those who belong, knowingly or not, to the devil's party. The rumor that Debord *disappeared* after May '68 is based on the illusion that he had previously *appeared*. As Debord insists, "I have never appeared anywhere."[13] The spectacle equates the refusal of celebrity with terrorism. "The mere fact that I have not at all wanted to be around the dreary celebrities of the day would give me, if there were such a need, a sufficient prestige around those who have the unfortunate obligation of having to be around them."[14] Not the least of Debord's achievements was to appear in the spectacle only as its negation.

Two things in particular make Debord's relation to Lebovici appear unacceptable. The first is the gift. Lebovici gave Debord the means to live well, to write, to make his films. In 1983 Lebovici even purchased the Studio Cujas cinema, where Debord's films were the only ones screened, whether anyone showed up to watch them or not. As Martine Barraqué puts it, "people used to say that Guy Debord was Gérard Lebovici's *ballerina*."

One of the more extraordinary documents of Debordiana is the *Contracts*, which codify the agreements between Debord and Lebovici's film company for *Society of the Spectacle, In Girum* and a film on Spain that was never made. While the first reads indeed like a contract, they become increasingly like a détournement of legal documents. In the last contract, for the Spain film, Lebovici gives and Debord agrees to nothing in return. It is if anything the negation of the contract. No consideration is offered in return for the gift.[15] Or rather, it is the very offering of nothing in return, except the explicit statement that nothing is owed, which permits Lebovici's gift to approximate to the state of being a pure donation.[16]

Debord once claimed the virtue of having "invented some crimes of a new type."[17] Principal among which was the refusal to appear within the spectacle on command. Where this tactic confers on most who try it nothing but obscurity, Debord succeeded in pulling off a uniquely anti-spectacular fame. This strategy was not without its dangers. To the state of a disintegrating spectacle, those who will neither stay in obscurity nor affirm the spectacle with their presence can only be categorized as traitors to the state. As the spectacle disintegrates, it grows far less tolerant of those who refuse it. As Gracián says, the state can counter almost any challenge to itself, but not mockery.

In November 2008 French anti-terrorist police arrested Julien Coupat (b. 1975) and held him for several months without trial. As a condition of his release Coupat had to surrender his passport and identity papers. He was the last to be released of a group that Interior Minister Michèle Alliot-Marie called *anarcho-autonomous*. The government failed to secure any convictions on terrorist charges. The arrests were triggered by the attempted sabotage of a high-speed train. A group protesting the transporting of radioactive waste in Germany had already claimed responsibility for the sabotage. Coupat described his imprisonment as "petty revenge" in the face of the complete failure of the police action that rounded up him and his friends. Giorgio Agamben: "The only possible conclusion to this shadowy affair is that those engaged in activism against the (in this case debatable) way social and economic problems are managed today are considered ipso facto as potential terrorists, even when not one act can justify this accusation."[18]

Just as the spectacle took Debord's refusal of its charms for a threat to its existence, so too with Coupat. "Anti-terrorism," Coupat writes, "contrary to what the term insinuates, is not a means of fighting against terrorism, it is the means by which it positively produces the political enemy as terrorist." This is not the least aspect that connects the Coupat affair to the Situationist legacy. Coupat wrote a paper on the Situationists while at university. He may have been a member of the *Tiqqun* group, which was not unfamiliar with certain figures who once moved in Debordian circles. He may or may not be one of the authors of a text called *The Coming Insurrection*, and which may be the real reason for his arrest. Coupat declares that "unfortunately, I am not the author of *The Coming Insurrection*, and the whole affair will end up convincing us of the essentially policing role of the author-function." He also notes that "In France one can't remember power becoming so fearful of a book in a long time."

Whatever its provenance, *The Coming Insurrection* is surely the first notable political text to pick up where the Situationists left off.[19] Published in the name of the Invisible Committee, it revives the glamour of the spectral party, the devil's party. It takes the refusal of existing power, and its attendant everyday life, as far as the rejection even of the so-called leftist versions within it. It takes it as given that even the ruling class has lost its way. It shows a keen interest in urban affairs, but sees this as a time in which the metropolis has all but engulfed its rural peripheries. The creation of a life in the cracks of the commodity form has to remove itself from its major achievement—the modern city. Hence the group that was arrested with Coupat were known as the Tarnac 9, after the small town of some three-hundred-odd inhabitants in the Limousin region where they ran a cooperative store. Like Debord, late in life, they had withdrawn from the space of the city, to contemplate it from without, to act upon it from without.

26 Guy Debord, His Art and Times

Reputation is more about stealth than deeds.
Baltasar Gracián

It was in the Auvergne region, just east of Limousin, where in 1992 Brigitte Cornand met Guy Debord. He was living in a house there, near the village of Champot, that Lebovici had bought for him. "At that time he was totally broke. He had no money," Cornand says. "Lebovici was shot in the parking lot. Then the wife said 'I keep going, giving you money,' then she died. She passed away two or three years later. Then immediately, no more money. They had the Champot place. So they went there and abandoned Paris because it was too expensive. Hard times, really."[1]

Cornand had been making video works about artists for the Canal+ television station. These were not documentaries, they were "artist films, like a story, like a poem."[2] She made one that détourned the text of *In Girum*, that "gave a perfume, a flavor of it." Via her friend Gil Wolman she wrote to Debord about it, and after it screened, Debord wrote back. When a book collector who knew Debord planned a trip to the Auvergne to see him, he took Cornand along, and at their initial meeting a possible collaboration was floated for the first time.

Cornand: "The idea was to describe a no-future situation. Something like that. He had the idea to show a very dark and very impossible situation for humankind, so he asked me [to find] a list of different extracts from news, and with specific dates, and after that the duration depends on the intensity of each segment. The idea was to make a film only with documents from the television networks." Not that Debord was much of a television watcher himself. "Through conversations he heard about things. He heard something." He would give Cornand lists with dates and subjects, and she would locate the television footage at the archives of the Audio-Visual Institute.

What distinguishes the Cornand video collaboration from Debord's film work is that it takes the freshly sprouting world of multichannel television as its theater of operation. Henri Lefebvre: "The reign of the global would also be the reign of a gigantic tautology, which would kill all dramas after having exploited them shamelessly." Writing in the sixties, Lefebvre thought this final stage of what he alternately called the Spectacle, the Great Pleonasm, and the Thing of Things, was a long way off. Yet it was a tendency to be feared: "It would be a closed circuit from hell, a perfect circle in which the absence of communication and communication pushed to the point of paroxysm would meet and their identities would merge."[3] Debord's last work, made specifically for television, indulged the possibility that this Thing of Things had finally come to pass.

There is no voice-over in *Guy Debord, His Art and His Times* (1995). The spectacle speaks for itself. Debord intervenes through title cards, over which plays the accordion music of Debord's contemporary, Lino Léonardi (b. 1928), from his settings for poems by François Villon. "The accordion means Saint Germain, the fifties," says Cornand. It is the sound of the provincial hoodlum descended upon Paris, among whom Debord counted himself.[4]

The first section, which is very brief, is about his art. Cornand: "For me he is not a filmmaker but an artist. We can see that in the film. People said *filmmaker* because he was using films, but in fact the films are very poetic, very rhythmic, totally personal, not at all a film like Hollywood or a documentary, it is not that. But at the time people were unable to say he was an artist, because he was in a circle of literature. You have different drawers for culture in France. You are put in one box." *Guy Debord* is now included in the boxed set of Debord's films.[5]

A bunch of French literary men discuss Debord's *Comments on the Society of the Spectacle* on a France 2 TV talk show. The most obviously odious of these, Franz-Olivier Giesbert, remarks that "it legitimizes violence," and that Debord "tells us democracy is breaking down … and yet one feels democracy is advancing all over. All you have to do is read the papers!" If this is the taste and judgment of public opinion, all the better to maintain one's distance from it.[6] What Debord avoided is precisely having to live amid such company. Whether it is a work of art or not, it is certainly not cinema, or anti-cinema. It is perhaps television, or rather anti-television.

The accordion plays. Blocky letters scroll: "Guy Debord has made very little art, but the little he has made is extreme." The graffiti "Never work!" is the first of these few art works. Also mentioned is *Howls for Sade* (1952). After Stéphane Mallarmé and the blank white page, after Kazimir Malevich and the white on white canvas, Debord's silent white screen is a fitting extension of extremity into a new form.[7] "Debord has since maintained the same indifference toward the tastes and judgments of public opinion. And he has been reproached for many other immoralities. In particular, for almost always having been rather interested when easy money was involved. Having regularly obeyed the principle, 'never look a gift horse in the mouth.'" It's a perfect statement of indifference to conventional taste and opinion.

Guy Debord contains the now standard Debordian panegyric to the comrades of his youth, in block-lettered inter-titles: "This fine band of hoodlums, his constant entourage, have also been a great influence on his excesses." Only this last tribute is briefer than any others, as if the memory of them was already slipping away. In between Ivan Chtcheglov (1933–98) and Asger Jorn (1914–73), Gil Wolman (1929–95) appears. Of all the comrades from Debord's early days, he was one of the most talented, one of the first to be excommunicated, and one of the last to be rehabilitated.[8] The efforts of this motley crew at not working compare favorably to a promotional film détourned later in *Guy Debord*, which extols the virtues of French prison labor—no absenteeism! Debord pays tribute to those who absented themselves, as much as it is possible, from the prison house of the spectacle.

"And now I will attempt to be as anti-televisual in form as I have been in content." The rapid edits of *Society of the Spectacle* give way to painfully long excerpts from television current affairs and news shows. Yet there is still a strategy to the relation between the détourned videos. A title card quotes Lautréamont: "I will write down my thoughts in orderly fashion, in a pattern devoid of confusion. If they are right, the first to come will be the consequence of the others. That is the true order."[9] The true order cuts video about the artists Christo and Jean-Claude, who wrapped the Pont Neuf in plastic sheets, with another on the disappearance of the Aral Sea, already two-thirds gone thanks to Soviet-era hydrological engineering. The failure of art and the failure of science are for Debord two sides of the same spectacular coin.

Guy Debord contains some truly disturbing images, of a kind rarely seen anymore, at least on American television. They are perhaps from a very particular moment in the unraveling of the spectacle, a moment when those who produced it as much as those who consumed it could watch agog at the spectacle of its own disintegration.

Before showing us lynchings, dead and dying children, nuclear disaster, or the no less terrifying remnants of contemporary art, Debord remarks that for journalists and media producers, such images are "an occasion to discuss in ethical terms about a deontology they might perhaps choose to impose on themselves in certain extreme cases: should such images be shown? Or why should one deprive oneself from showing them?" The Kantian duty of the journalist can only be one of exposure. No image can remain secret, only its reasons for coming into being in the first place remain outside the realm of appearances. The spectacle's categorical imperative is that the showing of something is always the highest good, and good without qualification. But this showing of the particular is the not-showing of the totality to which it belongs, a totality accessible only to historical thought and action.

Debord: "The professionals have all firmly concluded that nothing of the world's sorrows should be hidden. No bogus oversensitivity on the public's part should prevent one from broadcasting what one has the merit and opportunity to record; and even more so when, for once, it is something true. The *media* thus want to prove that they are, in every respect, intent to the extreme on showing the truth, and quite convinced that any detail, put under close enough scrutiny, is usually a perfect and unequivocal model of truth." Only the relations between such details remains a mystery. *Guy Debord* draw attention to the absence of such relations.

Here is a Japanese wrestler in her tiny apartment. She is a premonition of what labor will be like when everyone is the performance artist of their own ritual humiliation, not so much reality television as televisual reality. Here is an oil derrick drilling under the Arboretum of Versailles. No monument of history can withstand the production of value from the destruction of nature and culture. Here is the dynamiting of sub-Corbusian tower blocks, as if to vindicate at last the Situationist critique of them. "What has been built so badly must be demolished even faster." Here is acid rain in Bavaria. "We thought economy was a science; we were obviously wrong. We now know it would be neither the first, nor the last, of the *enemy's sciences* to prove itself deceptive."

Acid rain seems such a period pollutant, now, not the fashionable new pollution. A 2006 study by UCLA scientists found that Hollywood was responsible for sending 140,000 tons of pollutants into the air each year. Most of it came from the diesel emissions of trucks and generators, but the pyrotechnic explosions from special effects scenes were also a cause. An economist for the city advised against regulating Hollywood effluent: "'There would be a risk because you have other states out there quite anxious to get a piece of the film industry.'"[10] In any case, movie-made smog is not a *cause célèbre* among movie-made celebrities at this time.

A brief historical recap on the spectacle of power from Hitler to JFK: "The *democratic* state has become stranger." The opening minute of French 24-hour television news channel, on the model of CNN. The spectacle has become baroque enough to produce its own in-curling commentary on itself, in *real time*. A man stands in front of a line of tanks near Tiananmen Square.[11] The old Soviet guard attempts a coup against Russian president Boris Yeltsin. Riots in Haiti, Algeria, a woman attacked as she flees through a street market in Somalia: "The unverifiable world." An astonishingly long extract from a documentary about the crisis in the schools in the immigrant suburbs around Paris. "The most modern developments of historical reality have illustrated very precisely how Thomas Hobbes thought man's life must have been before he knew civilization and the state: lonely, dirty, devoid of pleasure, dimwitted, brief." The same neighborhoods would erupt in riot and fire in 2005.

Some light relief: Arthur Cravan, Dada poet, boxer, deserter of several nations, nephew of Oscar Wilde, here in some rare footage being pummeled by a much smaller opponent. He fought the great Jack Johnson, the first black man to be world heavyweight champion, even if the Cravan-Johnson bout was something of a scam. Cravan is one of the enduring sources of the Debordian way of life: "The people I respected more than anyone alive were Arthur Cravan and Lautréamont."[12] Debord, who lived his whole life as if answerable to nobody, holds himself answerable to the friends of Cravan and Lautréamont, friends he would lose with any slippage into mere official art or scholarship. And were he to lose such friends, how could he console himself with any others?

If there is a false friend to Arthur Cravan, to what matters about Dada, it is Daniel Buren, who became something of an official artist in the years of the Mitterrand presidency. In *Les Deux Plateaux* (1986), Buren replaced a parking lot at the Palais-Royal with two levels of striped columns, of varying height. Debord has the cheek to compare them to a barcode. The art historian Benjamin Buchloh, after a quasi-Debordian take-down of what became of the avant-garde, offers this apologia for a related Buren work: "Quite unlike recent examples of public monumental sculpture, which pretend to have solved the contradictions between individual aesthetic producer and collective labor conditions, reflected in the transgression of their work from individual sculptural unit to the monumental structures bordering on architecture, Buren's work maintains these contradictions precisely because of its painterly decorative dimensions that dialectically negate the successful achievement of an architectural dimension of public space."[13] Or, in short, even a distinguished spokesman for the neo-avant-garde cannot do much more with it than champion its own acknowledgement of its failure.

But there is a more sinister side to contemporary art as the decoration of power. Shots of sculptures of sheep near the Cattenom power plant, which in 2005 exposed eight workers to radiation. "Nuclear power likes to be surrounded by its favorite animal. Magritte might have written: this is not a sheep." If this is the art that decorates French state power, what does it say for that power?

"Every time Bernard Tapie speaks of himself, one wonders what dishonesty he could ever have been reproached for." Tapie is one of a series of political figures who appear, mostly without much comment, but who are emblematic of a kind of secret history of the disintegrating spectacle. Bernard Tapie was a French businessman, politician and occasional actor, singer and TV host. From 1986 to 1994, he was president of the Marseille Olympic soccer club. He was minister of city affairs in the Bérégovoy government until his indictment for complicity in corruption and the subornation of witnesses. After a high-profile case he was convicted and spent about six months in prison. French politics is a curious affair.

News footage of the full state funeral for Socialist Prime Minister Pierre Bérégovoy. He died after being found in a coma with two bullets in the head. A coronial inquiry ruled his death a suicide. The second bullet was attributed to a *nervous reflex*. Bérégovoy was under investigation over a one-million-Franc interest-free loan by businessman and friend Roger-Patrice Pelat, who had died of a heart attack on March 7, 1989, less than one month after being found guilty in the Pechiney-Triangle affair. Bérégovoy's suicide came on the eve of the opening of a new trial concerning the acquisition of Triangle by Pechiney.

Was Bérégovoy assassinated? Curious similarities exist between his death and that of other figures close to Mitterrand, including: René Lucet, the head of the Social Security public health system, shot twice through the head on March 4, 1982; François de Grossouvre, Mitterrand's adviser, shot in the head twice at the Élysée Palace on April 7, 1994; and Pierre-Yves Guézou, responsible for a phone tapping scandal at the Élysée, found hanged in his home on December 12, 1994. The curious death of Gérard Lebovici seems less curious in such company.

ACT UP protests the indifference of the French state to the AIDS crisis. AIDS had a special resonance for Debord: "Immune defense is a thing of the past on earth." He offers instead his own philosophy of personal health. For those on the AIDS cocktail of drugs: "no drinking, no smoking. Are you kidding?" By early 1985, an American process to heat blood supplies to neutralize the AIDS virus was available to the French authorities, who instead decided to wait until a French product was ready. They continued to distribute blood knowing that the odds were that some was contaminated. A judicial inquiry acquitted Socialist Ministers Georgina

Dufoix and Laurent Fabius of all personal moral responsibility in the matter.

In Girum featured lovingly photographed images of the waters of Venice. But in *Guy Debord*, the river has become a raging torrent. A TV news video shows a caravan floating in flood waters and crashing through a bridge. Some holiday! Cut to a computer-generated image of an estuary landscape, where gleaming glass towers sprout. Having demolished the worst of the tower blocks that once housed the working class in the seventies, in the nineties a new vertical landscape will flourish. It's the same old sub-Corbusian blocks of raw concrete, only this time with a *high-end* kitchen and a veneer of marble in the bathroom. The landscape that disorganized labor refused is now the chosen habitus of the spectacle's young favorites—bankers, lawyers, media execs.

Near the very end, images of François Mitterrand, clutching the red rose of socialism, as he commences his inauguration. *Guy Debord* has already shown the murky venality into which the Socialist government descended, vindicating Debord's refusal to join the more ambitious '68-ers in playing bit parts in that regime. And at last, bringing up the rear, Bill Clinton jogging in the streets of Naples, in town for the 1994 G7 summit, some years before anyone had thought of using such summits as sites of confrontation with a now post-national spectacular power.[14]

In January 2006 boatloads of armed Ijaws overran a Shell oil facility in the Niger delta and took several hostages. World oil prices ticked up briefly on the news. In February they seized a barge and took more hostages, blew up an oil pipeline, a gas pipeline and a loading terminal. In June they took over a rig forty miles out to sea and took yet more hostages. They called themselves the Movement for the Emancipation of the Niger Delta (MEND). An American journalist describes meeting some of them: "One was naked except for his ammunition and a pair of dirty white briefs. They had painted their faces with white chalk to signify purity, and they had tied amulets around their arms and necks and foreheads for protection from bullets." MEND runs its network on cheap cellphones, plastic speedboats and guns bought at floating arms bazaars with ransom money that the oil companies vigorously deny paying them.

The people of the Niger delta scratch out a living from fish caught in its polluted streams. They have no clean drinking water. A MEND member who goes by the name of Brutus: "This is modern day slavery." Sometimes there's no electricity for days. A Shell employee and former MEND hostage observes from the safety of an oil industry compound: "This is obscene. They are looking through the fence at golf courses and tennis courts where the floodlights are on at midnight." Says MEND spokesperson Jomo Ghomo: "We are not communists, or even revolutionaries. We're just extremely bitter men."[15]

São Paulo is one of the favored capitals of the disintegrating spectacle, where money goes to frolic, managed from the computer terminals of shiny high-rise towers, unfettered by regulation or taxation. One weekend in May 2006, a wave of bombings, burnings and shootings hit the city. It wasn't a riot, a revolt or a revolution, but something else. Anonymous people came out of the crowd and set fire to buses and banks. They didn't loot, but they did kill around forty police officers.

The May attack was the work of the PCC, or First Command of the Capital, a network of autonomous cells funded by the drug trade, which controls the inmates of most of Brazil's prisons and extends into the favelas as well. It made no demands. "It denied the government the power to even concede." The attacks just stopped. Nobody knows why, although one rumor has it that the state eventually agreed to provide PCC inmates with flat screen TVs on which to watch the World Cup football matches. The police retaliated with death squads in the favelas and killed over four hundred.

The PCC started out as a prison football team. After killing a rival team, it morphed into a prison gang. Then it became adept at using cellphones to manage itself and became more like a swarm. Its members swear allegiance to a sixteen-point manifesto, the last of which declares "we will revolutionize the country from inside the prisons, and our strong arm will be the Terror of the powerful." Like MEND, the PCC became, for millions of slum dwellers, the law, a substitute for the state in the state's absence.[16] *Guy Debord* is an intimation of this world, a world no longer all that novel or interesting, and so mostly unremarked, where the criminal, the political and the entrepreneurial become identical within the spectacle.

Near the start of *Guy Debord* is a shot of a page from Debord's early work *Mémoire*, a work composed entirely of détourned phrases, including this one: "The organization of the words that produces a discourse transforms things within the world order by way of an action on the consciences: both the one that frames it as well as those who receive it. It is the breach through which a moment of eternity is consumed in a world that darkly rolls to its loss." Debord follows this text with the fragment "How far are we." It's a neat summation of what remains of the Letterist method of his youth, even in late Debord. The moment of eternity, the moment of fire, which sparks amid all that is borne away on the current of time.

The execrable language of his century is that language of the edit, of the organization of pre-existing units, be it of images, sounds or words. In *Guy Debord*, Guy Debord and Brigitte Cornand show the power of the method, one last time. *Guy Debord* screened on Canal+, together with *Society of the Spectacle*, *Refutation of All Judgments* and *Latcho Drom* (1993) by the Algerian-born Romany filmmaker Tony Gatlif (b. 1948), who like Debord enjoyed the patronage of Lebovici. Debord put his affairs in order, then shot himself in the heart.

27 A Romany Detour

When your opponent sees into your reasoning like a lynx, conceal your thoughts like an inky squid.

Baltasar Gracián

When François Mitterrand became president of France in 1981, it appeared for many on the left as if the seeds of May '68 had finally flowered. Debord was not convinced. This was not the longed-for entry of socialists into the state, but the final entry of the state into the Socialist Party. In other words, it was a faded repeat of the final colonization of the Italian Communist Party by the Italian state in the late seventies that Sanguinetti so elegantly exposed. The spectacle was changing form. The diffuse and concentrated spectacles gave way to the integrated spectacle, which combined some attributes of both. The definitive response to May '68 would be the spectacular incorporation of the signs of leftism into the state as a tactical measure. While leftish intellectuals enjoyed a brief honeymoon with the new government, Debord chose to absent himself from the scene even more.

He spent more time out of Paris. From 1981 to 1987 Debord summered in Arles. Perhaps it was at Arles that he became acquainted—or re-acquainted—with Gypsies. The region around Arles has many connections to Gypsies. The nearby town of Saintes Maries de la Mer is home to Sara, patron saint of the Gypsies, around whom there is a famous celebration every May. The popular band the Gypsy Kings formed in the early eighties out of musicians whose families fled civil war in Spain and settled around Arles. While this would hardly be the kind of Gypsy culture that would appeal to Debord, it is a spectacular residue of the significance of Arles in Gypsy life.

Born in Shanghai in 1941, Alice Becker-Ho met Debord in 1963. Her father was in the German Navy, but he deserted. He was from the border province of Alsace-Lorraine and considered himself French. He became a banker in Shanghai but was obliged to move his family to France when the Maoists arrived. Alice came in contact with Debord through hanging around the Socialism or Barbarism group, with which the Situationists were in dialogue at the time. They were married in 1972.

"Guy married me so that I could have the benefit of his work if ever he died or went to jail," she told Debord biographer Andrew Hussey. "We loved each other and sometimes we loved other people, but we had no respect for the institution of marriage."[1] And sometimes they loved the same things. Such as the Gypsies, avatars of everyday life outside of property and the bourgeois family. The Gypsies would be the subject of the first of a remarkable series of books Becker-Ho would later publish. The Gypsies are an evocative figure in many ways for a way of life outside the spectacle.

The Gypsies call themselves Rom and call everyone else Gaje. Here they will be called by the name Gaje give them—and not always kindly—Gypsies. Debord writes in *Panegyric*: "The Gypsies rightly contend that one is never obliged to speak the truth except in one's own language; in the enemy's language the lie must reign."[2] This reads like a détournement of a passage from a famous book about them, by an even more famous author. Jan Yoors (1922–77) writes in *Gypsies*: "In Romani they said, 'Tshatshimo Romano' (The truth is expressed in Romani). It was the Gaje who, by forcing the Rom to speak a foreign language, made the Gypsy lie. The Rom said, 'Mashkar le gajende leski shib si le Romeski zor' (Surrounded by the Gaje the Rom tongue is his only defense)."[3]

Yoors should know: by his own admission, he ran away from home at the age of twelve to live with Gypsies, and did so on and off for many years. The British made him an agent during the war with a special mission to liaise between Gypsies and the Resistance in occupied France. Later he moved to New York, established himself as an artist working in tapestry, and wrote books about his adventures.

On Yoor's account, the Rom are active perpetuators of the myth of the Gypsy. "They created an aura of fearful superstition around their race, convincingly pretending to possess mysterious powers … Gypsy men and women were conscious of the image they projected, and amongst themselves they joked about the fear they inspired in the Gaje." Their gift to the Gaje would be exoticism, romance, nostalgia, dreams, longings, mystery. But all this would be carefully managed appearances.

Yoors sums it up in this story, which he presents as told to him by a Rom elder: "whenever the representatives of authority wanted to interfere with Gypsy affairs, the first step was to capture and incarcerate their King, in the belief that this would destroy the Gypsies' social organization, being convinced that the King was the fierce autocrat they were led to believe him to be—whereas in fact life went on much as before with the exception of the foolish and fooled King." The Rom have no kings, but the appearance of having kings could have its uses: "there are lies more believable than truth."[4] One could say much the same about Debord, *King of Situationism.*

It isn't hard to see what might attract Debord's attention in Yoors' story. There is a certain unspoken subtlety about it. Perhaps the Rom deceived Yoors as they deceived other Gaje, merely giving him the impression of unfettered access to their culture. Perhaps Yoors did really belong to the Rom community, but was really not so able to free himself from the Gypsy image of themselves that the Rom project upon the Gaje for their own benefit. Perhaps Yoors belonged to the Rom, but in writing for Gaje, adopted their prudent policy of mystification.

Yoors' account is premised on a certain strategy in which the playfulness of language directed at power shields something quite different: a language that is not playful at all, but discreet, even clandestine. This presents something of a double bind: Is his book a truthful account of deception or a deceptive version of the facts? Interestingly, where Yoors writes of the Rom, Debord writes of Gypsies. Yoors apparently reveals secrets; Debord frankly has something to hide.

The Rom approach to everyday life might have much to recommend it to Situationists, or Post-Situationists, if there is such a thing. Yoors presents them as a federation of autonomous *kumpania*. Relations between kumpania were renewed from time to time with ritual celebrations, gifts and by inter-marriage. Each kumpania is a fluid association, always gathering and scattering as new alliances form and old relationships expire. They may dissolve at any time by mutual consent. There is no political superstructure. Rom justice is decided by the *Kris*, which may meet when necessary to settle contractual disputes or breaches of the conventions of purity.[5] It is a striking account of the conditions of possibility of life outside the state.

The law of the land is not to be transgressed so much as finessed. Yoors does not deny that the Lowara kumpania, among whom he lived and traveled, had their own distinctive approach to private property. "Stealing from the Gaje was not really a misdeed as long as it was limited to taking basic necessities, and not in larger quantities than was needed at that moment."[6] Many a chicken that crossed their path ended up in a Romani pot. Wealth is for spending, not accumulating. "Communism and capitalism alike were merely reflections of the foolish Gaje's fixation on the accumulation of things, which in time enslaved men."[7]

For the Lowara, Gaje were to be outwitted, but not needlessly provoked. As the Romani proverb has it: "it is easier to milk a cow that stands still."[8] Yoors contrasts them to another kumpania who were caught up in a vicious cycle of hostility from Gaje which prompts the Rom to aggressive thieving, which in turn provokes more Gaje hostility. This allows Yoors' to contrast his *good* version of the culture with a *bad* one, which impeded the Gypsies' ability to live off the land and move freely. "Above all it was their mobility which spared them. They did not fight back; they simply moved away."[9]

Slovenia seems, in the early twenty-first century, to have escaped its past and become a suburb of Europe. Even in the little town of Ambrus there are new cars in the driveways, kitchen renovations. Yet this is where townspeople allegedly surrounded the house of the Strojans, a Gypsy family, shouting, "Kill the Gypsies!" The Strojans hid out in nearby woods for five days. The locals claim their house was built without permits, even though the Strojans have lived there since the sixties.

The interior minister said that the Strojans would not be allowed to return to their house, but that the government would find them a new one elsewhere. When Slovenia's human rights ombudsman raised the matter with the Council of Europe's human right's commissioner, the Slovenian prime minister accused him of "denigrating Slovenia's name."[10] Borderless Europe may if anything be a harder world for the Gypsies today than the bordered one of the thirties about which Yoors writes. Debord: "One cannot go into exile in a unified world."[11]

Yoors' Lowara are indifferent to the ownership of property that does not have immediate use, but they do love a lavish party. The *patshiv* can occur whenever different kumpania meet and are occasions for grand displays of generosity that bring respect to the host. "A patshiv must convey good will to one and all, without exception: the most humble on such occasions must be treated as kings."[12] Yet the Rom are not the libertines of Gaje legend.[13] Yoors describes a rigorous set of ritual obligations, an elaborate concern with separating the pure from the impure, and a distinctive mode of justice. They only appear to the Gaje as disorderly, as the Gaje cannot comprehend that they have a different rigor.

The Gypsies may outwardly acknowledge the God of Islam or Christianity to appease the Gaje. More recently, Saint Sara, the patron saint of the Gypsies, seems to fascinate the Gaje more because some see in her worship traces of ancient rituals the Gypsies have brought with them from India.[14] But for Yoors, the Gypsies only really honor the *Mule,* or ancestors. Interestingly, the Mule are not eternal. The Gods of the ancestors live on only as long as they are remembered. Yoors' Gypsies are an oral culture, passing on strategies for negotiating life through elaborate forms of storytelling and everyday proverbs, not a few of which deal with ways of outwitting Gaje.

The procedures of the state are likewise both accepted and flaunted. For instance, the surnames invented for official documents were often ribald jokes, unintelligible to Gaje in any country but good for a laugh among the Rom. A Romani riddle runs: "A white meadow, some black ewes—they talk continually as they go by, but they don't recognize us." The answer: a document.[15] The Rom appear in written records as Gypsies, but that appearance is a strategy for maintaining as much scope as possible for autonomous action.

Yoors experiences Rom autonomy through the quality of time in everyday life. While bound by rigorous codes and enduring hardship and danger, Yoors finds with the Rom a certain quality and intensity, which collapses, when he writes of it, into banalities. "To the Rom life was an endless flow, like a torrent without form or goal, beyond good or evil, and man's place in it was like a process of self-definition, forbidding the all too human cowardice of weariness and doubt. With a driving urge to seek out what was elemental in life, man was free to react in his own way to its challenges, be what he could make of himself. This was his freedom."[16]

This sounds more like warmed-over Jean-Paul Sartre than the Rom speaking, as if they lived without the *bad faith* of doing things because they are supposed to, were happily *condemned to freedom,* and other existentialist commonplaces. Nevertheless there is something here that points to a reading of Yoor's Gypsies as constructors of situations out of whatever they can borrow as they detour through a world which, in Yoors' time, is already passing into the spectacle.

THE PRINCES DO NOT GIVE UP. This was the graffiti, quite possibly written by René Viénet, that during May '68 earned the Situationists the respect of Tony Gatlif. The Rom might be without a king but the men at least think of themselves as princes. Gatlif came into the same patronage orbit as Debord when he sought Lebovici's help in finishing his first feature film, *The Princes* (1983). Its setting is the same extra-urban transitional zones that so fascinated the Impressionists, only now it is a post-industrial landscape in decline. The factories are closing. Nara, a Rom who no longer wanders, makes a living of sorts stripping valuable scrap from abandoned workhouses.

Nara is harassed not only by the police and by Gaje but also by his daughter, mother and estranged wife. Gatlif's narrative is male-centered but hardly flattering. His women characters all comment on and delimit Nara's aggressive sense of self. A red Mercedes appears bearing three princes in gangster-sharp suits, who turn out to be his wife's three brothers. Nara spurned their sister, and they would kill him for this, only she confirms what is in Nara's eyes her offense: she let some social worker persuade her to go on the pill. Romany women exist in Nara's world to bear children. "You live like our grandparents. You haven't changed," as one of the princes says to him. His own mother claims she lost fourteen to the Nazi camps.

Only the world has changed. Nara has only one sickly white horse, which at the start of the film stands tied up outside a crumbling housing estate. He doesn't get much of a price for it, and returns home shortly after with a TV set. The spectacle is beyond the range of things he can turn to his advantage. Throughout the film he finds odd-jobs, gets out of scrapes: "We don't beg, we *take*," as he says. But he can't finesse the journalist who comes to take down his story.

There's a certain satisfaction in the scene where a tourist takes his picture and Nara responds by beating the crap out of him. The viewer feels the guilty pleasure of taking Nara's side in the attack while knowing at the same time that to view the film at all is to take part in the spectacularization of Rom life that the film both admits and yet tries to finesse. Like Yoors, Gatlif plays at revealing and concealing, seducing and refusing. It's a translation into cinema of what Alice Becker-Ho calls the *language of discretion*. For while not much may remain in the lees of the disintegrating spectacle, there may still be codes of conduct for those in the know.

28 The Language of Discretion

The consummate person—wise in speech, prudent in deeds—is admitted to, and even desired by, the singular society of the discreet.

Baltasar Gracián

At a Nicaraguan school for the deaf, founded in 1977 under the Somoza dictatorship and expanded by the Sandinistas, teachers noticed that students were ignoring their Spanish lessons and were instead developing their own system of signs for talking with each other. This discreet language has been developed further as older children pass it on to younger ones.[1] While this is a remarkable achievement, the Gypsies kept their clandestine language alive across and beyond Europe, and for more than half a millennia. In *The Princes of Jargon,* Alice Becker-Ho quotes the great Dutch historian and Situationist favorite Johan Huizinga: "It is not surprising that the people of Paris should have believed in the tale of the Gypsies, who presented themselves in 1427 ... They came from Egypt, they said; the pope had ordered them, by way of penance for their apostasy, to wander about for seven years."[2]

The story about the pope is a fabrication, a manipulating of what Yoors would call Gaje appearances. Yoors is cited more than once in Alice Becker-Ho's *The Princes of Jargon,* but her book has a different purpose. She argues there that Romani language is one of the sources of the linguistic tactics of the dangerous classes—their jargon, argot, slang or cant. This in turn she claims accounts for the origins of far more words in French and other European languages than conventional linguists credit. She follows in the footsteps of Marcel Schwob, the symbolist writer, friend to Oscar Wilde, uncle to Claude Cahun, and Schwob's pioneering Gypsy etymologies.[3]

Where it is respectable to look for the imprint left in language by the great cities of Greece or Rome's powerful empire, Becker-Ho embarks upon a counter-etymology, looking for the traces of those who resisted the state with their own kinds of clandestine organization. Gypsies have "elected to confront the world with ancient weapons (slang, word magic, tribal spirit). To put it succinctly, their history, their memory and their 'writing' are wholly contained in their language which is a language of struggle."[4] They set the standard for discreet uses of language, even of the common tongue.

This might apply also, for example, to the slang of late-nineteenth-century homosexual subculture that Wilde embedded even in his most popular plays. *The Importance of Being Earnest* means one thing to the bourgeois theater audience and quite another to men who earnestly seek unmentionables with other men.[5] Whether it is a question of hiding in a distinct language, such as Romani, or hiding in a jargon made out of the common language, such as cant, it is a tactic for creating a unity of thought and life within and against the language and the power of the state.

Becker-Ho: "The gypsies are our middle ages preserved: dangerous classes from another age."[6] As they traveled across hundreds of miles and hundreds of years, the Gypsies fell in and fell out with other marginal groups, few of which lasted as long or ranged as far as they did. They are the continuous thread through the counter-history of living outside states, faiths and territories. In modern times they become the most persistent of those dangerous classes who constitute themselves through an act of refusal: "You are not born dangerous class. You become so the moment you cease to acknowledge the values and constraints of a world from which you have broken free: we are basically referring here to the necessity of wage-labor."[7]

The Coquillards are one example of organization among the dangerous classes which Becker-Ho thinks borrowed linguistic tactics from the Gypsies. While lacking their elaborate oral culture, the Coquillards included among them the literate. While not above highway robbery, the Coquillards included tavern clerks, capable of forging charters and decrees or passing as pilgrims, and not without some success, at a time when, as Huizinga says, "doubt and rationalistic interpretation alternate with the blindest credulity."[8]

The Coquillards are the dangerous classes' version of the kinds of guild organization that in the late middle ages came up against the rise of individualism and the commodity form.

The legend of the Coquillards remains because they numbered among them the poet François Villon. He made them famous, not least with his *ballades* in the Coquillard jargon. While there is no lack of learned commentary on them, some details remain obscure. Villon's English translator writes: "These poems are notoriously resistant to decipherment (and, some readers may think, scarcely worth the effort required)."[9]

One ballade in jargon includes the lines: "Companions in living it up / keep on taking white for black."[10] Does this refer to counterfeit coins, or does it refer to which road to take to avoid the law? The Coquillard Colin de Cayeux and his associates get their due in Villon's more respectable "Testament." "You handsome lads, you stand to lose / The loveliest rose that's in your crown."[11] Unable to talk his way out of a jam, de Cayeux hung for his crimes.

In *Panegyric* Debord will use Villon's tribute to de Cayeux and other lost children as a *memento mori* for Ghislain de Marbaix, a somewhat shady character whom he knew in his youth.[12] But with the passing of the Situationists, Debord and Becker-Ho sought a discreet way of passing on a certain knowledge of how to use language to organize an inside and an outside to being within the spectacle, which is perhaps of even more interest as this spectacle disintegrates.

True slang, like that of the Coquillards, is minoritarian and centripetal; it is coined for particular use, and uses whatever swims into its orbit. Fake slang is spectacular and centrifugal; it issues from the media and ripples outwards. Becker-Ho: "The slang of times past and its usage signaled one's membership of a particular world. Nowadays people harbor illusions that they are in touch with a host of different worlds."[13] The spectacular circulation of slang allows respectable people to drop into conversation jargon from prison, drug dealing and so on. Becker-Ho: "A language wrought of ingenious tricks, devised for its own use, is today being co-opted by the world which is diametrically opposed to it."[14] True that.

Slang was once an elusive language, of value to a quite select company. Lacenaire: "a thief who doesn't know the slang is nobody."[15] The opposite of fashionable coinage, slang had a quite different purpose. "Nowadays, due to the fact that poetry is no longer practiced, some people think that they can detect it anew in slang, where the share of poetry remains small. Metaphors are to slang what the image of the Gypsy is to the Gypsy."[16] The second term in this parallel, Gypsy/slang, is not the truth of the first, metaphor/image-of-Gypsy. It is rather its secret. The problem with contemporary slang—and poetry, and theory—is that it no longer has anything to hide.

Giorgio Agamben: "Gypsies are to a people what argot is to language."[17] From Becker-Ho's research he derives a larger principle: "We do not have, in fact, the slightest idea what a people or a language is." One of romanticism's least helpful notions was that of the identity of a language and a people. This alleged identity becomes the legitimating ruse of the modern state. The state claims to be founded on language that it has imposed upon its peoples by force. Only by breaking the nexus of people and language can praxis and thought undo the seamless appearance of the state.

Even at the elementary level of the word, sometimes even of the particles of sound, language is détournement, a borrowing of borrowings. Becker-Ho: "Who does the borrowing from whom of a word itself on loan?"[18] The very concept of a loan-word presupposed that language is somebody's property. Argot is then not a language but rather a particular series of techniques that can be used on any linguistic material. Agamben: "All peoples are gangs and coquilles, all languages are jargons and argot." This is where his otherwise pertinent essay over-reaches. While there is no people in perfect identity with a language that is its special property, it is not then the case that we are all Coquillards. It is only the case that we are potentially so.

Agamben misses the far-reaching implications of Becker-Ho's apparently modest study. Jargon, like any kind of language, is nobody's property, but the practice of jargon is part of a practice of life. Becker-Ho: "What comprises dangerous-class *nous* is the continual ability to detect who is on one side of the line or the other."[19] The Coquillards acquire it from the Rom; Villon acquires it from the Coquillards; Becker-Ho acquires it from the practices of all of the above. To practice language as argot, and thus to undo the apparent identity of language and people, takes a certain discretion.

Creating and sustaining a secret language is an acquired art. It is not a quality that can be claimed to dignify, say, the treatises of professors of philology. The jargon of academics is a quite different practice to that of the Coquillards. Academic jargon does not produce a different relation to the world. Becker-Ho: "On the contrary, it defends and reinforces a world based on the division of labor by protecting the privileges of a caste, extending their protection even to the words the latter uses."[20]

In the disintegrating spectacle, argot is likely to proliferate, but in the favelas and refugee camps rather than the lecture halls. "Slang is making a comeback with the creation of as many ghettos as there are cities still standing."[21] This is where Becker-Ho locates the possibility of that language which Debord characterized as "the language of contradiction, which has to be dialectical in form as well as in content."[22] Argot is the language of negation, where words can be turned to show an opposite or complimentary meaning.

Becker-Ho proposes an approach to language that is at odds with both the objectively scientific and the subjectively poetic. Language is conflict, ruse, strategy. Linguistic discovery is not innocent of power. Michel Foucault is drawn to the study of language as power, identifying, classifying, ordering and authorizing; Becker-Ho sides with those for whom language can only be a ruse or a trick. She insists that these marginal and excluded language practices have their own coherence. "It is essential to be able to distance oneself from ordinary social values as well as from the vocabulary that their expression requires."[23] From the point of view of power they can only be defined negatively, as *resistance*, whereas to Becker-Ho they have their own secretive forms and practices.

In 2003 Swiss courts agreed to hear a case brought by a coalition of groups representing the Gypsies against IBM, subsidiaries of which they allege "helped the Nazis automate the Holocaust."[24] Whether the company is responsible or not, it is certainly true that the Nazis used Hollerith machines sold by an IBM subsidiary to tabulate census data and manage the logistics of transporting people to the camps. A similar claim by Jewish survivors was dropped amid negotiations with Germany and Switzerland over compensation.

Gypsy groups say that Gypsy survivors and their descendants, who number about 1.2 million, have been left out of these compensation agreements. Already in the thirties, when Yoors traveled with his beloved Lowara, the document was getting harder to dodge. The "ancient weapons" of the Gypsies may be no match for computerized logistics, but a new breed of cypherpunks may carry on the language of discretion into the new world of code.

Writing in the nineties, Becker-Ho was prescient about the influence of computerization on language, a *big data* project receiving considerable investment at the time. She is particularly scathing about linguists who imagine that having access to a vast digitized corpus of a language will answer all their questions about linguistic origins and use. She does not see the incorporation of language into the archive on this granular level as a neutral fact of merely scientific interest, but nor does she reduce its possible effects to a question of control. Becker-Ho: "All this will bear mainly on the definition of new property rights, whence those 'considerable' economic interests since realized by Google."[25]

If the problem was once the illusion that a language was the property of a people, the problem may soon become that language is the very real property of particular private interests. Take the example of the activists who convened a conference on *radical media,* only to receive a cease and desist order from a media company that has trademarked the name @radicalmedia and thus claims a rather exorbitant proprietary right over the very concept.

By stepping outside the *panoptic* of power, Becker-Ho also steps outside its forensic approach to the marginal. The language of the dangerous classes is not to be freely exposed to just anyone. "If there is a game with words, and to an even greater extent a game going on with their meaning, the real truth lies elsewhere, for the use of the initiated, of those who have already chosen sincerity."[26] What might outwardly appear as a playful approach to language is a ruse designed to shield a relative stabilization of meaning for other purposes. Becker-Ho: "In slang, the indisputably poetic element within it must be situated after, not before its formation ... Poetry's route is through culture, slang's is through deception."[27]

Which is why "the playful content increases the further away one gets from serious matters."[28] By the time it becomes modern poetry, playfulness has forgotten its original purpose. "This form of playful diversion (or *détournement*) gives that popular and good natured character to slang, thus helping to mask the latter's primitive technical aspects and at the same time toning down its savagery. The weapon that others have used turns up here with the primer removed; we are left with the game, the contest of words, the release of pent up energy."[29]

Considered as an interiority, as a caché for discreet significance, slang has no author, and no authority. It is not creative or spontaneous. It is not playful for its own sake. It is poor in ideas but abounds in synonyms, as these are a useful way of stabilizing a pattern of terms which can be understood by those in the know. For example, when the Coquillards speak of *marriage*, they have in mind not nuptials, but the noose. Slang is an artificial language meant to be unintelligible to certain people. It doesn't change much or too quickly until it loses its underpinnings in clandestine use. "Slang is language disguised."[30] The more a clandestine group needs to fight and to hide, the more elaborate becomes its slang.

Here is where Becker-Ho also takes her distance from those like Julia Kristeva who focus on the exterior qualities of the poetic and playful attributes of language, and make this exteriority a radical resource in itself.[31] It is the case that in its early days the Situationist International valued poetry as the *anti-matter* of the spectacle, but by this they always mean not just Lautréamont and Fourier but also the wildcat strike.[32] They did not imagine avant-garde poetics, which draws attention to the perverse productivity of language, as an analogy for labor in general. In any case, what is distinctive about the whole Situationist and Post-Situationist project is that it is a certain poetics that it wants to make instrumental. They make use of modern poetry as a resource in the same way the Coquillards used what they could glean from Romani language practices.

As Becker-Ho writes, "the closed realm of slang, encompassing a discreet language and the community that speaks it, has been a continual source of inspiration for many writers past and present."[33] Debord, for instance, uses the words *cave* (sucker) and *baron* (stooge) in *Comments on the Society of the Spectacle*, and in *Panegyric* writes a whole paragraph in the jargon of the Coquillards as a way of gesturing toward his own use of a language that both perpetuates his own appearances and yet has something to hide. Debord chooses to write in a language "generally accessible to those in the know."[34]

Becker-Ho may as well be speaking of Debord's own use of language with her elusive remark that "Historical knowledge allows those things that ought not to be explained in too much detail to be nonetheless presented in the light most appropriate to them."[35] A historical knowledge, in turn, of the language of the Gypsies and the slang of the Coquillards might be a discreet way of describing certain silences in Debordian languages.

Debord's paragraph in Coquillard jargon might these days be his most easily understood. Becker-Ho quotes the writer Pierre Mac Orlan, a longtime Debord favorite: "The last few years have seen argot become an academic jargon destined for little use outside the Sorbonne where candidates in cant studies will thereby be adding a new jewel to their crown. The crown in question here though is no longer the one made of roses that Master François [Villon] referred to whenever a housebreaking would prompt celebration in verse of the chaplets of roses sported by 'his fine lads' from Montpipeau ... Language, whether in the form of argot or of the pure, time honored classical variety, cannot hold out against changes in social conditions, above all when changes are of the type we are presently experiencing."[36] Now that there are scholars of Coquillard, not to mention of *Situationism*, it may be time for another tactic. Debord makes use of what one might call the irony of the spectacle: that a classical written language becomes something like a secret language, outside of the spectacular language both high and low, of left and right.

Debord and Becker-Ho's strategy with language is in the end one of participating in a broad front of practices that make language discreet, which allow it to separate out an internal from an external sense. In a world so devoted to useless exposure, this might be something of an achievement in its own right. "There is in the very use of slang a sense of unadulterated pleasure that already comprises a first result: in the act of poking fun at the uninitiated, it is already in itself a deception, fully the first step on the road to deceit and the initial satisfaction thus engendered. Moreover, there is nothing peculiar to the dangerous classes about this, since it is a feature of any jargon that goes hand in hand with a class consciousness."[37]

In a world that so values the *public intellectual,* who has conceded in advance to be part of the spectacle, there might be something to be said for the *private intellectual,* whose interests remain separate from it. Private here would not be in the sense of the domestic, the familial, the home or bourgeois private property, but rather a discreet kind of sociability, a different and undisclosed code. "I must take care not to give too much information to just anybody," as Debord says. Certain pages will need to be interpolated into his writing, like the secret codicils of certain treaties.[38] The private intellectual is at the same time the *public idiot,* speaking an idiolect known to some but not all.

It may seem strange that Debord and Becker-Ho would celebrate both François Villon and Niccolò Machiavelli, given that one was a thief and the other a secretary of state. They at least had in common that they were both tortured, even if for rather different crimes. In the end, the writers that matter embody strategies, either in the service of the state or against it, and there is something to learn from both. While Machiavelli has his followers, Debord and Becker-Ho's project is a rare one in so thoroughly refusing to identify itself either with the existing state or with the ideal state so beloved of reforming intellectuals. Clément Marot wrote in 1533: "As for the jargon, I leave its correction and exegesis to Villon's successors in the art of the crowbar and the hook."[39] Debord and Becker-Ho's exegesis hewed to different but no less ancient tools.

29 Game of War

The trick is to know what cards to discard.
Baltasar Gracián

"We play an effigy of war, and battles made like / real ones, armies formed from boxwood, and play realms, / As twin kings, white and black, opposed against each other, / Struggle for praise with bicolored weapons."[1] These are the opening lines of the 1527 poem "Scacchia Ludus" by Marcus Hieronymus Vida. That strategic genius, in any field, is the only thing worth commemorating is a characteristically Debordian note. The word *effigy* might appeal to Debord in its modern sense, given how careful he was to preserve his bad reputation.[2] But here it might mean something else: that the game is a form, a mold—an allegory, perhaps—for a certain kind of strategic experience.

One of the strangest entries in Guy Debord's bibliography is the 1987 book in which he and Alice Becker-Ho record the rules of the board game Debord designed, variously known as the *Jeu de la Guerre*, *Kriegsspiel* and *Game of War*. The bulk of the book is a move-by-move account of a game between the two of them. *Game of War* is first mentioned in Debord's writings in 1956. In 1977 Debord entered into a partnership with his then-publisher Gérard Lebovici in a company to make board games, of which it was to be the first. A craftsman was commissioned to make four or five sets in copper and silver.[3] On this account, the game was a part of Debord's life for more than thirty years.

Debord was not a casual gamer. As he writes: "And so I have studied the logic of war. Moreover, I succeeded, a long time ago, in presenting the basics of its movement on a rather simple board game: the forces in contention as well as the contradictory necessities imposed on the operations of each of the parties. I have played this game and, in the often difficult conduct of my life, I have drawn a few lessons from it—I also set myself rules and I have followed them. The surprises of this kriegsspiel seem inexhaustible; and I fear that this may well be the only one of my works that anyone will dare acknowledge as having some value."[4]

The record of the playing of the game is both a tribute to his enduring interest in strategy and a remarkable testament to Debord and Becker-Ho's relationship. As Debord writes: "the nature of our collaboration resides in the 'game of war' that we played."[5] Are not all relationships games? Played by more or less adequate rules, and with more or less cheating? As for who won this game, and whether there was cheating, some facts and conjectures will follow in due course.

Game of War is a strategy game, and to see this as a major rather than minor part of his legacy is to insist that above all else Debord was a strategist. Jacqueline de Jong: "He was a great strategist." Giorgio Agamben: "Once, when I was tempted (as I still am) to consider Guy Debord a philosopher, he told me: 'I'm not a philosopher, I'm a strategist.' Debord saw his time as an incessant war, which engaged his entire life in a strategy."[6]

Unlike the scholar, the strategist is not the proprietor of a field of knowledge, but rather assesses the value of the forces aligned on any available territory. The strategist occupies, evacuates or contests any territory at hand in pursuit of advantage. Where philosophers came of late to concern themselves with endless green fields of ineffable traces and immanent virtualities, strategists take their chances against mundane necessity. Debord: "The world of war at least presents the advantage of leaving no room for the silly chatter of optimism."[7] In this regard he is remote from Fourier, and perhaps even from Marx.

The avant-gardes have a long-standing connection to games. The Surrealists invented several. Marcel Duchamp famously gave up art for chess. He even coauthored a book about it. François Le Lionnais: "What [Vitaly] Halberstadt and Duchamp perfected was the theory of the relationship between squares which have no apparent connection, *Les Cases Conjugées*, which was a sort of theory of the structure of the board. That is to say, because the pawns are in a certain relationship one can perceive invisible connections between empty squares on the board which are apparently unrelated."[8] Like the Surrealists, Debord invented his own game, and like Duchamp, it took the form of a sustained effort to create via the game a conception of how events unfold in space, a "schematic representation of the overall agonistic process." Its ambition is nothing less than "the dialectics of all conflict."[9]

Game of War includes more or less plausible parameters of movement and engagement for infantry, cavalry and artillery. Besides the arsenals, two per side, *Game of War* also includes units for communication. With the possible exception of the communication units, it works in much the same way as classic nineteenth-century kriegsspiel, of the kind popularized in the training of the Prussian officer class. Debord claims his is modeled on classic war games and is consistent with the famous treatise *On War* (1832) of Carl von Clausewitz.[10] Its rules capture the essential movements of warfare from the time of Napoleon to the Paris Commune. *Game of War* is a détournement, then, but since what it plagiarizes is essentially an algorithm, a set of rules for a game, then the result is a little different from other instances of détournement. The distinctive correction Debord offers to an understanding of strategy comes out in the specifics of game play.

Debord's ambition seems to be to create a game which has possibilities for play that are as great as chess but which conceives of play in a different manner. As Alex Galloway writes, it is something like "chess with networks."[11] *Game of War* does not enclose space within strategy as chess does. Space is only ever partially included within the range of movement of the pieces. Some space remains smooth and open. The game is also subject to sudden reversals of fortune less common in chess. Debord: "In fact, I wanted to imitate poker—not the chance factor in poker, but the combat that is characteristic of it."[12] Each side makes its initial deployments in ignorance of those of the enemy, introducing at least an element of the unknown characteristic of poker.

The game requires attention to the tactical level of defending each of one's units, since once one starts losing them more pieces can quickly fall. However, units cannot move or engage unless they remain in communication with their arsenals, directly or via relays, making lines of communication particularly vital. Players are usually more concerned with breaking the adversary's lines of communication than with offensive action directed against either the adversary's arsenal or fighting units. Outside of the quantitative struggle between blocks of fighting units is a qualitative struggle, in which a force suddenly loses all its power when the enemy cuts off its communications; "thus the outcome of a tactical engagement over just one square may have major strategic consequences."[13]

Each player has to keep three quite different aspects of the game in mind: fighting units, arsenals, lines of communication. While attempting to maintain freedom of action, each side is also obliged to make difficult choices between qualitatively different kinds of operations, the means for the realization of which are always in short supply. One may have the means but not the time, or the time but not the means. "Each army must strive to keep the initiative, compensating for shortfalls in troop strength by the speed with which it can concentrate its forces at a decisive point where it must be the stronger: strategic maneuvers succeed only when victory yields an immediate return, so to speak, in terms of tactical confrontation."[14]

Among the particular qualities of *Game of War* is that it is not a territorial game. It does not conceive of space as property, to be conquered and held. Antonio Gramsci famously juxtaposed the concepts of the *war of position* and the *war of maneuver*. For Gramsci the war of maneuver is associated with syndicalist approaches to political conflict, with Rosa Luxemburg, and with the events of the October Revolution in Russia. He associates the war of position with mature Leninism and the lessons of the defeats suffered across Europe by the revolutionary movement that the October Revolution was supposed to spark. Gramsci: "In the East, the state was everything, civil society was primordial and gelatinous; in the West, there was a proper relation between state and civil society, and when the state trembled a sturdy structure of civil society was at once revealed. The state was only an outer ditch, behind which there stood a powerful system of fortresses and earthworks."[15]

For Debord this line of thinking can only justify the bureaucratic apparatus of the Communist parties and their obsession with creating one institutional bunker after another, from the trade unions to the official Communist art perpetuated by former Dadaists and Surrealists such as Tristan Tzara and Louis Aragon in their waning years. The Italian Communist Party pursued this war of position with particular vigor after the Liberation. Sanguinetti shows that all that resulted was the co-option of the party by the state. *Game of War* is a refutation of this whole conception of strategy. Debord: "This is a war of movement … a war in which territory per se is of no interest."[16]

In their film disquisition on *Game of War,* the London-based Class Wargames group goes so far as to claim that "*Game of War* is Debord's answer to the political enigma of Bolshevism."[17] They read, or rather they play, *Game of War* as Debord's meditation on the 1917 Russian revolution, the signal event that shaped the times into which he was born, and which for Debord is a historic defeat of the revolutionary movement. It was through the militarization of daily life that the Soviet experiment degenerated into the concentrated spectacle. "Then as now, radical intellectuals had to ask themselves the key question: do they have the moral strength to resist the temptations of Bolshevism?" Class Wargames sees the four cavalry units as effigies of the Leninist vanguard party, "the new class of warrior intellectual." The cavalry pieces move the fastest, so they can quite literally function as the avant-garde, but this avant-garde is there to be thrown into the maw of time. "In this game, the players must learn how to make the best use of these elite troops on the social battlefield without becoming Bolsheviks themselves."

In the war of position, tactics are dictated from above by strategic concerns with taking and holding institutions across the landscape of state and civil society. *Game of War* refutes this territorial conception of space and this hierarchical relation between strategy and tactics. Space is always partially unmarked; tactics can sometimes call a strategy into being. Some space need not be occupied or contested at all; every tactic involves a risk to one's positions. "It makes sense to move against the enemy's communications, but one's own will be stretched in the process."[18]

Debord moves the conception of conflict away from the privileging of space that persists in Gramsci's war of position. Key to *Game of War* is the question of judging the moment to move from the tactical advantage to the strategic exploit. Tactics and strategy do not have a hierarchical and spatial relation, but a mobile and temporal one. Plans have to be changed or abandoned in the light of events. Debord: "The interaction between tactics and strategy is a continuing source of surprises and reverses—and this often right up to the last moment."[19]

Prussian *kriegsspiel* were often fought using actual maps of contested borders. *Game of War* offers a rather more abstract terrain. Each side has an L-shaped mountain range and a pair of arsenals, but in different positions. The asymmetrical board offers different strategic opportunities to the two sides, which are labeled simply North and South. Class Wargames: "Players who lack a profound knowledge of psychogeography will find themselves at a loss, while their opponents weave the disruption of the mountains and the bulwark of the forts into a more proficient command of the terrain as a whole." This asymmetry is perhaps Debord's way of encoding something key to Clausewitz's understanding of war, namely that the two sides in conflict always confront each other as something incommensurable. Calculation is clearly a key to Clausewitzian conduct, but he does not treat the world of war as a closed one in which calculation replaces strategic intuition.

Game of War is a rigorous and schematic presentation of conflict, if missing certain qualities. The spatial field is asymmetrical but unchanging. The moment of surprise comes only once, when each side reveals to the other the initial disposition of its forces. In documenting the playing of a single game for their book, Debord and Becker-Ho present each move on a diagram that outlines as a static figure the changing disposition of forces, but this gives no real sense of the ebb and tension in time of game play. Still, the ambition of documenting the play-by-play with these diagrams of *Game of War* is clear: "Before they went to the printers, the figures looked like a truly dazzling puzzle awaiting solution, just like the times in which we live."[20]

30 The Strategist

Never reveal the final stratagems of your art.
Baltasar Gracián

Debord is a strategist, not a philosopher. History is a matter of will, luck and calculation, of "the simultaneous consideration of contradictory requirements."[1] There is nothing ineffable or sublime about it. Here he differs from a great deal of modern leftist thought. Writing of the Iranian revolution, Michel Foucault declared: "The man in revolt is ultimately inexplicable."[2] Alain Badiou persists in an irrational fidelity to the event of Mao's Cultural Revolution.[3] When not admiring Robespierre, Slavoj Žižek dreams of repeating Lenin, who seems to cause him indigestion. While Foucault, like his friend Gilles Deleuze, prefers the ineffable revolt to revolution, Badiou and Žižek put their faith in the memory of great leaders, whose proper names seem strangely to occlude, not to say occult, thinking about historical time itself. In either case, leftist philosophers react against what Žižek calls "the reinscription of a revolt into the process of strategic-political calculation."[4]

But from whose point of view is revolt itself a lawless event, or a dissolute moment where the Real and the Symbolic have illicit congress? From the point of view of the priest—and the police. The movement of revolt is no exception to the fluid dynamics of historical time. Debord is quite clear on this: *Game of War* is a practice he found useful for the difficult conduct of the whole of his life. There is nothing ecstatic about *Game of War*, and that perhaps makes it the better legacy of the late twentieth century's lessons in action.

Strategic thought confronts the gap between the possible and the actual, without the silly chatter of the impossible intruding. Boris

Groys: "The irreducible, unhomogenizable, infinite, virtual empire of heterogeneities and differences is actually nothing but bourgeois pluralism without market losers, capitalism as utopia ... a neo-theological opiate of the people."[5] Or more succinctly—Clausewitz: "there is a great difference between possibility and fact."[6]

Above all, Debord is not someone who ever went looking for this theological utopia in the moment of revolt. Such times are in a certain sense playful, but they aren't festivals, and still less sacred rites. The strategist's world is necessarily secular. The strategist enacts the gap between the known and the unknown in tactics. Debord: "Though the basic principles are certain, their application is always a matter of doubt."[7] To the strategist, unlike the philosopher, the event comes as no surprise.

While *Game of War* distances itself from the incalculable time of the romantic left, it also differs from the closed world of cold war strategy. This brought together advances in mathematics such as game theory, the modern programmable computer, and global surveillance and intelligence gathering, all in an attempt to rationalize strategic thinking. The fog of war would dissipate under the combined attack of a vast expansion in information gathering, computing power capable of analyzing this data with cool efficiency, and, above all, centralized command. The defense intellectuals who embarked on this path brought the specialized tools of social science to bear on problems of fighting the strictly spectacular war of nuclear deterrence.[8]

The ancestor of what becomes the dominant model of the defense intellectual was not so much Carl von Clausewitz (1780–1831) as his contemporary Antoine-Henri Jomini (1779–1869).[9] Where the former stressed the continuity between war and politics, and between calculation and intuition, Jomini treated war as a thing apart, a thing governed by ratios of *mass x velocity.*

Unlike Jomini, von Clausewitz has a supple sense of the array of facts that compose a situation and the difficulties they put in the way of action. Clausewitz: "In war, action is like swimming against the tide, where normal attributes are insufficient to achieve even mediocre results."[10] One difficulty is what we might now think of as the network of information relayed both to and from the front lines. In *Game of War,* Debord tries to capture the effect of tidal friction by allowing a limited number of pieces to be moved in each turn. No grand strategy can unfold all at once. While the pieces have different values, all must remain in line of sight contact.

Clausewitz writes of war as "a wonderful trinity, composed of the original violence of its elements, hatred and animosity, which may be looked upon as blind instinct; the play of probabilities and chance, which make it a free activity of the soul; and of the subordinate nature of a political instrument, by which it belongs purely to the reason."[11] For Clausewitz, the first element (instinct) is the people, the second (probability) is the General and the last (reason) is the calculus of state power. In cold war decision science, everything collapses into calculation. Where leftist philosophers take refuge in the incalculable event like the good humanists they somehow remain, the cold war scholars of the *inhumanities* delight in making history disappear completely into the algorithms of the rationalization of choice.

Clausewitz is famous for *On War*, which appears at times to distill military experience into axioms. But when he writes about actual campaigns, particularly those he witnessed, there is more subtlety to how he presents the situations of war. Here he is, for instance, on Napoleon's main strategic innovation: "Bonaparte was the first to risk everything on a single great battle. This use of the word *risk* does not imply that more would be risked than if the forces and actions were divided, for there can be situations in which dividing them could be a thousand times more hazardous than risking them in a single battle. Rather, it is a gamble because, forgetting all rational calculation, the human mind is reluctant to concentrate a decision of enormous consequence in a single moment, as a battle requires. It is as if the mind felt restricted by such a limited amount of time. A vague feeling arises that if only given time, additional strength from within would be found, all of which, if it is not based on objective facts but instead only on feelings, is just natural human weakness."[12] Here the situation is neither objective nor subjective, aleatory nor determined, rational nor irrational. All has to be considered at once, but yet with clarity and precision. By considering the subjective as an objective factor, Napoleon, as Debord observes, was able to "use victories in advance, on credit."[13]

The art of *Game of War* may lie in maintaining the properly

Clausewitzian dimension within which strategy operates, which is not susceptible to capture by the techniques of either poetics or mathematics. Debord's understanding of Clausewitz restores the *aesthetic* dimension, if one can call it that, of assessing situations and determining courses of action. Rather than Jomini meets the computer, Debord offers von Clausewitz crossed with their contemporary Stendhal (1783–1842).

In Stendhal's astonishing account of the Battle of Waterloo, the fog of war becomes a veritable shroud, and despite the fine weather. Our hero Fabrizio wanders about in the train of Marshall Ney, not even sure if what he is experiencing is an event at all, shocking though it is: "What he found horrible was a horse all covered in blood that was struggling on the ploughed soil, its feet caught up in its own entrails. It was trying to follow the others; the blood was flowing into the mud."[14]

Having believed all day in victory, Stendhal's army of Napoleon finally retreats in disarray, with many casualties, and among them obedience. Debord: "There is simply no way of obtaining cast-iron certainty as to what should be done, and this holds true even after crushing numerical superiority has been achieved, for there are circumstances in which a seemingly defeated army may still launch decisive actions against its opponent's communications."[15] Perhaps the strongest lesson Debord encodes in *Game of War* is that even the most powerful adversary has as a weakness the communication of the parts with the whole. The successful counter-attack is on communication, which is to say, on the *totality*.

The plane on which all the particular units move has its own temporality, in which mass and speed are bound in the kind of reciprocal relationship Jomini would have understood. The larger the mass one fields against the enemy, the slower it moves; the faster it moves, the smaller the mass. When a particular unit engages not another particular unit, but the line of communication, it touches instead on another plane. This other plane is the network of communication, where so long as the lines are not broken, communication is instantaneous and direct. As Class Wargames counsels players of *Game of War*: "if the coherence of their networks of communication breaks down, they will experience a kind of vertigo, whereby the stability of their psychogeographic perception is disrupted." Debord's dialectic of conflict steers the gamer toward the conduct of struggle on the plane of communication where cutting the lines can afford a quick victory. The plane of communication is the plane of the totality. Cutting communication disables not a particular unit but the network connecting units. The plane of communication is one of simultaneous and homogeneous time, or of what Debord in *Society of the Spectacle* (1967) conceives of as *spectacular time.*

So while it looks like its nineteenth-century ancestors, *Game of War* is also a diagram of the strategic possibilities of spectacular time. Debord: "The bourgeoisie has thus made irreversible historical time known and has imposed it on society, but it has prevented society from using it. 'Once there was history, but not anymore,' because the class of owners of the economy, which is inextricably tied to economic history, must repress every other irreversible use of time because it is directly threatened by them all. The ruling class, made up of specialists in the possession of things who are themselves therefore possessed by things, is forced to link its fate with the preservation of this reified history, that is, with the preservation of a new immobility within history."[16] This very totality of homogeneous time becomes at once the spectacle's great strength and its fatal weakness—its Achilles' heel.

One could add Debord to that list of modern figures who never quite got over Napoleon Bonaparte. His conquest of Europe is the breech that establishes the nascent form of the bourgeois state. His campaigns absorb the masses into history in their wake. Georg Lukács: "What previously was experienced only by isolated and mostly adventurous-minded individuals ... becomes in this period the mass experience of hundreds of thousands, of millions."[17] For Lukács, the lessons of this time remain in the great historical novels, those of Stendhal included, in which the bourgeoisie narrates to itself the relation between individual experience and historical totality.

Debord, whose *Society of the Spectacle* often reads like détourned Lukács, looks elsewhere here, to Clausewitz, not to Lukács, or Hegel, or Stendhal. Even though he pays tribute to that Stendhal who, as "second lieutenant in the 6th Dragoons Regiment in Italy, captured an Austrian battery."[18] Nor does Debord turn so much to Fourier as Vaneigem does. The form Debord chooses to memorialize the lessons of the great bourgeois epoch is neither philosophy nor the novel nor utopia, but the kriegsspiel. Not the legacy of the bourgeois scholar, artist or prophet, but that of the officer class.

Game of War also contests the popular legacy of the Napoleonic era in the world of games. Keith Sanborn: "Compared to its popular contemporary American formulation of Napoleonic warfare, the game of *Risk*, the Debord and Becker-Ho game is vastly more complex. In *Game of War*, evaluating lines of communication, geographical position, logistics, and the relative speed and strength of different units all factor into the outcome. In *Risk*, the meaning of geographical position is reduced largely to simple topological adjacency; the concentrated quantities of armies and their offensive and defensive coefficients determine the stochastic representation of their force. Dice are thrown and the final outcome of battle is then determined largely by the law of large numbers. Individual player intervention has fairly minimal effect. *Risk* is, thus, an historical reflection of the global outlook of cold war technocracy. The statistically oriented logistical bias of that outlook appears on the horizon of military history as a positivistic misreading of the construct of total war."[19]

This is the context in which to recognize the historical stakes at work in not only Debord's efforts to publish his game, but also the strange interest of the publishing house founded by his friend Gérard Lebovici in reissuing works by Jomini, but particularly by Napoleon and Clausewitz. Napoleon's maxims put alternating stress on the logical and sensory aspects of war. Clausewitz's account of Waterloo has the temerity to vivisect the mistakes of the winning side.[20] If there is a literature to which Debord aspires to append his own modest contributions, it is the strategic thought of those who, whether they had major or minor roles in it, and whether they were on the winning side or the losing, adjoined themselves to their specific historical moment.

Game of War likewise offers an understanding of conflict that, unlike *Risk*, draws on what might be called a certain style of *participant observation*. Curiously, *Risk* (1957) was also invented by a filmmaker, Albert Lamorisse. Whatever the merit of *White Mane* (1953) and *The Red Balloon* (1956), both of these noted children's films offer idealized and magical solutions to conflict, and reintroduce the theological dimension that Debord tries valiantly to exclude.

In a remarkable reading of Debord and Becker-Ho's account of a single game, Galloway makes two striking claims: That the unidentified player who wins the game is Becker-Ho; that the losing player, Debord, broke the rules. Galloway claims that in *Game of War*, optimal troop deployments have crystalline shapes such as lattices, ladders and crosses. "If a gamer is sufficiently experienced with the rules of a game he or she will learn the point of maximal exploitation and, since it is in his or her interest, will enact these techniques of optimal exploitation as often as possible." And that is what the losing side—South—does. South, Galloway asserts, plays as if they had intimate knowledge of the algorithm of the game and of the formations its rules favor. And yet all is for naught, for North out-plays South in the end. An ill and ageing Debord is outplayed by, and will be outlived by, his younger partner. In spite of his best efforts, he cannot outwit his times.

Morale is a constant theme in the writings of both Clausewitz and Napoleon himself. Something no calculation of *mass x velocity* can measure is the morale of the forces themselves. If there is a key to understanding the experience of a *situation*, it is that its openness to setting the course of events one way or another depends to an immeasurable degree on courage. The specific talent of the strategist is in assessing morale as much as in calculating the mechanics of circumstance.

Philosophy detracts from the strategist's art by excesses of both optimism and pessimism. On the one hand, its gay combinations of language make everything seem possible; on the other, its disappointment with the actual world leaves a bleak and metallic aftertaste. It is as if philosophy could do nothing but binge-drink on hope and bemoan its historical hangovers. Vaneigem: "Revolt has less need of metaphysicians than metaphysicians have of revolt."[21] The legacy of the Post-Situationists points toward something quite different, to tactics that might open toward strategies, starting from the most minor moments of the everyday. It is a low theory that moves from the everyday to the totality, rather than a high theory that institutionalizes the mere thought of extremes.

Perhaps the last word should be that of Alice Becker-Ho: "Need we add again, to that which we'd stated in the preamble, that all play is first and foremost free action … is liberty? It appears the answer to this question is yes. This, at any rate, is what the preceding pages have attempted to emphasize. The finest players having been those who, free until the very end, conducted a game in which they themselves fixed the rules, guided by this virtue so badly perceived nowadays: loyal, before all else, to oneself."[22]

31 The Inhuman Comedy

Know how to forget. It takes more luck than skill.

Baltasar Gracián

The spirit of American capital at its peak in the twentieth century can be summed up in the famous statement: "What's good for General Motors is good for America." In the twenty-first century, one might say, rather: "What's good for Goldman Sachs is none of your fucking business." The spectacle of disintegration no longer bothers much with keeping up appearances. It is as if, having realized that commodified life offers nothing of much value to anyone, that which might be of some use is to be withdrawn so that a few, a miserable few, might at least hoard its paltry splendors in the most extravagant fashion. It can't last, so why worry? Keynes had it almost right: In the long run we're all dead, and the long run itself is running poorly.

Which makes it all the more puzzling why critical thought has not seized upon the moment to at least offer a few glowing embers of clarity. But that would require a mode of thought as total as the inhuman comedy that confronts it. For that mode of thought to exist would require a coalition of practices in which everyday life could be brought to consciousness of itself in a language—whether earthy or rarified it hardly matters—which refuses the separate compartments of the intellectual division of labor and comports itself discreetly.

Perhaps the wrong turn was to pay too much attention to Louis Althusser, whose brilliant and seductive project had the dubious merit of making it possible to assume that one could practice critical thought inside the academy without confronting the intellectual division of labor that is the law of the land there. Althusser sliced the totality into separate instances: economic, political, ideological, each as *relatively autonomous* as the university departments that claimed one of these territories for itself. Each was to have its privileged technical terms and scientific techniques. Thus one could comfortably adopt the language of one's discipline but inflect it with a *marxisant* flavor, which itself becomes increasingly hard to savor.

In Althusser's world, this division of labor was presided over by a master-discipline, which naturally was his own—philosophy—that became a sort of police agent assuring that in each of the other levels the practices that obtained were intellectually lawful. Whether what is ventured is a concept or a practice, the voice that hails from the other side of the street or the back of the hall with a "hey you!" is that of the Althusserian. So much so that we internalize this philosophical cop in advance. It is by Althusser himself that we are interpolated. As T. J. Clark once noted, it is no accident of timing that Debord's *The Society of the Spectacle* came out in 1967, just after the start of the Althusserian boom.[1]

Just as the entry of the worker's parties into the state turned out really to mean the entry of the state into the worker's parties, so too with this entrist project in the realm of knowledge. We became what we beheld. Critical thought did not take over the academy; the academy took over critical theory. It became hypocritical theory, the bad conscience of the scholar who knows too much to take the game all that seriously. Obvious though this is, one is not supposed to admit it; this in itself becomes a barrier to thought.

Having, like Napoleon, crowned itself at the head of this empire of knowledge, what a dismal business philosophy ends up being! The philosophers have only interpreted the world, Marx said. And his would-be inheritors complete the thought thus: the point, however, is to interpret those philosophers. The philosophy of history becomes merely the history of philosophy. The ruthless criticism of all that exists is replaced by the apostolic succession, of great men succeeded by great men, as if this view of history had not been soundly exposed as fairy tales in every other domain in which it once prevailed.[2]

While hardly recognizing the sovereignty of philosophy, those other knowledges which attempt critique more often than not do so only in the language of their discipline, and direct themselves at that level of the totality over which their discipline claims proprietary rights. Thus the disintegrating spectacle finds itself confronted with fragments of specialized knowledge that cannot but think in the fetishizing terms of the disciplines that birth it.

The serious business of the critique of political economy continues, but it is usually a humorless affair, uncomfortable with just how fictional the business of business has become. Meanwhile, the political becomes the precious object at the center of a whole cult of discourse, rendering it impossible to ask the prior question of whether politics can really be said to still exist.

It seems the height of philistinism to quote that notorious fascist phrase: when I hear the word culture I reach for my revolver. These days what remains of the ruling class is quicker on the draw, not to mention trigger-happy. It requires no such pretext. Yet culture continues to be the magic kingdom in which most critical intellectuals spend their days. When we hear revolvers we reach for our culture.

Against all of which, perhaps a different path—or different paths—could be carved through the critical practices of the late twentieth century. But it requires some back-tracking to find the way. What Debord called "the repugnant seventies" appear as a turning point where battles were lost, where what appeared to be strategic advances turned out to be retreats into dead ends.[3]

Hence the backward <->> forward itinerary of this book. As a first step, a return to the bourgeois revolution as precursor, to open up the question of what is living and what is dead in the memory of it. Through the work of T. J. Clark, an aesthetic economy emerges, via the concept of spectacle, as a domain in which the two categories have to be thought together, grounded in a Marxist sense of class struggle, and one not severed from its anarchist double. But Clark himself ends up boxed in to the aesthetic as the domain of mourning for a lost art of critical practices.

And so: Vaneigem, who opens up toward the imbrication of the struggle in and against the spectacle more properly in everyday life. This also is the occasion for broaching the value of the utopian as a practice of the everyday, extending and permutating on its possibilities. Vaneigem rediscovers and revises Fourier's great discovery:

a language of the passions practiced as a totality that excludes the necessity of sacrifice.

In René Viénet, the Fourierist and Marxist critiques come together in comedic interventions in the struggles of his time, where earthy humor mixes with heretical critique. Viénet thought all Situationists should know the basics of film production. He advances a critical embrace of a technics; he thought and practiced outside of specialization and its professional guilds. Nothing could be easier in the twenty-first century, and yet this supposed democratizing of the means of communication usually lacks his historical sense.

Viénet also has the merit of his relentless attack on one of the great mythic recuperations of radical energy, the Maoist dictatorship and the civil wars it spawned. In the disintegrating spectacle, historical thought has declined so far that the fantastic legends about Lenin and Mao, long since exposed as spectacular doubles of genuine popular struggles, have resurfaced among would-be leftists in search of saints to venerate.

A more plausible story is found in the struggles of disorganized labor in Italy through the seventies and after. Sanguinetti provides a counter-history, and one that considers more closely what transpires within the ruling class at this time. The people make history, but the properties of that history are recovered by the more skillful agents of the ruling class and subsumed within the history of property, the closest thing to a history that can be officially acknowledged.

And yet the ruling class appears to have lost the ability to think historically.[4] This distinguishes the disintegrating spectacle from its predecessors. Having gone on the offensive, and had victories aplenty in its advance, the ruling class comes to believe its own legends. At the acme of its power we see the acne in its beauty.

Today's ruling class are such philistines that they collect contemporary art. They seem dimly aware that the joke is on them and gamely laugh along to pulled-punch lines they don't get. One has to admire the gumption of the gallerists who convince them to part with millions for such bric-a-brac. Even Jeffrey Deitch, one of the great carnival barkers of this art world circus, could be amazed to find a Courbet worth less than a Warhol.[5] This is not a great age for patrons.

In the overdeveloped world, the ruling class no longer sees the point of maintaining vast cultural and educational institutions for the edification of the masses, and whether by increments or sudden cuts, their state withdraws from them. There shall be no social practice for the evaluating of the world outside the market. It is quite possible that for those canny enough to search for a modus vivendi in this world, the editorial, curatorial and educational professions might no longer provide it. This leaves, as in previous ages, the art of seducing patrons. One has to admit: Debord had a talent for this; and Lebovici, in turn, had a talent for being talent's patron. Let his name not be forgotten. What a friend to his friends! He made of the profits of the spectacle itself a gift for something of far greater interest than mere art or literature.

Let us not get too carried away with substituting a rogues' gallery for the usual lives of the saints. There is a certain tactical use to be made of naming tavern clerks and vagabonds in the place of the great thinkers of an age. Above all, let's not hoist Guy Debord into the pantheon. That is why in *The Spectacle of Disintegration* he at least appears in the company of some supposedly minor figures. It's a gesture toward the proposition that what's of enduring interest is always collaborations, practices, situations, moments, forms of everyday life, not the great and their singular works. What matters in the end are not the proper names but the improper names, which announce that voice which can denounce this world.[6]

When the holy spectacle subsumes even the signs of its enemies into its nave of all knavery, when all other practices retreat to the margins, it is time for the devil's party. There's nothing that isn't in somebody's database, somewhere. While refusing the vanity of assuming that one is under surveillance by any agency of consequence, one should perhaps be a little discreet about what one says to just anybody. Socrates had a point when he suggested that the written word goes out like an orphan into the world. Some thoughts should be kept within that other family of those who adopt each other for the sole purpose of carving out quiet spaces for the practice of life.

And yet it's a great age for détournement. This is not the same as the remix culture that proliferates so wildly, working and reworking any and every fragment of text, sound or image. Détournement imbues such practices with a strategy that is quite distinct from their usual raison d'être. As Debord's late works in (anti)film and (non)television demonstrate, détournement has no particular style or flavor. It is rather a matter of connecting the fragments of spectacular culture in such a way as to reveal the absence of the historical trajectory which those fragments both embody and refuse. As Courbet realized with *A Burial at Ornans*, the means are present within the tensions of existing signs to construct a proxy for the destiny of which they protest their innocence.

If there are strategies of revealing that détournement proffers, there are also strategies of concealing, of which argot is an exemplar, as Alice Becker-Ho's researches show. A language made for everyone has nothing left of it but the dogmas and doxas that the spectacle leaves like used shopping bags in the corners of the everyday. A language made for anyone is something else, a language which conceals something of its intentions for those not in the know. A language for anyone, but not for everyone, conveys a subtle other sense for those who discreetly accept the principles of historical thought and action.

These days, the devil's party may be impossible to spot. Everything about them, like their language, looks at first glance like everyone else. Yet one knows from certain details just whom one is dealing with, if one knows where to look. The devil's party is not entirely anonymous. It works silently to create a certain seductive aura around a version of what it is in itself that deflects attention from what it is for itself. The key to which is the passions and their expression within everyday life. The knowledge the devil's party values is accorded no prizes, for it can only be valued otherwise.

The problem with politics is that one spends too much time on the phone. And to organize what? Sometimes it seems the intellectuals are the last to know. How else to explain the fascination with The Political just at that time when it has all but ceased to exist? Like a species of endangered owls, the philosophers hoot about The Political as if such a habitat still existed. The Political was always that aspect of the state most encrusted with ideological escutcheons. Better to turn to the discourse of strategy, which while hardly free from decorative effects, nevertheless is obliged from time to time to speak not of the emblem but of the shield behind it.

In the realm of strategy one finds in a more general form principles to be discovered via the practice of applied art and writing. On the one side is the folly of a free poetics, a great tumbling acrobatics in which anything seems possible. On the other side is a pure objective calculation, which relieves its functionaries of the necessity of decision. Professional life in the disintegrating spectacle is built on the separation of the two into distinct orders of discipline: the creative and the technical. Both are relieved of responsibility for action: the first by appeals to romantic authority; the second by resignation to objective functions. Strategy takes as its domain what lies between.

Strategy is part calculation and part inspiration, part objective conditions and part empathetic intuition. Its domain is the situation, which can be only partly known, but is not for all that a mystical event. Strategy is the ordering of actions within a situation that reveals its contours via a form of engagement. The disintegrating spectacle can get by just fine without the High Theories which would either poeticize or rationalize its totality, for the bitter truth is that it is a totality without either poetry or reason. But it cannot get by without strategies.

Perhaps one could, like Censor, apply oneself to the study of what strategy this ruling class ought to pursue if it were still capable of forming one. At the level of the individual firms and their contestations over the future of the commodity form, the disintegrating spectacle is a world of brilliant campaigns and honorable defeats. At the level of the aggregation of interests among the ruling parties via the state that might ensure the long-term survival of the world on which it feeds, this ruling class has failed the ultimate test, that of historical thought in action. What is at work in the world is the punning of history, the invention of ever-new slogans and brands for the inability of competing forces to find the terrain on which their conflicts could be resolved in a more capacious form. Perhaps because the forms for which history calls are finally those beyond the commodity itself.

The Situationist International dissolved itself in 1972. Let's call the various projects attempted after that by various former members Post-Situationist, in the double sense of coming after and yet still marked by and indebted to that which it succeeded. *The Spectacle of*

Disintegration attempts to pick up the threads of these diverse and incommensurable projects, to find what in them might speak to a world they allegorize and foreshadow but do not fully inhabit. Their ideas, it turned out, really were on everybody's minds, and their influence turns up, for good or ill, far and wide.

Let's pick up just two strands to mark where one might advance a critical project in their wake, and along quite different paths to the rut in which hypocritical theory now runs about. Let's conclude with one instance of a renewal of critical theory (which was also a practice) and one instance of a critical practice (which of course also experimented in new concepts). As an instance of the former, the journal *Tiqqun*; as an instance of the latter, Occupy Wall Street.

If there is a place where the Post-Situationist current was revived in an original way, it was in the two issues of the journal *Tiqqun*, which appeared in 1999–2000, and which challenged *Internationale Situationiste* in both style and substance, if not longevity. While in some ways *Tiqqun* was an advance, the Post-Situationists who precede them also provide certain correctives to *Tiqqun*. In the writings of *Tiqqun*, there is a slippage from revulsion against the party of the working class to revulsion at the working class itself. These new narodniks make of the dangerous classes a romantic image only, one no longer subject to the kind of street ethnography of which Debord—let alone Fourier—was once capable. There is a slippage also from the terrain of capital and spectacle to spectacle and police, and finally to an exclusive interest in the police—or in *biopower*.

Like the Situationists and Post-Situationists, *Tiqqun* sees the working-class movement as caught up within the styles and forms of capital. Labor became what it beheld. But their own trajectory is to advance, in negative, a whole mess of petit bourgeois desires. The stylish business, the select company, even the country house—all the trappings of petit bourgeois life—are rejected in *Tiqqun*, and yet leave their mark. Their *imaginary party* repeats the devil's party, with more footnotes and less discretion.

Still: if it is the case, as *Tiqqun* proposes, that the more doctrinaire Autonomists are just the idealists of the managerial class, then it is also the case that the Situationists became the fantasy other life of the so-called creative class.[7] If the Post-Situationists are a corrective to some of *Tiqqun*'s foibles, *Tiqqun* in turn is a corrective gift in return. It is not unlike Clark's anarchist-Marxist dialogue, transposed to another time and conjuncture.

One of *Tiqqun*'s lesser-known works provides a real extension of Post-Situationist thought: the critique of the figure of The Girl. Here they advance onto the terrain of the critique of the overdeveloped world on its own terms, as if taking that sage Situationist advice not to hanker after the garb of situations past. For is it not the case that hypocritical thought is still traumatized by the past, and not even the past of 1968, but the past of the early twentieth century?

Between them, Žižek and Badiou on the one hand, and Hardt and Negri on the other, seem to repeat the debates of the inter-war period: The Leninist party without the popular front; the popular front without the Leninist party. The Great War, the Russian Revolution, the jazz age and the Great Depression seem to constitute the locus of several breaks with bourgeois thought's self-regard. The left-Heideggerians can only manage a melancholy remembrance of the most hideous consequences of this sequence of events.[8] Out of the shards of a fracturing order they claim only the most grisly: the Nazism of the camps and the terrible vision of those philosophers attracted like moths to the flames: Ernst Jünger, Martin Heidegger, Carl Schmitt. Meanwhile, the psychoanalysts seem puzzled by the "decline in symbolic efficiency" that comes after the inevitable eclipse of the father figures who supposedly stood above it all, not least the declining efficiency of the invocation of father Freud himself.

It's true enough that the Situationists had their version of this period, alighting instead upon the Kronstadt rebellion and particularly on the Spanish Civil War. What they attempted to salvage from the wreckage was critique in action. They built their critique on the lessons learned from the defeat of the Spanish Revolution, and on the limits to Surrealism's intuitive and impassioned critique of colonialism. In this age of the Lesser Wars and the Lesser Depression, the early twentieth century might indeed offer up some avatars for a renewal of critical thought. Not perhaps the Surrealism of Breton and friends, but of more marginal figures like Claude Cahun and Mina Loy.[9]

It is time to draw together a thread from this *Spectacle of Disintegration* that has so far eluded a coherent critique. One finds it in the split between Pissarro's peasant women and Manet's shopgirls. It reappears in both Debord and Viénet's films as the split between the image of The Girl that they détourn from popular magazines and pulp movies, and the words they appear on screen to voice, like ventriloquist dummies. Mina Loy and Claude Cahun saw her coming and tried to speak otherwise, from everyday life rather than from this cool abstraction. Vaneigem acknowledged that the whole spectacular order rested on the struggle for which she was a body double.[10]

Little sister is watching you. She stares out at you from billboards, magazines, screens large and small. Behind the production of her image is not some quirky dictator and his nervous minions, but a small army of stylists, hair dressers, photographers and, of course, models.[11] Whole industries exist to find and groom actual bodies who might embody this abstract, ultimately philosophical figure, who is one of the central modes of the contemporary world of images. She has a privileged place within the spectacle. She won't send the secret police to kick down your door in the middle of the night, but she might send you to the mall to get new shoes—and quite possibly in your sleep.

The Girl hasn't much to do with actual women, although women might or might not feel obliged to mark their distance from her. The Girl is not even necessarily female or even all that young. Sometimes men's bodies or older bodies populate the images that constitute her. She isn't always white. She isn't always human. Sometimes she is a robot or a cartoon or a flower. The norms around which she gravitates are geometrical.

The Girl is the marker of the success and the failure of feminism. Like most social movements, its gains come at the price of a certain incorporation into the very order it opposes. The women's liberation movement begat, as an unintended consequence, *girl power*. *Tiqqun*: "The supposed liberation of women has not consisted in their emancipation from the domestic sphere, but rather the extension of that sphere over the whole of society."[12]

It is not the factory that was extended across the social domain, but the boudoir. Life in the overdeveloped world is not a social factory, but a social boudoir. It even extends itself into the workplace, which now harbors rituals of tact and gestures of politeness that could be worthy of Vienna and the Dancing Kid. In the overdeveloped world, labor became affective labor. Politics became family drama. Art became interior decoration. The struggle over the remaking of the form of social life became kitchen renovation.

It's not that women are to blame for any of this, although a certain misogynistic tendency might have it that way. Rather, it is that the image of The Girl becomes the emblem through which this modification in the world of images is managed and felt. That modification of the world of images corresponds in turn to an extension and modification of the spectacle. The demise of the concentrated spectacle lays the groundwork for the supersession of Big Brother by the little sisters. She first surfaces in the diffuse spectacle, but puts paid to her rivals only after the integrated spectacle starts to disintegrate. She is the figurehead nailed to the prow of its disintegration.

The omnipresence of The Girl only shows that the legend of the intimacy of woman with nature has found a new home, that of second nature, or the spectacular world of finishes and veneers. The Girl's utopia is domestic, but the domicile of the domestic is imagined as the whole world. The Girl makes every scene an interior, as if any place in the world could be made her private domain by her presence.

Her power to create this domain is her beauty. She is sequestered in her own beauty. A certain moralizing tone in contemporary discourse holds somewhat paradoxically that beauty is only skin deep and at the same time what matters is really inner beauty. But, like the Greeks, the world of the contemporary spectacle regards beauty as having both spiritual and philosophical import. Debord: "what is good appears; what appears is good."[13] The good that appears—beauty—is outside of time. Experience, ageing, memory—in short, history—is not to appear. Time is marked out by the structural permutations of the fashion cycle.

The Girl is quite naturally not just about beauty but also about sex. Or rather, she is about sexuality, a sexiness detached from any particular sex act. Sexual liberation did not free people to have sex in all the Fourierist permutations. Rather, sexual liberation liberated sex from people. It even liberated sex from the human. Ever since Manet's *Olympia*, The Girl has had an embarrassing relation to the specifics of sex, not to mention the specifics of money. She is not supposed to be locatable in any particular intercourse of either kind. The Girl is about *seduction* more than sex.[14]

And yet there is a certain nobility about The Girl which is not supposed to be questioned. She stands, as embodiment of beauty, on the one side for venal seduction, but on the other for romantic love. Love is the last unquestionable ideology of the disintegrating spectacle. After the death of God comes the death of the oedipal father-figures who are His stand-ins, including Big Brother. No third term mediates any more between the self and what appears to it. Yet romantic love lives on. Pop songs still speak endlessly of it, declaring their loves to "you, you."

The Girl is only partly there as the object of desire, as stand-in for the commodity. *Tiqqun*: "The Girl is the dominant social relationship, the central form of the desire of desire, within the spectacle."[15] As Kojève parses Hegel: I don't desire the other as a thing. I desire the other's desire. Or to translate that into pop: "I want you to want me / I need you to need me." The Girl is a commodity that appears to desire its acquirer. Or rather, she might desire us. The suspension is key. The universal and eternal seduction projected by The Girl might or might not alight specifically on us. She is available to be available, but she isn't cheap: "Because I'm worth it!"

One could read a lot of hypocritical theory and not find any mention of The Girl, or any of the other handful of figures who populate the disintegrating spectacle and do the work—or something like it—of all the Holy Fathers, Big Brothers and Fraternal Functionaries who used to populate it. Debord and Viénet's films appear transitional in this respect.[16] Which is why, to go forward, the best way is to go back, back at least to the Post-Situationist moment, when everyday life was still the ground of an attempt at the critique of the totality, expressed in acts.

Speaking of acts: On September 17, 2011, a small band descended on Zuccotti Park, a little square of concrete planter boxes in downtown Manhattan, and declared that they had "occupied Wall street." They hung on long enough for it to turn into a situation that, if not on the scale of May '68, at least gave the ruling class something to think about.

Organized labor got involved. Labor has been in retreat for decades in the overdeveloped world, so mobilizing ten thousand people, as they did on October 5, 2011, is something of a rearguard action. Still, it is unusual for New York, if not for Paris, and at least seemed to confuse the police for a while. So I want to end *The Spectacle of Disintegration* with some notes, tentative though they are, recorded from the occupation. I have kept them in the present tense for reasons that will become obvious.

The confrontations with the police usually get the most attention, but they're not the only thing going on at Occupy Wall Street. I went down to Zuccotti Park at about 9 p.m. on Wednesday, October 5, 2011, after putting the kids to bed. I was alarmed by stuff on the Twitter feed that telegraphed incidents of contact with the police but which were not clear about the location. I wanted to make sure our park was still there.

Just off the subway, and heading down Church street, I catch a glimpse of a march going north, up the street parallel to the east. I see a mass of closely ranked bodies and banners and hear some vigorous chants. I'm not sure where they'd be going, as Wall Street is to the south. I decide to keep going down Church to Zuccotti Park and maybe catch up with that group later.

I hear the park before I see it. At the western end, about a hundred people are chanting, singing, dancing, banging on drums. I hang out with them for a while. This crowd is young, fun, and a bit crusty. The financial district is usually so dead after working hours. Even the idea of a party at night here is something.

It is hard to work my way into the park. Piles of stuff are arranged around the planting beds. Mostly disassembled tents. The police are pretty clear that they will not tolerate "structures" without a permit, and apparently a tent is a "structure."

A young man lies flat on his back in a sleeping bag. I narrowly miss kicking him in the head on my way by. He looks exhausted, as do a few others in sleeping bags that I find in the west end of the park, just past the drum circle at its westerly end.

Under the sound of the drumming is the thrum of a generator. A small knot of young men crouch around it, powering up devices. Most of the signs of organized activity are east of the crumpled tents and random sleepers. Knots of people cluster around tables dedicated to one function or other of keeping the park running.

Here was where I find people you might think of as "anarchists," if only in the sartorial sense. People who have some experience at self-organization. Otherwise the crowd is mostly dressed like any other crowd of college or post-college age young people in New York City, although here and there you find older people as well.

A young woman explains what is "problematic" about the occupation to two friends, and allows me to listen in on their conversation for a while. There are a lot of small groups talking amongst themselves. A man in a business suit raises a red and black flag while talking to another man in a track suit and hoodie.

A woman smiles at a man sitting on one of the stone benches. She parts her thighs and plants herself on his lap. He kisses her; she kisses him back. Her hands are in his hair. I thought of that line in Raoul Vaneigem about those who go on and on about class struggle without speaking of love. They speak with a corpse in their mouth, he says.

An older group, earnest, weathered, holds up signs about class struggle so that the TV crew on the southern side can see them. They do not have the curious, expectant, hesitant look of some of the younger people. Not everybody finds all this so surprising. As René Viénet put it: our ideas are on everybody's minds.

At the eastern end of the park is a group, about the same size as the drum circle, who prefer to chant slogans. They are standing tightly packed in an oval, doing call-and-response chants of the popular memes of the occasion.

It strikes me as curious how the park is polarized between these two ambiences: the drum circle at one end and the chanters at the other. The drum circle understands the place as something like a festival. They aren't for or against anything; they just are. Here, in this improbable, unlikely place.

The chanters feel more in need of a binding ritual that would settle at least for the moment who we are and who we aren't. They seemed more interested in making explicit the terms of the cleaving to and the cleaving from.

The northern side is strangely bare. It is supposed to be an area for art and signs, but something about that part of the park doesn't seem appealing, even though people are tightly packed into the middle. Along the northern edge are handmade posters, arranged so they can be seen in a stroll down that side. My favorite is "the medium is the message." Done rather patiently in several colors.

Someone wades in with a stack of pizzas. The food carts that are usually here anyway are still open. I would like to know what they made of it all, but they are doing a fairly brisk business and I don't want to hold anyone up. Both cops and occupiers line up for coffee, and perhaps a few office workers held back late.

A police truck arrives and barriers are slid off and erected down the southern side. Quite a few people get up to watch. A palpating rise in the level of tension. Who knows who ordered the new barriers or why? It could just be to make people a little tense.

The police seem relaxed, however. A policewoman leans against the barriers on the north side and chats on her cellphone. A cluster of maybe ten blue-shirted officers lean against the wall outside the Brooks Brothers store on the other side of the street. A white-shirted officer rests his bullhorn on the barriers for a moment. It isn't always like this, of course. I saw police arrest three people in broad daylight on the morning of September 20. At this moment, all is calm. Nothing is forever in these kinds of situations.

Wandering around the park, I talk briefly to a few people. I steer away from people who looked like old hands. I am interested in those people who seem in a sort of a fugue state. Mostly, they can not quite find words to describe the sensation. There is just something about this moment in space and time that is hard to describe.

It isn't obvious what one should be doing. It isn't work; it isn't leisure. There's nothing to buy. The union-organized marchers are long gone by the time I get there, so there isn't really any protesting to be done. In the park at this moment there are no police to confront. If you want to make the moment intelligible to yourself, you have to find your own way to do it.

The chanters and the drummers are two ways to go about it. Or perhaps it is a good moment just to try and sleep. There's always something to organize. There are always points to debate. Or, you could just *be there*. In some ways that's the hardest part. To just be there, in a moment carved out of the division of daily life between the time of work and the time of leisure. In a space that is supposed to be where office workers go for coffee and a cigarette on their breaks.

There's a division of the space of the park into functions, and usually this does sort of function. At night, with such a big crowd in it, the space starts to redefine itself a bit, and more by ambience than function. People arrange themselves in it more according to how they felt about it. There is an unanswerable question in the air, or so it seems to me, about what forms of life are possible. In different parts of the park people gravitate toward different answers. This is what you might call the *psychogeography* of the place.

When there's nobody really watching, when there's nothing to confront, when there's nothing to debate—this is what's left: How is it possible to create forms of life for ourselves, even if it's in the shadow of tall buildings that cast long shadows?

I sit for a while writing these notes, then I prepare myself to leave the Park and head back to the subway. I have to get up the next morning to get the kids off to school. People drift away, although it is clear that a fairly large group will stay on for most of the night. And others will be back in the morning.

Not many people can inhabit this place outside of work time, but a lot of people come to visit, and to glimpse something of another way in which the city might function. Other lives are possible; sometimes they even actually exist.

No matter what happens here next day or next week, I just want to record the fact that this actually happened.

Zuccotti Park, October 5, 2011

Notes

Leaving the Twentieth Century: Situationist Revolutions

1 There's a third, short book, with pictures, that presents a lecture based on this work: *Fifty Years of Recuperation*, New York: Princeton Architectural Press, 2008. I've *détourned* its three best sentences in this new introduction.

2 If I was to change one thing, I'd decenter the start of the story from Paris to the Belgian Surrealists, and Marcel Mariën's extraordinary project for a making the revolution on credit by founding an advertising agency. See McKenzie Wark, "Marcel Mariën," *Public Seminar*, January 27, 2016.

1 Street Ethnography

1 Simone de Beauvoir, *Force of Circumstance*, Paragon House, New York, 1992, p. 128.

2 See Boris Vian, *Manual of Saint-Germain-des-Prés*, Rizzoli, New York, 2005. His fake American crime novels are *I Spit on Your Graves*, Tam Tam Books, Los Angeles, 1998, and *The Dead All Have the Same Skin*, Tam Tam Books, Los Angeles, 2008. His *literary* novel *Autumn in Peking*, Tam Tam Books, Los Angeles, 2006, is perhaps his quasi-surrealist take on postwar culture, and *Foam of the Daze*, Tam Tam Books, Los Angeles, 2003, includes a delirious scene about the morbid enthusiasm for the celebrity philosopher Jean-Sol Partre.

3 For the Anglophone invader's perspective, see Elaine Dundy, *The Dud Avocado*, New York Review Books Classics, New York, 2007, p. 84 ff.

4 Simone Signoret, *Nostalgia Isn't What It Used to Be*, Harper and Row, New York, 1978, p. 43.

5 The classic study is Stanley Cohen, *Folk Devils and Moral Panics: The Creation of Mods and Rockers*, Routledge, New York, 2002. For a more contemporary assessment of the concept, see Catharine Lumby, "Sex, Murder and Moral Panic: Coming to a Suburb Near You," *Meanjin*, Vol. 58, No. 4, 2000.

6 Dick Hebdige, *Subculture: The Meaning of Style*, Routledge, London, 1988. Hebdige uses Jean Genet as his touchstone for a literature of subculture. The Situationists despised Genet, and not without reason, as his romance of negativity all too neatly worked as a spectacle of negation, rather than as negation of the spectacle.

7 Here moral panic could be read in the terms proposed by Slavoj Žižek, *The Sublime Object of Ideology*, second edition, Verso, London, 2009. The teen existentialists are a threat to bourgeois enjoyment either because they enjoy too much (sexual depravity, amorality, and so forth) or too little (political seriousness, asexual relations between the genders, and so on).

8 Quoted in Gianni Menichetti, *Vali Myers: A Memoir*, Golda Foundation, Fresno CA, 2007, p. 20. For Patti Smith's recollection of Myers, see her *Just Kids*, Ecco Press, New York, 2010. It seems appropriate for Myers to be reading Gorky. As Lukács once said of Gorky and his time, but in a way also applicable to postwar Paris and the Saint-Germain milieu: "neither the revolutionary nor the modern bourgeois ideology were born simply and immediately out of the dissolution of the old ideologies. On the contrary; as in every period of disintegration, the process begins with an ever greater perplexity of the great masses concerned; the weak sink into apathy or fritter away their strength in short-lived outbursts of senseless revolt." George Lukács, *Studies in European Realism*, Howard Fertig, New York, 2002, p. 212.

9 The dangers of appropriating the term *tribe* in such an urban context are neatly sidestepped in Wu Ming, *Manituana*, Verso, London, 2009. In this novel, Mohawk warriors visit London as representatives of the Iroquois Federation. The Federation has been loyal to the British Crown but seeks assurances that the alliance is mutual before joining forces against the American revolutionaries. While in London they are presented with an appeal from the London Mohocks, fierce exemplars of the dangerous classes, who suggest instead an alliance with them, as both have been dispossessed of their lands and their traditional way of life by British power. To be *tribal*, then, is not to exist in a state before colonial contact, but rather to have been dispossessed by that contact, whether at the antipodes of empire or at its very center.

10 Ed van der Elsken, *Love on the Left Bank*, Dewi Lewis Publishing, Stockport, UK, 1999, unpaginated. Tennessee Williams describes the Vali Myers look in his play *Orpheus Descending*. See *The Rose Tattoo and Other Plays*, Penguin Books, London, 2001, p. 252. For the Plimpton, Pomerand and the unattributed observation, see George Plimpton, "Vali," *Paris Review*, No. 18, 1958, pp. 43–47. For Plimpton and the permanent invader culture of Saint-Germain, see Nelson Aldrich (ed.), *George Being George*, Random House, New York, 2008, p. 83 ff; Juan Goytisolo, *Forbidden Territory: The Memoirs of Juan Goytisolo, 1931–1956*, translated by Peter Bush, North Point Press, San Francisco, 1985, p. 177. Goytisolo recounts in the same volume his wandering with Bernstein and Debord, pp. 205–6. Perhaps the most remarkable record of the time is Guy Debord, *Mémoires*, Editions Allia, Paris, 2004, in which Debord détourns both van der Elsken photos and a phrase from Goytisolo. See Boris Donné, *Pour mémoires*, Editions Allia, Paris, 2004. Also worth mentioning among memoirs of the time is Maurice Rajsfus, *Une enfance laïque et républicaine*, Editions Manya, Levallois, 1992.

11 *Class warfare*, Vian, *Manual*, p. 38; *closed group*, Ralph Rumney, *The Consul*, translated by Malcolm Imrie, City Lights, San Francisco CA, 2002, p. 63.

12 The Situationists spotted this convergence of the bourgeois and bohemian fairly early. See "On the Poverty of Student Life," in Ken Knabb (ed.), *Situationist International Anthology*, Bureau of Public Secrets, 2007, and Guy Debord and Giancarlo Sanguinetti, *The Real Split in the International*, Pluto Press, London, 2003.

13 The community of difference is advanced, though with considerably more subtlety than is possible here, in Maurice Blanchot, *The Unavowable Community*, Station Hill Press, Barrytown NY, 1988. Blanchot's reference points are Georges Bataille's Acéphale group, Breton's surrealists, and Marguerite Duras, a Saint-Germain identity not mentioned by Vian, for the obvious reason that she was still identified with the Communist Party, to which she adhered during the Resistance.

14 Jean-Paul Sartre, *What is Literature? And Other Essays*, Harvard University Press, Cambridge MA, p. 174; Georges Bataille, "La Divinité d'Isou," *Œuvres complètes*, Vol. 11, Gallimard, Paris, 1988, p. 379. See also André Breton, *Manifestoes of Surrealism*, University of Michigan Press, Ann Arbor, 1972, p. 298.

15 Isidore Isou, *L'Agrégation d'un nom d'un Messie*, Gallimard, Paris, 1947; Isidore Isou, *Introduction à une nouvelle poésie et une nouvelle musique*, Gallimard, Paris, 1947. It was Greil Marcus who really put Isou into this story, not least for Anglophone readers, but not without a certain embarrassment. On the Romanian connection in Dada, see Tom Sandqvist, *Dada East: The Romanians of Cabaret Voltaire*, MIT Press, Cambridge MA, 2006.

16 Isidore Isou, "Manifesto of Letterist Poetry" (1942), in Mary Ann Caws, *Manifesto: A Century of Isms*, University of Nebraska Press, Lincoln NE, 2001, p. 545. *American Speech*, Vol. 26, No. 3, 1951, notes references to Letterism turning up in *Time*, the *New Yorker* and the *Spectator* in the late 1940s. Isou's manifestos did not go entirely unnoticed.

17 Isou, "Traité de Bave et d' éternité (Venom and Eternity)", *Avant Garde 2: Experimental Cinema 1928–1954, Films from the Raymond Rohauer Collection*, Kino International, New York, 2007. This 111-minute version is based on the 1953 version produced by Raymond Rohauer and Leon Vickman, with 30 minutes of material restored from Isou's four-hour version. See also Allyson Field, "Hurlements en faveur de Sade: The Negation and Surpassing of Discrepant Cinema," *Substance*, No. 90, 1999, and Jacques Donguy's interview with Isou in *Art Press*, No. 269, 2001. Isou's relation to Dada is rather more complicated than there is room to explore here.

18 Gabriel Pomerand, *Saint Ghetto of the Loans: Grimoire*, translated by Michael Kasper, Ugly Duckling Press, Lost Literature Series No. 1, Brooklyn NY, 2006. Originally published as *Saint Ghetto des Prêts: Grimoire*, OLB, Paris, 1950. Needless to say the literal renderings of lines from the book which follow here hardly do it justice. Interestingly, Vian also draws a link between Saint-Germain and the Jewish ghetto, perhaps with less warrant.

19 Jules Romains, *Donogoo Tonka*, Princeton Architectural Press, New York, 2009. Romains started a movement called Unamism, based on the idea of collective consciousness and group behavior, and Pomerand's invocation of him is of interest in this connection as well as for his handling of the exotic. For an illuminating discussion of the relation between fiction and ethnography, see James Buzard, *Disorienting Fiction*, Princeton University Press, Princeton NJ, 2005.

20 Jean-Michel Mension, *The Tribe*, City Lights, San Francisco, 2001, p. 41. For a seminal if slightly later study of deviance, see Howard Becker, *Outsiders*, Free Press, New York, 1963. The most excluded among the Saint-Germain tribe were probably those taking ether, the aroma of which is all too telling.

21 Louis-Ferdinand Céline, *Journey to the End of the Night*, New Directions, New York, 2006, p. 5. This novel and its sequel, *Death on the Installment Plan*, New Directions, New York, 1971, describe the same miserable outer suburban Paris of Debord's early childhood. Céline had something of a paranoid break and turned anti-Semitic in the 1930s. He escaped execution as a collaborator and was back in Paris by 1952, where his outsider status, but not his political deliriums, gave him a certain alternative currency. Even after the war Sartre could write, only half joking: "Perhaps Céline will be the only one of all of us to remain" (*What is Literature*, p. 244). Debord détourns the epigram from *Journey* in his *Mémoires* (1958), reprinted in facsimile by Editions Allia, Paris, 2004.

22 On bohemia in general, see Elizabeth Wilson, *Bohemians: The Glamorous Outcasts*, Rutgers University Press, New Brunswick NJ, 2001. My thanks to Tony Moore for his insights into bohemian cultural formations.

23 Ivan Chtcheglov, "Formulary for a New Urbanism" (1953), in Ken Knabb (ed.), *Situationist International Anthology*, revised edition, Bureau of Public Secrets, San Francisco, 2006, pp. 1–8.

24 The Letterist International had two distinct phases with quite different memberships, which need not concern us too much here.

25 "Next Planet," *Potlatch*, No. 4, July 1954, in Libero Andreotti and Xavier Costa (eds), *Theory of the Dérive and Other Situationist Writings*, Museu d'Art Contemporani de Barcelona, 1996, p. 43; Guy Debord, *présente Potlatch*, Gallimard, Paris, 1996, p. 32.

2 *No More Temples of the Sun*

1 Georges Bataille, "The Obelisk," in Allan Stoekl (ed), *Visions of Excess: Selected Writings 1927–1939*, University of Minnesota Press, Minneapolis, 1985, pp. 213 ff.

2 See Michel Surya, *Georges Bataille*, Verso, London, 2002. A particularly interesting attempt to make Bataille relevant again as the philosopher of a symbolic, rather than material consumption of surplus, is Alan Stoekl, *Bataille's Peak: Energy, Religion, and Postsustainability*, University of Minnesota Press, Minneapolis, 2007.

3 A great account can be found in the seminal Greil Marcus, *Lipstick Traces*, Harvard University Press, Cambridge MA, 1989, p. 279 ff. See Michel Mourre, *In Spite of Blasphemy*, John Lehman, London, 1953. Like Dada founder Hugo Ball, Mourre found his way in spite of himself back to the church, and to a position of power within it. It recalls in its own way Sartre's story "Childhood of a Leader." As Marcus says, "He sought a bolt of lightning and gained the right to light a candle."

4 Le Corbusier, *Towards an Architecture*, Getty Research Institute, Los Angeles, 2007, p. 95. André Breton had polemicized against Le Corbusier long before Chtcheglov. See *Position politique du surréalisme*, Editions du Sagittaire, Paris, 1935.

5 Jacques Rancière, *The Politics of Aesthetics*, Continuum, London, 2004, p. 12.

6 *Tigers in a cage*, Le Corbusier, *Towards an Architecture*, p. 97; *unifying management*, ibid., p. 233. The Parthenon and Roman form feature more heavily in this book, but Luxor rates a mention.

7 See also de Chirico's novel, *Hebdomeros*, Exact Change Press, Cambridge MA, 1992. Debord was also fond of the landscapes of Claude Lorrain. Céline already makes literary use of Lorrain's landscape techniques in *Journey to the End of the Night*, p. 66.

8 Lev Kassil, *The Black Book and Schwambrania*, translated by Fainna Glagoleva, Progress Publishers, Moscow, 1978, pp. 13, 20. On Kassil see Inessa Medzibovskaya's essay in *Russian Children's Literature*, Routledge, London, 2008. On Kassil and Chtcheglov, see Jean-Marie Apostolidès and Boris Donné, *Ivan Chtcheglov: Profil perdu*, Editions Allia, Paris, 2006.

9 See Robert McNab, *Ghost Ships: A Surrealist Love Triangle*, Yale University Press, New Haven, 2004, for a usefully geographic account of the surrealists' relation to wandering, travel and colonialism. The seminal essay on surrealist ethnography is in James Clifford, *The Predicament of Culture*, Harvard University Press, Cambridge MA, 2002. See also the *Visual Anthropology Review* Spring 1991 special issue on ethnographic surrealism, and Martin Roberts, "The Self and Other: Ethnographic Film, Surrealism, Politics," *Visual Anthropology*, Vol. 8, pp. 77–94, for a critique of the rather depoliticized surrealism at work in Clifford.

10 Debord, *présente Potlatch*, p. 241; Andreotti & Costa, *Theory of the Dérive*, p. 60.

11 Knabb, *Situationist International Anthology*, p. 7.

12 Michèle Bernstein, "Dérive by the Mile," *Potlatch*, No. 9, 1954, Andreotti & Costa, *Theory of the Dérive*, p. 47; Debord, *présente Potlatch*, p. 65. The dérive is different from the amblings of the flâneur, a more exclusively masculine figure for whom the street

is to be seen as a thing apart, rather than a succession of atmospheres and adventures to participate in. See Griselda Pollock, *Vision & Difference,* Routledge, London, 1988. However, the dérive certainly derives from the flâneur as a vehicle for remaking literary form. See Eric Hazan, *The Invention of Paris*, Verso, London, 2010, p. 315 ff which traces a line from Restif via Balzac to Baudelaire.

13 Interview with Jacqueline de Jong, Algonquin Hotel, New York, October 17, 2009. See also Andrew Hussey, *The Game of War: The Life and Death of Guy Debord*, Jonathan Cape, London, 2001, p. 82.

14 Henry Lefebvre, *Critique de la vie quotidienne I,* L'Arche Editeur, Paris, 1977 second edition, p. 197; *Critique of Everyday Life, Vol. 1,* Verso, London, p. 182. This 1947 volume has much more to say about rural than urban life. Only after his encounter with the Situationists would the city emerge as the great theme of his writing. No wonder they accused him of plagiarism.

15 "On the Role of the Written Word," *Potlatch,* No. 23, 1955; Andreotti & Costa, *Theory of the Dérive*, p. 55; Debord, *présente Potlatch*, p. 203. The slogan was détourned from the Belgian surrealists.

16 Rumney, *The Consul*, p. 58.

17 Debord, "The Big Sleep and Its Clients," in Tom McDonough (ed.), *Guy Debord and the Situationist International,* MIT Press, Cambridge MA, 2004, p. 21 ff; Debord, *présente Potlatch*, p. 104 ff.

18 Patrick Straram, *Les Bouteilles se couchent,* edited by Jean-Marie Apostolidès and Boris Donné, Editions Allia, Paris, 2006, p. 17. The original version known to Debord was lost. This edition is a reconstruction by the editors. See also Patrick Straram, *Lettre à Guy Debord*, Sens & Tonka, Paris, 2006.

19 Straram, *Les Bouteilles se couchent*, p. 92.

20 *Critical practice:* the term is borrowed from friends at Chelsea College of Art and Design. The critique of the commodification of everyday life was taken up by Lefebvre's assistant Jean Baudrillard, among others. See *The System of Objects*, Verso, London, 2006.

21 Here we concentrate on the writing of the dérive. Perhaps its best expressions were maps and diagrams. See Simon Sadler, *The Situationist City*, MIT Press, Cambridge MA, 1999, p. 82 ff for a careful reading of Debord and Jorn's *Naked City* (1957).

22 On leisure and the labor movement, see Brian Rigby, *Popular Culture in Modern France*, Routledge, London, 1991.

23 See *Internationale Situationniste*, No. 8, January 1963, p. 42.

24 Friedrich Nietzsche, *The Gay Science*, Vintage, New York, 1974; *Thus Spoke Zarathustra*, Penguin, 1983. Both translations by Walter Kaufmann.

25 An influential source for nomadism is René Grousset, *The Empire of the Steppes: A History of Central Asia*, Rutgers University Press, New Brunswick NJ, 1970. Originally published in French in 1939, it was reissued many times after the war.

26 Gilles Deleuze and Félix Guattari, *Anti-Oedipus: Capitalism and Schizophrenia*, University of Minnesota Press, Minneapolis, 1983, p. 2. The connection between Situationist and what would be known in English as Post-structuralist thought is developed in Sadie Plant, *The Most Radical Gesture: The Situationist International and After*, Routledge, London, 1992. On dérive in relation to surrealism's Freudian legacy, see Tom McDonough, "Delirious Paris: Mapping as Paranoid-Critical Activity," *Grey Room*, Spring 2005.

27 See Kristin Ross, *The Emergence of Social Space*, Verso, London, 2008, on the politics of geography, and on the counter-school of the communard and anarchist Elisée Reclus. Debord does not appear to draw on Reclus directly, but Ross makes an

excellent case for a continuity of spatial practices and concepts. See also John P. Clark and Camille Martin (eds), *Anarchy, Geography, Modernity: The Radical Social Thought of Elisée Reclus*, Lexington Books, Oxford, 2004.

28 An earlier expedition had produced Michel Leiris's *L'Afrique fantôme*, Gallimard, Paris, 1981. In a literal way, the Situationists *pass over* the interest in exoticism of the surrealists.

29 See Rolf Lindner (ed.), *The Reportage of Urban Culture: Robert Park and the Chicago School*, Cambridge University Press, Cambridge, 1996.

30 Bataille, *Visions of Excess*, p. 34. Here Bataille compares Icarus, soaring up above, with the old mole, burrowing underground.

31 See Anthony Vidler, "Terres Inconnues: Cartographies of a Landscape to Be Invented," *October*, No. 115, Winter 2006; Tom McDonough, "Situationist Space," *October*, Vol. 67, Winter 1994; Brian Newsome, *French Urban Planning 1940–1968*, Peter Lang, New York, 2009; Paul-Henry Chombart de Lauwe, *Paris et l'agglomération parisienne*, Presses Universitaires de France, Paris, 1952.

32 See also Walter Benjamin, "Surrealism," in *Selected Writings, Vol. 2*, Harvard University Press, Cambridge MA, 1999, pp. 207–21.

33 *Abstract*: letter from Constant, quoted in Aldo van Eyck, *Writings: Collected Articles and Other Writings*, Sun, Amsterdam, 2008, p. 64; *Saint-Germain*: see Mark Wigley, *Constant's New Babylon: The Hyper-Architecture of Desire*, Witte de With Center for Contemporary Art and 010 Publishers, Rotterdam, 1998, p. 134. Constant was on the mailing list for free copies of *Potlatch*.

34 *Las Vegas Review-Journal*, May 3, 2003. See also Mike Davis, *Dead Cities*, New Press, New York, 2003.

35 The moving city is from: "Unitary Urbanism at the End of the 1950s," in Sussman, *On the Passage of a Few People*, p. 144; *Internationale Situationniste*, No. 3, December 1959, p. 13. An early, avant-garde incarnation of this ecological model would be Paolo Soleri, *Arcology: The City in the Image of Man*, MIT Press, Cambridge MA, 1973.

36 Borrowed (or burrowed) from *Hamlet*, Marx used the figure of the old mole most famously in the "Eighteenth Brumaire of Louis Bonaparte," in Karl Marx, *Surveys from Exile*, Penguin, 1973, p. 237. Bataille contrasts the old mole to "Icarian" thought, such as Hegel's, which soars above materiality, surveying it from outside. See Bataille, *Visions of Excess*, p. 32 ff. It also appears in Viénet, *Enragés and Situationists*, pp. 15, 73.

37 On Siasconset: *New York Times*, July 8, 2007; George E. Stuart, "The Timeless Vision of Teotihuacan," *National Geographic*, Vol. 188, No. 6, December 1995, p. 11.

38 Guy Debord, "Introduction to a Critique of Urban Geography," in Knabb, *Situationist International Anthology*, p. 10. It originally appeared in the journal edited by Belgian surrealist Marcel Mariën, *Les Lèvres Nues*, No. 6. September 1955. The complete run is reprinted by Editions Allia, Paris, 1995.

39 Sadler, *Situationist City*, p. 98. This could be the place to mention Owen Hatherley's defense of the brutalist wing of social democratic urban planning, *A Guide to the New Ruins of Great Britain*, Verso, London, 2010. While quite possibly informed by Chtcheglov and Constant, New Brutalist architects like the Smithsons developed their own critique of the failures of modernist social housing, coming up with networks, labyrinths, intersections and other means of producing social experiences. As Hatherley shows, such building, whatever its limitations, was a damned sight better than the more recent policy of turning over social housing to the private sector. Hatherley shows how the punk and postpunk critique of social housing in Sheffield and Manchester led mostly to property development and speculation,

whereas it is to the credit of social housing that, when combined with a certain subcultural knowledge, it once gave rise to whole creative scenes of much greater interest than the "creative industries" real-estate scams that replaced it.

40 Knabb, *Situationist International Anthology*, p. 9.

3 *The Torrent of History*

1 *Slate*, January 11, 2002; *New York Times*, February 23, 2002.

2 Comte de Lautréamont, *Maldoror and the Complete Works*, Exact Change Press, Cambridge MA, 1994: *old discoveries*, p. 313, *direction of hope*, p. 260; *one can be just*, p. 249; *plagiarism is necessary*, p. 240; *pyramids*, p. 85; *umbrella*, p. 193, *starlings*, p. 159.

3 See Tom McDonough, *The Beautiful Language of My Century*, MIT Press, Cambridge MA, 2007, and Maurice Saillet, *Les Inventeurs de Maldoror*, Les temps qu'il fait, Paris, 1992. This section was inspired by a paper McDonough gave at Binghamton University in 2001, and is indebted also to his book.

4 Paul Nougé, *Works Selected by Marcel Mariën*, Printed Head, Volume 3, No. 8, Atlas Press, London, 1985. See also Patricia Allmer and Hilde van Gelder, *Collective Inventions: Surrealism in Belgium*, Leuven University Press, Leuven, 2007.

5 Gil J. Wolman, "The Anticoncept," in Marc'O (ed.), *Ion: Centre de Création*, No. 1, April 1952, reprinted by Marc-Gilbert Guillaumin, Paris, 1999, p. 167 ff. This translation is by Keith Sanborn. See also Jean-Michel Mension, *The Tribe*, City Lights Books, San Francisco, 2001, pp. 61–64; Gérard Berréby and Danielle Orhan (eds), *Gil Joseph Wolman: Défense de Mourir*, Editions Allia, Paris, 2001 and Bartomeu Mari and João Fernandes, *Gil Wolman: I Am Mortal and Alive*, Museu d'Art Contemporani, Barcelona, 2010.

6 Guy Debord and Gil J. Wolman, "Pourquoi le Lettrisme?", in Debord, *présente Potlatch*, p. 175.

7 Lemaître, who speaks English, claims the status of co-inventor of Letterism under the nose of Isidore Isou, who clearly can't understand a word that Lemaître and Welles exchange. Thanks to Allan Stoekl for the Welles suggestion.

8 Molière, *Les Précieuses Ridicules*, Hachette, Paris, 2006.

9 Détournement may be less about surrealist collective imagination and closer to a conscious practice of what Halbwachs called collective memory. See Maurice Halbwachs, *On Collective Memory*, University of Chicago Press, 1992.

10 Karl Marx and Friedrich Engels, "Manifesto of the Communist Party," in Karl Marx, *The Revolutions of 1848: Political Writings Volume 1*, edited by David Fernbach, Penguin Books, Harmondsworth, 1978, p. 71. See Martin Puchner, *Poetry of the Revolution: Marx, Manifestos and the Avant-Gardes*, Princeton University Press, Princeton NJ, 2006. Puchner gives an excellent account of the influence of the Communist Manifesto on its avant-garde successors. Less convincing is his reading of the Situationists in the context of Tel Quel poetics.

11 McDonough, *The Beautiful Language of My Century*, p. 49. On Letterist and Situationist détournement, see Astrid Vicas, "Reusing Culture," *Yale Journal of Criticism*, Vol. 11, No. 2, 1998. On intertextuality, see Julia Kristeva, *Desire in Language: A Semiotic Approach to Literature and Art*, Columbia University Press, New York, 1980. Debord's "Mort de J. H. ou Fragiles Tissus (En Souvenir de Kaki)" (1954) is reproduced as plate 043 in Stefan Zweifel, et al. (eds), *In Girum Imus Nocte et Consumimur Igni: The Situationist International (1952–1972)*, JRP, Zurich, 2006.

12 *Times*, London, January 13, 2008. Tom McCarthy's *Remainder*, Vintage, New York, 2007, is a novel that could be read as a detailed working through of the consequences

of quotation, rather than détournement, being the dominant form of acknowledging the past in the space of the present.

13 Michel Foucault, "What Is an Author?," in *Language, Counter-Memory, Practice*, Cornell University Press, Ithaca NY, 1977.

14 This is the difference between détournement and the creative commons approach. See Lawrence Lessig, *Remix*, Penguin, New York, 2008; Yochai Benkler, *The Wealth of Networks*, Yale University Press, New Haven, 2006.

15 The question of history in Marxist thought is handled with considerably more subtlety in Martin Jay, *Marxism and Totality*, University of California Press, Berkeley CA, 1984.

16 Richard Barbrook, *Imaginary Futures: From Thinking Machines to the Global Village*, Pluto Press, London, 2007. Barbrook's historical narrative encompasses not only the American and Soviet versions of history, but also the social-democratic "third way" versions. As he shows, all draw on a common Marxist stock to very different ends.

17 Gregory Elliott, *Althusser: The Detour of Theory*, Verso, London, 1987, is a rare account of Althusser which includes the Maoist context for his thinking. Régis Debray, *Praised Be Our Lords: The Autobiography*, Verso, London, 2007, presents in condensed form Debray's own account of his adventures and misadventures. For a critique of these deviations from Marx's economic thought, see Meghnad Desai, *Marx's Revenge: The Resurgence of Capitalism and the Death of State Socialism*, Verso, London, 2004. Jean-François Lyotard, *The Postmodern Condition: A Report on Knowledge*, University of Minnesota Press, Minneapolis, 1984, is famously where Lyotard abandons the Marxist *grand récit* of history.

18 For the script see: Guy Debord, *Complete Cinematic Works*, translated and edited by Ken Knabb, AK Press, Oakland CA, 2003. On this first film in the context of Debordian cinema, see Tom Levin's classic essay "Dismantling the Spectacle: The Cinema of Guy Debord," in McDonough (ed.), *Guy Debord and the Situationist International*. And in the context of Debord's other early works, see Vincent Kaufmann, *Guy Debord: Revolution in the Service of Poetry*, University of Minnesota Press, Minneapolis, 2006, pp. 1–78, in the course of which he describes the Situationist project, not without justice, as "like a rereading of Marx by Peter Pan" (p. 6).

4 *Extreme Aesthetics*

1 Of course it is Plato who puts this figure in the mouth of Aristophanes: Plato, *The Symposium*, translated by Christopher Gill, Penguin, London, 1999.

2 C. J. L. Almqvist, *The Queen's Tiara*, Arcadia, London, 2001. "When, however, Jorn identifies the development of [eroticism] he does not follow this through, as he does with other essentially aesthetic emotions, into a consequent curiosity which, by exploring the unknown, would make it feasible to expand the possibilities and awareness of sexual identities. In effect, he imposes an unnecessary a priori upon himself." Peter Shield, *Comparative Vandalism: Asger Jorn and the Artisitc Attitude to Life*, Ashgate, Aldershot, 1998, p. 202. Not that this should stop us.

3 T. J. Clark, *Farewell to an Idea*, Yale University Press, New Haven, 2001, p. 389. A passing remark in the context of an extended discussion of Jackson Pollock. An exception would be Peter Wollen, *Raiding the Icebox: Reflections on Twentieth-Century Culture*, Verso, London, 2008. Fabian Tompsett and Stewart Home have also done much to promote the memory of Jorn in various avant-garde circles.

4 On Cobra, see Willemijn Stokvis, *Cobra: The Last Avant-Garde Movement of the Twentieth Century*, Lund Humphries, London, 2004.

5 See the autobiographical novel by Christian Dotremont, *La Pierre et l'oreiller*, Gallimard, Paris, 1955, p. 172.

6 Max Bill, *Form, Function, Beauty = Gestalt*, Architectural Association of London, London, 2010: *Bauhaus principles*, p. 42; *concrete design*, p. 9; *from the spoon to the city*, p. 9; *good form*, p. 31; *parasite*, p. 46; *art is an order*, p. 47. See also *Max Bill: No Beginning, No End: A Retrospective*, Museum Marta Herford & Verlag Scheidegger & Spiess, 2008, and Nicola Pezolet, *Le Bauhaus Imaginiste contre un Bauhaus Imaginaire*, Université Laval, Quebec, 2008. On Jorn, Bill and the Letterists, see Craig Saper, *Networked Art*, University of Minnesota Press, Minneapolis, 2001, p. 91ff.

7 Asger Jorn, *Pour la forme: Ebauche d'une méthodologie des arts*, Paris, Editions Allia, 2001, pp. 34–44. The following quotations are from Alan Prohm's translation of the chapter "On the Cult of the New in Our Century," in *Crayon*, No. 5, 2008, pp. 216–31. I am indebted also to his commentary.

8 On Sottsass, see Barbara Radice, *Ettore Sottsass: A Critical Biography*, Norton, New York, 1993, although his connection to Imaginist Bauhaus is passed over in silence. See also Mirella Bandini, *Pinot Gallizio e il Laboratorio Sperimentale d'Alba*, Galleria Civica d'Arte Moderna, Turin, 1974.

9 Graham Birtwhistle, *Living Art: Asger Jorn's Comprehensive Theory of Art between Helhesten and Cobra*, Reflex, Utrecht, 1986, p. 57. A work to which this chapter is heavily indebted. See also Peter Shield, *Comparative Vandalism:, op cit.*

10 Birtwhistle, *Living Art*, p. 85. For Apollo and Dionysus, see Friedrich Nietzsche, *The Birth of Tragedy*, translated by Shaun Whiteside, Penguin, London, 1994. A striking contemporary version of the Apollonian as fear of popular power is Christoph Spehr's film *Free Cooperation* (2004).

11 Birtwhistle, *Living Art*, p. 63. Jorn could be usefully compared to Brian Massumi, *Parables of the Virtual: Movement, Affect, Sensation*, Duke University Press, Durham NC, 2002.

12 Friedrich Engels, *Anti-Dühring*, Progress Publishers, Moscow, 1975. Engels's scientism plays a controversial role in both Eastern and Western Marxism. See Helena Sheehan, *Marxism and the Philosophy of Science*, Humanity Books, Amherst NY, 1993. What is distinctive about Jorn is that he is more interested in a parallel aesthetic practice, alongside science as practice, than in a philosophy of either art or science.

13 One could make an interesting comparison here between Jorn's genealogy of a radical modernism and that of another former Situationist with a deep interest in art history: T. J. Clark's *Farewell to an Idea*. Unlike Clark, Jorn at mid-century still thought of an affirmative role for aesthetic practice. It could be more than the spectacle in negative.

14 Friedrich Engels, *Socialism: Utopian and Scientific*, International Publishers, New York, 2004, p. 51.

15 *New York Times*, January 5, 2009.

16 *Entangled and chaotic truth*, Birtwhistle, *Living Art*, p. 69; *transformation of nature*, ibid., p. 72.

17 Ibid., p. 97. Jorn's attempt at a mystic materialism self-consciously recalls that of another Scandinavian artist in Paris: August Strindberg, *Inferno*, Penguin, Harmondsworth, 1979.

18 Birtwhistle, *Living Art*, p. 76.

19 *Art of naïve adults*, Birtwhistle, *Living Art*, p. 181. On the Modifications show, see "Modifications Peinture Détournée", in Gérard Berréby (ed.), *Textes et Documents Situationnistes 1957–1960*, Editions Allia, Paris, 2004, p. 102 ff; Claire Gilman, "Asger Jorn's Avant-Garde Archives," in McDonough, *Guy Debord and the Situationist International*.

20 Birtwhistle, *Living Art*, p. 93. While Ralph Rumney takes credit for introducing Debord to Huizinga, André Breton had also picked up on him as early as 1954. Huizinga becomes central to the understanding of the Situationists in Libero Andreotti, "Play-tactics of the Internationale Situationniste," *October*, Winter 2000.

21 Benedict de Spinoza, *Ethics*, Penguin, London, 1996, pp. 24–5, 33, S2.

22 Gilles Deleuze and Félix Guattari, *A Thousand Plateaus*, University of Minnesota Press, Minneapolis, 1987, p. 10.

23 Birtwhistle, *Living Art*, p. 92.

24 Ibid. Like Jorn, Huizinga was raised in an austere Christianity, and reacted with a certain willful aestheticism. See Robert Anchor, "History and Play: Johan Huizinga and His Critics," *History and Theory*, February 1978.

25 Alfred Jarry, *Exploits and Opinions of Dr Faustroll, Pataphysician*, Exact Change Press, Boston, 1996.

26 See Perry Anderson, *Considerations on Western Marxism*, New Left Books, London, 1977, the book which really consolidated the idea of Western Marxism. See also Perry Anderson, *In the Tracks of Historical Materialism*, Verso, London, 1985 for later reconsiderations.

27 *Organized movement*, Birtwhistle, *Living Art*, p. 100; *air currents*, ibid.; *Pyrric victory*, ibid., p. 35, *pact*, ibid., p. 103. Jorn's critique of Isou, "Originality and Magnitude," can be found in Asger Jorn, *Open Creation and Its Enemies*, Unpopular Books, London, 1994, originally published in *Internationale Situationniste*, No. 4, June 1960.

28 See Paul Klee, *The Diaries of Paul Klee, 1898–1918*, University of California Press, Berkeley, 1973; Viktor Shklovsky, *Mayakovsky and His Circle*, Pluto Press, London, 1974.

29 Birtwhistle, *Living Art*, p. 114. On the diagram, see Gilles Deleuze, *Foucault*, University of Minnesota Press, Minneapolis, 1988.

30 *Class society*, Birtwhistle, *Living Art*, p. 152; *nature's way*, ibid., p. 157.

31 Ibid., p. 161. Jorn's approach to prehistory is not unlike Vere Gordon Childe, *Man Makes Himself*, Mentor Books, New York, 1951.

32 Birtwhistle, *Living Art*, p. 161; compare to Engels on "primitive communism," *Origins of the Family, Private Property and the State*, Progress Publishers, Moscow, 1978.

33 *Art is cult*, Birtwhistle, *Living Art*, p. 166; *lost our paradise*, ibid., p. 173. One could see Bill and Jorn's disagreement as two readings of Kleist's famous essay on the marionettes. If paradise is locked, and yet there may be still be a way to enter around the back, is the key to be form or movement? Heinrich von Kleist, *Selected Prose*, Archipelago Books, Brooklyn NY, 2009, p. 264 ff.

34 See Guy Atkin, *Jorn in Scandinavia: 1930–1953*, Wittenborn, New York, 1968.

35 Jean-Paul Sartre, *Being and Nothingness*, Washington Square Press, New York, 1956, pp. 620–28. *Resisting world*, p. 621; *condemned to freedom*, p. 623; *empirical and practical concep*t, p. 624; *curfew*, p. 625; *free upsurge*, p. 628.

36 Louis Althusser, *For Marx*, Verso, London, 2006; Louis Althusser and Etienne Balibar, *Reading Capital*, Verso, London, 2009. The English edition of the latter leaves out the contributions of Jacques Rancière and Roger Establet. A rare work which takes an interest in Jorn as radical theorist is Richard Gombin, *The Radical Tradition*, St. Martin's Press, New York, 1979, pp. 119–25.

5 *A Provisional Micro-Society*

1 A generous selection of Rumney's Cosio photographs are included in my *50 Years of Recuperation of the Situationist International*, Princeton Architectural Press, New York, 2008.
2 Debord to Jorn, September 1, 1957. Debord's *Correspondance* is published by Fayard. The first volume is also in English as: Guy Debord, *Correspondence: The Foundation of the Situationist International*, Semiotext(e), Los Angeles, 2009.
3 Ivan Chtcheglov, "Lettres de Loin," *Internationale Situationniste* No. 9, August 1964, p. 38.
4 Debord to Straram, October 3, 1958.
5 Debord to Constant, September 7, 1959.
6 Guy Debord, *Panegyric*, Verso, London, 1991, p. 59.
7 *Our official organ*, Debord to Korun, June 16, 1958; *never work*, Debord to Wyckaert, June 22, 1960; *Lumaline*, Debord to Jorn, July 16, 1960.
8 *Heavy hand*, Debord to Ovadia, March 30, 1960; *all material*, Debord to Straram, November 12, 1958.
9 *I reproach you*, Debord to Olmo, October 18, 1957; *any real work*, Debord to Rumney, March 13, 1958.
10 For Guggenheim's side of the story, see Mary V. Dearborn, *Mistress of Modernism: The Life of Peggy Guggenheim*, Houghton Mifflin Harcourt, Boston, 2004. She was not entirely wrong in seeing Rumney as an irresponsible alcoholic.
11 Ralph Rumney, "The Leaning Tower of Venice," in Simon Ford, *The Situationist International: A User's Guide*, Black Dog, London, 2005, and also *Vague*, No. 22, 1990, pp. 33–35. Rumney was involved with the ICA in London where Alloway was assistant curator from 1955–60, but Rumney's thinking took a very different direction to Alloway and the Independent Group, of which he was a prominent member. See Lawrence Alloway, *Imagining the Present*, Routledge, London, 2006. See also Alan Woods, *The Map Is Not the Territory*, Manchester University Press, Manchester, 2000, which contains Rumney's later elaboration on the distinction between game and play.
12 Debord to Constant, June 21, 1960.
13 *New Yorker*, June 9, 2008. On contemporary art as the art of the market, see Isabelle Graw, *High Price: Art between the Market and Celebrity Culture*, Sternberg Press, Berlin, 2010.
14 *Jorn the first partisan*, Debord to Constant, June 2, 1960; *I without the we*, Debord to Melanotte, February 10, 1959.
15 *Objective criteria*, Debord to Frankin, January 26, 1960; *good will*, Debord to Korun, June 16, 1958; *neither freedom nor intelligence*, Debord to Straram, August 25, 1960.
16 Or so Blanchot proposes. See Blanchot, *The Unavowable Community*.
17 *False disciples*, Debord to Gallizio, January 13, 1957; *perspectives*, Debord to Straram, November 12, 1958; *Situationism*, Debord to Simondo, August 22, 1957; *dogmas*, Debord to Gallizio, November 23, 1957. On Simondo: Cristiana Campanini, "Simondo Inedito," *Arte*, May 2004.
18 *Internal propaganda*, Debord to Constant, September 16, 1959; *artistically old men*, Debord to Constant, October 16, 1959.
19 *Most urgent problem*, Debord to Constant, March 3, 1959; *specialized collaborators*, Debord to Constant, February 28, 1959.
20 Cardinal de Retz, *Mémoires*, Société des Bibliophiles, Paris, 1903, p. 215.
21 Giorgina Bertolino et al. (eds), *Pinot Gallizio: Il laboratorio della scrittura*, Charta, Milan, 2005, p. 20. On Gallizio, see Nicola Pezolet, "The Cavern of Antimatter,"

Grey Room, Winter 2010, Frances Stracey, "Pinot Gallizio's Industrial Painting," *Oxford Art Journal*, No. 28, 2005.

22 Bertolino, *Pinot Gallizio*, p. 164. On the Alba conference, see Nathalie Aubert, "Cobra after Cobra and the Alba Congress," *Third Text*, March 2006.

23 Michèle Bernstein, "In Praise of Pinot Gallizio," in McDonough, *Guy Debord and the Situationist International*, p. 70 and Berréby (ed.), *Textes et documents*, pp. 64–68. See also Mirella Bandini, "An Enormous and Unknown Chemical Reaction," in Sussman, *On the Passage of a Few People*, p. 72. Gallizio's praxis beyond play and labor might be at the roots of what is now called in its recuperated form *playbor*, in which value is extracted from the very ambiguity of action's interests and motives. See Nick Dyer-Witheford and Greig de Peuter, *Games of Empire*, University of Minnesota Press, Minneapolis, 2009.

24 *Tumult*, Debord to Gallizio, January 30, 1958; *deficiency*, Debord to Constant, May 20, 1959; *sickening arrivisme*, Debord to Constant, June 2, 1960. *Fight their own glory*, Guy Debord, *Considerations on the Assassination of Gérard Lebovici*, Tam Tam Books, Los Angeles, 2001, p. 78.

25 Debord to Constant, November 26, 1959.

26 Constant & Debord, "Amsterdam Declaration," Andreotti & Costa, *Theory of the Dérive*, pp. 80–81; *Internationale Situationiste* No. 2, December 1958, pp. 31–32.

27 Alice Becker-Ho, *Princes of Jargon*, Edwin Mellen Press, Lewiston NY, 2004, p. 39. For Constant's account, see Andreotti and Costa, *Theory of the Dérive*, p. 154.

28 Constant, "On Our Means and Our Perspectives" (1958), in *The Decomposition of the Artist*, Drawing Center, New York, 1999, p. 7. See also Debord's letter to Constant, September 25, 1958.

29 Constant, "On Our Means and Our Perspectives," Andreotti & Costa, *Theory of the Dérive*, p. 77; *Internationale Siuationniste*, No. 2, 1958. Constant was already familiar with Henri Lefebvre's 1947 edition of *Critique of Everyday Life*, which is also a significant influence.

30 *No painting*, Debord to Constant, September 25, 1958; *any spirit of the "pictorial,"* Debord to Constant, August 8, 1958.

31 *Really experimental faction*, Debord to Constant, August 8, 1958; *I don't have the right*, Debord to Constant, September 7, 1959.

32 Debord to Constant, April 4, 1959. See Frank Manuel, *The Prophets of Paris*, Harper, New York, 1965, on the utopians Debord accuses Constant of resurrecting.

33 Ibid. See Raoul Vanegeim, 'Comments against Urbanism', in *Internationale Situationiste*, No. 6, August 1961, also in McDonough, p119ff. An attack on Chombart, it also closes the book on utopia adventures in built form for the Situationists.

34 *Passion*, Debord to Constant, June 21, 1960; *indecision*, quoted in Debord to Jorn, July 6, 1960; *choose the terrain*, Debord to Constant, June 21, 1960.

35 Marcel Mauss, *The Gift*, Norton, New York, 2000; Georges Bataille, *The Accursed Share, Vol. 1*, Zone Books, New York, 1989. Claude Lefort, a key figure in the Socialism or Barbarism group, also took up the figure of the gift, but Debord had very little taste for Lefort and his interest in the group postdates Lefort's departure from it in 1958.

36 Jacques Derrida, *Given Time: 1. Counterfeit Money*, translated by Peggy Kamuf, University of Chicago Press, Chicago, 1991. *Nothing else*, p. 28; *presents itself*, p. 15; *subject and object*, p. 24. See also Douglas Smith, "Giving the Game Away: Play and Exchange in Situationism and Structuralism," *Modern & Contemporary France*, November 2005; Scott Cutler Shershow, *The Work and the Gift*, University of Chicago Press, Chicago, 2005, for a very helpful overview of the whole terrain of work and gift in twentieth-century social thought.

37 Claude Lévi-Strauss, *Tristes Tropiques*, New York, 1965, p. 62. Sartre is the proximate enemy here.

38 Debord to Constant, June 2, 1960.

6 *Permanent Play*

1 Charles Fourier, *The Theory of the Four Movements*, Cambridge University Press, Cambridge, 1996, p. 111. This chapter is interested in a classic Marxist approach to the relations between the genders, drawing on Fourier and centrally concerned with asking the property question. For the now more common approach, more concerned with representation, see Kelly Baum, "The Sex of the Situationist International," *October*, No. 126, Fall 2008. On the collapse of the critique of representation into consumer feminism, see Nina Power, *One Dimensional Woman*, Zero Books, Winchester, UK, 2009.

2 Kristin Ross, *Fast Cars, Clean Bodies*, MIT Press, Cambridge MA, 1995, p. 148. For the characters in Bernstein's novels, it is more like fast bodies, clean cars.

3 On de Scudéry's map and the spatial politics of its time, see Joan DeJean, "No Man's Land: The Novel's First Geography," *Yale French Studies*, No. 73, 1987. See also the introduction to Madeleine de Scudéry, *The Story of Sappho*, translated by Karen Newman, University of Chicago Press, Chicago, 2003. Anthony Vidler, "Terres Inconnues", *October* No. 115, Winter 2006, usefully connects the *Carte de Tendre* to psychogeography. For a far more contemporary version of the (anti-) novel of (Sapphic) desire, see Eileen Myles, *Inferno*, O/R Books, New York, 2010.

4 Debord to Straram, October 10, 1960. The possibilities of détourning novels as a transitional tactic are discussed in "Détournement: A User's Guide," in Knabb, *Situationist International Anthology*, p. 18.

5 Carol Hanisch, "The Personal is Political," in Shulamith Firestone and Anne Koedt (eds), *Notes from the Second Year*, Women's Liberation, New York, 1970. Debates rage over who actually coined the phrase.

6 Maurice Blanchot, *Friendship*, translated by Elizabeth Rottenberg, Stanford University Press, Stanford CA, 1997, p. 70. *Pure spectacle,* Henri Lefebvre, *Introduction to Modernity*, Verso, London, 1995, p. 337.

7 Debord to Frankin, July 15, 1959.

8 Xavier Canonne, *Surrealism in Belgium 1924–2000*, Mercatorfonds, Brussels, 2007, p. 142. Mochot was the stepdaughter of the brother of another Belgian surrealist, Paul Bourgoignie.

9 Michèle Bernstein, *La Nuit*, Buchet-Chastel, Paris, 1961, p. 40.

10 *They pass beside a column*, Bernstein, *La Nuit*, p. 18; *in a labyrinth*, ibid., p. 92.

11 Arthur Adamov, *Ping-Pong: A Play in Two Parts*, Grove Press, New York, 1959.

12 Asger Jorn, "La Création ouverte et ses ennemis," *Internationale Situationniste*, No. 5, p. 45; translated by Fabian Tompsett as *Open Creation and Its Enemies*, Unpopular Books, London, 1994, p. 39.

13 Debord and Wolman, "Détournement: A User's Guide."

14 On networks, distributed and otherwise, see Alex Galloway, *Protocol*, MIT Press, Cambridge MA, 2004.

15 Choderlos de Laclos, *Dangerous Liaisons*, Penguin, London, 2007; Michel Feher (ed.), *The Libertine Reader: Eroticism and Enlightenment in Eighteenth-Century France*, Zone Books, New York, 1997.

16 Debord to Straram, November 12, 1958.

17 Michèle Bernstein, *Tous les chevaux du roi*, Editions Allia, Paris, 2004, p. 116; *All*

The King's Horses, translated by John Kelsey, Semiotext(e), Los Angeles, 2008, p. 108.

18 Odile Passot, "Portrait of Guy Debord as a Young Libertine," *Substance*, No. 3, 1999, p. 77. Odile Passot is a pseudonym; this text was actually written by Jean-Marie Apostolidès. See his *Les Tombeaux de Guy Debord*, Flammarion, Paris, 2006.

19 See Marcel Carné, *The Devil's Envoys (Les Visiteurs du soir)*, 1942, with script by Jacques Prévert and Pierre Laroche.

20 Bernstein, *Tous les chevaux*, p. 36 ; *King's Horses*, p. 42.

21 Len Bracken, *Guy Debord Revolutionary*, Feral House, Venice CA, 1997, p. 245. Not the most reliable biography, but one with spirit.

22 Asger Jorn and Noël Arnaud, *La Langue verte et la cuite. Etude gastrophonique sur la marmythologie musiculinaire*, (Bibliothèque d'Alexandrie Vol. III), Jean-Jacques Pauvert Editeur, Paris, 1968. It received a surprisingly warm and astute review in *Man*, Vol. 4, No. 4, December 1969, p. 667.

23 Greil Marcus, *Lipstick Traces*, p. 423. Marcus offers a pioneering account of the Situationists, including insights into many of the figures of interest here (Wolman, Trocchi, Bernstein).

7 *Tin Can Philosophy*

1 Abdelhafid Khatib, "Attempt at a Psychogeographical Description of Les Halles," Andreotti & Costa, *Theory of the Dérive*, pp. 72–6 ; *Internationale Situationniste* No. 2, December 1958, p. 13ff. His Les Halles can be compared to that of Gérard de Nerval, "October Nights," in *Selected Writings*, Penguin, London, 1999, p. 204 ff.

2 See Martin Evans, *The Memory of Resistance*, Berg French Studies, New York, 1997; Todd Shepard, *Inventing Decolonization*, Cornell University Press, Ithaca NY, 2006.

3 Anselm Jappe, *Guy Debord*, University of California Press, Berkeley, 1999, is an excellent reading of the Hegelian-Marxist Debord. For the wider context, see Mark Poster, *Existential Marxism in Postwar France: From Sartre to Althusser*, Princeton University Press, Princeton NJ, 1975; see also V. I. Lenin, "Left-Wing Communism, an Infantile Disorder," *Collected Works*, Vol. 31, Progress Publishers, Moscow, 1964.

4 In "L'Internationale Situationniste, Socialisme ou Barbarie, and the Crisis of the Marxist Imaginary," *Substance* No. 90, 1999, Stephen Hastings-King offers a more subtle account of the various stages of Debord's relation with the Socialism or Barbarism group. When key members of the latter, particularly Castoriadis, turned away from Marxism towards a new kind of critique, Debord took his distance, and in Hastings-King's view, tried to supplant them as *the* revolutionary expression of the proletariat. However, Hastings-King does not quite see how *Society of the Spectacle* is a détournement of the contending texts influential on the left at the time. Lukács is subverted more than idolized in this famous text.

5 See Debord to Jorn, July 16, 1960.

6 Asger Jorn, *The Natural Order and Other Texts*, translated by Peter Shield, Ashgate, Farnham UK, 2002, p. 139. Jorn added new material to his 1960 "Critique" for the book *Value and Economics* (1962), which is included in this volume. References are to both the Shield translation of the later text, and to the original French text where the quote appears in both.

7 C. Wright Mills, *The Power Elite*, Oxford University Press, Oxford, 1957. On Mills:

Daniel Geary, *Radical Ambition: C. Wright Mills, the Left and American Social Thought*, University of California Press, Berkeley, 2009.

8 Jorn, *The Natural Order*, p. 135.

9 On Mauss and his critique of the Soviet economy, see David Graeber, *Toward an Anthropological Theory of Value*, Palgrave, London, 2001.

10 On Marx's love affair with capital, see Marshall Berman, *All That Is Solid Melts into Air*, Penguin, New York, 1988; Jean-François Lyotard, *Libidinal Economy*, Indiana University Press, Bloomington, 1993.

11 Asger Jorn, "Critique de la politique économique- Suivie de la lutte finale," *Internationale Situationniste*, May 1960, p. 25; *The Natural Order*, p. 132. Jorn anticipates another attempt to deepen the critique of political economy, see Jean Baudrillard, *The Mirror of Production*, Telos Press, St. Louis, 1975.

12 Jorn, *The Natural Order*, p. 126.

13 Jorn, *Critique*, p. 10; *The Natural Order*, p. 130.

14 Jorn, *Critique*, p. 11; *The Natural Order*, p. 139.

15 Jorn, *Critique*, p. 13; *The Natural Order*, p. 141.

16 Jorn, *Critique*, p. 28; *The Natural Order*, p. 135. A Jornian reading of Warhol immediately suggests itself, as an art of pure container value.

17 Jorn, *Critique*, p. 16; *The Natural Order*, p. 136. Compare to Georges Bataille, *The Accursed Share, Vol. 1*, Zone Books, New York, 1991. *Scarcity* would become a key term in Sartre's *Critique of Dialectical Reason.*

18 *State as container*, Jorn, *Critique*, p. 29 ; *The Natural Order*, p. 138. *Assault on the universe*, Henri Lefebvre, *Introduction à la modernité: Préludes*, Les Editions de minuit, Paris, 1962, pp. 37–8. See also Susan Buck-Morss, *Dreamworld and Catastrophe: The Passing of Mass Utopia in East and West*, MIT Press, Cambridge MA, 2002. The most remarkable writing on Stalin's assault on the universe is surely by Andrey Platonov: see *Soul and Other Stories*, NYRB Classics, New York, 2007 and *The Foundation Pit*, NYRB Classics, New York, 2009.

19 Debord to Jorn, July 6, 1960.

20 Jorn, *The Natural Order*, p. 142.

8 The Thing of Things

1 Lefebvre, *Introduction à la modernité: Préludes*, pp. 131–34 (hereafter *Modernité*); translated as Henri Lefebvre, *Introduction to Modernity*, Verso, London, 1995, pp. 128–30 (hereafter *Modernity*).

2 Henri Lefebvre, *Critique de la vie quotidienne II – Fondements d"une sociologie de la quotidienneté*, L'Arche Editeur, Paris, 1961, p. 51 (hereafter *Quotidienne II*). Translated as Henri Lefebvre, *Critique of Everyday Life, Volume 2*, Verso, London. 2008, p. 49 (hereafter *Everyday 2*).

3 Henri Lefebvre, *The Explosion*, Monthly Review Press, New York, 1969, p. 104. Andrew Merrifield, *Henri Lefebvre: A Critical Introduction*, Routledge, London, 2006. For Lefebvre's settling of accounts with his past, see *La Somme et le reste*, Economica, Paris, 2008.

4 Henri Lefebvre, *Key Writings*, Continuum, London, 2003, p. 167.

5 Kristin Ross, "Lefebvre on the Situationists: An Interview," in McDonough, *Guy Debord and the Situationists*, p. 268.

6 "Letters from Henri Lefebvre," *Norbert Guterman Papers*, Box 1/Folder 1953–1962; Rare Book and Manuscript Library, Columbia University Library, Paris 31-12-1958.

7 *To know the everyday*, *Quotidienne II*, p. 102, *Everyday 2*, p. 98; *transduction*, *Quotidienne II*, pp. 121–22, *Everyday 2*, p. 105. See Adrian Mackenzie, *Transductions: Bodies and Machines at Speed*, Continuum, London, 2006 for more on transduction, which Lefebvre borrows from Gilbert Simondon.

8 Like many of Lefebvre's concepts, it may be more of a collective production. In the case of the theory of needs, Lefebvre drew on the work of Dionys Mascolo, *Le Communisme: Révolution et communication*, Gallimard, Paris, 1953. Mascolo and Lefebvre joined forces with other non-party Marxists in 1956 in the journal *Arguments*. See Mark Poster, *Existential Marxism in Postwar France*. Poster puts Lefebvre's work after leaving the Communist Party in the context of the reception of Sartre's work and the development of *Arguments*, which is probably far more important than his brief association with Debord.

9 Henri Lefebvre, *Everyday Life in the Modern World*, Transaction Publishers, New Brunswick NJ, 2007, p. 13. Written in 1967, this was a summary of the projected third volume of *The Critique of Everyday Life*, which, when it eventually appeared, took on a quite different character. In it Lefebvre extends his analysis further into the great pleonasm of consumer culture, in which it is the consumers who come to suspect that they are what is consumed, and in which signs float free of their referents. "One might just as well say that all referentials have vanished and what remains is the memory and the demand for a system of reference." One can find here the kernel of the project of Lefebvre's most talented assistant. See Baudrillard, *The System of Objects*.

10 Eugene Thacker, *After Life*, University of Chicago Press, Chicago, 2010. *Every ontology*, p. x; *animating principle*, p. 12. Eugene points out to me that Raoul Vaneigem's *Movement of the Free Spirit*, Zone Books, New York, 1998 could be considered an attempt to radicalize the metaphysics of life as spirit.

11 See John Bellamy Foster, *Marx's Ecology: Materialism and Nature*, Monthly Review Press, New York, 2000. Where Thacker makes Aristotle the touchstone for his three metaphysics of life (time, form, spirit), perhaps one has to look, as Marx and Darwin did, to Lucretius and the Epicurians for materialist life.

12 Lefebvre, *Quotidienne II*, p. 17; *Everyday 2*, p. 11.

13 Lefebvre, *Modernité*, p. 100; *Modernity*, pp. 93–4.

14 Lefebvre, *Quotidienne II*, p. 79; *Everyday 2*, p. 75. Debord will develop cyclical and linear time further in the "Time and History" chapter of *Society of the Spectacle.*

15 Lefebvre, *Quotidienne II*, p. 84; *Everyday 2*, p. 81.

16 Lefebvre, *Quotidienne II*, p. 229; *Everyday 2*, p. 227. See Gayatri Spivak, *A Critique of Postcolonial Reason*, Harvard University Press, Cambridge MA, 1999. Lefebvre constructs a concept of modernity without reference to the colonial other.

17 Lefebvre, *Quotidienne II*, p. 138; *Everyday 2*, p. 134. Mention of *agôn* and *aléa* seems to suggest a familiarity with Roger Caillois, *May, Play and Games*, University of Illinois Press, Champaign IL, 2001. Lefebvre's comrade in the *Arguments* group Kostas Alexos developed the theme of play (and in a playful style) in *Vers la pensée planétaire*, Editions de Minuit, Paris, 1964; *Le Jeu du monde*, Editions de Minuit, Paris, 1969. On the everyday reduced to the tactical, see Michel de Certeau, *The Practice of Everyday Life*, University of California Press, Berkeley CA, 2002. De Certeau deals only with tactics, excluding the strategic dimension. De Certeau's study, so influential for cultural studies, was commissioned by the French state secretary of culture. See Derek Schilling, "Everyday Life and the Challenge to History in Postwar France," *Diacritics*, Spring 2003, p. 37, and also John Roberts, *Philosophizing the Everyday*, Pluto Press, London, 2006.

18 Lefebvre, *Modernité*, p. 125; *Modernity*, p. 121. On the development of game theory

and other cold war social sciences, see Philip Mirowski, *Machine Dreams: Economics Becomes a Cyborg Science*, Cambridge University Press, Cambridge 2002; Manuel de Landa, *War in the Age of Intelligent Machines*, Zone Books, New York, 1991; Paul Edwards, *The Closed World: Computers and the Politics of Discourse in Cold War America*, MIT Press, Cambridge MA, 1997; Lydia Lin, *The Freudian Robot*, University of Chicago Press, Chicago, 2011, addresses the (mis) translations between American and French Information theory.

19 Lefebvre, *Quotidienne II*, p. 196; *Everyday 2*, p. 193. Huizinga's was an essentially cultural but nevertheless entirely scathing critique of modernity, not least modern broadcasting and journalism. Debord and Lefebvre were probably not aware that he had preceded them in the critique of the spectacle. See R. L. Colie, "Johan Huizinga and the Task of Cultural History," *American Historical Review*, Vol. 69, No. 3, 1964. Peter Geyl, "Huizinga as Accuser of His Age," *History and Theory*, Vol. 2, No. 3, 1963, is a critical account by a contemporary.

20 Lefebvre, *Quotidienne II*, pp. 137–8; *Everyday 2*, p. 134. Fredric Jameson, in *Archaeologies of the Future*, Verso, London, 2006, p. 243, writes that only in Sartre, and in Laclau and Mouffe, is the problem of the group put back at the center of political thought. But perhaps another way opens up if one takes Lefebvre's rather less precise thinking about groups and the practice of the Situationists together.

21 Lefebvre, *Quotidienne II*, p. 205; *Everyday 2*, p. 203. On the latter-day consequences of the curious ontological status of games, see Jesper Juul, *Half Real: Video Games between Real Rules and Fictional Worlds*, MIT Press, Cambridge MA, 2005.

22 Lefebvre, *Quotidienne II*, p. 168; *Everyday 2*, p. 160. Lefebvre does not achieve the formal clarity of Derrida's famous essay, "Structure, Sign and Play," in *Writing and Difference*, Routledge, London, 2001. Instead there is a practical sense of the implications of play in Lefebvre.

23 *Discourse strives for totality*, Lefebvre, *Modernité*, p. 13, *Modernity*, p. 5; *every totalization*, *Quotidienne II*, p. 186, *Everyday 2*, p. 183 ; *insistence upon totality*, *Quotidienne II*, p. 184, *Everyday 2*, p. 181. A representative work of the so-called new philosophers would be André Glucksmann (b. 1937), *The Master Thinkers*, Harper Collins, 1980.

24 Lefebvre, *Quotidienne II*, p. 242 ; *Everyday 2*, p. 240. One branch of media and cultural studies has indeed tended towards an uncritical embrace of the popular, and a populism which upholds consumer choice against the centralizing tendencies of an older form of spectacle. See Henry Jenkins, *Fans, Bloggers, and Gamers: Media Consumers in a Digital Age*, NYU Press, New York, 2006.

25 Lefebvre, *Quotidienne II*, p. 264; *Everyday 2*, p. 262. A critique that could apply to Jean Baudrillard, for example. Lefebvre's reversible alienation seems curiously like territorialization and deterritorialization in Deleuze and Guattari.

26 Lefebvre, *Quotidienne II*, p. 343; *Everyday 2*, p. 343.

27 BBC News, August 10, 2005.

28 Lefebvre, *Quotidienne II*, p. 355; *Everyday 2*, p. 356.

29 Lefebvre, *Quotidienne II*, p. 356; *Everyday 2*, p. 357.

30 On *situation*, see Gerald Raunig, *Art and Revolution: Transversal Activism in the Long Twentieth Century*, Semiotext(e), Los Angeles, 2007. If, for Raunig, Hegel subsumes the situation too quickly into the dialectics of conflict, perhaps Raunig dissolves conflict too much into proliferating difference. See also Roberto Ohrt, *Phantom Avantgarde*, Galerie Van de Loo, Munich, 1990, p. 163 ff.

31 *The moment*, Lefebvre, *Quotidienne II*, p. 351, *Everyday 2*, p. 353; *the difficulty*, Debord to Frankin, February 22, 1960. This letter is the basis for a later article "Théorie des moments et construction des situations," *Internationale Situationniste*, No. 4, pp. 10–11; Andreotti & Costa, *Theory of the Dérive*, pp. 100–101.

32 Debord to Jorn, July 2, 1959.
33 Lefebvre, *Modernité*, p. 128; *Modernity*, p. 123. See also Henri Lefebvre, "The Everyday and Everydayness," *Yale French Studies*, No. 73, 1987 for a succinct statement of Lefebvre's more pessimistic approach to the everyday.
34 *Something worse*, Lefebvre, *Modernité*, p. 174, *Modernity*, p. 173; *ghost of revolution*, *Modernité*, p. 233, *Modernity*, p. 237. The hauntological quality of modernity, and Marxism's catalyzing role at the séance is the subject of Jacques Derrida, *Specters of Marx: The State of the Debt, The Work of Mourning & the New International*, Routledge, London, 2006.
35 Lefebvre, *Quotidienne II*, p. 81; *Everyday 2*, p. 77.
36 *Great Pleonasm*, Lefebvre, *Quotidienne II*, p. 165, *Everyday 2*, p. 164; *Thing of Things*, *Modernité*, p. 168, *Modernity*, p. 167; *faked orgasm*, *Modernité*, p. 255, *Modernity*, p. 259.
37 Lefebvre, *Modernité*, p. 277, *Modernity*, p. 283. This could be usefully compared to Roland Barthes, *Mythologies*, Noonday Press, New York, 1972. Barthes undoubtedly achieves closer and more illuminating readings, but at the price of losing Lefebvre's grasp of the totalizing tendencies of modernity.
38 Lefebvre, *Modernité*, p. 280; *Modernity*, p. 286.
39 Lefebvre, *Modernité*, p. 286; *Modernity*, p. 283. See also Michael Löwy: *Morning Star: Surrealism, Marxism, Anarchism, Situationism, Utopia*, University of Texas Press, Austin TX, 2009.
40 Constant attests to Debord's love of American comics in *HuO: Hans-Ulrich Obrist: Interviews*, Charta, Milan, 2003.
41 Lefebvre, *Modernité*, p. 294; *Modernity*, p. 302.
42 Lefebvre, *Quotidienne II*, p. 227; *Everyday 2*, p. 225.
43 Lefebvre, *Modernité*, pp. 236–37; *Modernity*, p. 364.
44 Lefebvre, *Modernité*, p. 298; *Modernity*, p. 306.

9 *Divided We Stand*

1 thinkproperty.com, September 8, 2008, accessed via Google Earth.
2 Charles Dickens, *The Mystery of Edwin Drood*, Everyman's Library, London, 2004.
3 Interview with Jacqueline de Jong, Algonquin Hotel, New York, October 17, 2009. All other quotes from de Jong not otherwise identified are from this interview. See also the contributions by de Jong and Karen Kurczynski to Mikkel Bolt Rasmussen and Jakob Jakobsen, *Expect Anything, Fear Nothing: The Situationist Movement in Scandanavia and Elsewhere*, Autonomedia, New York, forthcoming.
4 On the aborted Amsterdam show, see Sadler, *The Situationist City*, p. 115 ff. The show turned the museum into a labyrinth opening out towards the city, extended even further by a three-day dérive, coordinated by walkie-talkies. Part of the plan was published as "Die Welt Als Labyrinth," *Internationale Situationniste*, No. 4, June 1960, pp. 5–7.
5 Matta is quoted in Guy Atkins, *Asger Jorn, The Crucial Years 1954–1964*, Borgens Forlag, Copenhagen, 1977, p. 56. On Spur, I rely largely on the account of Diedrich Diederichsen, "Persecution and Self-Persecution: The Spur Group and Its Texts," *Grey Room*, Winter 2007.
6 Gruppe Spur, "Manifest," in Berréby (ed.), *Textes et Documents*, p. 90. On the role Adorno played in postwar German culture, see Stefan Müller-Doohm, *Adorno: A Biography*, Polity, Cambridge, 2009, and his surprise bestseller, Theodor Adorno, *Minima Moralia: Reflections on Damaged Life*, Verso, London, 2006. Unlike his

contemporary Lefebvre, he abandoned faith in the proletariat. Not surprising, given the divergent historical experiences of France and Germany in the 1930s.

7 Vincent Kaufmann, *Revolution in the Service of Poetry*, University of Minnesota Press, Minneapolis, 2006, p. 93. This excellent study might stand in for a host of others, some not quite so excellent, which effect the recuperation of *situationism* as either aesthetics or biography, or, in this case—both.

8 Vaneigem makes his presence felt in *Internationale Situationniste* from issue No. 6, but especially with a series of texts titled "Basic Banalities," starting in No. 7. See Knabb, *Anthology*, pp. 117–30, 154–72. He claims never to have met Constant. See Hans Ulrich Obrist, "In Conversation with Raoul Vanegeim," *e-flux journal*, No. 6, May 2009.

9 Atkins, *Asger Jorn, The Crucial Years*.

10 From a letter by Jorn to Debord, July 12, 1960, quoted as a postscript to a letter from Debord to Jorn, July 16, 1960.

11 Debord to Jorn, August 23, 1962. The Jorn quote is attributed to the pseudonym Jorn used, George Keller, in "La Cinquième Conférence de l'I. S. à Göteborg", from *Internationale Situationniste*, No. 7, April 1962, p. 30.

12 Debord to Vaneigem, February 15, 1962. See also letter to Tom Levin, November 1989. This is in Bill Brown's translation.

13 "Danger! Do Not Lean Out!", *Situationist Times*, No. 1.

14 "The Struggle for the Situcratic Society," signed by Nash, de Jong, et al., *Situationist Times* No. 2, 1962.

15 See Howard Slater, "Divided We Stand: An Outline of Scandinavian Situationism," *Infopool*, No. 4, 2001, p. 31. Slater makes a good case for the value of the Nashists, and I am indebted to it. See also Howard Slater, "The Spoiled Ideas of Lost Situations," *Infopool*, No. 2, 2000.

16 Jens Jørgen Thorsen, "The Communicative Phase in Art," in *Situationister 1957–1970*, Jørgen Nash et al. (eds), Bauhaus Situationist, 1966. Quoted in Slater, "Divided We Stand," p. 31. One could see Thorsen's communicative art as a precursor to the recuperated form of relational aesthetics. See Nicholas Bourriaud, *Relational Aesthetics*, Les Presses du réel, Paris, 1998, and for a critique: Claire Bishop, *Artificial Hells: Participatory Art and the Politics of Spectatorship*, Verso, London, 2011.

17 The head disappeared again in 1998: *New York Times*, March 21, 1998.

18 See Slater, "Divided We Stand," p. 32.

19 *Situationist idea*, interview in *Aspekt*, No. 3, Copenhagen, 1963, translated by Jakob Jakobsen for infopool.com; *chiliastic serenity*, T. J. Clark, *The Painting of Modern Life*, Princeton University Press, 1984, p. 10.

20 Jacqueline de Jong, "Critic on the Political Practice of Détournement," *Situationist Times*, No. 1, 1962.

21 Ibid.

22 Ibid.

23 Noël Arnaud, *Les Vies parallèles de Boris Vian*, 10/18, Paris, 1970. On the College of Pataphysics, see Alastair Brotchie (ed.), *A True History of the College of Pataphysics*, Atlas Press, London, 1995.

24 Benjamin Buchloh writes: "Dufrêne would orient himself toward a more disillusioned and skeptical acceptance of the social compartmentalization of transgressive activities … it led to a paradoxical position suspended between this pessimism concerning the revolutionary potential of the neo-avantgarde and an insistence upon radical gestures of opposition: to transform the internal structure of the aesthetic object; to emphasize the collaborative nature of the artistic project; and to demonstrate the relocation of artistic practice in the collective urban space of advanced

industrial consumer culture." Benjamin Buchloh, *Neo-Avantgarde and Culture Industry*, MIT Press, Cambridge MA, 2003.

25 See Emily Apter, *The Translation Zone: A New Comparative Literature*, Princeton University Press, Princeton, 2005, p. 226 ff. In "The Master of the Revolutionary Subject," *Substance* No. 90, 1999, Roberto Ohrt makes the point that, whatever their failings, the Situationists were much more international than many of the avant-garde groups of their time.

26 "Renseignements Situationnistes," *Internationale Situationniste*, No. 7, April 1962, pp. 49–54.

27 A theme taken up ably by Eduardo Rothe, "The Conquest of Space in the Time of Power," *Internationale Situationniste* No. 12, September 1969; Knabb, *Situationist International Anthology*, p. 371 ff. Rothe later worked for the Ministry of Communication in Venezuela.

28 On Jorn and topology see Wark, *50 Years of Recuperation*. After completing the manuscript for this book, I discovered Fabian Tompsett's translation and commentary: Jorn, *Open Creation and Its Enemies*, which had blazed the trail through Jorn's difficult texts, if only I had known it.

29 Jacqueline de Jong, "The Times of the Situationists," in Zweifel et al, *In Girum Imus Nocte et Consumimur Igni*, p. 239.

30 Atkins, *Asger Jorn, The Crucial Years*, p. 127. Atkins was a fascinating character in his own right. Comparing Atkins to Jorn's famous paintings, de Jong says that "his whole life was a Modification." Some of his early life story can be found in William Stevenson, *Spymistress: The Life of Vera Atkins*, Arcade, New York, 2006.

31 Asger Jorn et al., *Signes gravés sur les églises de l'Eure et du Calvados*, Borgen, Copenhagen, 1963, including an interesting essay by Jorn on the morphology of symbols and an elaborate working-out of his *triolectic* diagrams.

32 Two volumes that give a real sense of his intentions are: Asger Jorn et al., *Bird, Beast and Man in the Nordic Iron Age*, Walther König, Munich, 2005; Asger Jorn et al., *Men, Gods and Masks in the Nordic Iron Age*, Walther König, Cologne, 2008 (Jorn is quoted from p. 10).

33 *Polydimensional*, Jorn, "La création ouverte et ses ennemis," p. 327; *all my outpourings* and *Jorn's texts*, Shield, *Comparative Vandalism*, Borgen p. xxiii, Ashgate, p. 19. This is the standard work on Jorn's mature thought. As de Jong pointed out to me, Jorn did not think of his writing as art at all, but as something quite separate.

34 *Situationist Times*, No. 3, p. 30.

35 Slater, "Divided We Stand," p. 8.

36 *Dionysian dance*, Lefebvre, *Modernité*, p. 19; *most brilliant Situationists*, ibid., pp. 236–37.

37 Jorn, *Pour la forme*, p. 71; Terry Smith, "Spectacle Architecture Before and After the Aftermath," in Anthony Vidler (ed.), *Architecture Between Spectacle and Use*, Clark Studies in the Visual Arts, Williamstown MA, 2008.

10 An Athlete of Duration

1 Alexander Trocchi, *Invisible Insurrection of a Million Minds: A Trocchi Reader*, edited by Andrew Murray Scott, Polygon, Edinburgh, 1991, p. 196. Trocchi did not know that the right-wing Brazilian Integralist Action Party had used "sigma" as its emblem in the 1930s. *Accretions*, p. 181; *unpopular*, p. 177; *grids of expression*, p. 178; *ancestral bones*, p. 181. On the *modern* nature of the October revolution, see Leon Trotsky, *The History of the Russian Revolution*, Vol. 3, Ch. 43, "The Insurrection." "The

Invisible Insurrection" appeared as "Technique du coup du monde" in *Internationale Situationniste*, No. 8, January 1963, p. 48 ff.

2 Trocchi quotes Williams from an essay by kitchen sink dramatist Arnold Wesker (b. 1932), founder of the rival Center 42: "Secret Reins," *Encounter*, Vol. 18, No. 3, March 1962, p. 5. The Williams quote appears in *Internationale Situationniste*, No. 8, January 1963, p. 52. On Williams of this period, see Dai Smith, *Raymond Williams: A Warrior's Tale*, Parthian Books, London, 2009. Williams's argument for the public ownership (but not state control) of the means of cultural production are most forcefully made in *The Long Revolution*, Columbia University Press, New York, 1961, pp. 335–47, although the exact sentences Wesker and Trocchi quote are not to be found there.

3 Alexander Trocchi, *Invisible Insurrection*, p. 195. See Katherine Chaddock Reynolds, *Visions and Vanities: John Andrew Rice of Black Mountain College*, Louisiana State University Press, Baton Rouge, 1988, on the famous college.

4 Vladimir Lenin, "Dual Power," *Collected Works*, Progress Publishers, Moscow, 1964, pp. 38–41.

5 Hubertus Bigend makes an appearance in William Gibson's novels *Pattern Recognition* (2003), *Spook Country* (2007), and *Zero History* (2010) See *Spook Country*, pp. 74–75.

6 See Andrew Murray Scott's fantastically unreliable biography *Alexander Trocchi: The Making of the Monster*, Polygon, Edinburgh, 1991, and also Allan Campbell, *A Life in Pieces: Reflections on Alexander Trocchi*, Rebel Publishing, Edinburgh, 1997. On Girodias, see John de St. Jorre, *Venus Bound: The Erotic Voyage of the Olympia Press*, Random House, New York, 1996.

7 Alexander Trocchi, *Helen and Desire*, Rebel Inc, Edinburgh, 1997: *the sea*, p. 6; *alluvial sensations*, p. 33. Kathy Acker's détournement of it is in Amy Scholder (ed.), *Essential Acker: The Selected Writings of Kathy Acker*, Grove Press, New York, 2002.

8 Trocchi, *Helen and Desire*, p. 154. Compare to Deleuze and Guattari on becoming imperceptible in *A Thousand Plateaus*, University of Minnesota Press, Minneapolis, 1987.

9 Alexander Trocchi, "The Barbeque," from the *Moving Times* poster collected in Sigma Portfolio: A New Dimension in the Dissemination of Informations, privately duplicated, 1964.

10 Alexander Trocchi, *Cain's Book*, foreword by Greil Marcus, introduction by Richard Seaver, Grove Press, New York, 1992: *pinball*, p. 60; *chemistry*, p. 33. A rare appreciation of Trocchi as Situationist writer is: Michael Gardiner, *From Trocchi to Trainspotting: Scottish Critical Theory Since 1960*, Edinburgh University Press, Edinburgh, 2006. Malcolm Lowry was a favorite not only of Debord but of Lefebvre as well. See Malcolm Lowry, *Under the Volcano*, Penguin, London, 2000 and *The Voyage That Never Ends: Fictions, Poems, Fragments, Letters*, NYRB Classics, New York, 2007.

11 *New York Times*, April 3, 2007.

12 Trocchi, *Cain's Book*, p. 72.

13 James Campbell, *Syncopations: Beats, New Yorkers, and Writers in the Dark*, University of California Press, Berkeley CA, 2008, p. 204.

14 See Michael Duncan and Kristine McKenna, *Semina Culture: Wallace Berman and His Circle*, DAP, New York, 2005 and Wallace Berman, *Photographs*, Rose Gallery, Santa Monica CA, 2007.

15 *Under the eyelids*, "Potlatch: an interpersonal log," *Portfolio* No. 4; *new dimension*, "Subscription Form," *Portfolio* No. 12.

16 "Potlatch: an interpersonal log," *Portfolio* No. 4.

17 For critical responses to blog as media, see Geert Lovink, *Zero Comments*, Routledge, London, 2008; Jodi Dean, *Blog Theory*, Polity Press, 2010.

18 "Sigma Informations," *Portfolio* No. 5.
19 Based on the "Situationist Manifesto," originally published in *Internationale Situationniste*, No. 4, June 1960.
20 "Project: projects," *Portfolio* No. 22.
21 Martin Heidegger, *Parmenides*, Indiana University Press, Bloomington, 1992, p. 81.
22 Constant, "Discipline or Intervention?", in Mark Wigley, *Constant's New Babylon: The Hyper-Architecture of Desire*, Witte de With, Rotterdam, 1998, p. 142. I am greatly indebted to this almost priceless work. Almost priceless, in that at the time of writing secondhand copies change hands for over 1,000 euros.
23 Irving Rosenthal, *Sheeper*, Grove Press, New York, 1967, pp. 217–37.
24 Jeff Nuttall, *Bomb Culture*, Dell, New York, 1968, p.150. Dutch Beat sensation Simon Vinkenoog also assisted Trocchi on sigma for a time, and through his sigma Center connects it to Provo: Jaap van der Bent, "O fellow travellers I write you a poem in Amsterdam," *College Literature*, Vol. 27, No. 1, 2000.
25 Stewart Home, *Tainted Love*, Virgin Books, London, 2006, p. 162. The chapter from which this is taken also neatly describes the process of fabricating legends for the consumption of journalists.
26 Constant, "New Babylon: Outline of a Culture," in Wigley, *Constant's New Babylon*, p. 160. Hereafter cited as Wigley.

11 New Babylon

1 Interview with Constant by Linda Boersma and Sue Smit, *Bomb*, No. 91, Spring 2005. On the influence of wartime bombing and postwar reconstruction on Constant, see Tom McDonough, "Metastructure: Experimental Utopia and Traumatic Memory in Constant's New Babylon," *Grey Room*, Fall 2008. Constant's friend Armado also wrote about a German city and the memory of the war: *From Berlin*, Reaktion Books, London, 1997.
2 Constant had assistants for the New Babylon work, including Debord himself and Constant's son Victor. For Constant's reflections on his life shortly before his death, see Maarten Schmidt and Thomas Doebele, *Constant, avant le départ*, Icarus Films, 2006. See also Victor Nieuwenhuijs and Maartje Seyferth, *New Babylon de Constant*, Moskito Film, 2005.
3 Wigley, p. 132. Hilde Heynen in "The Antimonies of Utopia," *Assemblage*, April 1996, does consider it a utopia, with predictable results.
4 Asger Jorn, "On the Cult of the New in Our Century," translated by Alan Prohm, *Crayon*, 2008, p. 188.
5 Aldo van Eyck, *Writings: Collected Articles and Other Writings*, Sun, Amsterdam, 2008, p. 66. Of course there are other influences. Constant's thinking on the relation between art and architecture also stems from a negative reaction to a Mondrian show he saw in Amsterdam in 1946. See Adrian Lewis, "Constant and Hilton in Correspondence," *Burlington Magazine*, Vol. 140, No. 1145, August 1998.
6 *House-like city*, van Eyck, "Beyond Visibility," *Situationist Times*, No. 4, pp. 79–85; *awareness of duration*, van Eyck, *Writings*, p. 74. The contrast between objective clock time and intuited duration is perhaps a reference to Bergson. See Henri Bergson, *Key Writings*, Continuum, New York, 2005. Lukács drew on Bergson and Max Weber's iron cage to form a general theory of reification.
7 *Exteriorize man from time*, van Eyck, *Writings*, pp. 74–75; *at home nowhere*, ibid., p. 87. The (anti)utopia of Superstudio, surely a critique of Constant among others, is an infrastructure for a global homelessness. See Peter Lang and William Menking,

Superstudio: Life without Objects, Skira, Milan, 2003. And for a brilliant account of Italian utopian architecture and critical theory, Pier Vittorio Aureli, *The Project of Autonomy: Politics and Architecture within and against Capitalism*, Princeton Architectural Press, New York, 2008.

8 Le Corbusier, *The City of Tomorrow and Its Planning*, Dover, New York, 1987. Vertical separation of flows is just one of Corbusier's techniques for transforming the city so as to *preserve* its ruling order. Constant's détournement is a reversal, and as Debord and Wolman said, the direct reversal of the significance of an element is not always the most effective. Constant was not alone in borrowing the separation of flows. Van Eyck's Team 10 colleagues the Smithsons made particular use of it. See Sadler, *The Situationist City*.

9 See Larry Busbea, *Topologies: The Urban Utopia in France 1960–1970*, MIT Press, Cambridge MA, 2007; Jean Baudrillard, *Utopia Deferred: Writings from Utopie 1967–1978*, Semiotext(e), New York, 2006; Paul Virilio, *Bunker Archaeology*, Princeton Architectural Press, New York, 2008; Paul Virilio and Sylvère Lotringer, *Crepuscular Dawn*, Semiotext(e), New York, 2002. Manfredi Nicoletti, "The End of Utopia," *Perspecta*, Vol. 13, 1971, puts Constant in the context of twentieth-century utopian architecture as a whole.

10 Constant, "Lecture Given at the ICA, London" (1963), *The Decomposition of the Artist*, p. 12(a). Levittown, the original suburban tract development, a civilian application of techniques learned during the war for the mass production of airstrips, was a prime exhibit for the Situationists of spectacular architecture.

11 Friedrich Engels, *The Condition of the Working Class in England*, Oxford University Press, 2009; William Morris, *News from Nowhere and Other Writings*, Penguin, London, 1994; Edward Bellamy, *Looking Backward*, Oxford University Press, 2007. H. G. Wells, *The Time Machine*, Penguin, London, 2005, while clearly referencing the utopian literature, foregrounds the technological question, and interestingly plays on the spatial figure of above and below ground. Wells extrapolated the underground factory from aerial bombing, something which, as Paul Virilio points out, Albert Speer would render concrete in the dying days of the Nazi regime. Constant's underground factories thus have a rather more sinister genealogy than he allows. See Rosalind Williams, *Notes on the Underground: An Essay on Technology, Society and the Imagination*, MIT Press, Cambridge MA, 2008 to see just how deep the rabbit hole goes.

12 Norbert Wiener, *The Human Use of Human Beings*, second edition, Doubleday Anchor, Garden City, New York, 1954, p. 52. Wiener was somewhat more pessimistic than Constant: "In a very real sense we are the shipwrecked passengers on a doomed planet … we shall go down, but let it be in a manner to which we may look forward as worthy of our dignity" (p. 40).

13 Wigley, p. 234. On the transformation of capitalist relations of production by automation, see David F. Noble, *America by Design: Science, Technology and the Rise of Corporate Capitalism*, Oxford University Press, New York, 1979, and *Forces of Production: A Social History of Industrial Automation*, Oxford University Press, New York, 1986.

14 Wigley, p. 233. Automation was a controversial topic for the left in the postwar period. Constant shares the optimism of those like Serge Mallet that automation led to the development of a truly social production, which nevertheless did not lead to the ideological co-option of labor within capitalism, but on the contrary might give rise to a new form of working-class militancy. See Serge Mallet, *The New Working Class*, Spokesman Books, London, 1975.

15 *Bloomberg Businessweek*, November 24, 2010.

16 Wigley, p. 209. The motif of spatially separate networks for different kinds of travel

has a long history. Sanford Kwinter credits Antonio Sant'Elia (1888–1916) with being the first to establish movement and circulation as the first principle of spatial design. Movement isn't something added after the fact to inert space, but rather that from which architecture is built. See Sanford Kwinter, *Architectures of Time*, MIT Press, Cambridge MA, 2002, p. 91. On experimental geography in the twenty-first century, see Trevor Paglen, "Experimental Geography," *Brooklyn Rail*, March 2009; Nato Thompson (ed.), *Experimental Geography*, Melville House, Hoboken NJ, 2009.

17 Wigley, p. 161. The most vivid image of the global alienation of space is a story by Lawrence Alloway's friend J. G. Ballard, "The Concentration City," in *The Best Stories of J. G. Ballard*, Picador, London, 2001. See *Re/Search*, No. 8/9, 1984, a special issue on Ballard.

18 Wigley, p.161. On wandering: Rebecca Solnit, *Wanderlust: A History of Walking*, Verso, London, 2006; Simon Pope and Claudia Schenk, *London Walking: A Handbook for Survival*, Ellipsis Arts, London, 2001; Francesco Careri, *Walkscapes*, Editorial Gustavo Gili, 2005.

19 Wigley, p. 162. On power and networks, see Alexander Galloway, *Protocol: How Control Exists after Decentralization*, MIT Press, Cambridge MA, 2006, and Wendy Hui Kyong Chun, *Control and Freedom: Power and Paranoia in the Age of Fiber Optics*, MIT Press, Cambridge MA, 2008.

20 Constant, "Lecture Given at the ICA, London" (1963), *The Decomposition of the Artist*, p. 13 (a). Antonio Negri, *Time for Revolution*, Continuum, London, 2003, contains two texts which are the antithesis of New Babylon, in their radical affirmation of *living labor*.

21 Here New Babylon reaches towards what would now be called the posthuman. See Dominic Pettman, *Human Error: Species-Being and Media Machines*, University of Minnesota Press, Minneapolis, 2011.

22 Johan Huizinga, *Homo Ludens*, Beacon Press, Boston, 1950; Jean-François Lyotard, *Just Gaming*, University of Minnesota Press, Minneapolis, 1985, offers a quite different revival of the figure of the game, via a détournement of Wittgenstein's *language game*. In neither Huizinga, Lefebvre, nor Constant is there a privileging of language, however. The revival of Schmitt owes a lot to Chantal Mouffe, *The Democratic Paradox*, Verso, London, 2000. See Gopal Balakrishnan, *The Enemy: An Intellectual Portrait of Carl Schmitt*, Verso, London, 2002.

23 Constant, "The Rise and Decline of the Avant Garde" (1964), *The Decomposition of the Artist*, p. 26 (a).

24 Wigley, p. 232. See Raoul Vaneigem and Attila Kotányi, "Basic Program of the Bureau of Unitary Urbanism, " in Knabb, *Situationist International Anthology*, p. 86 ff; *Internationale Situationniste*, No. 6, 1961, pp. 16–19, for the subsequent direction of the Situationist International after Constant's departure.

25 Wigley, p. 233. See Richard Kempton, *Provo: Amsterdam's Anarchist Revolt*, Autonomia, New York, 2007. For the Situationist take on the Provos, see Franklin Rosemont and Charles Radcliffe, *Dancin' in the Streets: Anarchists, IWWs, Surrealists, Situationists and Provos in the 1960s*, Charles H. Kerr, Chicago, 2005: "As it is the only reflection their poetry and taste for adventure has found in official theory is in Constant's New Babylon, where it appears as an abstract appendage to his plans for a fully modernized concentration camp, the world, he assures us, of homo ludens. Constant is about as 'ludic' as an ox" (p. 422).

26 Wigley, p. 232. The Situationists once described the Beats, and not without justification, as "mystical cretins," but Allen Ginsburg's contemporaneous critique of "Moloch whose mind is pure machinery" is perhaps most relevant here.

27 Leslie T. Chang, *Factory Girls*, Speigel and Grau, New York, 2008, p. 6. This

daughter of Chinese nationalists offers a politically dubious account, the strength of which is its attention to the everyday lives of factory workers.

28 *New York Times*, March 7, 2009. See Giovanni Arrighi, *Adam Smith in Beijing: Lineages of the 21st Century*, Verso, London, 2009.

29 Wigley, p. 60.

30 Constant, "Lecture Given at the ICA, London" (1963), *The Decomposition of the Artist*, p. 9 (a).

31 Wigley, p. 235.

32 Walter Benjamin, *The Work of Art in the Age of Mechanical Reproducibility and Other Writings on Media*, Harvard University Press, Cambridge MA, 2008. Benjamin clearly prefigures the concept of détournement in his writings on media, particularly the famous "Work of Art" essay. A topic for another time.

33 Among thinkers of technology Gilbert Simondon is undergoing something of a revival, even if the main undercurrent is a regrettable overdependence on Martin Heidegger. The former is too technocratic even for Constant, and for the latter, famously, only the Gods can save us. See Adrian MacKenzie, *Transductions: Bodies and Machines at Speed*, Continuum, London, 2006, for a useful introduction to Simondon, and Bernard Stiegler, *Technics and Time*, Stanford University Press, Stanford CA, 1998 for a striking synthesis.

12 The Beach Beneath the Street

1 "The Decline and Fall of the Spectacle-Commodity Economy," in Guy Debord, *Sick Planet*, Seagull Books, 2008, p. 5, also in Knabb, *Situationist International Anthology*, p. 195; *Internationale Situationniste*, No. 10, March, 1966, p. 3; Ronald Porambo, *No Cause for Indictment: An Autopsy of Newark*, Melville House, Hoboken NJ, 2007. Originally published in 1971.

2 Wigley, p. 162. See *The Memoirs of Lacenaire*, Staples Press, London, 1952. The poet-criminal Lacenaire was a celebrated figure, and everyone from Dickens to Stendhal wrote about him. He inspired the character of Raskolnikov. His legend spans the romantic, surrealist and Situationist movements. Interestingly, Foucault chose to publish *I, Pierre Rivière, Having Slaughtered My Mother, My Sister, and My Brother: A Case of Parricide in the 19th Century*, University of Nebraska Press, Lincoln, 1982, in part to counter the Lacenaire legend. Like Porambo, Lacenaire was a far better writer than he was a criminal.

3 Gerald Horne, *Fire This Time: The Watts Uprising and the 1960s*, Da Capo, New York, 1997, p. 129. Horne calls it a "potlatch of destruction among those denied the dream" (p. 15).

4 Janet Abu-Lughod, *Race, Space, and Riots*, Oxford University Press, New York, 2007, p. 293.

5 Guy Debord, *Society of the Spectacle*, Zone Books, New York, 1994, Ch. 1, section 17. It's an elegant paragraph, in which Debord connects Marx to Sartre with admirable economy.

6 Wigley, p. 236.

7 It was Georges Sorel (1847–1922), that unreliable fellow traveler of the syndicalist movement, who proposed the central role of the myth of the general strike: *From Georges Sorel: Essays in Socialism and Philosophy*, edited with an introduction by John L. Stanley, translated by John and Charlotte Stanley, Oxford University Press, 1976.

8 Debord to Vaneigem, February 1966.

9 Viénet, *Enragés and Situationists*.

10 De Retz, *Mémoires*. One of the chapter epigrams of Viénet's *Enragés* is from de Retz, p. 25.

11 *The scene,* Viénet, *Enragés,* p. 21; *whiff of cordite,* Dominque Lecourt, *Mediocracy: French Philosophy since 1968,* Verso, London, 2001, p. 22. Lecourt juxtaposes the "brand image" of Althusserianism with Debord's "cult book" as setting the scene for May 1968 (pp. 17–22); *place of damnation,* Lefebvre, *The Explosion,* p. 104.

12 BBC News, March 27, 2002. On the living dead, see Evan Calder Williams, *Combined and Uneven Apocalypse,* Zero Books, Winchester, UK, 2011.

13 Bernard Stiegler, *Acting Out,* Stanford University Press, Stanford CA, 2008: *enormous suffering,* p. 41, *consumer's disgust,* p. 60. Far from being an individualistic society, the disintegrating spectacle produces the herd—Durn's "living dead." Like the Situationists, Stiegler conceives of desire as a kind of unlimited horizon. This infinite quality of desire is what pushes its frail vehicle, the body and its needs, on. This desire is fantastic, but it grounds the possibility of individuation. The spectacle subordinates the free time in which desire might find itself to the synchronic time of the contemplation of the world as a world of things. The spectacle disarms desire. Its goal for Stiegler is not to channel desire but rather to forestall *disgust*. It can only stave off "the coming slowdown of consumption, caused by the consumer's disgust." Would this impasse appear, however, were it not for the failed revolution of 1968? Perhaps it was doomed to fail. Perhaps it was always impossible, a desire out of joint with need. But without the very possibility of that impossible, look at what we are left with: the Nanterre of Richard Durn, rather than of the Enragés.

14 *Negation of the state,* Viénet, *Enragés,* p. 32. For his own account, see Daniel and Gabriel Cohn-Bendit, *Obsolete Communism: The Left-Wing Alternative,* AK Press, San Francisco, 2000. Danny the Red later became Danny the Green, as a member of the European Parliament.

15 René Reisel (b. 1950) was the son of the Communist militant, and a member of the Situationist International from 1968 until his exclusion in 1971. Later he became a sheep farmer and an activist in the Peasant Federation. See René Reisel and Jaime Semprún, *Catastrophisme, administration du désastre et soumission durable,* Editions de l'Encyclopédie des Nuisances, Paris, 2008. The Encyclopédie des Nuisances is a not unworthy continuation of the Situationist legacy.

16 *Self-respect,* Viénet, *Enragés,* p. 58. A note in Debord's handwriting giving the members of the Committee for the Maintenance of the Occupation is reproduced in Zweifel et al., *In Girum Imus Nocte et Consumimur Igni,* p. 62. One of Stiegler's concerns is the intergenerational, on which score alone the composition of this little group is interesting.

17 *Millions of people,* Viénet, *Enragés,* p. 76 ; *people strolled, dreamed,* ibid., p. 77.

18 Michael Hardt and Antonio Negri have attempted to displace Marx's Shakespearan figure of the old mole, with its implications of a surface behind which something is hidden, in favor of a more two dimensional metaphor. But there is no essence and appearance at work in the figure of the old mole. Rather, it's an apt image for materialism itself, in which necessity always reveals itself too late. As Hegel says somewhere: hell is truth seen too late. See Hardt and Negri, *Empire,* Harvard University Press, Cambridge MA, 2000, p. 52 ff.

19 *Despair,* ibid., p. 92; *isolated,* ibid., p. 59; *backwardness,* ibid., p. 86.

20 Hegel, Preface to *The Philosophy of Right*.

21 Alain Badiou offers the attractive notion of fidelity: of Lenin's to the Paris Commune, of Mao's to Lenin, and so forth, except that his very examples tend mostly to be betrayals. Détournement is the opposite of fidelity. Moreover, is there not some-

thing disturbing in how often Badiou, like his friend Slavoj Žižek, invokes the great leaders of the Third International rather than the movements they "led"?

22 For example, Buchloh, *Neo-Avantgarde and Culture Industry*. While acknowledging the diminishing returns of avant-garde gestures in the postwar context, Buchloh remains wedded to them, and, like them, to the institutions of the art world. This now seems even more of a dead end than Jorn's expressionism. For a Marxist reading of Debord, see Anselm Jappe's excellent *Guy Debord* and more recently Richard Gilman-Opalsky, *Spectacular Capitalism*, Autonomedia, New York, 2011.

23 Lefebvre, *Introduction à la modernité. Préludes*, pp 29–30; Henri Lefebvre, *The Sociology of Marx*, Random House, New York, 1968, p. 110. Quoting Karl Marx, *Theories of Surplus Value*, translated by Emile Burns, Foreign Language Publishing House, Moscow, 1969, p. 376. As Lefebvre remarks, this is clearly a Marxian reading of Balzac.

24 More or less from Shakespeare, *Henry IV Pt. I*, Act 5, Scene 2. Debord uses it for an epigram in *Society of the Spectacle*. *People* magazine (December 14, 2010) wonders about the limo ambush: "will the royal wedding be safe?"

25 Roberto Bolaño, *2666*, Farrar, Strauss, Giroux, New York, 2008, p. 105. Or to give another example: Thomas Pynchon, *Inherent Vice*, Penguin, New York, 2009, the epigram to which is "Sous les pavés, la plage!" (Beneath the pavement, the beach!)

26 Simon Critchley, *Infinitely Demanding: Ethics of Commitment, Politics of Resistance*, Verso, London, 2008, p. 1; Jacques Rancière, *Short Voyages to the Land of the People*, Stanford University Press, Stanford CA, 2003.

27 Writing to Frankin on August 8, 1958, Debord observes that the proletariat is the hidden God of the Socialism or Barbarism group. The reference is to the reading by Lucien Goldmann (1913–1970) of Pascal, *The Hidden God*, Routledge, London, 1964, but one might extend the critical move further. The unifying principle, or rather the alibi, that absolves us of the necessity to think and act for ourselves, yet which is nowhere actually present, might these days take the name of *power*.

28 René Viénet, "The Situationists and New Forms of Action Against Politics and Art," in Knabb, *Situationist International Anthology*, pp. 273–77. When it appeared in *Internationale Situationniste*, No. 11, 1967, pp. 32–36 it was illustrated by frames from André Bertrand's détourned comics, including the famous *Return of the Durruti Column*.

29 On which see Wark, *A Hacker Manifesto*, and David Berry and Giles Moss, *Libre Culture*, Pygmalion Books, Winnipeg, 2008.

30 On which see Wark, *Gamer Theory*, and Eugene Thacker and Alex Galloway, *The Exploit*, University of Minnesota Press, Minneapolis, 2007. Given the Situationist predilection for pinball, one might wonder what becomes of play in the age of the gamer. Both of these are, unlike most of *game studies*, critical accounts. See also Sven Lütticken, "Playtimes," *New Left Review*, No. 66, November 2010.

31 This is one of the great questions addressed in Trevor Paglen, *Invisible*, Aperture, New York, 2010. Work which also, incidentally, ups the ante as far as the détournement of Chombart's aerial surveillance goes.

32 On the "new international," see Derrida, *Specters of Marx*. Attractive as it sounds, it offers something less than the practice of the Situationist International, precisely on the question of the forms of free association that might yet bind those without status, without form, without party, without country, without nation, without citizenship, without common belonging to a class.

33 Jorn's insistence that there are two classes, respectively makers of form and content under commodity production, might be more helpful than the idea of an internal differentiation between material and immaterial labor, not least because there is no

immaterial labor. The problem of communicating between different situations of struggle becomes clearer when one understands this as one of the qualitative differences. See Hardt and Negri, *Empire*, pp. 3–63. For those familiar with the opening gambits of the fabulous book, let's just say that this is why our owl and old mole have not become a snake or an eagle.

34 Manuel Castells, *The Urban Question*, MIT Press, Cambridge MA, 1979. Lefebvre responded to Castells's critique in *The Survival of Capitalism*, Schocken Books, New York, 1981. Biopower has since become a whole academic industry, the key text of which remains Giorgio Agamben, *Homo Sacer*, Stanford University Press, Stanford CA, 1998. Following Heidegger and late Foucault, the trouble once again is *metaphysics*, in this case within political theory, where sovereignty becomes power over life. When did those who went looking for an unassailable power within discourse fail to find it? A century after the death of God, one still awaits the death of its avatar, power, which has been *proven not to exist* time and time again. Take the 2011 events in Egypt and Tunisia, for example. Mehdi Belhaj Kacem: "January 2011 is a May '68 carried through all the way … it was the first Situationist revolution in history … that is, carried out by the people directly." (A Tunisian Renaissance: Interview with Mehdi Belhaj Kacem," by Alex Galloway, *Lacanian Ink*, January 31, 2011.

13 The Critique of Everyday Life

1 Debord, *In Girum Imus Nocte*, p. 54. See also: *In girum imus nocte et consumimur igni*, Gallimard, Paris, 1999, p. 42, or *Oeuvres*, p. 1382.

2 "Now the SI," in Knabb, *Anthology*, p. 177; *Internationale Situationiste*, No. 9, August 1964, p. 5: "pour sortir du vingtième siècle."

3 See Tom McDonough (ed.), *Guy Debord and the Situationist International*, MIT Press, Cambridge MA, 2004; Georgina Bertolino et al., *Pinot Gallizio*, Charta, Milan, 2005.

4 Of the figures from the later, "political" phase of the Situationist International, Raoul Vaneigem has attracted particular attention: Pol Charles, *Vaneigem l'insatiable*, L'Age d'Homme, Laussane, 2002; Grégory Lambrette, *Raoul Vaneigem*, Libertaires, Brussels, 2007; Larent Six, *Raoul Vaneigem*, Éditions Luce Wilquin, Avin, 2005.

5 Some versions of the Debord biography: Literary version: Vincent Kaufmann, *Guy Debord*, University of Minnesota Press, Minneapolis, 2006; Marxist version: Anselm Jappe, *Guy Debord*, University of California Press, Berkeley, 1999; philosophical version: Jean-Marie Apostolides, *Tombeau de Guy Debord*, Exils, Paris, 1999.

6 *Le Monde*, June 14, 2009; *Le Monde*, June 17, 2009; *Libération*, June 17, 2009. The Library eventually succeeded in acquiring these materials.

7 See Simon During, *Exit Capitalism*, Routledge, London, 2009.

8 Guy Debord, *Panegyric*, Verso, London, p. 68; *Oeuvres*, p. 1685.

9 Guy Debord, *Considerations on the Assassination of Gérard Lebovici*, Tam Tam Books, Los Angeles, 2002, p. 37; *Oeuvres*, p. 1557.

10 Debord, *Considerations on the Assassination*, p. 79; *Oeuvres*, p. 1577.

11 *What other success?*, Debord, *Considerations on the Assassination*, p. 79; *Oeuvres*, p. 1577. *At war with the whole world, In Girum*, p. 44; *Oeuvres*, p. 1373.

12 Alice Becker-Ho, *The Princes of Jargon*, Edwin Mellen Press, Lewiston NY, 2004, p. 7.

13 Art history has lately come to undo the category of the originary author, even in its most canonic locus, the art of the Renaissance. The pressure of past forms, seeping into present expressions, comes into play even there. But that signs of this at work

in art are instances also of détournement as popular practice has not yet broken into the light of day among historians. See Alexander Nagel and Christopher Wood, *Anachronistic Renaissance*, Zone Books, New York, 2010.

14 "Guy Debord's Widow Threatens NYU Professor with Copyright Violation," *Chronicle of Higher Education*, April 28, 2008; see also *Artforum*, November 1, 2008, pp. 167–8.

15 Some versions: Pomo version: Sadie Plant, *The Most Radical Gesture*, Routledge, London, 1992; punk version: Greil Marcus, *Lipstick Traces*, Harvard University Press, Cambridge MA, 2009; art version: Elizabeth Sussman (ed.), *On the Passage of a Few People Through a Rather Brief Moment in Time*, MIT Press, Cambridge MA, 1989; anarchist version: David Graeber, *Direct Action: An Ethnography*, AK Press, Oakland CA, 2009; new left version: Peter Wollen, *Raiding the Icebox*, Verso, London, 1993; Paris-centric version: Patrick Marcolini, *Le Mouvement Situationiste: Une histoire intellectuelle*, L'Échappée, Paris, 2012.

16 Guy Debord, writing to Constant on April 26, 1959. See Guy Debord, *Correspondence*, Semiotext(e), Los Angeles, 2008, pp. 242–5.

17 Debord, *Considerations on the Assassination*, p. 31; *Oeuvres*, p. 1553.

18 Cardinal de Retz, *Mémoires*, Société des Bibliophiles, Paris, 1903, p. 236; quoted in Debord, *Panegyric*, p. 18; *Oeuvres*, p. 1665.

19 See Alberto Toscano, *Fanaticism: The Uses of An Idea*, Verso, London, 2010, on the rhetorical function of the fanatic in liberal politics.

20 Simon Critchley, *Infinitely Demanding*, Verso, London, 2008; Alain Badiou, *The Century*, Polity, Cambridge, 2007; Jacques Rancière, *The Future of the Image*, Verso, London, 2009.

21 Debord, *Panegyric*, p. 40; *Oeuvres*, p. 1673.

22 Debord, *Panegyric*, p. 29; *Oeuvres*, p. 1668.

23 Louis-Ferdinand Céline, *Journey to the End of the Night*, New Directions, New York, 2006, p. 18.

24 "Le monde dont nous parlons," *Internationale Situationiste*, No. 9, August 1964, p. 6; Sussman, *On the Passage of a Few People*, p. 154.

25 Debord, *In Girum*, p. 24; *Oeuvres*, p. 1354.

14 Liberty Guiding the People

1 Clark, *The Sight of Death*, p. 185.

2 T. J. Clark and Donald Nicholson-Smith, "Why Art Can't Kill the Situationist International," in McDonough (ed.), *Guy Debord and the Situationist International*, p. 485.

3 Kathryn Tuma, "In Conversation: T. J. Clark with Kathryn Tuma," *Brooklyn Rail*, November 2006.

4 Clark, *The Sight of Death*, p. 114; see also p. 239.

5 T. J. Clark, *The Painting of Modern Life: Paris in the Art of Manet and His Followers*, Knopf, New York, 1985, p. 36. A book that seemed untimely in the "postmodern" moment in which it was published, but that context will be ignored here.

6 See Michel Foucault, *Discipline and Punish: The Birth of the Prison*, Vintage, New York, 1995. Foucault takes oblique aim at Debord in the overture to this famous book, which sees the spectacle end with the spectacle of the scaffold, replaced by the new order of visibility of disciplinary institutions like the prison. But perhaps it's more an instance of anxiety of influence: Is not Debord the one who had first asked seemingly Foucauldian questions about regimes of visibility? Is it not Debord who

notices first asymmetries of who sees who or what? In breaking with Marxism in the Stalinist mode—still a powerful force in seventies France—Foucault erases the traces of his debt to the non-Stalinist left.

7 T. J. Clark, *Farewell to an Idea*, Yale University Press, New Haven CT, 1999, pp. 7–8. Released the year of renewed activism around the World Trade Organization, Clark was again somewhat untimely.

8 T. J. Clark, *Image of the People: Gustave Courbet and the 1848 Revolution*, Thames & Hudson, London, 1982, p. 10.

9 Clark, *Farewell to an Idea*, p. 28.

10 Ibid., p. 47.

11 Ibid., p. 34.

12 Ibid., p. 48.

13 T. J. Clark, *The Absolute Bourgeois: Artists and Politics in France 1848–1851*, Thames & Hudson, London, 1982, p. 19.

14 Clark, *Image of the People*, p. 19. See also T. J. Clark, "A Bourgeois Dance of Death," *Burlington Magazine*, April 1969.

15 See Jerrold Seigel, *Bohemian Paris: Culture, Politics and the Boundaries of Bourgeois Life, 1830–1930*, Johns Hopkins, Baltimore, 1999.

16 Clark, *Image of the People*, p. 33.

17 Ibid., p. 14.

18 Ibid., p. 34. On over-identification, see Slavoj Žižek, *Metastases of Enjoyment*, Verso, London, 2005, pp. 70–3. Perhaps the best case for it as an avant-garde strategy is Alexei Monroe, *Interrogation Machine: Laibach and NSK*, MIT Press, Cambridge MA, 2005.

19 On total semantic field, see Henri Lefebvre, *Introduction to Modernity*, Verso, London, 1995, p. 239; *Introduction à la modernité. Préludes*, Les éditions de minuit, Paris, 1962, p. 235. On Lefebvre's attempt to redeem romanticism, see McKenzie Wark, *The Beach Beneath the Street*, Verso, London, 2011.

20 Karl Marx, "The June Revolution," in Karl Marx, *The Revolutions of 1848: Political Writings Volume 1*, edited by David Fernbach, Penguin, Harmondsworth, 1978, p. 131. Marx here makes romantic imagery politically productive again.

21 Clark, *Image of the People*, p. 74.

22 All of these Thailand stories are sourced from news.bbc.co.uk.

23 Clark, *Image of the People*, p. 159.

24 Ibid., p. 73. Compare to Debord's classic statement on détournement: *Society of the Spectacle*, paras. 206–11. The practice of détournement is itself détourned. Debord détourns Lautréamont (207), but interestingly chooses to quote from Kierkegaard. Debordian détournement arises from Lautréamont and his contact with Belgian Surrealism. The quote from Kierkegaard (206) is perhaps a nod to his old friend Asger Jorn, who always preferred to source his ideas from his fellow Scandinavians.

25 Clark, *Image of the People*, p. 140.

26 Ibid., p. 149.

27 Ibid., pp. 160–1.

28 Clark, *The Painting of Modern Life*, p. 15.

29 Ibid., p. 44. On moral panic, see the classic work by the late Stanley Cohen, *Folk Devils and Moral Panics*, Routledge, London, 2003. Of the many books on Paris, see David Harvey, *Paris, Capital of Modernity*, Routledge, New York, 2005, which engages with, and usefully enriches, Clark's account.

30 Clark, *The Painting of Modern Life*, p. 69. See Louis Chevalier, *The Assassination of Paris*, University of Chicago Press, Chicago, 1994. Originally published in 1977,

this conservative historian's lament for the city struck a chord with Debord. See *Panegyric*, p. 39.

31 "Theses on the Paris Commune," in Knabb, *Anthology*, p. 400. See also the classic study: Prosper-Olivier Lissagaray, *History of the Paris Commune*, translated by Eleanor Marx Aveling, Verso, London, 2012.

32 Henri Lefebvre, "Excerpt from *The Proclamation of the Commune*," in Tom McDonough (ed.), *The Situationists and the City*, Verso, London, 2009, p. 175.

33 Clark, *Image of the People*, p. 154.

34 Clark, *The Painting of Modern Life*, p. 69.

15 *The Spectacle of Modern Life*

1 Clark, *The Painting of Modern Life*, p. 49. On modernity and the city, see Marshall Berman, *All That Is Solid Melts Into Air*, Penguin, New York, 1988.

2 The early twenty-first-century Olympia might well be Sasha Grey, porn star and actor. On the question of the black supplicant with flowers in this painting, see the work of artist Mickalene Thomas.

3 *New York Magazine*, July 10, 2005.

4 It would be worth pausing here over the agency of Victorine Meurent, and of models in general. See Wendy Steiner, *The Real, Real Thing: The Model in the Mirror of Art*, University of Chicago Press, Chicago, 2010, and Eunice Lipton, *Alias Olympia*, Cornell University Press, Ithaca NY, 1999.

5 Clark, *The Painting of Modern Life*, p. 108.

6 Ibid., p. 128.

7 One might begin here with: Laura Mulvey, *Visual and Other Pleasures*, Palgrave Macmillan, London, 2009. Clark's distance from other leftist cultural critics of the time, such as Mulvey, can be measured via T. J. Clark, "Preliminaries to a Possible Treatment of Olympia," *Screen*, Vol. 21, No. 1, 1980.

8 Clark, *The Painting of Modern Life*, p. 147.

9 Ibid., p. 165.

10 Ibid., p. 164.

11 Ibid., p. 203.

12 *ABC News*, September 20, 2006.

13 Clark, *The Painting of Modern Life*, p. 229. See also the fine essay by Greil Marcus, "The Dance That Everybody Forgot," *New Formations*, No. 2, Summer 1987.

14 Clark, *The Painting of Modern Life*, p. 236.

15 Ibid., p. 229.

16 Ibid., p. 236.

17 Ibid.

18 Ibid., p. 205.

19 See Mark Andrejevic, *Reality TV: The Work of Being Watched*, Rowman and Littlefield, Lanham MD, 2007; Jodi Dean, *Publicity's Secret*, Cornell University Press, Ithaca NY, 1988.

20 Clark, *The Painting of Modern Life*, p. 253.

21 See for example Kai Fikentscher, *You Better Work! Underground Dance Music in New York City*, Wesleyan, Hanover NH, 2000.

22 *New York Magazine*, April 4, 2010.

16 *Anarchies of Perception*

1 Clark, *Farewell to an Idea*, Yale University Press, New Haven CT, p. 104.
2 *Every act*, and *folding of parts*: Clark, *Farewell to an Idea*, p. 180.
3 Clark, *Farewell to an Idea*, p. 62. See also Félix Fénéon, *Novels in Three Lines*, New York Review of Books Classics, New York, 2007.
4 Kojin Karatani, *Transcritique*, MIT Press, Cambridge MA, 2003, also attempts to rethink the logic of the Marxist-anarchist split and repair it.
5 Clark, *Farewell to an Idea*, p. 103.
6 Clark, *Farewell to an Idea*, p. 121. On the institutionalizing of geography in France and an anarchist social geography, see Kristin Ross, *The Emergence of the Social*, Verso, London, 2008, p. 75ff.
7 See J. M. Bernstein, *Against Voluptuous Bodies*, Stanford University Press, Stanford CA, 2006, and Eric L. Santner, *The Royal Remains*, University of Chicago Press, Chicago, 2011. These two erudite books read Clark in the context of critical theory and psychoanalysis, respectively, and are concerned to place Clarkian aesthetics in readings of modernity based on sovereignty and rationalization, respectively. Yet what is distinctive about Clark, and this connects him to the Situationist current, is the question of aesthetics considered not from above but from below. Or rather: how popular forces pushing from below do so, in part at least, via the struggle over the means of representation, and not just over what is pictured within it. See also Gail Day, *Dialectical Passions: Negation in Postwar Art*, Columbia University Press, New York, 2011, which places Clark more in the history of New Left aesthetics.
8 Debord, *Comments*, p. 3; *Oeuvres*, p. 1595. Clark argues that Debord avoids periodizing the spectacle in *Society of the Spectacle*, but in the light of this later text this might not be strictly the case. See T. J. Clark, "Origins of the Present Crisis," *New Left Review*, No. 2, March–April 2000.
9 Debord, *Society of the Spectacle*, s. 100. Jonathan Crary manages to embellish this simple point nicely; see McDonough (ed.), *Guy Debord and the Situationist International*.
10 T. J. Clark, "Foreword," Anselm Jappe, *Guy Debord*, p. viii.
11 *Brooklyn Rail*, November 2006.
12 Retort, *Afflicted Powers: Capital and Spectacle in a New Age of War*, Verso, London, 2006, pp. 3, 5.
13 Ibid., pp. 28, 37.
14 Ibid., p. 20.
15 Clark, "Foreword," pp. ix–x.
16 Ibid.

17 *The Revolution of Everyday Life*

1 Hans Ulrich Obrist, "In Conversation with Raoul Vaneigem," *e-flux journal*, No. 6, May 2009.
2 Debord to Vaneigem, March 8, 1965, in Guy Debord, *Correspondance*, Vol. 3, Fayard, Paris, 2003.
3 Vaneigem, *The Revolution of Everyday Life*, p. 13. On the Provos, see Richard Kempton, *Provo: Amsterdam's Anarchist Revolt*, Autonomedia, New York, 2007. Henri Lefebvre goes to some lengths to debunk the popular idea that Herbert Marcuse was the prophet of '68, in part to bolster his own claim. See *The Explosion*, Monthly Review Press, 1969, surely a candidate for the honor of being his worst book.

4 From the 1991 preface to *The Revolution of Everyday Life*.
5 Laurence Remilla, "In Conversation with Raoul Vaneigem," *The Idler*, No. 35, Spring 2005, p. 82.
6 From Vaneigem's resignation letter, in Guy Debord and Gianfranco Sanguinetti, *The Real Split in the International*, translated by John McHale, Pluto Press, London, 2003, p. 142. Friedrich Hölderlin, *Hyperion*, translated by Ross Benjamin, Archipelago Books, Brooklyn NY, 2008, see p. 172. Georg Lukács, in *Goethe and His Age*, Merlin Press, 1968, makes the case for Hegel's supersession of the political instincts that he shared with Hölderlin in their youth. Vaneigem's writings are more in the spirit of Hölderlin than Hegel, and on this point he differs from Debord.
7 Regarding Vaneigem on heresies, see Alexander Galloway, Eugene Thacker and McKenzie Wark, *Excommunication*, University of Chicago Press, Chicago, 2013.
8 The standard work on Debord's relation to Hegelian Marxism is Anselm Jappe, *Guy Debord*.
9 Lefebvre, *Critique of Everyday Life*, Vol. 2, p. 288; *new life*, Lefebvre, *Introduction to Modernity*, p. 69.
10 Raoul Vaneigem, "Some Theoretical Topics That Need To Be Dealt With Without Academic Debate or Idle Speculation," Knabb, *Anthology*, p. 221; *Internationale Situationiste*, No. 10, 1966, p. 42.
11 André Breton, *Ode to Charles Fourier*, translated by Kenneth White, Cape Goliard Press, London, 1970. See Theodor Adorno, *Prisms*, MIT Press, Cambridge MA, 1988, p. 34. The Fourier of liberated desire was taken up in the United States by Norman O. Brown and Herbert Marcuse.
12 Guy Debord, letter to the Italian section, March 12, 1969, in Guy Debord, *Correspondance Volume 4, 1969–1972*, Fayard, Paris, 2005.
13 Roland Barthes, *Sade / Fourier / Loyola*, Farrar, Straus and Giroux, New York, 1976, p. 87.
14 See *Topique*, October 1970, with contributions by Maurice Blanchot, Michel Butor and Pierre Klossowski; and Emile Lehouck, "La Lecture surréaliste de Charles Fourier," *Australian Journal of French Studies*, Vol. 20, No. 1, 1983, pp. 26–36.
15 Raymond Queneau, "Dialectique hégélienne et series de Fourier," *Bords*, Paris, 1963. Walter Benjamin, *Charles Baudelaire*, Verso, London, 1985, pp. 159–60. Italo Calvino, *The Uses of Literature*, Harcourt Brace, New York, 1986.
16 Fredric Jameson, *Archaeologies of the Future*, Verso, London, 2007, p. 251.
17 From an email interview with Vaneigem, conducted in May–June 2011.
18 Charles Fourier, in Jonathan Beecher and Richard Bienvenu, *The Utopian Vision of Charles Fourier: Selected Texts*, Beacon Press, Boston MA, p. 268; Francois Bott, "Raoul Vaneigem," *Le Monde*, September 12, 2003.
19 Vaneigem, *Revolution of Everyday Life*, p. 84.
20 Vaneigem, *Revolution of Everyday Life*, p. 190.
21 Raoul Vaneigem, *A Cavalier History of Surrealism*, AK Press, Oakland CA, 1999, p. 8. Vaneigem's surrealism is a Paris-centric parade of white guys, even if (at least) one of them was not so straight. A usefully decentering resource is Franklin Rosemont and Robin D. G. Kelley, *Black, Brown and Beige: Surrealist Writings from Africa and the Diaspora*, University of Texas Press, Austin TX, 2010.
22 Vaneigem, *A Cavalier History*, p. 5.
23 Ibid., p. 10.
24 Ibid., p. 12.
25 Ibid., p. 74.
26 Ibid., p. 54.

27 René Crevel, *My Body and I*, Archipelago Press, Brookyn NY, 2005, p. 83, written when he was twenty-five and ten years before his suicide.
28 Vaneigem, *A Cavalier History*, p. 73.
29 Ibid., p. 113.
30 Michel Leiris, *Manhood*, University of Chicago Press, Chicago, 1992. See the essay on Leiris by John Conomos in *Flesh*, Intervention Publications No. 22, Sydney 1988.
31 Vaneigem, *A Cavalier History*, p. 100.
32 Jonathan Beecher and Richard Bienvenu (eds), *The Utopian Vision of Charles Fourier: Selected Texts*, Beacon Press, Boston MA, p. 289.
33 Fourier, *The Utopian Vision*, p. 158.
34 Ibid., p. 157.
35 Charles Fourier, *The Theory of the Four Movements*, edited by Gareth Steadman Jones and Ian Patterson, Cambridge University Press, Cambridge, 1996, p. 233. Actually, he thought there were thirty-six kinds of bankruptcy, that being the magic number in his series. See Charles Fourier, *The Hierarchies of Cuckholdry and Bankruptcy*, translated by Geoffrey Longnecker, Wakefield Press, Cambridge MA, 2011.
36 Fourier, *The Utopian Vision*, p. 142.
37 Vaneigem, *The Revolution of Everyday Life*, p. 258.
38 Raoul Vaneigem, "Basic Banalities Part 1," in Knabb, *Anthology*, p. 123; *Internationale Situationiste*, No. 7, April 1962, p. 36.
39 Vaneigem, *The Revolution of Everyday Life*, p. 46.
40 Charles Fourier, *Harmonian Man: Selected Writings*, edited by Mark Poster, Anchor Books, New York, 1971, p. 77.
41 Crevel, *My Body and I*, p. 124.
42 Leiris, *Manhood*, p. 120.
43 Vaneigem, *The Revolution of Everyday Life*, p. 22.
44 Rémila, "In Conversation with Raoul Vanegeim," p. 82.
45 Fourier, *The Utopian Vision*, p. 148.

18 Détournement as Utopia

1 Raoul Vaneigem, *The Book of Pleasures*, translated by John Fullerton, Pending Press, London, 1983, p. 28.
2 Fourier, *The Utopian Vision*, p. 145.
3 Fourier, *The Theory of the Four Movements*, p. 200.
4 Vaneigem, *The Revolution of Everyday Life*, p. 185. He borrows the idea from Brecht's Herr Keuner stories.
5 Vaneigem, *The Revolution of Everyday Life*, p. 264.
6 Eric Santner, "The New Idolatry," pressblog.uchicago.edu, September 6, 2011. See also Eric Santner, *The Royal Remains*. Santner sees this as part of a heretical extension of the properly religious into the secular domain. For Vaneigem, the heretical procedure of extending sacred poetics in every direction is not an excessive margin but the very center of sacred practice, for good and ill. For Vaneigem, as for Fourier, it's not a question of pushing sacred sacrifice back into its proper box but of overturning its logic in all domains.
7 Imaginal, rather than an affect of the imaginary or the imagination, in that the imaginal is not the opposite of reason but the field within which reason is possible. The imaginal is social rather than merely individual. It constructs not just an imagi-

nary bond between self and other, but the field of possible unities and connections. Détournement, which not only copies but corrects in the direction of hope, synthesizes aspects of both classical and romantic practices of imagination. See Chiara Bottici, *A Philosophy of Political Myth*, Cambridge University Press, Cambridge, 2010.

8 Herman Melville's story "Bartleby, the Scrivener" (1853) turns up as an exemplar of a certain kind of praxis in Gilles Deleuze, *Essays Critical and Clinical*, Minnesota University Press, Minneapolis, 1997, in Slavoj Žižek, *The Parallax View*, MIT Press, Cambridge MA, 2006, and in Michael Hardt and Antonio Negri, *Empire*, Harvard University Press, Cambridge MA, 2000, and also in Giorgio Agamben, *Potentialities*, Stanford University Press, Stanford CA, 1999. And this is to name just the most prominent examples. When it comes to the Bartelbization of theories of praxis, "I prefer not to."

9 Jonathan Beecher, *Charles Fourier: The Visionary and His World*, University of California Press, Berkeley, 1986, p. 490.

10 Vaneigem, *The Revolution of Everyday Life*, p. 187.

11 See J. D. Bernal, *Science in History*, Vol. 2, MIT Press, Cambridge MA, 1971. While Bernal is far more respectful of, and knowledgeable about, Newton's achievements, he is nevertheless alert to how implicated they were in the trade and industry of the time and the role they played in the rise of bourgeois thought. Fourier was not wrong to want to build on but diverge from Newton.

12 Fourier, *Harmonian Man*, p. 51.

13 Ibid., p. 49.

14 Jameson, *Archaeologies of the Future*, p. 248. I am indebted to Jameson's reading of Fourier throughout this chapter.

15 *Unlimited philanthropy*, Fourier, *Harmonian Man*, p. 83; *prodigal*, Fourier, *Harmonian Man*, p. 88.

16 Alice Becker-Ho, *The Essence of Jargon*, translated by John McHale, typescript, 2007, p. 28.

17 Fourier, *The Utopian Vision*, p. 200.

18 *Minimum of satisfaction*, Fourier, *The Utopian Vision*, p. 337; *the ravages it causes*, Fourier, *The Utopian Vision*, p. 339.

19 *Prohibition and contraband*, Fourier, *Harmonian Man*, p. 238; *poor in pleasure*, Fourier, *Harmonian Man*, p. 80.

20 A claim not actually the case with Fourier. T. J. Clark, "For a Left With No Future," *New Left Review*, No. 74, March–April 2012, p. 68. Here Clark turns from realist to tragic, but a form of tragedy that has not broadened—despite a nod toward Platonov—toward the popular. See Susan Watkins' reply in the same issue.

21 Fourier, *Harmonian Man*, p. 75.

22 Ibid., p. 83.

19 Charles Fourier's Queer Theory

1 Charles Fourier, *Des Harmonies Polygames en Amour*, Payot & Rivages, Paris, 2003, with a preface by Raoul Vaneigem.

2 On Fourier and Restif, see Mark Poster, *The Utopian Thought of Restif de la Bretonne*, New York University Press, New York, 1971. On Fourier in the French utopian continuum, see Frank Manuel, *The Prophets of Paris*, Harper & Row, New York, 1962. For Rabelais' utopian order of the Themeites, see *Gargantua and Pantegruel*, translated by M. A. Screech, Penguin, London, 2006, p. 362ff. However, Fourier really stands alone in terms of sexual freedom and equality.

3 Vaneigem, *The Book of Pleasures*, p. 54.
4 Raoul Vaneigem, "Basic Banalities Part 2," in Knabb, *Anthology*, p. 167; *Internationale Situationiste*, No. 8, January 1963, p. 44.
5 For an account of aristocratic cultural forms of the kind Fourier détourns, see Johan Huizinga, *The Waning of the Middle Ages*, St. Martin's Press, New York, 1924.
6 Fourier, *Harmonian Man*, p. 262.
7 Ibid., p. 267.
8 Ibid., p. 263.
9 Ibid., p. 271.
10 For a fine—Rabelaisian—satire on civilized sex among the supposedly progressive middle classes, see Christina Stead, *Letty Fox: Her Luck*, New York Review Books, 2001. It hardly needs updating.
11 Fourier, *Harmonian Man*, p. 272.
12 See Raoul Vaneigem, *La Resistance au christianisme; les heresies, des origines au xviii siècle*, Fayard, Paris, 1993, ch. 7.
13 Fourier, *Harmonian Man*, p. 28.
14 Barthes, *Sade / Fourier / Loyola*, p. 78.
15 Rather like the coded color handkerchiefs worn at Mattachine square dances. See Stuart Timmons, *The Trouble with Harry Hay, Founder of the Modern Gay Movement*, Alyson Publications, Boston, 1990.
16 Stendhal, *De L'Amour*, Flammarion, Paris, 1992.
17 Beecher, *Charles Fourier*, p. 12.
18 Fourier, *Harmonian Man*, p. 40.
19 Vaneigem, *The Revolution of Everyday Life*, p. 26.
20 Nikolai Chernyshevsky, *What Is to Be Done?*, translated by Michael Katz, Cornell University Press, Ithaca NY, 1989.
21 See for example Jane McGonnigal, *Reality Is Broken: Why Games Make Us Better and How They Can Change the World*, Penguin, New York, 2011.
22 Francois Bott, "Raoul Vaneigem," *Le Monde*, September 12, 2003.
23 See Luc Boltanski and Eve Chiapello, *The New Spirit of Capitalism*, translated by Gregory Elliot, Verso, London, 2007.
24 Tiqqun, *Introduction to Civil War*, Semiotext(e), Los Angeles, 2010, p. 28, s. 8 (gloss), originally published in *Tiqqun*, No. 2, 2001, p. 5. The difference would lie in that itch *Tiqqun* can't help but scratch: critique of metaphysics. They spend more time worrying away at predicates than developing a mode of writing based on penchants.
25 "Premiers Matériaux pour une Théorie de la Jeunne-Fille," *Tiqqun*, No. 1, 1999.
26 Raoul Vaneigem, in *Charles Fourier, Des Harmonies Polygames en Amour*, edited by Raoul Vaneigem, Rivages, Paris, 2003, p. 7.
27 Raoul Vaneigem, "Aiming for Practical Truth," in Knabb, *Anthology*, p. 279.
28 Raoul Vaneigem, "Notice to the Civilized Concerning Generalized Self Management." The title, and some of the text, is a détournement of Fourier. Knabb, *Anthology*, p. 365.
29 See Paul Lafargue, *The Right to Be Lazy*, AK Press, Oakland CA, 2011.
30 Raoul Vaneigem, *Voyage à Oarystis*, illustrated by Giampiero Caiti, Éditions Estuaire, Brussels, 2005, p. 101.

20 The Ass Dreams of China Pop

1 Letter to Viénet, June 21, 1961, in Guy Debord, *Correspondance Volume 2*, 1960–1964, Fayard, Paris, 2001.

2 Meaghan Morris, "Transnational Imagination in Action Cinema: Hong Kong and the making of a global popular culture," *Inter-Asia Cultural Studies*, Vol. 5, No. 2, 2004.

3 My thanks to Julia P. Carrillo for pointing this out.

4 Jacques Rancière argues that Althusser's critique of ideology legitimated those within the French Communist Party who took the student revolt aspect of May '68 to be just a petit bourgeois tantrum. His own break with Althusserianism came at a time (1974) when it was being repurposed, against its will, as a prop for a return to intellectual order. He classifies it alongside the theory of spectacle as one of those doctrines based on "the idea that the dominated are dominated because they are ignorant of the laws of domination. This simplistic view assigns to those who adopt it the exalted task of bringing their science to the blind masses. Eventually, though, this task dissolves into a pure thought of resentment" (*Althusser's Lesson*, Continuum, London, 2010, p. xvi). Against this, Rancière insists on the equality of intelligences of the dominated with the dominators. While this break might have been welcome, Rancière makes it only by invoking a most fantastic version of the Chinese Cultural Revolution as its authenticating flag. The "penitentiary realities" of that movement he is still unable to quite acknowledge as late as 2010. Rancière almost always identifies the Situationist project with Debord's *Society of the Spectacle* (book and film), or his later texts: "The trajectory of Situationist discourse ... is undoubtedly symptomatic of the contemporary ebb and flow of aesthetics and politics, and of the transformations of avant-garde thinking into nostalgia" (*The Politics of Aesthetics*, Continuum, London, 2004, p. 9). That this "Situationist project" was also, and already, seeding the very counter-practices he wanted to celebrate, and without recourse to the authority of the bloody flag of the Maoist violence, consistently eludes him. Not surprisingly, the originality of détournement as method also eludes him. The doctrine that "aesthetics has its own politics" (*The Politics of Aesthetics*, p. 60) is helpful if one wants to find an apparently legitimate reason to still be reading Flaubert, but it doesn't confront the Situationist proposition, at the heart of détournement, that aesthetics has its own *political economy*. Embarrassment at Maoism's "excesses" aside, there is still no retreat in Rancière from its fetishizing of the political.

5 http://sexdrugsandbottleservice.tumblr.com, February 14, 2009.

6 This and subsequent quotes are from René Viénet, *Can Dialectics Break Bricks?* (1973), most readily available at ubu.com.

7 Rey Chow, *Writing Diaspora*, Indiana University Press, Bloomington IL, 1993, p. 20. For a more affirmative account of specifically western Maoism, see Andrew Ross, *Nice Work if You Can Get It*, New York University Press, New York, 2010; Kristin Ross, *May '68 and Its Afterlives*, University of Chicago Press, Chicago, 2004. Smug liberal version: Richard Wolin, *The Wind from the East*, Princeton University Press, Princeton NJ, 2010.

8 On the genres and subgenres Viénet draws upon here, see Chris Desjardins, *Outlaw Masters of Japanese Film*, I. B. Taurus, London, 2005.

9 René Viénet, *The Girls of Kamare* (1974), most readily seen at ubu.com. Following Viénet quotes are also from this film.

10 "Address to Revolutionaries of Algeria and of All Countries," Knabb, *Anthology*, p. 189.

11 Mustapha Khayati, "Setting Straight Some Popular Misconceptions About Revolutions in the Underdeveloped Countries," Knabb, *Anthology*, p. 285.

12 ABC News, April 30, 2009; *New York Times*, August 11, 2009.

13 Other works by Poussin at the National Gallery were defaced in 2011.

14 Francis Deron et al., *Revo. Cul dans la Chine Pop: Anthologie de la presse des Gardes rouges*, Éditions 10/18, Paris, 1974. It was over censorship of Deron's writing about the "Maoist graveyard" that Viénet resigned as editor of *Monde Chinois* in 2008.

21 *Mao by Mao*

1 René Viénet, "Preface" to Simon Leys, *Les habits neufs du Président Mao*, Champ Libre, Paris, 1971. Viénet's other main source is Harold Isaacs, *The Tragedy of the Chinese Revolution*, Haymarket Editions, Chicago, 2009. For Leys, the Chinese Communists cease to be a revolutionary force when Mao tries to apply tactics from the guerrilla period to economic reconstructions, with disastrous results, during the Great Leap Forward. For Isaacs, the Communists had ceased being a revolutionary party in the 1920s, with the defeat of the Chinese labor movement. On this point, Viénet follows Isaacs.

2 See Elizabeth Perry and Li Xun, *Proletarian Power: Shanghai in the Cultural Revolution*, Westview Press, Boulder CO, 1997.

3 Francis Deron, René Viénet, Wu Zingming, *Mao by Mao*, 1977. The film represented France in the short film category at Cannes in 1977.

4 Avaliable on ubu.com as *Chinois, encore un effort pour être révolutionnaires, (a.ka. Peking Duck Soup)*, English version by "Professor Stone," with narration by John G. Simmons, Archie Taylor and Jo Bouvier. Subsequent unattributed Viénet quotes in the text are from this film.

5 Debord, letter to Sanguinetti, April 25, 1972, in Debord, *Correspondance Volume 4: 1969–1972*.

6 The extent of the great famine in the wake of Mao's Great Leap Forward is only now coming to light. See Zhou Xun (ed.), *The Great Famine in China 1958–1962: A Documentary History*, Yale University Press, New Haven CT, 2012.

7 See Victor Serge, *Memoirs of a Revolutionary*, New York Review Books Classics, New York, 2011. Serge was also a perceptive critic of the Bolsheviks' China policy.

8 Li Yi Zhe, *Chinois, si vous saviez*, Christian Bourgeois, Paris, 1976. Published by Viénet and Deron in their Biblioteque Asiatique series, once it moved from Champ Libre. For an English translation, see Li Yi Zhe, "On Socialist Democracy and the Legal System," in Gregor Benton and Alan Hunter, *Wild Lily, Prairie Fire: China's Road to Democracy*, Princeton University Press, Princeton NJ, 1995.

9 Richard McGregor, *The Party: The Secret World of China's Communist Leaders*, Harper, New York, 2012.

10 *New York Times*, December 25, 2004.

11 Debord to Viénet, November 17, 1964, in Debord, *Correspondance Volume 2: 1960–1964*.

22 *The Occulted State*

1 *Now Public*, June 14, 2007.

2 Gianfranco Sanguinetti, *On Terrorism and the State*, translated by Lucy Forsyth and Michel Prigent, B. M. Chronos, London, 1982, p. 59; Gianfranco Sanguinetti, *Del Terrorismo e Dello Stato*, Sanguinetti CP, Milan, 1979, p. 33.

3 Retort, *Afflicted Powers*, p. 79. Retort is a San Francisco–based group including Iain Boal, Joseph Matthews, Michael Watts and T. J. Clark.

4 Retort, *Afflicted Powers*, p. 131.

5 Debord to Gallizio, July 17, 1958, Debord, *Correspondence*.

6 Debord, *Panegyric*, p. 51; *Oeuvres*, p. 1678.
7 Debord, *Considerations on the Assassination*, p. 60; *Oeuvres*, p. 1568.
8 Debord, *Panegyric*, p. 50; *Oeuvres*, p. 1677.
9 Guy Debord, *Preface to the Fourth Italian Edition of the Society of the Spectacle*, Chronos Publications, London, 1983, p. 12.
10 Debord to Sanguinetti, April 21, 1978, Guy Debord, *Correspondance Volume 5, 1973–1978*, Fayard, Paris, 2005.
11 Andrew Hussey, *The Game of War: The Life and Death of Guy Debord*, Jonathan Cape, London, 2001.
12 Sanguinetti, *On Terrorism*, p. 14; from the preface to the French edition: Gianfranco Sanguinetti, *Du Terrorisme et de l'Etat*, 2e edition, Groupment Graphique Gamma, Paris, 1980, p. 7.
13 Sanguinetti, *On Terrorism*, pp. 19–20; *Du Terrorisme*, p. 14. Sanguinetti is here a useful counterpoint to the range of views included in the seminal English-language document of the Autonomist movement: Sylvère Lotringer and Christian Marazzi (eds), *Autonomia: Post-Political Politics*, Semiotext(e), New York, 2007. See also Paolo Virno and Michael Hardt (eds), *Radical Thought in Italy: A Potential Politics*, University of Minnesota Press, Minneapolis, 2006. Given the Situationist interest in the critique of urban planning, a book of particular interest is Pier Vitorio Aureli, *The Project of Autonomy: Politics and Architecture Within and Against Capitalism*, Princeton Architectural, New York, 2008. But what is often lacking in the global celebration of autonomist writings is the immediate political context within which it was formed, something which this chapter seeks at least in part to remedy.
14 Particularly instructive here is Antonio Negri, *Books for Burning: Between Civil War and Democracy in 1970s Italy*, Verso, London, 2006, which reprints Negri's texts of the period. The break with Leninism is slow, painful, and perhaps somewhat incomplete.
15 Tiqqun, *This Is Not a Program*, Semiotext(e), Los Angeles, 2011, p. 21; "Ceci n'est pas un programme," *Tiqqun*, No. 2, p. 240.
16 *New York Times*, June 5, 2006. On conspiracy theories: Debord, *Comments*, p. 59; Jodi Dean, *Aliens in America: Conspiracy Cultures from Outer Space to Cyberspace*, Cornell University Press, Ithaca NY, 1998; Jack Bratich, *Conspiracy Panics: Political Rationality and Popular Culture*, SUNY Press, Albany NY, 2008.
17 Debord, *Comments*, p. 24; *Oeuvres*, p. 1607.
18 William Gibson, *Spook Country*, Putnam, New York, 2007, p. 74.
19 It sometimes appears as if more has been written about Wikileaks than the volume of documents they actually released. See Micah Sifry, *Wikileaks and the Age of Transparency*, O/R Books, New York, 2011. See also Suelette Dreyfus and Julian Assange, *Underground*, Random House Australia, Sydney, 2011, a reprint of an earlier study of the hacker culture from which Wikileaks sprang. Perhaps this could have been seen coming: McKenzie Wark, *A Hacker Manifesto*, Harvard University Press, Cambridge MA, 2004, the first version of which appeared in 2000.
20 *New York Times Magazine*, November 26, 2000.
21 *Highest ambition*, Debord, *Comments*, p. 11. On La Boétie, cf. *Comments*, p. 61. Now that journalists in Rupert Murdoch's employ have been caught tapping cellphone calls, and Scotland Yard caught sitting on what it knew of this, Debord's chiasmus might thus be amended: Yet the lowest achievement of the disintegrating spectacle is to turn journalists into cops and cops into journalists.
22 Sanguinetti, *On Terrorism*, p. 58; *Del Terrorismo*, p. 32.
23 Debord, *Comments*, p. 82; *Oeuvres*, p. 1642.

24 Debord, *In Girum*, p. 65; *Oeuvres*, p. 1391. This statement is accompanied in the film by movie images of naval warfare. The image of war is itself the image of the war of images.
25 *Washington Post*, July 19, 2010.
26 Debord, *Comments*, p. 84.

23 The Last Chance to Save Capitalism

1 See Michel Foucault, *The Birth of Biopolitics*, Palgrave, London, 2008.
2 Censor (Gianfranco Sanguinetti), *Véridique Rapport sur les dernières chances de sauver le capitalisme en Italie. Traduit de l'italien par Guy Debord (suivi de Preuves de l'inexistence de Censor par son auteur)*, Ugo Mursia Editore, Milan, 1975 / Champ Libre, Paris, 1976, p. 147.
3 Censor, *Véridique Rapport*, p. 31.
4 Ibid., p. 128. After the war, the Italian Communist Party cached at least some of its weapons from the partisan struggle against fascism, but in 1948 renounced the option of armed insurrection.
5 Censor, *Véridique Rapport*, pp. 50–1, 48–9, 58.
6 Ibid., p. 68.
7 Ibid., p. 80; See Baltasar Gracián, *The Art of Worldly Wisdom*, Doubleday, New York, 1991, s. 40, s. 160. Gracián would put it more in terms of prudence, the measured use of the truth and the avoidance of outright lies.
8 Ibid., p. 91. This, for the Situationists, was the lesson of the Spanish Civil War.
9 Ibid., p. 94. See Gracián, *Art of Worldly Wisdom*, s. 214.
10 Ibid., pp. 106–10. See also Guy Debord, *A Sick Planet*, Seagull Books, Oxford, 2008.
11 Ibid., pp. 155–7. One could seek an explanation for the rise of contemporary art here.
12 Giuseppe di Lampedusa, *The Leopard*, translated by Archibald Colquhoun, Pantheon, New York, 1960, p. 40.
13 *Daily News*, August 11, 2010.
14 Debord, *Society of the Spectacle*, s. 2.

24 Anti-Cinema

1 The dissolution is documented in Debord and Sanguinetti, *The Real Split in the International*.
2 Champot, where he played *Game of War*, is lovingly described in *Panygeric*, p. 48.
3 Thomas Y. Levin, "Dismantling the Spectacle: The Cinema of Guy Debord," in Sussman, *On the Passage of a Few People*, p. 108. I am much indebted to this classic essay.
4 In this respect, Debord doesn't really belong in Martin Jay, *Downcast Eyes: The Denigration of Vision in Twentieth Century French Thought*, University of California Press, Berkeley, 1994. "The reigning deceptions of the time are on the point of making us forget that the truth may also be found in images. An image that has not been deliberately separated from its meaning adds great precision and certainty to knowledge." Debord, *Panegyric*, Vols 1 & 2, p. 73.
5 See McKenzie Wark, "Détournement: An Abuser's Guide," *Angelaki*, Vol. 14, No. 1, April 2009, *Special issue: Plagiarism! (from work to détournement)*, edited by John Kinsella and Niall Lucy.
6 *Philadelphia Inquirer*, December 26, 2008.

7 Isidore Isou, "Treatise on Slime and Eternity," in *Avant-garde 2: Experimental Cinema*, Kino Cinema, New York, 2007.

8 Interview with Martine Barraqué-Curie by Julia Carrillo and McKenzie Wark, April 27, 2009. Actually, the later film adds some material as well, not least on the Carnation Revolution in Portugal.

9 Lefebvre, *Critique de la vie quotidienne II*, p. 86. See the remarkable document by the Tiqqun group, "Premiers matériaux pour une théorie de la Jeune-Fille," *Tiqqun*, January 1999, reprinted as a separate text, VLCP, 2006.

10 See John Hartley, *Tele-ology: Studies in Television*, Routledge, London, 1992, p. 218ff, for a fine essay whose starting point on this is the birth of Kylie Minogue in 1968. Hartley detected early on the almost dialectical quality of what I will call The Girl, as both a controlling, patriarchal image for women, but also a surface on which a sense of the public coalesced. I followed in his footsteps in McKenzie Wark, *Celebrities, Culture and Cyberspace*, Pluto Press, Sydney, 1998. Hartley sheered the critical and francophone side of cultural theory away and relied on a nuanced and interpretive orientation to popular publics (derived in part from Terry Hawkes). His choice of Kylie over the Situationists in *Tele-ology* is something of a manifesto. My writings on the Situationists are among other things a belated dialogue with that strand of Anglophone cultural studies of which Hartley is a leading exemplar.

11 One should note that in Alain Badiou's *The Meaning of Sarkozy*, the Trotskyite remnants of the seventies come in for a brisk dismissal, but only some of the Maoist currents. Like his mentor Louis Althusser, Badiou remains relentlessly Maoist in not only political but also theoretical formation. Mao's injunction to "put politics in command" and reject Marxism as a critique of political *economy* has done lasting damage to critical thought.

12 Jaime Semprun, *La Guerre sociale au Portugal*, Champ Libre, Paris, 1975. See also Loren Goldner, *Ubu Saved from Drowning: Class Struggle and Statist Containment in Portugal and Spain, 1974–1977*, Queequeg Publications, New York, 2011.

13 Debord, *Complete Cinematic Works*, p. 223; *Oeuvres*, p. 1412.

14 *Correspondence* (to Frankin, July 15, 1959). See Gilles Deleuze, *Cinema 1: The Movement Image*, Continuum, London, 2005.

15 Debord, *Complete Cinematic Works*, p. 49; *Oeuvres*, p. 1203. See Julian Graffy, *Chapaev: Kinofile Filmmakers' Companion*, No. 11, I. B. Taurus, London, 2009.

16 Russian friends old enough to remember the Soviet era recall that *Chapayev* was détourned in everyday life via a series of jokes, often ribald or in dubious taste. See also Victor Prevelin, *Buddha's Little Finger*, Penguin, New York, 2001.

17 The parable does not quite appear in this classic form in Aesop. See Leslie Kurke, *Aesopic Conversations*, Princeton University Press, Princeton NJ, 2010, which finds the traces of a popular counter-knowledge in the fables of "classical" times.

18 On the suppression of the revolution by the Communists in Spain, the classic first-hand account is George Orwell, *Homage to Catalonia*, Penguin, London, 2000. It was published as *Hommage à la Catalogne 1936–1937*, Champ Libre, Paris, 1981.

25 The Devil's Party

1 Debord, *In Girum*, p. 50; *Oeuvres*, p. 1377. Actually the "name writ on water" is from Keats' epitaph for himself, détourned from Fletcher's "Philaster," but it is borrowed again by Shelley in "Adonais" and "Fragment on Keats," as well as by Christina Rossetti and Oscar Wilde. Shelley was indeed shipwrecked, and the shipwrecked above all perhaps have their names written on water. 'Shipwreckers'

both détourns and corrects the thought. See Richard Cronin, *Romantic Victorians*, Palgrave Macmillan, London, 2002.

2 Debord, *Panegyric*, p. 15; Oeuvres, p. 1633.

3 Terence, "Homo sum: humani nil a me alienum puto," *Heauton Timoroumenos*, line 77.

4 Will Baker, *Jacques Prévert*, Twayne Publishers, New York, 1967; Edward Baron Turk, *Marcel Carné and the Golden Age of French Cinema*, Harvard University Press, Cambridge MA, 1989. The female lead in both films is Arletty.

5 Debord, *In Girum*, p. 33; *Oeuvres*, p. 1362.

6 *The Memoirs of Lacenaire*, translated by Philip John Stead, Staple Press, London, 1952, pp. 157–9. Here sounding as if he is détourning the Gospel of Matthew: "I come not to bring peace but the sword." Lacenaire is also mentioned in *Panegyric*, p. 7. Foucault compares Lacenaire unfavorably to another criminal-writer of the time: "No, I think that one must compare Rivière with Lacenaire, who was his exact contemporary and who committed a whole heap of minor and shoddy crimes, mostly failures, hardly glorious at all, but who succeeded through his very intelligent discourse in making these crimes exist as real works of art, and in making the criminal, that is Lacenaire himself, the very artist of criminality. It's another tour de force if you like: he managed to give an intense reality, for dozens of years, for more than a century, to acts that were finally very shoddy and ignoble. As a criminal he was a rather petty type, but the splendor and intelligence of his writing gave a consistency to it all." Sylvère Lotringer (ed.), *Foucault Live: Collected Interviews, 1961–1984*, Semiotext(e), Los Angeles, 1996, pp. 203–6.

7 Adorno, *Minima Moralia*, p. 111; Vaneigem, *The Revolution of Everyday Life*, p. 31.

8 Karl Marx and Fredrick Engels, *Collected Works, Volume 4*, International Publishers, New York, 1976, p. 82. Or as Lefebvre says, "man moves 'wrong foot forward.'" *Introduction à la modernité. Préludes*, Les éditions de minuit, Paris, 1962, p. 146.

9 Olivier Assayas, *A Post-May Adolescence: Letter to Alice Debord*, translated by Adrian Martin and Rachel Zerner, Synema, Vienna, 2012, pp. 49–50, 77, 101. See also Debord, *Considerations on the Assassination*, pp. 5–6. Assayas produced the DVD edition of Debord's films, and not much else of value in this context, except perhaps *demonlover* (2007). Of course, there were in actuality many "authors" of the Champ Libre editorial direction. See Éditions Champ Libre, *Correspondance Tome 1*, editions Ivrea, Paris, 1996.

10 Debord, *Considerations on the Assassination*, p. 3; *Oeuvres*, p. 1540.

11 Debord, *Considerations on the Assassination*, p. 9; *Oeuvres*, p. 1543.

12 "He smelled as if he hadn't bathed in days." *New York Times Magazine*, January 26, 2011. For Assange in his own words: Hans Ulrich Obrist, "In Conversation with Julian Assange," *e-flux journal*, No. 25, May 2011, e-flux.com, and Julian Assange et al., *Cypherpunks*, O/R Books, New York, 2012.

13 Debord, *Considerations on the Assassination*, p. 23; *Oeuvres*, p. 1550.

14 Debord, *Considerations on the Assassination*, p. 44; *Oeuvres*, p. 1560.

15 Guy Debord, *Des Contrats*, Le temps qu'il fait, Cognac, 1995; *Oeuvres*, p. 1843ff.

16 See Jacques Derrida, *Given Time*, University of Chicago Press, Chicago, 1996. Derrida's critique is of the Christian-bourgeois idea of the gift as an unmotivated, selfless charity. But for ethnographers, and Situationists, the gift is always a stake in a game among rivals. See Jean Baudrillard, *Fragments*, Verso, London, 1997, pp. 127–8.

17 Debord, *Panegyric*, p. 17; *Oeuvres*, 1664.

18 See the documents collected and translated at tarnac9.wordpress.com, including an interview with Coupat from *Le Monde*, June 4, 2009; Giorgio Agamben, "Ter-

rorisme ou tragic-comédie," *Libération*, November 19, 2008; Alberto Toscano, "The War Against Preterrorism," *Radical Philosophy*, No. 154, March–April 2009.

19 The Invisible Committee, *The Coming Insurrection*, Semiotext(e), Los Angeles, 2009. See also Benjamin Noys (ed.), *Communization and Its Discontents*, minor compositions, London, 2011. Most of the contributors to the latter are highly critical of *Tiqqun* and its offspring, such as the Invisible Committee, and pursue more theoretically rigorous concepts of an immanent Communism. Both a certain quality of the prose, and certain practical commitments, make *The Coming Insurrection* more germane to our story here, but interested readers can pursue these more *rigorous*, not to say *dogmatic*, versions of a Post-Situationist practice according to taste.

26 Guy Debord, His Art and Times

1 Interview by McKenzie Wark with Brigitte Cornand, New York, April 17, 2009.

2 See for example Cornand's later work on Louise Bourgeois.

3 Lefebvre, *Critique de la vie quotidienne II*, p 81; *Critique of Everyday Life* Vol. 2, p. 77. See Debord, *Panegyric*, p. 74; *Comments*, p. 19.

4 Letter to Leonardi, October 6, 1994. The music is from Monique Morelli, *Musique de Leonardi, François Villon*, Chevance, 1974.

5 Guy Debord, *Oeuvres Cinematographiques Completes*, produced by Olivier Assayas, Gaumont, Paris, 2005. See Keith Sanborn, "Return of the Suppressed," *Artforum*, February 2006, on some quirks of this DVD edition. Quotes from the film are from the English-language edition produced by Cornand and not included in the Gaumont box set. My thanks to Cornand for my copy.

6 Besides several books on French men of state, Franz-Olivier Giesbert is the author of *The American: A Memoir*, Pantheon, New York, 2005.

7 It would be amusing to compare the readings of Mallarmé offered by Debord to Quentin Meillassoux, *The Number and the Siren*, Urbanomic and Sequence Press, New York, 2012. There is no cult of contingency in Debord, for whom the rattle of the dice has more to do with the exigencies of historical time than the contingencies of cosmic time. Debord is no nihilist. Historical time is always an open invitation to roll the dice and take a chance on another way of life, if only for the pleasure of watching the blocks fall. We begin again, from the beginning, with neither hope nor resignation, but with a keen calculation of the chances, and for a chance to act in and against our time, for the ages. See also Debord, *Considerations on the Assassination*, p. 32; *Panegyric*, p. 15.

8 See Gil Joseph Wolman, *Défense de mourir*, Éditions Allia, Paris, 2001.

9 Comte de Lautréamont, *Maldoror and the Complete Works*, Exact Change Press, Cambridge MA, 1994, p. 234.

10 *The Australian*, November 16, 2006.

11 See McKenzie Wark, *Virtual Geography: Living with Global Media Events*, Indiana University Press, Bloomington IN, 1995.

12 Debord, *Panegyric*, p. 12; *Oeuvres*, p. 1662; cf. *Comments*, p. 78; *Oeuvres*, p. 1639 and *In Girum*, p. 33; *Oeuvres*, p. 1662; *Considerations on the Assassination*, p. 26. See Arthur Cravan, *Oeuvres: articles, lettres*, Éditions Gérard Lebovici, Paris, 1987; Carolyn Burke, *Becoming Modern: The Life of Mina Loy*, University of California Press, Berkeley CA, 1997, is probably the best English-language source on Cravan, whom Loy married shortly before he died. A suitably unreliable source on Cravan is Mike Richardson and Rick Geary, *Cravan: Mystery Man of the Twentieth Century*, Dark

Horse, Milwaukie OR, 2005, which includes the delicious speculation that Cravan became the novelist B. Traven.

13 Benjamin Buchloh, *Neo-Avantgarde and Culture Industry*, MIT Press, Cambridge MA, 2000, p. 137. Interestingly, this volume contains an essay on Jacques Villeglé (who would have rubbed shoulders with Debord in the Saint-Germain heyday) which includes a brief appreciation of François Dufrêne, who departs from the Letterist International directly into the neo-avant-garde. Cf. Debord, *Comments*, p. 77.

14 See the Bernadette Corporation video, *Get Rid of Yourself*, 2003.

15 *Vanity Fair*, February 2007.

16 *Vanity Fair*, April 2007.

27 A Romany Detour

1 Hussey, *The Game of War*, p. 283.

2 Debord, *Panegyric*, p. 9; *Oeuvres*, p. 1660.

3 Jan Yoors, *The Gypsies*, Simon & Schuster, New York, p. 51.

4 Yoors, *The Gypsies*, pp. 31, 82, 116.

5 Ibid., pp. 121, 23, 135.

6 Ibid., *The Gypsies*, p. 34.

7 Ibid., *The Gypsies*, pp. 122–3.

8 Ibid., *The Gypsies*, p. 53.

9 Ibid., *The Gypsies*, p. 123.

10 *New York Times*, November 13, 2006.

11 Debord, *Panegyric*, p. 40; *Oeuvres*, p. 1673.

12 Yoors, *The Gypsies*, p. 93.

13 A certain caution is called for in any deployment of the figure of the "gypsy," a caution Becker-Ho and Debord don't always observe. See Adrian Marsh et al., *Gypsies and the Problem of Identities*, Transactions, Istanbul, 2006.

14 Isabel Fonesa, *Bury Me Standing: The Gypsies and Their Journey*, Knopf, New York, 1995, pp. 106–7.

15 Becker-Ho, *The Princes of Jargon*, p. 67.

16 Yoors, *The Gypsies*, p. 159.

28 The Language of Discretion

1 *New York Times*, September 21, 2004.

2 Becker-Ho, *The Princes of Jargon*, p. 41; J. Huizinga, *The Waning of the Middle Ages*, St. Martin's Press, New York, 1984, p. 10.

3 See Jonathon Green, "Romany Rise," *Critical Quarterly*, Vol. 41, No. 3, 1999.

4 Becker-Ho, *The Princes of Jargon*, p. 153.

5 Christopher Hitchens, *Unacknowledged Legislators: Writers in the Public Sphere*, Verso, London, 2000, pp. 3–9.

6 Becker-Ho, *The Princes of Jargon*, p. 67.

7 Alice Becker-Ho, *The Essence of Jargon*, translated by John McHale, typescript, 2007, p. 23.

8 Becker-Ho, *The Princes of Jargon*, p. 37. On the modern extension of the con from the Coquillards to Benjamin Marks to spam, and their relation to the development of transport and communication, see Graham Parker, *Fair Use: Notes from Spam*, Book-works, London, 2008.

9 François Villon, *Complete Poems*, edited by Barbara Sargent-Bauer, University of Toronto Press, Toronto, p. 299.
10 Ibid., p. 309.
11 Ibid., lines 1667–8.
12 On Ghislain de Marbaix, see Jean-Michel Mension, *The Tribe*, Verso, London, 2002, p. 75ff.
13 Becker-Ho, *The Princes of Jargon*, p. 61.
14 Becker-Ho, *The Essence of Jargon*, p. 16.
15 *The Memoirs of Lacenaire*, p. 144.
16 Becker-Ho, *The Princes of Jargon*, p. 161.
17 Giorgio Agamben, *Means Without End*, University of Minnesota Press, Minneapolis, 2000, pp. 63–72.
18 Becker-Ho, *The Essence of Jargon*, p. 33.
19 Ibid., p. 23.
20 Ibid., p. 18.
21 Ibid., p. 21.
22 Debord, *Society of the Spectacle*, s. 204, quoted in Becker-Ho, *The Essence of Jargon*, p. 23. Debord distinguishes this approach to language from Roland Barthes' writing degree zero, the avant-garde of the time.
23 Becker-Ho, *The Princes of Jargon*, p. 143. See also Michel de Certeau's review essay on Foucault in *Heterologies: Discourse on the Other*, University of Minnesota Press, Minneapolis, 1986, which raises a similar point but settles for a more generic and less "dangerous" field of everyday practices.
24 *New York Times*, February 5, 2003. See also Edwin Black, *IBM and the Holocaust*, Dialog Press, New York, 2008.
25 Becker-Ho, *The Essence of Jargon*, p. 6.
26 Becker-Ho, *The Princes of Jargon*, p. 159.
27 Becker-Ho, *The Essence of Jargon*, p. 33.
28 Becker-Ho, *The Princes of Jargon*, p. 159.
29 Ibid., p. 159.
30 Ibid., p. 145.
31 Julia Kristeva, *Revolution in Poetic Language*, Columbia University Press, New York, 1984.
32 See for example "All the King's Men," in Knabb, *Anthology*, p. 152.
33 Becker-Ho, *The Princes of Jargon*, p. 17.
34 Debord, *Panegyric*, p. 24; *Oeuvres*, p. 1667.
35 Becker-Ho, *The Princes of Jargon*, p. 19.
36 Ibid., p. 47.
37 Ibid., p. 143.
38 Debord, *Comments*, pp. 1–2; *Oeuvres*, p. 1593.
39 Becker-Ho, *The Princes of Jargon*, p. 137; François Villon, *Complete Poems*, p. 299.

29 *Game of War*

1 Thanks to Michael Pettinger for this translation. Vida was the Bishop of Alba, where the inaugural conference of the Situationist International took place.
2 See Guy Debord, *Cette mauvaise réputation*, Gallimard, Paris, 1993; *Oeuvres*, p. 1796ff.
3 Alice Becker-Ho, "Historical Note (2006)," in Alice Becker-Ho and Guy Debord, *A Game of War*, translated by Donald Nicholson-Smith, Atlas Press, London, 2007, p. 7. See also *Oeuvres*, p. 285.

4 Debord, *Panegyric*, pp. 55–6; *Oeuvres*, p. 1679.
5 Becker-Ho and Guy Debord, *A Game of War*, p. 9.
6 *Strategist*: Jacqueline de Jong, in Stefan Zweifel et al. (eds), *In Girum Imus Nocte et Consumimur Igni: The Situationist International 1957–1972*, JRP-Ringier, Zurich, 2006, p. 240; Giorgio Agamben, in ibid., p. 36.
7 Debord, *Panegyric*, p. 61; *Oeuvres*, p. 1682.
8 On Surrealist games, see Susan Laxton, *Paris as Gameboard: Ludic Strategies in Surrealism*, PhD dissertation, Columbia University, 2004. Duchamp's book on chess is Marcel Duchamp and Vitali Halberstadt, *Opposition und Schwesterfelder (Gebundene Ausgabe)* Tropen, Berlin, 2001. François Le Lionnais is quoted in Allan Woods, *The Map Is Not the Territory*, Manchester University Press, Manchester, 2000, p. 199. Le Lionnais (1901–84) was a mathematician, chemical engineer, and a founder of the Oulipo group.
9 Becker-Ho and Debord, *A Game of War*, pp. 25, 26.
10 See Ed Halter, *From Sun Tzu to Xbox*, Thunder Mouth Press, New York, 2006.
11 Alexander R. Galloway, "Debord's Nostalgic Algorithm," *Culture Machine*, Vol. 10, 2009. On the one occasion Galloway and I played *Game of War*, on Alice Becker-Ho's own set, no less, the game ended in a draw. My position was weak, and I don't doubt Alex would have won had there been more time.
12 Becker-Ho and Debord, *A Game of War*, p. 156.
13 Ibid., p. 19.
14 Ibid., p. 21.
15 Antonio Gramsci, *Selections from The Prison Notebooks*, translated by Quintin Hoare and Geoffrey Nowell Smith, International Publishers, New York, 1971, p. 238. Of course Gramsci could also be wrong just on the facts. On the depth of Russian civil society's institutions, see Wayne Dowler, *Russia in 1913*, Northern Illinois University Press, Dekalb IL, 2010.
16 Becker-Ho and Debord, *A Game of War*, p. 24.
17 Class Wargames, *Guy Debord's Game of War*, 2009; Richard Barbrook and Fabian Thompsett, *Class Wargames Presents: Guy Debord's Game of War*, Unpopular Books, London, 2009. See classwargames.net. See also Richard Barbrook, *Class Wargames: Ludic Subversions Against Spectacular Capitalism*, manuscript, 2012. I should point out that on the one occasion I played *Game of War* against Class Wargames, I was soundly thrashed.
18 Becker-Ho and Debord, *A Game of War*, p. 22.
19 Ibid., p. 24.
20 Guy Debord, "Preface to the First Edition," in Becker-Ho and Debord, *A Game of War*, p. 9.

30 The Strategist

1 Becker-Ho and Debord, *A Game of War*, p. 26.
2 See Janet Afary and Kevin Anderson, *Foucault and the Iranian Revolution*, University of Chicago Press, Chicago, 2005, p. 263.
3 See Alain Badiou, *The Communist Hypothesis*, Verso, London, 2011, p. 101, where he describes Maoism as "the only true political creation of the sixties and seventies." Compare to the Chinese "new left" sociologist Wang Hui, *China's New Order*, Harvard University Press, Cambridge MA, 2003, pp. 148–9, who describes how Mao "used the socialist system of public ownership to establish a prosperous and

powerful modern nation-state while at the same time working towards his principal goal of equality." The latter may have some justification, having to operate as a loyal opposition within the Chinese academy, for using the government's own official history against it. Viénet is a useful counterweight to the persistence of Mao idolatry in the West. A more consistent critical account of this history would be a much vaster and more demanding project.

4 Slavoj Žižek, *In Defense of Lost Causes*, Verso, London, 2008, p. 111.
5 Boris Groys, *The Communist Postscript*, Verso, London, 2010, p. 99.
6 Carl von Clausewitz, *On Wellington: A Critique of Waterloo*, translated and edited by Peter Hofschröder, Oklahoma University Press, Norman OK, 2010, p. 171.
7 Becker-Ho and Debord, *A Game of War*, p. 24.
8 See Manuel DeLanda, *War in the Age of Intelligent Machines*, Zone Books, New York, 1991; Paul Edwards, *The Closed World*, MIT Press, Cambridge MA, 1997; Fred Kaplan, *The Wizards of Armageddon*, Stanford University Press, Stanford CA, 1991.
9 Antoine de Jomini, *Précis de l'Art de la Guerre*, Champ Libre, Paris, 1977. The influence of Jomini on cold war strategy is also noted in Paul Virilio and Sylvère Lotringer, *Pure War*, Semiotext(e), Los Angeles, 2008.
10 Clausewitz, *On Wellington*, p. 105.
11 Carl von Clausewitz, *On War*, Penguin Classics, London, 1982, p. 121. An edition with few merits, other than the introduction by Anatol Rapoport, which shows exactly how *On War* was taken up in limited fashion in the world of game theory.
12 Clausewitz, *On Wellington*, p. 59.
13 Debord, *Comments*, p. 86; *Oeuvres*, p. 1644.
14 Stendhal, *The Charterhouse of Parma*, translated by John Sturrock, Penguin Books, London, 2006, p. 47.
15 Becker-Ho and Debord, *A Game of War*, pp. 25–6.
16 Debord, *Society of the Spectacle*, s. 143.
17 Georg Lukács, *The Historical Novel*, translated by Hannah and Stanley Mitchell, Merlin Press, London, 1989, p. 24.
18 Guy Debord, *Panegyric*, p. 57; *Oeuvres*, p. 1680.
19 Keith Sanborn, "Postcard from Berezina," in Napoleon, *How to Make War*, edited by Yann Cloarec, translated by Keith Sanborn, Ediciones La Calavera, New York, 1998, pp. 103–4.
20 Napoléon, *Comment faire la guerre*, Textes rassemblés par Yann Cloarec, Champ Libre, Paris, 1973; Carl von Clausewitz, *Campagne de 1815 en France*, Champ Libre, Paris, 1973.
21 Vaneigem, *The Revolution of Everyday Life*, p. 165.
22 Alice Becker-Ho, *Du jargon héretier en Bastardie*, Gallimard, Paris, 2002, p. 161.

31 *The Inhuman Comedy*

1 Clark and Nicholson-Smith, "Why Art Can't Kill the Situationist International," in McDonough, *Guy Debord and the Situationist International*, p. 467.
2 To cite just one classic version of history from below: E. P. Thompson, *The Making of the English Working Class*, Penguin, London, 2002.
3 Debord, *Panegyric*, p. 39; *Oeuvres*, p. 1673.
4 Loretta Napoleoni, *Maonomics: Why Chinese Communists Make Better Capitalists Than We Do*, Seven Stories, New York, 2011, tries to make the case that China won the

cold war, that Deng Xiaoping's development strategy was essentially Marxist, and that the Chinese Communist Party is playing the historical long game. The attention to Deng-era China is at least a relief from Maoist nostalgia. Mao-era China does not much resemble the overdeveloped world in the twenty-first century. On the other hand, China in these same times does look a bit like the France and Italy of the postwar period. Rapid industrialization, transfer of populations from country to city, growing boredom with factory life, attempt by the integrated spectacle to compensate by expanding consumption and at the same time with selective repression. Situationist theory of history might have a certain ongoing relevance.

5 *New Yorker*, November 12, 2007.

6 For the idea of the improper name, I am indebted to Marco Deseriis, and his work on, and with, improper names, from Luther Blissett to the Yes Men.

7 Tiqqun, *This Is Not a Program*, Semiotext(e), Los Angeles, 2011, p. 117; *Tiqqun*, No. 2, p. 266.

8 See for example Gianni Vattimo and Santiago Zabala, *Hermeneutic Communism: From Heidegger to Marx*, Columbia University Press, New York, 2011.

9 Mina Loy, *Stories and Essays*, Dalkey Archive, Champaign IL, 2011; Claude Cahun, *Écrits*, Jean-Michel Place Éditions, Paris, 2002. See also Penelope Rosemont, *Surrealist Women: An International Anthology*, University of Texas Press, Austin, 1998.

10 Tom Levin claims that Dušan Makavejev's film *Sweet Movie* (1974) is dedicated to Vaneigem. If one takes that to be so, then it can be appended to the (anti-)canon of Situationist film as a quite astute analysis of The Girl. Interestingly, rather than find the Big Brother of the concentrated spectacle hidden in the diffuse spectacle, his analysis proceeds in reverse: he finds little sister's eastern double.

11 See Michael Gross, *Model: The Ugly Business of Beautiful Women*, Harper, New York, 2003. Wendy Steiner, *The Real Real Thing: The Model in the Mirror of Art*, University of Chicago Press, Chicago, 2010, restores some agency to the figure of the model, if only in the context of the art world. Jon Stratton, *The Desirable Body: Cultural Fetishism and the Erotics of Consumption*, University of Illinois Press, Urbana IL, 1996, takes some steps beyond the standard conflation of Marxian and Freudian theories of fetishism to consider The Girl as produced out of spectacular social relations. Still, the best thing on this subject is Ann K. Clark, "The Girl: A Rhetoric of Desire," *Cultural Studies*, Vol. 1, No. 2, 1987.

12 "Premieres matériaux pour une théorie de la Jeune-Fille," *Tiqqun: Organe Conscient du Parti Imaginaire*, Paris, 1999, p. 101.

13 Debord, *Society of the Spectacle*, p. 12.

14 Jean Baudrillard, *Seduction*, Macmillan, London, 1991. Baudrillard gives an account of his—oblique—relation to the Situationists in *Utopia Deferred*, Semiotext(e), Los Angeles, 2006, pp. 13–30. See also Craig Buckley and Jean-Louis Violeau, *Utopie: Texts and Projects 1967–1978*, Semiotext(e), Los Angeles, 2011. The Utopie group, in which he was an elusive presence, picked up the critique of architecture, design and the everyday from the early Situationists and took it somewhere else than the return to council communism advocated by the latter Situationists. Seduction is one of the keys via which Baudrillard extracts himself from rhetorics of production and desire to re-establish a low theory of the everyday outside of such well-policed languages.

15 "Premieres matériaux," p. 105; Alexandre Kojève, *Introduction to the Reading of Hegel*, Cornell University Press, Ithaca NY, 1969.

16 Compare Debord's film to DJ Rabbi, *Society of the Spectacle (A Digital Remix)*, 2004, Djrabbi.com.

Index

INDEX